Developing Narrative Advertising and Marketing Discourse in the AI Era

Recep Yılmaz
https://orcid.org/0000-0003-3406-2755
Ondokuz Mayis University, Turkey

IGI Global
Scientific Publishing
Publishing Tomorrow's Research Today

Vice President of Editorial — Melissa Wagner
Director of Acquisitions — Mikaela Felty
Director of Book Development — Jocelynn Hessler
Production Manager — Mike Brehm
Cover Design — Jose Rosado

Published in the United States of America by
IGI Global Scientific Publishing
701 East Chocolate Avenue
Hershey, PA, 17033, USA
Tel: 717-533-8845 | Fax: 717-533-7115
Website: https://www.igi-global.com E-mail: cust@igi-global.com

Library of Congress Cataloging-in-Publication Data

Names: Yılmaz, Recep, 1982- editor
Title: Developing narrative advertising and marketing discourse in the AI era / [edited by] Recep Yılmaz.
Description: Hershey, PA : IGI Global Scientific Publishing, [2026] | Includes bibliographical references and index. | Summary: "This book addresses the current challenges and developments in narrative advertising and marketing discourse in the context of artificial intelligence. It presents original ideas, theoretical models, and illuminating perspectives that substantially advances scholarly understanding and practical applications in the field"-- Provided by publisher.
Identifiers: LCCN 2025035293 (print) | LCCN 2025035294 (ebook) | ISBN 9798337356662 hardcover | ISBN 9798337356679 paperback | ISBN 9798337356686 ebook
Subjects: LCSH: Artificial intelligence--Marketing applications | Advertising--Technological innovations | Marketing--Technological innovations
Classification: LCC HF5415.125 .D48 2026 (print) | LCC HF5415.125 (ebook) | DDC 658.8--dc23/eng/20260123
LC record available at https://lccn.loc.gov/2025035293
LC ebook record available at https://lccn.loc.gov/2025035294

British Cataloguing in Publication Data
A Cataloguing in Publication record for this book is available from the British Library.

To my wife Nurten and my daughter Nil Rüya,

for their endless love, unwavering faith, and the light they bring to every page of my life.

Editorial Advisory Board

Table of Contents

Detailed Table of Contents

Section 2
AI, Narrative Transformation, and Media Shift

While AI comprises stages such as creative idea development, script writing, cast selection, set design, shooting, post-production, and versioning in traditional advertising production, the integration of AI-based tools is reshaping this structure. The research technically examines the impact of AI-supported creative idea development systems, automated script generators, AI-based consumer insight analysis tools, and visual design models on decision-makers during the pre-production phase.During the production phase, innovations such as virtual production technologies, AI-optimized lighting and camera placement systems, digital actors and performance production, and automated production planning algorithms were evaluated. In the post-production phase, the time/cost efficiency impact of tools such as AI-assisted editing, color correction, sound design, scene cleanup, face replacement, and rapid variant generation was analyzed.

This chapter examines the impact of artificial intelligence (AI) tools on advertising production processes and the construction of narratives from the perspective of advertising professionals. Drawing on a phenomenological qualitative design, in-depth interviews were conducted with 16 advertising practitioners integrating AI into creative workflows. The findings indicate that AI is mainly conceptualized as a supportive assistant rather than an autonomous creator. While AI enhances speed, efficiency, and idea generation, participants emphasize that originality, emotional depth, and narrative authenticity remain human-driven. The study reveals a shift toward hybrid creativity, where routine tasks are increasingly delegated to AI, yet strategic thinking and insight development remain human-centered. Although concerns regarding standardization and superficiality persist, AI is largely perceived as transformative rather than disruptive. The sustainability of advertising practice depends on balancing algorithmic efficiency with human imagination and cultural sensitivity.

Artificial intelligence (AI) technologies are also considered a communication and meaning-making practice that transforms the structure of the narrative relationship that brands establish with consumers. AI systems, which offer personalized stories to consumers, are expanding the scale of marketing narratives. This comprehensive process carries risks, including ethical violations, algorithmic bias, and implicit forms of manipulation. This research critically analyzes AI-powered marketing narratives from the perspective of meaning-making and discursive persuasion. The research adopts a qualitative and theoretical approach and utilizes narratology and digital marketing literature to analyze the impact of AI-powered narratives on brand discourse, consumer persuasion, and perception. The study reveals that AI plays a pioneering role in marketing communication, at the levels of narrative epistemology and ethical responsibility. The study presents an approach that centers narrative responsibility for ethical and sustainable AI-based brand communication.

In contemporary contexts, sustainability has evolved beyond environmental responsibility or corporate social responsibility to become a central element of strategic management, value creation, and brand identity. This study examines silence strategies in sustainability communication during crisis periods, focusing on greenhushing through a discourseanalytic approach. Global crises such as pandemics, economic instability, and armed conflicts often lead brands to intentionally reduce or suspend sustainability narratives. Adopting a qualitative research design, the study analyzes publicly corporate reports, official websites, social media content, and press releases of national and international brands using thematic discourse analysis. The findings suggest that although greenhushing may serve as a short-term risk-avoidance strategy, it creates long-term challenges for ethical consistency and public trust. The study argues that silence in sustainability communication should be reconsidered not only as a crisis management tool but also as a key issue in ethical public relations practice.

All forms of communication are being redesigned through digitalization and transferred into everyday life, shaping individuals' modes of thinking. The perception of the ideal body and beauty conveyed through digital media has become increasingly widespread with the emergence of artificial intelligence applications. Brands, by integrating new technologies into their communication strategies, aim to reach their consumer audiences through these tools. In this context, the fashion industry is undergoing a profound transformation in its advertising and visual content production processes by adopting AI-powered digital twin technology. This technology has gained particular prominence as global brands create digital avatars of real models to use in advertising campaigns. The aim of this study is to evaluate how women are represented in media environments where reality is reproduced through artificial intelligence, drawing on Baudrillard's concept of "hyperreality."

This chapter conceptualizes corporate communication as a temporally structured narrative system and examines the shift from retrospective corporate social responsibility (CSR) discourse to future-oriented sustainability narratives. While CSR legitimizes organizations through past performance, sustainability communication constructs meaning by projecting the future within present discourse. The chapter introduces the Proleptic Corporate Narrative Model, composed of four layers: temporal projection, future value construction, predictive persuasion, and narrative mediation. The framework shows how sustainability communication functions not only as information but as a narrative architecture shaping expectations and institutional positioning through future-oriented meaning production. An analysis of Brandverse campaigns indicates that corporate communication increasingly relies on proleptic narrative logic, constructing legitimacy through future projection.

Foreword

The rapid expansion of artificial intelligence across communication systems has not only transformed the operational mechanisms of marketing but has also begun to reshape the epistemological foundations upon which narrative persuasion is constructed. In this context, Developing Narrative Advertising and Marketing Discourse in the AI Era offers a rigorous and timely contribution to a field undergoing profound structural change.

This book approaches advertising narratives not simply as persuasive instruments, but as structured meaning systems increasingly mediated by algorithmic intelligence. By foregrounding the intersection of narrative theory, marketing communication, and artificial intelligence, the book moves beyond the prevailing technical and instrumental perspectives that dominate current AI discourse. Instead, it situates artificial intelligence within a broader communicative and epistemic transformation—one that reconfigures how narratives are generated, structured, interpreted, and operationalized in contemporary marketing environments.

A distinctive strength of this book lies in its ability to integrate theoretical reflection with practical transformation. Across its chapters, the book traces how artificial intelligence alters the architecture of advertising narratives, from linguistic and semiotic construction to production processes, consumer interpretation, ethical responsibility, and strategic communication. The progression from conceptual foundations to technological transformation, and from critical reflection to strategic foresight, provides a coherent intellectual trajectory that culminates in a comprehensive narrative framework. This framework not only synthesizes the theoretical insights developed throughout the book but also offers a forward-looking projection of how narrative advertising and marketing discourse may evolve in the near future.

Having closely followed Recep Yılmaz's sustained and systematic efforts to bridge narrative theory and communication studies, I view this work as a significant continuation of a broader intellectual trajectory. His scholarship consistently seeks to understand narrative not merely as a textual or representational structure, but as a dynamic system of meaning-making embedded in communication practices.

In this book, this perspective is extended into the domain of artificial intelligence, where narrative becomes both a theoretical construct and an operational architecture shaping contemporary marketing discourse.

The book's interdisciplinary orientation, conceptual coherence, and methodological diversity make it valuable for scholars, researchers, and practitioners seeking to understand the structural transformation of narrative persuasion in the age of artificial intelligence. More importantly, it invites readers to reconsider the future of marketing communication through the lens of narrative—now increasingly mediated by intelligent systems.

This book stands as an important contribution to the evolving dialogue between narrative, communication, and artificial intelligence, and it offers a meaningful framework for understanding the future trajectory of narrative advertising and marketing discourse.

M. Nur Erdem
Ondokuz Mayıs University, Turkey

Preface

INTRODUCTION

The increasing centrality of artificial intelligence in marketing communication has transformed not only the technical mechanisms of advertising but also the narrative and discursive structures through which meaning is produced, mediated, and operationalized. This volume emerged from the need to understand this transformation at a deeper theoretical level and to situate the evolving relationship between narrative, discourse, and artificial intelligence within a coherent conceptual framework. Beyond describing technological change, the book seeks to theorize how AI reshapes the architecture of narrative persuasion and to integrate these transformations within a model-oriented perspective.

Existing research on artificial intelligence in marketing communication largely concentrates on optimization, automation, and technical performance. While these approaches offer valuable insights, they rarely address the narratological dimensions of communication. Conversely, narrative studies have historically focused on textual and representational structures without sufficiently incorporating the structural and epistemological implications introduced by intelligent systems. This volume is positioned at the intersection of these two domains. It aims to bridge the gap between narrative theory and AI-driven communication by examining how algorithmic systems reshape the production, circulation, and interpretation of marketing narratives.

One of the central challenges encountered during the editorial process was the relative absence of a well-established connection between narrative and communication in contemporary scholarship. The relationship between artificial intelligence and narrative is still emerging, and integrating this relationship into an already underdeveloped narrative–communication framework required a systematic and theoretically consistent approach. This volume represents an attempt to construct that connection by organizing diverse perspectives within a coherent intellectual structure.

The book is organized into four interconnected sections, each reflecting a stage in the conceptual progression of AI-mediated narrative transformation.

SECTION OVERVIEWS

Section I: Conceptual and Theoretical Foundations, Chapters 1-4 establishes the linguistic, semiotic, and theoretical groundwork of AI-driven narrative communication. It examines the limits and potentials of algorithmic creativity, the role of storytelling in building brand loyalty, semiotic mechanisms of meaning production in AI-supported advertising narratives, and the evolving logic of measurement and optimization in narrative-based marketing strategies. Together, these chapters provide the conceptual vocabulary necessary for understanding narrative as a dynamic and measurable communicative system.

Section II: AI, Narrative Transformation, and Media Shift, Chapters 5-8 focuses on the structural transformation of advertising and communication processes under the influence of artificial intelligence. It explores how AI reshapes production workflows, creative decision-making, and narrative construction, while also examining the effects of AI-driven narratives on consumer decision-making and behavioral response. This section demonstrates that artificial intelligence does not merely accelerate communication processes but reconfigures the architecture through which narratives are generated and experienced.

Section III: Critical, Ethical, and Strategic Dimensions, Chapters 9-11 addresses the normative and critical implications of AI-mediated narrative communication. It examines ethical risks, algorithmic bias, and narrative responsibility, alongside strategic silence in sustainability communication and the construction of hyperreal representations through digital twin technologies. These discussions situate AI-driven narrative transformation within broader debates on ethics, representation, and communicative accountability.

Section IV: Advanced Narrative Architecture and Strategic Futures, Chapter 12 culminates in a model-oriented synthesis of the preceding discussions. The final chapter conceptualizes corporate communication as a temporally structured narrative system and introduces the Proleptic Corporate Narrative Model, which explains how future-oriented meaning construction increasingly shapes contemporary marketing discourse. This framework positions artificial intelligence as a mediating layer that enhances predictive narrative capacity and transforms the logic of narrative persuasion.

CONCLUSION

Taken together, the volume proposes that artificial intelligence is not merely a technological tool but a structural and epistemological force that reshapes narrative advertising and marketing discourse. By integrating theoretical reflection, empirical inquiry, and strategic analysis, the book aims to provide both conceptual depth and practical relevance.

This work is intended for a diverse audience, including scholars, graduate students, and practitioners in communication, marketing, media studies, and artificial intelligence. Through its interdisciplinary orientation and model-based approach, the volume seeks to contribute to the theoretical grounding of narrative advertising in the age of artificial intelligence and to offer a framework for understanding its future trajectory.

Recep Yılmaz
Ondokuz Mayıs University, Turkey

Acknowledgment

I would like to express my sincere gratitude to the IGI Global family for their continuous support, professionalism, and dedication throughout the development and publication of this book. Their guidance and editorial support played a significant role in completing this project.

I would like to express my deep gratitude to the members of this book's editorial advisory board members, *Ebru Gökaliler, Sevimece Karadoğan Doruk, Sevgi Kavut, İsa Sarı, İdil Sayımer, Füsun Topsümer, Melike Üzüm,* and *Şenay Yavuz*, for their valuable collaboration, intellectual contributions, and commitment to maintaining the academic quality and consistency of this book; and, of course, I would like to express my sincere thanks to the highly valued authors who contributed to perfecting the content of the book: *Elif Yılmaz, Erkan Hirik, Ebru Özgen, Esennur Sirer, Farheen Sayyad, Melike Üzüm, Mustafa Aydın, Nilay Tan Çakır, Nursel Bolat, Oğuzhan Alın, Özge Uğurlu Akbaş, Özgenur Güler, Suman Vij, Tugay Sarıkaya, Yeter Demir,* and *Yogeshwari Patil*. Their academic competence, dedication, and intellectual rigor enabled this book to take shape and be published.

On a special note, I would like to express my deepest gratitude to my family. My wife and daughter's patience, encouragement, and unwavering support gave me strength throughout this challenging process. Their presence has been a constant source of strength and inspiration for me.

Recep Yılmaz
Ondokuz Mayıs University, Turkey

Section 1
Conceptual and Theoretical Foundations

Chapter 1
Artificial Creativity? A Morpho-Semantic Investigation of Neologisms and Wordplay in AI-Driven Advertising Discourse

Erkan Hirik
http://orcid.org/0000-0001-6978-8981
Samsun University, Turkey

ABSTRACT

This study investigates the "algorithmic creativity paradox" in advertising, asking whether AI can produce the rule-changing creativity that effective slogans demand or whether it remains confined to rule-governed statistical repetition. Although AI applies Turkish morphological rules with near-perfect accuracy, it struggles to recreate the intentional deviations and culturally embedded wit of human copywriters. The analysis suggests AI is generally risk-averse, favoring dictionary-attested forms and safe similes over the metaphor-rich, culturally grounded puns seen in campaigns such as "Biraver." AI therefore functions as a powerful derivational engine, generating virtually unlimited morphological variants and sometimes producing hallucinations that look creative, yet without an intent to break rules meaningfully. The study concludes that AI is best used for inspiration and ideation, with humans selecting and refining outputs to secure semantic depth and pragmatic impact.

INTRODUCTION

Advertising is, at its core, the management of an attention economy, and language is the most effective instrument for governing that economy. While the standard language aims at social consensus and intelligibility, advertising language exists by

DOI: 10.4018/979-8-3373-5666-2.ch001

strategically violating that consensus, that is, by producing linguistic deviations. In a flat, linear, fully rule-bound communicative environment, the advertising message is liable to get lost in the noise. For this reason, copywriting operates as a field of creative deformation in which the grammatical, syntactic, and semantic limits of language are deliberately pushed, words are effectively reinvented, and meaning is detached from its habitual context and rebuilt.

Yet in the first quarter of the twenty-first century, a new actor has entered this creative arena from outside the human mind: *Artificial Intelligence* (AI). Large Language Models (LLMs), trained on datasets containing billions of words, have acquired the capacity to imitate human language, generate text, and even produce outputs presented as "creative." This is precisely where the study's central problem emerges, namely, the algorithmic creativity paradox. The paradox points to an ontological tension between the nature of creativity and the operating logic of AI: *can a system that functions through the statistical repetition of past data break linguistic rules in a genuinely creative manner? Or are its outputs ultimately no more than an advanced collage assembled from what already exists?*

Pragmatic Deviation versus Grammatical Perfection

Although AI demonstrates outstanding performance in applying existing linguistic rules, it faces an ontological difficulty when producing the "rule-external" (agrammatic) structures that advertising often requires.

Advertising discourse is built on elliptical clauses, inverted word order, and neologisms. For instance, the slogan "Aç kapa, aç kapa. Artema" (a Turkish faucet advertisement) is grammatically incomplete, yet it pragmatically conveys a fully formed message. AI models (ChatGPT, Gemini, Claude, and others) tend to generate an "average" variety of language, a tendency that may contribute to reduced linguistic diversity and increasing standardisation (Pedreschi et al., 2025). Unless explicitly requested in the prompt, an AI system typically avoids taking the risk of turning meaningless sound clusters such as "Aganigi naganigi" (Fiskobirlik: a well-known hazelnut advertising slogan/hazelnut promotion campaign catchphrase in Türkiye) into a coherent marketing message. This caution follows directly from the model's operating principle: within a given context, it produces the output with the highest probability. Advertising creativity, by contrast, often depends on forging low-probability, surprising connections (Boden, 1998, pp. 348-349).

- "Yok aslında birbirimizden farkımız ama biz Osmanlı Bankası'yız." (There's no real difference between us, but we're Osmanlı Bankası.)

The paradox in this slogan lies in its logic: it claims there is no difference while simultaneously foregrounding difference. As a piece of formal reasoning, it is contradictory. As advertising, it is striking. Because AI is trained around logical consistency and truth-oriented objectives (Barut, 2025, p. 162), it may struggle to produce, or even to recognise, rhetorical figures of this kind, especially irony. In Boden's (1998) well-known discussion of AI and creativity, such systems most often display combinational creativity. In other words, they recombine existing ideas or data in new configurations. What results, however, is less genuine novelty than a large-scale collage of prior material. Since AI-generated texts reflect patterns present in the training data, the system's capacity to produce historical creativity (H-creativity, understood as something no one has produced before) remains a contested issue (Kim, 2022, p. 64).

In advertising, neologism is not merely a matter of joining words. It also involves loading the new form with cultural and affective connotations (Batı, 2002). Human cognition can turn a brand name into a generic product category, as in the case of "Pimapen" (PVC window brand) and "Selpak" (paper tissue brand), which refer to paper tissues in general. AI, by contrast, can learn such semantic shifts only after they enter its training data. In this sense, AI does not lead linguistic change; it follows it.

It is therefore reasonable to argue that AI's linguistic outputs remain largely confined to what Chomsky would call *rule-governed creativity*. In contrast, the rule-breaking character of advertising still marks a frontier for machine learning. An AI system may break rules "by accident" through hallucination (Banh & Strobel, 2023, p. 63). What it cannot easily reproduce is the deliberate, goal-directed, and persuasive deviation that a copywriter produces, because that deviation presupposes culturally and pragmatically grounded intent.

Two Faces of Linguistic Creativity: A Chomskyan Distinction

To evaluate AI performance in advertising texts, especially in slogan writing and neologism production, one must first clarify how "creativity" is defined in linguistics. In Chomsky's (1965) account of linguistic capacity, creativity is not a mechanical by-product; it is a form of generativity specific to the human mind. In this context, two widely cited notions of creativity become relevant: rule-governed creativity and rule-changing creativity. If the present paradox is to be made analytically tractable, the starting point is this duality built into the linguistic definition of creativity. Drawing on the competence-performance distinction, Noam Chomsky uses the term rule-governed creativity to refer to the human ability to generate an unlimited number of sentences from a limited set of rules (McGilvray, 2001, p. 6; Zawada, 2005, p. 20). On this view, any physiologically healthy speaker can both produce and understand sentences they have never previously heard, precisely because they possess this capacity. Turkish grammar, for example, permits a perfectly well-formed sentence aligned with subject-object-verb order and vowel harmony: "Yarın akşam eve erken geleceğim." (I will come home early tomorrow evening). This sentence is produced entirely within the existing rule system. Owing to their training on massive datasets, AI models can execute this kind of rule-governed production with remarkable accuracy. Indeed, it has been observed that AI may exhibit near-flawless grammar (Nazlı, 2022b, p. 197) and commit fewer syntactic errors than human writers. Advertising and literature, however, demand movement beyond this rule-governed system. They call for rule-changing creativity. In Boden's typology, this corresponds to transformational creativity, namely creativity that pushes against, or reshapes, the boundaries of an existing conceptual space (Boden, 1998, p. 348). Advertising language departs from the morphological, syntactic, and semantic conventions of the standard language in order to attract attention and persuade.

- "Biraver" (Efes Pilsen advertisement) or "Çokomik" (Şokella advertisement). (Lembet, 2012, p. 59)

Here, a morphological deviation is created by combining "bira" (beer) with "semaver" (samovar) or "çoko" (chocolate) with "komik" (funny). The item "biraver" does not appear in the TDK Güncel Türkçe Sözlük 'Turkish Language Association Contemporary Turkish Dictionary' and runs counter to ordinary derivational expectations. Yet in advertising terms, the "error" functions as a creative neologism. This is where the core paradox becomes concrete: *how can a system designed to predict the statistically most likely word produce a statistically unlikely mistake that is nonetheless meaningful and functional?*

Rule-Governed Creativity and AI's Comfort Zone

In Chomsky's (1965) framework, the creativity that is emphasised is fundamentally rule-governed. It refers to a speaker's ability to use a finite set of grammatical rules (phonology, morphology, syntax) to generate an infinite number of sentences that they have never heard or uttered before. A Turkish speaker, for example, can produce and understand the sentence "Yapay zekâ, bahçedeki mor çiçekleri sulayan robotu izliyordu." (The AI system was watching the robot watering the purple flowers in the garden.) even without prior exposure to it. The productivity at work here remains faithful to the rules of the language.

AI models display a near-superhuman capacity in this domain. They learn syntactic regularities and morphological patterns from large-scale data, and they apply Turkish agglutinative morphology, vowel harmony, and canonical word order with mathematical consistency. In that sense, AI excels at producing grammatically well-formed and acceptable sentences. Advertising, however, asks for more than grammatical correctness. If a bank advertisement states "Güveniniz bizim için önemlidir." (Your trust is important to us.) the sentence is rule-governed, correct, and readily interpretable. Yet, from an advertising standpoint, it is not creative. It is merely true. Contemporary AI architectures are optimised to produce precisely this kind of "correctness." The punch of advertising, by contrast, often lies in how truth is bent, not simply in how it is stated.

Rule-Changing Creativity and What Advertising Demands

The second kind of creativity, rule-changing creativity, exceeds the boundaries of the Chomskyan system and is more closely associated with literary and advertising language. It does not stop at generating new sentences by applying existing rules. It stretches, violates, or effectively redefines the rules.

As Leech (1966) argues, advertising language is characterised by deviations from the standard language. When a slogan uses "Yiyin gari" (Eat up, then!), (Lays advertisement), a regional dialect feature is brought into the standard register. The result is a rule violation that nevertheless captures attention. Likewise, when one says "Fanta'la"[1] (in the sense of "drink Fanta"), a brand name is verbalised, yielding a morphological formation that does not exist as a conventional item in the language. This is precisely the rule-changing creativity advertising exploits, and it is also where the paradox deepens. AI systems are trained through mechanisms that reward the selection of what is "correct," that is, what is most probable in context. Yet "Fanta'la" is, statistically speaking, low-probability, and from the standpoint of standard grammar, it can be labelled "incorrect." In advertising, "error" becomes style and a tool of effect. For AI, error is a loss to be minimised. For AI to become genuinely creative in advertising copy, it would have to work against its own truth-oriented optimisation and, in a paradoxical sense, learn to "err" well.

Statistical Parrot or Digital Artist?

One of the study's central concerns is whether the neologisms and wordplays produced by AI originate in genuine cognitive processes or amount to stochastic parroting (stochastic parrots, Bender et al., 2021).

The operating logic of AI is not so much to discover a new idea as to assemble fragments drawn from billions of prior ones. When an AI model is asked to produce a chocolate advertisement slogan, it effectively computes the distributional proximity between chocolate and terms such as *mutluluk* (happiness), *haz* (pleasure), *enerji* (energy), and *lezzet* (flavour), then arranges them into well-formed grammar. The output often takes the form of clichés such as "Mutluluğun tadı" (The taste of happiness) or “Enerji dolu bir ısırık.” (An energy-filled bite.) Creativity involves a movement toward the unknown. Algorithms are structurally inclined to repeat what is already known.

At times, AI produces non-existent words or connections through what is called hallucination. In advertising, such hallucinations can become an unexpected opportunity. If an AI model generates a meaningless word through a contextual error, can a human copywriter label it a neologism and convert it into a brand name? In that case, where should creativity be located: in the system that produced the mistake, or in the human agent who recognises the mistake as creative?

THE MORPHOLOGICAL CAPABILITIES OF TURKISH AND AI

Discussing the issues mentioned above through Turkish makes the problem even more intriguing. Turkish is highly conducive to the creation of neologisms due to its agglutinative structure. A large number of new words can be derived through combinations of roots and suffixes (for example: Göz → Gözlük → Gözlükçü → Gözlükçülük). Advertisers exploit this productivity, often creating forms in patterns such as “Word + sAl” (for example, Lezzetsel) or “Word + lA” (for example, Whatsapp’la).

Can AI use this “mathematical” morphology of Turkish to produce original neologisms that are semantically viable and persuasive in marketing terms? Or are AI-generated neologisms merely fabrications that look well-formed on the surface while remaining empty at the level of deeper meaning?

The “X + kafası” (X + head) pattern (Karadağ & Burnaz, 2021) is a metaphorical neologism template that has become popular in Turkish in recent years. It emerged from the mind’s need to categorise social experience. Is it possible for an AI model, working only on word-level operations without sensing the social context or the spirit of the time, to invent a new template with cultural traction comparable to “X + kafası”? Or will it simply mimic the existing pattern and generate derivative items such as “tatil kafası” (holiday head) and “yaz kafası” (summer head)?

The Need for Deliberate Deviation in Advertising Discourse

Advertising discourse must stop the reader or viewer in their tracks. To create the effect that Russian Formalists call *defamiliarization* (Maloku & Avdyli, 2023), it must break the automatised structure of language.

- Phonological deviations: sound play, alliteration, deliberate misspellings. (Because AI learns phonology primarily through writing rather than sound, it can remain mechanical in rhyme and rhythm.)
- Lexical deviations/neologisms: deriving words that do not exist in the language.
- Semantic deviations: metaphor, metonymy, oxymoron, including logically "impossible" yet meaningful expressions such as "Sıcak buz." (hot ice).
- Grammatical deviations: ellipsis and inverted structures.

Can AI "learn" such deviations? If machine learning systems encounter enough examples of deviation in their training sets, in other words, enough creative advertising copy, they can imitate those patterns of deviation. One might call this *stylised imitation.* Yet a fine line remains: *can AI distinguish between breaking a rule creatively and producing an erroneous sentence?*

When a human copywriter produces the neologism "biraver" (Efes Pilsen), the form draws together cultural codes, including the relation of the semaver 'samovar' to tea culture and the social setting associated with beer. For AI to achieve a comparable intertextual and cultural synthesis based solely on statistical data is arguably the most challenging aspect of the algorithmic creativity paradox. Humour and wordplay require not only linguistic competence but also deep world knowledge and a theory of mind. AI, therefore, does not "know" the addressee's reaction in any strong sense. It can only predict.

Against this theoretical background, the study advances the following thesis: AI models can apply language's morphological and syntactic rules with high precision, thereby generating high-quality variations and collages of existing advertising discourse. Yet they remain insufficient without human supervision and prompt engineering to produce the culturally grounded, pragmatically and semantically disruptive neologisms that constitute the core of advertising, namely, rule-changing creativity. AI creativity is best described as a capacity for statistical rearrangement. Advertising language, by contrast, demands resignification.

Accordingly, the study examines neologisms and wordplays in AI-generated advertising texts along two principal axes:

i. Morphological accuracy: conformity to the structural properties of Turkish.
ii. Semantic depth: polysemy and richness of association.

The central research terrain lies in how AI's tendency not to break grammar but to stabilise it aligns with or conflicts with the transgressive spirit of advertising language.

Dictionary-Attested Forms or Nonsensical Fabrication?

Examining how AI models produce lexical items in natural languages suggests that they tend to oscillate between two competing orientations: "guaranteed approach" and "morphological adventure." When prompted to generate a brand name or a slogan, the central question is whether AI simply retrieves a safe, already attested word from its immense lexical store, or instead draws on the derivational resources of Turkish to construct a new form that has no dictionary entry yet remains morphologically well-formed.

In general terms, AI's default orientation tends toward lexical and phraseological conservatism, a form of dictionary loyalty. It prioritises items that are statistically frequent and therefore more likely to be "correct." For instance, when prompted to name a coffee brand, the model's first impulse is often to offer already familiar and socially ratified compounds such as "Kahve Dünyası" (Coffee World), "Kahve Durağı" (Coffee Stop) or "Kahve Evi" (Coffee House) This tendency reflects the model's treatment of language not primarily as a site of creativity, but as the reiteration of patterns whose acceptability has already been established. However, when the prompt's context is framed around creativity, novelty, or futuristic resonances, the model tends to activate a mechanism of morphological analogy. At this point, AI ceases to function merely as a repository of words and begins to operate more like a lexical engineer. Owing to its "mathematical" structure, Turkish permits, through the combination of stems and suffixes, an effectively limitless number of formations, much like Lego pieces. AI analyses recurring word-formation patterns in its data and applies them to new stems. For example, it can infer the internal logic of "bilgisayar" (bilgi + sayar) (computer) and, for an emotion-analysis application, derive the unattested form "Duygusayar" (emotion computer?). In doing so, AI sometimes enters a domain that can be described as phonetically plausible nonsense. It produces lexical items that lack an established semantic counterpart in the language, yet conform flawlessly to Turkish phonotactics. Thus, in the food sector, it might coin "lezzetyum" (lezzet + an element-like suffix) (flavourium?) to evoke a scientific register, or propose dictionary-external formations such as "verisel" (data?, or statistical?) in a technology context. Although these items are fabricated, they sound Turkish and are not experienced as markedly alien. In this respect, AI does not merely select what already exists; it can also construct lexemes that are absent from dictionaries but appear plausible by modelling Turkish's grammatical resources.

i. Dictionary-Attested Word Formation (Safe Zone)

By default, AI typically adopts a risk-averse strategy. It tends to prefer items that are attested in the *TDK Güncel Türkçe Sözlük* 'Turkish Language Association

Contemporary Turkish Dictionary' or firmly established in common usage. Thus, when asked to propose a name for a coffee brand, it often recommends generic compounds such as "Kahve Dünyası" and "Kahve Evi" or standard derivations such as "Kahveci." This tendency follows from the model's orientation toward selecting the most probable answer, and therefore the most "correct" answer (Kolaç, 2025).

ii. Morphological Fabrication and the Courage of AI

When an AI model is prompted with parameters such as "creative," "previously unheard," or "futuristic," it begins to generate dictionary-external forms by mobilising Turkish's morphological rules. Two mechanisms are typically at work here.

Analogy: As Banguoğlu (2015) notes, new words can be formed by modelling existing patterns in the language. If the model has access to the word "bilgisayar," it can infer the compositional logic of *bilgi* + *sayar* and, on that basis, propose derivations for new domains. For a music application, it may offer "müzikçalar", which is already attested, or coin "duygusayar", which is new.

Functional generalisation of suffixes: AI also tends to extend the use of certain derivational suffixes beyond their conventional environments, particularly *+sAl, +vari, +ImsI*, and *+matik*. By attaching these suffixes to stems with which they are not ordinarily combined, it can produce forms that are semantically odd, yet still interpretable.

- "Lezzetsel" (*lezzet + sAl*). In Turkish, attaching *+sAl* to nouns of Arabic origin is common (as in *tarihsel* or *dinsel*). However, its combination with *lezzet* is not part of the standard lexicon. AI can nonetheless generate this item by exploiting phonetic plausibility, producing a form that sounds acceptable even if it is lexically unattested.
- "Çıtırvari." (*çıtır+vari*) Here, the Persian-origin element *+vari* is attached to the onomatopoeic Turkish base çıtır. AI can operate within this pattern as well and offer similar formations as plausible candidates.

What is often labelled "hallucination" in the literature may, in an advertising context, be treated not as an error but as a potential source of creativity (Yıldırım, 2025). At the same time, AI can lose semantic transparency when producing such formations. While the human mind can readily construct a metaphor upon hearing an expression with a pejorative meaning like "Kapçık Ağızlı," a randomly generated phrase such as "Ağızsal Döngü" may be grammatically well-formed yet remain semantically inert.

Sarı (2015) notes that, in recent years, word-formation processes such as *clipping, blending,* and *initial-based formations* have become more prevalent in Turkish. When

AI attempts to transfer the English logic of blending (breakfast + lunch = brunch) to Turkish, it often encounters difficulties due to vowel harmony constraints. For example, when combining *kitap* and *kafe*, a human speaker might coin "kitapfe,". In contrast, an AI typically prefers to remain with a compound-like option such as "KitapKafe" or may generate phonotactically ill-formed strings (e.g., "Kitfe").

In natural language processing (NLP) workflows, AI models commonly analyse lexical items by segmenting them into stems and affixes (stemming/lemmatization) (Boltayevich et al., 2023). However, Turkish's agglutinative structure provides a more complex terrain for AI than English. While new word formation in English often proceeds through the juxtaposition of lexical items, in Turkish, the meaning and even the grammatical category of a base can be substantially reshaped through the accumulation of multiple suffixes.

Existing studies further indicate that AI's *morphological awareness* varies across languages. For instance, in a study of a morphologically rich language such as Greek, AI was found to align more closely with human performance in derivation, but to struggle with compounding and blended neologisms. A primary reason appears to be that AI processes words based on form-based cues rather than semantic context (Georgiou, 2025).

In Turkish, many derivatives can be formed from a single lexical base. Based on the statistical frequency in the training data, AI can often deploy such derivatives appropriately. The situation shifts, however, once one moves to the level of *creative deviation* demanded by advertising. AI typically exhibits a regression-to-the-mean tendency, favouring the most common, most standardised, and lowest-risk structures available in the language (Pedreschi et al., 2025). This orientation makes it difficult to produce the striking, oppositional neologisms that advertising discourse often requires.

For example, it is unlikely that AI will spontaneously generate idiomatised, derogatory neologisms such as "kapçık ağızlı" or culturally and morphologically playful formations such as "biraver" (bira + semaver/ver-). The underlying reason is that AI is generally less flexible than human speakers in constructing semantically and culturally distant associations between lexical items. In a study on false equivalents, Barut (2025) reports that ChatGPT sometimes produced pseudo-words while defining concepts, yet most of these formations were semantically empty. This finding suggests that AI can apply morphological regularities, but it does not consistently secure semantic coherence.

Turkish is highly productive in deriving new words through suffixes such as *+sAl*, *+(I)msI*, *+vari*, and *-lA*. During the language reforms of the Republican period, items such as "okul" (school), "evren" (universe), and "birey" (person) were deliberately coined through such resources and subsequently became conventionalised in the lexicon (Röhrborn, 2001). Copywriters often proceed analogously. Since AI models have been trained on the distributional profiles of these suffixes, they are generally competent at attaching them to existing bases. Their success in genuine coinage, however, remains contested.

Many AI-generated "new words" can amount to low-quality, decontextualised output, frequently discussed under labels such as hallucination or *AI slop.*[2] (Chyrvonyi, 2025, p. 178). In human creativity, a sound sequence such as "aganigi" can be produced as a deliberate nonsense form with phonetic appeal, whereas nonsensical items generated by AI are more often the by-product of statistical misfires. At the same time, when *neologism learning* techniques are applied, that is, when the model is explicitly taught a new lexical item along with its usage context, it has been shown to produce content that appropriately aligns with the newly introduced concept (Hewitt et al., 2025). This suggests that AI can use neologisms when instructed, but it still depends on human direction for the spontaneous production of creative neologisms.

Related difficulties also appear in translation. It has been observed that AI may fall into *structural calque* errors when rendering neologisms into the target language. For instance, instead of translating the English concept "me-ism" as "kendincilik," it may produce semantically void, word-for-word replicas. This indicates that even when AI can parse morphological structure, it may struggle to grasp the culturally and metaphorically innovated meaning behind the form, in other words, the relevant process of *neosemy.*

MORPHOLOGICAL ANALYSIS: NEOLOGISMS

Neologism as the Foundation of Advertising Discourse

One of the principal mechanisms that sustains a language's vitality and enables it to adapt to social change is the expansion of its lexicon. In the linguistic literature, a *neologism* is commonly defined as either the creation of a new lexical item that did not previously exist in the language or the assignment of an entirely new meaning to an already existing item (Çelikten & Çelikten, 2020; Mehmandoust & Söylemez, 2023). Since advertising is structurally anchored in the management of attention, it must disrupt consumers' automated perceptual routines and produce a defamiliarizing effect. This disruption is typically achieved by moving beyond the constraints of the standard language, most often through neologisms that reframe what appears familiar, thereby rendering the message salient.

Advertising discourse does not merely promote a product; it also constructs a new conceptual field around that product. In this process, neologisms serve as instruments that encode the product's distinctiveness at the linguistic level. For instance, in the case of *Fiskobirlik* (Fındık Tarım Satış Kooperatifleri Birliği) 'Union of Hazelnut Farming Sales Cooperatives', hybrid formations created from the initial letters or syllables of institutional names through blending and acronymisation can, over time, move beyond the status of a brand label and come to operate as a generic designation. Similarly, the English item *brunch*, formed by blending *breakfast* and *lunch*, is a neologism that has entered Turkish lexical usage through global advertising and marketing discourse.

Analyses of neologisms in Turkish advertising discourse suggest considerable diversity, while also indicating that, in terms of frequency, they are typically produced through three major morphological pathways:

i. Derivation: formations created by attaching derivational suffixes to existing bases (e.g., "Bankamatik" = *banka* + *-matik*). (Bank + matik).
ii. Compounding and blending: formations produced by combining semantic or phonological segments of two items [e.g., "biraver" = *bira* + *ver-* (beer + to give) and with the associative pull of *semaver* (samovar)] (Cesur Kılıçaslan et al., 2012).
iii. Semantic shift: formations in which an existing item is repositioned through contextual reframing [e.g., "Yıldız" (star) beyond its astronomical sense, used as a popular-culture icon or as a branding element such as a logo] (Çelik, 1995; Sarı, 2015, p. 79).

Lembet (2012, pp. 59-60) note that advertisers manipulate the phonetic, morphological, and syntactic properties of language, reshaping words and even syllables in the process. Examples such as "Kekstra" (Kek + Ekstra) and "çokomik" (çok + komik) show how morphological boundaries can be stretched to strengthen a brand's auditory memorability. Today, AI has entered this *process of creative deformation* as a new actor. A key issue that warrants systematic investigation is how AI models trained on large datasets simulate, in Turkish, the kinds of formations that traditional copywriters produce through linguistic intuition and cultural knowledge.

Language, much like a living organism, is a structure that continuously changes, develops, and renews itself through internal dynamics. One of the most dynamic sites of this change is undoubtedly the lexicon. New objects, concepts, technological developments, and social transformations generate fresh naming needs within a language (Akyıldız & Tükel Kanra, 2022, p. 1450). In the linguistics literature, this phenomenon, termed neologism, is commonly defined as the creation of a new lexical item in a language or the assignment of a new meaning to an existing item (Rodríguez Guerra, 2016, p. 529).

Activating neologisms in advertising is not simply a matter of assigning a name. It functions as a strategic instrument that supports branding and aims to produce differentiation. Brands seeking a durable place in consumers' minds often attempt to secure a competitive edge by coining new lexical items that are absent from standard dictionaries, phonetically appealing, rhythmically memorable, and rich in semantic association. This brings into view a consequential question*: Can large language models (LLMs), which operate on statistical probability estimation, display the kind of derivational competence that the human mind exhibits, a competence that is at once "rule-breaking" and yet grounded in rules?*

A closer look at neologism formation shows that languages draw on different mechanisms depending on their morphological architecture. Turkish, by virtue of its agglutinative structure, has a substantial capacity to derive new words through the attachment of derivational suffixes to stems and bases. Advertising discourse exploits this potential to its fullest, at times even at the cost of violating grammatical expectations through linguistic deviation, in order to produce striking neologisms.

Neologisms frequently encountered in advertising and in the literature can be grouped as follows:

1. Blending/portmanteau. New items formed by combining segments of two or more words. In English, *brunch* (breakfast + lunch) and *smog* (smoke + fog) are classic examples (Lehrer, 2003). In Turkish advertising, this strategy is likewise highly productive.
    - "Fiskobirlik" (Fındık Tarım Satış Kooperatifleri Birliği), "Çokomik" (çok + komik, or alternatively çikolata + komik).
    - Items such as *Rakunk* (raccoon + skunk) or *Wolvog* (wolf + dog), used in Atwood's dystopian fiction, show that blending is also exploited in literature to build inventive worlds (Mehmandoust & Söylemez, 2023, p. 1137).
2. Compounding. The formation of a new concept through the combination of two full lexical items.
    - "Biçerdöver" "Gecekondu" "Bilgisayar." In advertising, brand names such as "Çokoprens" (çikolata + prens) also fall within this category.
3. Derivation/affixation. Formations created by attaching derivational suffixes to existing bases. Turkish is particularly rich in this domain.
    - "Tursilleyin" is derived from the brand name *Tursil* via the verbalising suffix *-lA*. Copywriters often verbalise brand names to turn the brand into action. "Vimlemek" similarly is a verb derived from the brand name *Vim*.
4. Semantic shift. The assignment of a new meaning to an existing lexical item.
    - "Yıldız" (astronomical object → celebrity), "Fare" (mouse) (animal → computer hardware). In advertising, the conversion of common nouns

into brand names, as in “Kelebek” (butterfly) (a furniture brand), is closely related to this category and aligns with processes of generalisation.

5. Coinage/ex nihilo formation. The creation of an item from scratch, not transparently derived from an identifiable base, and shaped primarily by phonetic appeal.
   - “Aganigi naganigi” (a semantically opaque but memorable sound sequence in a Fiskobirlik advertisement). Such neologisms draw attention by exploiting phonetic attractiveness and a degree of opacity or mystery.

Artificial Intelligence and Agglutinative Morphology

Turkish is exceptionally conducive to the formation of neologisms due to its “mathematical” structure and suffixal system. Turkish roots and stems, through derivational suffixation, have the potential to lexicalise an effectively unlimited range of new concepts. This potential, however, is constrained by phonological harmony requirements (vowel harmony, consonant assimilation) and by morphotactic rules, most notably the ordering of suffixes.

AI models learn language not as an explicit rule system but as a chain of probabilistic regularities (Bender et al., 2021). While in analytic languages such as English word formation is often realised through juxtaposition (compounding) or through a relatively limited inventory of affixes, Turkish can build word forms with clause-like informational density by attaching multiple suffixes to a single base.

Empirical work suggests that AI models display two recurrent patterns in relation to Turkish morphology:

i. Dominance of High-Frequency Suffixes: AI tends to rely on the suffixes it encounters most frequently in training data, especially *+lI, +sIz, +CI, +lIk*, and, more recently, *+sAl*. The suffix *+sAl*, criticised by Lewis (1999) as a “manufactured suffix,” appears with disproportionate frequency in AI outputs. A major driver of this tendency is the heavy presence of academic and formal registers in model training corpora. In advertising discourse, where naturalness and audience resonance are central, outputs such as *gelenekselleştirilmiş tat* (traditionalized taste) rather than *geleneksel lezzet* (traditional taste) may be morphologically well-formed but pragmatically unsuccessful.
ii. Tokenisation (Blockchain) Effects and Hallucinative Formations: AI does not process words in terms of syllables or morphemes; it processes them as segmented units referred to as tokens. Given Turkish’s agglutinative character, tokenisation can fragment word forms, thereby obscuring stem-suffix relations. As a result, AI may generate neologisms that sound Turkish and remain phonet-

ically plausible, yet do not conform to grammatical constraints, yielding items such as *parlangıç, duyumsar, veridaş,* and *yenilenik.*

As noted above, culturally sedimented templates such as "X+Kafası" (Karadağ & Burnaz, 2021) can be imitated with relative ease (for instance, "Tatil Kafası", "Yaz Kafası"). By contrast, AI typically struggles with multi-layered blending formations such as *biraver*, where *bira, ver-*, and *semaver* are simultaneously activated at the levels of sound and meaning. This is not only a morphological operation; it also requires the ability to execute a semantically and culturally grounded pun.

Overall, AI performs strongly within the domain of Rule-Governed Creativity. It can derive new forms by applying existing regularities. In the kind of creativity advertising discourse tends to reward, namely Rule-Changing Creativity, where norms are stretched or strategically violated, AI outputs often remain either overly standardised or slide into semantic vacuity.

Brand-Name Derivation Scenario

A "smart tea glass" was conceived in order to bring technology and culture into the same frame. Given the central place of tea in Turkish culture and its high level of everyday consumption, the aim was to gauge how far artificial intelligence can analyse and account for this cultural domain. For this reason, starting from the scenario of an intelligent tea glass, the model was asked to propose potential names for the product.

Scenario: For an "Akıllı Çay Bardağı" (Smart Tea Glass) ChatGPT-5.2 is asked to derive Turkish brand names. The task is formulated as follows: *Produce alternative Turkish brand-name alternatives for a tea glass with "smart" functionality.* [Prompt: Akıllı özelliğe sahip bir çay bardağı (Akıllı çay bardağı) için Türkçe marka adları alternatifleri üret.]

AI Outputs and Their Morphological Analyses

- "AkıllıBardak" / "SmartÇay"
    - These responses exemplify compounding, one of the strategies AI most frequently relies on. The model either concatenates "Akıllı" (smart) and "bardak" (glass) directly or inserts the English item "smart" into a Turkish construction, which constitutes code-switching. As noted in the literature, AI tends to privilege high-frequency items in its training data (for instance, *smart, akıllı, teknoloji*). The result is comparatively safe, but it remains distant from the kind of creativity advertising discourse

typically rewards. In particular, it does not satisfy the advertising principle of deviation.

- "Çaymatik" / "Demleyiver"
    - o "Çaymatik": The suffix "-matik" is a productive analogical device in Turkish, especially in technological contexts (e.g., "bankamatik", "dokunmatik"). AI appears to have internalised this pattern and applies it readily.
    - o "Demleyiver": This formation draws on the swiftness construction "-i ver", adding an "immediate/quickly" nuance (demleyen hemen). Together, these examples suggest that AI has substantial command of Turkish derivational resources. They also imitate the pathway through which a brand name can shift toward a generic label, as often discussed with items like "Bankamatik." Even so, they largely remain repetitions of existing templates.
- "Çayver" / "Isıtgel"
    - o In advertising discourse, imperatives are widely used [for example, "Susuzluğunu dinle, Sprite iç!" (Listen to your thirst, drink Sprite!) AI can reproduce such syntactic cues of advertising. What it struggles to achieve is the fine-grained sound-based similarity and wordplay that underpins formations like "biraver" (Efes Pilsen), where the interplay between "bira" and "semaver" supports a culturally resonant pun. AI will likely derive "Çayver" primarily as the literal imperative "Çay ver" (give/serve me tea) without activating the "semaver" reference. In other words, it has difficulty producing *intertextuality* of this kind.
- "TeknoÇay" / "DijitalDem"
    - o It takes the form of combining non-Turkish prefixes (Tekno-, Dijital-) with Turkish lexical items. AI has learned from its training data that English or internationalised technology registers can carry prestige in product naming. As a result, it often gravitates toward elements such as *smart*, *tech*, or *plus* when producing brand-like outputs for technological goods.
- "Çayzen" / "Bardakistan"
    - o Here, the model draws on borrowed formatives such as "-zen" (often glossed as an agentive element, Persian origin) or "-istan" (a place-forming element). This is the domain in which AI can sometimes appear creative, yet it is also where it most frequently misfires. Compared to "Neyzen" ("ney" player), "Çayzen" is morphologically possible but semantically odd, since the intended role ("çay yapan"? *tea maker) is culturally and pragmatically unclear. The model can satisfy formal morphology, but it cannot reliably evaluate whether the resulting item will

be perceived as culturally apt, pragmatically effective, or euphonically appealing in advertising discourse.

AI largely remains faithful to morphological regularities when deriving words in agglutinative languages such as Turkish. It applies stem-suffix compatibility and vowel harmony with considerable success. It nevertheless struggles to produce neologisms that display the semantic and associative depth required by advertising discourse. The human mind can operate a metaphor-driven neologism process, as in the "X+Kafası" template, which can extend from "Matematik kafası" to "Hollywood kafası." In this process, the noun "kafa" moves beyond its literal sense as a body part and becomes a metaphor for mindset. AI, by contrast, tends to process lexical items in their literal meanings. Its capacity to invent new words by integrating connotative meanings and cultural codes remains limited, and the neologisms it generates are often combinations of existing material or instances of structural imitation.

AI can, as a morphological tool, generate an effectively unlimited number of variants. Selecting, from among these possibilities, the form that is striking, memorable, and viable as a brand name, however, still belongs to the domain of human creativity and cultural intuition. AI can produce dictionary-external items (nonsense words). Yet it has not reached human-level competence in ensuring that such items are phonetically plausible and that they meaningfully fill a lexical gap.

Morphological Analysis of AI-Generated Brand Names

In this section, the outputs produced in response to specific brand-name derivation prompts given to the ChatGPT-5.2 model are analysed from morphological and semantic perspectives. The analysis aims to show how AI mobilises Turkish derivational suffixes and word-combination mechanisms within the context of advertising creativity.

Prompt: "Yapay zekâ destekli, kişiye özel vitamin üreten bir sağlık girişimi için Türkçe, fütüristik, tek sözcüklük ve daha önce duyulmamış marka isimleri türet." [Derive Turkish, futuristic, single-word, previously unheard brand names for a health start-up that produces AI-assisted, personalised vitamins.]

Below are the AI-generated candidates and their morphological analyses.

Table 1. Morphological Analysis of AI-Generated Brand Names

AI Suggestion	Morphological Analysis (Base + Suffix / Structure)	Type	Evaluation and Link to Sources
Vitazekâ	*Vita* (Latin: life, also associated with "vitamin") + Zekâ (Arabic-origin, Turkish usage)	Blending / hybrid formation	AI hybridises "Yapay Zekâ" (Artificial Intelligence) and "Vitamin." The result is comparable to "Fiskobirlik" -type blended formations. At the same time, it combines a Latin-based element with an Arabic-origin Turkish lexeme and aligns the outcome with Turkish naming and syntagmatic expectations.
Özelleş	Özel 'special' (noun/adjective base) + -le(ş) (denominal/ deadjectival verbaliser)	Derivation	A standard derivational operation. It verbalises the concept "kişiye özel" (personal), turning it into a call-to-action-oriented form. This aligns with the advertising discourse's preference for directive and action-framing structures (Nazlı, 2022a).
Sağlıksal	Sağlık 'health' (noun) + +sAl (denominal nominaliser)	Derivation (fabrication)	A typical overextension of *+sAl*, the suffix criticised by Lewis (1999). Instead of the idiomatic *sağlıklı* (healthy), the form *sağlıksal* aims to sound more technical or "scientific." Morphologically acceptable, pragmatically marked, and often perceived as a salient feature of "AI Turkish."
Genkod	Gen (biology) + Kod (software/ IT)	Compounding	It is a compound formed by combining two monosyllabic nouns. It follows a logic comparable to Turkish formations such as "Yeryüzü" (surface/earth) and "Buzdolabı" (fridge), although in this case the combination is suffixless. In advertising discourse, such short and punchy forms are often preferred for their memorability.
Bedenimsi	Beden 'body' (noun) + +(I)msI (similative suffix)	Derivation	Formally well-formed (*beden + -imsi*), but semantically problematic. The meaning "body-like" lacks positive fit for a vitamin brand and may reduce perceived credibility. This illustrates a pattern where morphological well-formedness is achieved, while semantic appropriateness is not.
Vitamatik	*Vita* + +matik (borrowed element; productive in Turkish)	Borrowed suffixation	The element *+matik* is productive in Turkish via analogical extensions (as in "Bankamatik"). AI applies this analogy effectively, yielding a techno-register brand candidate that remains morphologically plausible.
Hücresel	Hücre 'cell' + +sel	Standard derivation	This is an already attested word. Despite the prompt's "previously unheard" constraint, AI opts for a dictionary-attested, high-prestige scientific register item as a brand name. This reflects a safe-zone preference.
Akılhap	Akıl 'mind'+ Hap 'pill'	Compounding (suffixless noun-noun construction)	A compact compound with an intertextual resonance to idiomatic expressions (for example, "Akıl küpü" 'mind cube'). It signals a more associative naming move and can be read as an attempt at metaphor-driven branding.

Based on the data presented in Table 1, the following inferences can be drawn regarding AI's morphological operating logic:

i. "+sel/sal" Obsession

When asked to propose a futuristic or "scientific" brand name, AI shows a disproportionate preference for the Turkish suffixes *+sel/+sal* (for example, *sağlıksal, hücresel, vitaminsel*). This tendency can plausibly be linked to the heavy weighting of academic and formal registers in the model's training data. Much as in what is often labelled "Anglo-Saxon Turkish."[3] This suffix serves as a cue to the model's seriousness and scientificity. In advertising discourse, by contrast, *+sel/+sal* formations are often perceived as cold and distancing.

ii. Blending Success and Limitations

AI is relatively successful at forming new lexical items by combining two distinct concepts, as in "Vitazekâ." This strategy aligns with a common practice in Turkish advertising discourse (for instance, "Kekstra", "Probis"). AI nevertheless tends to hesitate when blending pressures Turkish phonological constraints, including harmony-related expectations. In such cases, it often defaults to straightforward concatenation rather than pursuing more integrated, phonologically optimised blends.

iii. Morphological Well-Formedness and Semantic Vacuity

The item "Bedenimsi" is one of the clearest illustrations of the algorithmic creativity paradox. Morphologically, the derivation *beden + -(I)msI* is fully well-formed in terms of segmental sequencing and vowel patterning. Semantically, however, a vitamin brand name that effectively means "body-like but not a body" is unlikely to be acceptable from a marketing perspective. AI can handle form with high precision, yet it does not consistently model the pragmatic consequences of content. This supports the claim by Grilli and Pedota (2024) that AI tends to display "combinatory creativity" rather than "conceptual creativity."

iv. The Functionalisation of Borrowed Affixal Material

The case of "Vitamatik" shows that AI can also exploit Turkish's flexibility in integrating borrowed material into its derivational system, either by attaching Turkish suffixes to foreign bases or by deploying borrowed, affix-like elements with Turkish roots. AI can recognise lexicalised formatives such as *-matik* and even *-büs* (as in "metrobüs"), and it can extend them into new naming contexts.

In advertising discourse, neologism involves more than producing a new word; it involves building a world through that word. The examples above indicate that AI can, at a technical level, handle Turkish agglutinative morphology with considerable competence. It often applies stem-suffix compatibility and phonological alternations (e.g., vowel deletion and consonant lenition) with a level of consistency relatively free of human error. Even so, the neologisms it produces typically remain within the domain of *Rule-Governed Creativity*. In other words, it applies existing derivational routines (Base + derivational suffix) in a primarily mechanical way. For the kinds of neologisms that advertising often needs, namely forms that are deliberately deviant, strategically "broken" and culturally resonant, AI still depends on human intervention. This includes cases where deviation is constitutive of the effect, such as the branding of an idiom-like form (for example, "Sulugöz"), culturally layered wordplay of the "Biraver" type, hybridisation of product labels such as "Biskolata" orthography-based effects that stylise an apparent "error" (for example, "bidolu"), or conversational and relational cues carried by items such as "hoşbeş." In such cases, the persuasive force emerges not from morphological well-formedness alone, but from intertextuality, cultural indexing, and pragmatic targeting.

AI can generate dictionary-external items that appear plausible within Turkish derivational space. It struggles, however, to calibrate the balance between phonetic appeal and semantic relevance, mainly because it lacks robust access to cultural context. In advertising copywriting, AI therefore functions less as an autonomous creator than as a powerful derivational engine capable of producing an effectively unlimited set of morphological variants. The human copywriter's task is to filter out semantically inert formations, such as "Bedenimsi," and to select and refine candidates, such as "Vitazekâ," that possess brand potential.

SEMANTIC ANALYSIS: PUN AND POLYSEMY

The Linguistic Basis of Humour and Wit

Advertising discourse frequently draws on humour and wit in order to enhance persuasiveness and secure memorability. When the linguistic underpinnings of humour are examined, the core mechanisms are typically seen to rest on *incongruity* and *semantic ambiguity*. As Uçar (2014) notes, puns are generally built on the comic effect produced by placing two or more mutually incompatible meanings within the same context. In this process, the most commonly exploited resources are *polysemy* and *homophony*.

Turkish is particularly well-suited to such play, given its phonological profile and its extensive capacity for verb formation. Kahraman (2015) emphasises that polysemy constitutes a linguistic resource and that the connotative meanings words acquire in context add depth to communication. Copywriters deviate from the standard language in order to attract attention, for example, by drawing on a regional dialect feature, as in "Yiyin gari" 'Eat up, then!' (a Lays advertisement), or by disrupting the structure of an idiom through deviation. Deploying a lexical item so that it activates both its literal and its figurative senses simultaneously can intensify the semantic density of an advertisement. For instance, in a bank advertisement, the phrase "Yüzünüzü güldürür." (It will make you smile). can allude to both "happiness" and an interest rate percentage. In Turkish, "yüz" functions both as a numeral meaning "one hundred" and as a noun referring to a person's face.

When AI is assigned a creative task, for example, when it is prompted with "Esprili bir slogan yaz" (Write a witty slogan.), semantic analysis of the resulting outputs can reveal where the model positions itself within the hierarchy between metaphor and simile. The literature highlights that metaphors increase persuasiveness in advertising discourse and render abstract qualities more concrete. Metaphor establishes a direct identity relation between two domains (X is Y), whereas a simile, via an explicit marker comparable to "gibi" (as/like), sets up a safer and more overt relation (X is like Y).

The outputs produced in response to the following prompt given to the ChatGPT-5.2 model are evaluated below: "Çok hızlı giden bir spor araba için esprili ve yaratıcı bir slogan yaz." [Write a witty and creative slogan for a very fast sports car.]

- AI Output 1: "Rüzgâr gibi hızlı, şimşek gibi çakar." [Fast as the wind, striking like lightning.]
    - This is a typical simile-based construction. By using the widespread Turkish marker "gibi," it likens the car's speed to wind and lightning. The result is safe, readily interpretable, but also formulaic. AI appears to have retrieved the statistically salient association "speed = wind/lightning" from its training distribution. The degree of creativity is limited, precisely because the output remains within a low-risk zone.
- AI Output 2: "Yolların efendisi, hızın yeni adresi." [The master of the roads, the new address of speed.]
    - This output relies on clichéd advertising phrasing. Lexical items such as "adres" (address), "efendi" (master), and similar high-prestige promotional markers are frequently encountered in advertising discourse and are therefore readily reproduced by the model. Here, AI does not generate a semantic deviation; instead, it reiterates established templates.
- Illustration of Human Creativity: "Uçak biletine para ödeme." (for a car advertisement) [Do not pay for a plane ticket.]
    - This human-produced slogan does not describe speed directly. Instead, it activates the concept of "uçak" (plane) and establishes an implicit comparison between the car's speed and the speed of air travel, while simultaneously leveraging the pragmatic implication of saving money by not buying a plane ticket. Producing this kind of indirect, inference-driven slogan spontaneously is difficult for AI. The model can only build

the car-plane ticket linkage reliably if that association is represented in the training data. For this reason, AI often struggles with metaphor and tends to default to explicit similes marked by "gibi."

AI's Contextual Fidelity and Its Aversion to Ambiguity

One of the most significant obstacles AI models (LLMs) face in advertising creativity is, paradoxically, their highly proficient language-processing capacity. In next-token prediction, AI is optimised to select the statistically most probable continuation and to converge on the most explicit, least ambiguous interpretation. Advertising, however, often calls for deliberate ambiguity.

Kolaç (2025) argues that AI-based language models are effective in handling the technical and cultural contexts that underlie dictionary definitions and meaning-making processes, yet they fail to match the flexibility of the human mind when confronted with abstract, multi-layered meanings. When AI detects ambiguity in a sentence, it tends to interpret it as a breakdown in communication or an error and typically moves toward *disambiguation*, that is, making the meaning more explicit.

For example, in the line "Korkma, sönmez bu şafaklarda..."[4] The imperative "korkma" (Fear not!) functions as an encouragement and carries the sense of "do not worry." When AI explains or translates such a form, it often reduces it to a single dominant meaning (König, 1994, p. 228). A copywriter, by contrast, may seek to generate a controlled tension of meanings in the audience's mind to provoke reflection. AI's excessive fidelity to context can close precisely the productive interpretive space that advertising needs, thereby weakening the effect of wit.

From an ontological perspective, one of AI's central problems in advertising discourse concerns its stance toward meaning blur and double meaning. In human communication, and especially in advertising, ambiguity is a deliberate strategy used to capture attention and to involve the addressee actively in interpretation (Hidalgo Downing, 2000, p. 74). Rather than presenting a message in an immediately consumable form, the copywriter increases impact by leaving a gap for the audience to complete. AI models, however, operate on statistical likelihoods in training data and on a principle of relevance, and therefore tend to treat ambiguity as noise or as an error that must be resolved (Wilson, 2016, p. 8). Programmed to align with Grice's Cooperative Principle, AI aims to provide information as clearly and accurately as possible. Advertising discourse, by contrast, often relies on the intentional violation of Gricean maxims, particularly the maxims of *Quality* and *Manner* (Wilson, 2016, p. 16).

Because AI adheres strongly to contextual probability, it typically selects the most salient and most likely meaning in polysemous structures. When it encounters a creative, indeterminate neologism such as "Mental Ground Zero," it may struggle to interpret it and produce a literal output, such as "Zihinsel Sıfır Mekân," which lacks semantic depth (Yetkin Karakoç, 2014, p. 1616). This neutralises the very ambiguity that the copywriter seeks to maintain. AI can estimate semantic distance between words, but it cannot reliably process the irony or culturally charged tension that that distance generates in terms of communicative intent. In sum, while the human mind can take pleasure in ambiguity, AI tends to eliminate it, and this constitutes a paradox for creative advertising.

The Grey Zone Between Error and Invention

In advertising, neologisms are among the most effective tools for foregrounding a product's or service's salient features, enhancing memorability, and establishing a brand-specific linguistic identity. In cleaning-product advertising, for example, the expression "tursilleyin" (Tursil + the verbalising suffix -lA + imperative morphology) is a deliberate formation that turns a brand name into an action. Likewise, examples such as "Çokomik" (Çok/Çikolata + Komik) and "Aganigi naganigi" (semantically opaque sound sequences) illustrate a creative stretching of the language's morphological and phonetic resources. Such productions are outcomes of the human mind's Rule-Changing Creativity and serve an identifiable communicative purpose (Lehrer, 2003, p. 370).

By contrast, when AI models "hallucinate," the result typically lacks communicative intent; it is more accurately described as a probabilistic deviation. For instance, when asked to produce a Turkish text, an AI model may substitute "görüngüsel" for "görüntüsel" in an inappropriate context, or coin a redundant, over-suffixed form such as "teknolojikselleşmek." The literature notes that these pseudo-words often mimic derivational patterns while lacking stable semantic content.

Illustrative Case 1 (Human Creativity): "Biraver" (Efes Pilsen)

- Here, there is a phonetic and semantic interplay between "bira" and "semaver" (and possibly the verb "ver-"). The *semaver* as a tap-equipped vessel associated with communal consumption is conceptually transferred onto a beer-related frame, yielding a newly designated object (biraver). This is a purposeful deviation.

Illustrative Case 2 (AI Hallucination): "Çaysal" or "Bardakımsı"

- When asked to coin a new label for a tea glass, an AI model may derive such forms by over-relying on the high frequency of suffixes like *+sAl* and *+(I)msI* in its training data. Yet "Çaysal" does not constitute a natural derivation in Turkish in the way that items like "kumsal" or "uysal" do; it tends to sound forced and artificial. The model applies a morphological operation, but it misses the "spirit" of the word and its pragmatic appropriateness. This is not a creative invention but an error shaped by statistical central tendency, often associated with what is labelled AI slop.

Illustrative Case 3 (Grey Area): AI producing "Lezzetmatik."

- The formative *+matik* is entrenched in Turkish through items such as "bankamatik" and "dokunmatik." Combining this element with "lezzet" can be received as a creative neologism. At the same time, the formation may be better explained not as conceptual innovation on AI's part, but as the reuse of an "X+matik" template learned from the training distribution.

A Linguistic Boundary: Phonotactic Well-Formedness and Euphony

The usability of fabricated words produced by AI (whether framed as neologisms or as hallucinations) in advertising largely depends on the extent to which these forms conform to Turkish phonotactic constraints. Turkish is governed by relatively strict regularities in sound harmony and syllable structure. For a coined item to be accepted by an audience, it must first "sound Turkish" since perceived phonological naturalness functions as a precondition for uptake.

Phonotactics and the Limits of AI: Turkish does not permit initial consonant clusters of the type found in many European languages, and it also avoids word-final /b, c, d, g/, which undergo devoicing to /p, ç, t, k/. Because AI models operate through tokenisation rather than morphemic or syllabic parsing, they may occasionally generate outputs that violate such constraints.

- If an AI model is prompted with "güçlü bir temizleyici ismi türet" (Derive a strong cleaning agent name.), the influence of English-heavy training distributions may lead it to coin a form such as "Strogüç" (Strong + Güç). This item violates Turkish phonotactics, as an onset cluster such as "St-" is not permitted. It is not a purposeful creative deviation but a phonotactic violation, and it is likely to strike Turkish speakers as unfamiliar and off-putting, that is, cacophonous.

By contrast, when AI produces items such as "Güçmatik" or "Parlaks," it can be seen to respect vowel harmony and syllable-structure constraints. At the same time, the literature suggests that AI's morphological awareness varies across languages and that, in agglutinative systems such as Turkish, the model can sometimes struggle to locate stem-suffix boundaries consistently.

Morphological Boundaries and Suffix Ordering: In Turkish, suffix sequencing (base + derivational suffix + inflectional suffix) is constrained by an essentially rigid ordering principle. When AI hallucinates, it may disrupt this order.

- "Evlerli" (Ev + -ler + -li).
  - With limited exceptions, derivational suffixes such as *+lI* attach before inflectional markers such as *+lAr* (for instance, "evli-ler"). If AI produces "Evlerli" with a meaning like "having houses," this constitutes a morphological error. In advertising, such forms are typically interpreted as defective Turkish unless they are explicitly framed as an intentional register choice, for example, as child-directed speech or baby-talk stylisation (as in childlike utterances used in some campaigns). Otherwise, such errors can undermine brand credibility.

Semantic Transparency and Fabrication: As Sarı (2015) notes, a "potential word" is a form derivable under the language's rules but that has not yet entered the dictionary. AI outputs that might plausibly count as creative should ideally be drawn from this space of potential words. For example, "Gözlüklemek" ("to put on glasses" or "to examine through glasses") is unattested, yet morphologically and phonotactically possible and semantically transparent (Sarı, 2015, p. 7). If an advertisement said "Hayatı yeniden gözlükleyin," it could function as a successful neologism. If, however, the model produced "Gözlüksel," the unnecessary deployment of *+sAl* would move the form closer to coinage in a pejorative sense and toward the commonly criticised category of linguistic pollution.

Ultimately, the hallucination-creativity tension between AI and advertising hinges on the difference between violating a rule and bending it. The copywriter can break a rule effectively because the rule is known and the transgression is purposeful. AI, by contrast, operates through probabilistic approximation and can therefore break rules in ways that are simply erroneous. For an AI-produced form to be considered creative, it must conform to Turkish phonetic and morphological aesthetics while still delivering a surprising novelty at the semantic level. Otherwise, the output remains liable to be perceived as AI slop.

HALLUCINATION OR CREATIVITY?

AI systems, and large language models (LLMs) in particular, are built on statistical probability. For that reason, they may at times produce outputs that do not align with reality, that are not attested in the training data, or that remain semantically underdetermined. In the literature, this phenomenon is termed hallucination and is generally treated as an error that undermines a model's reliability. Hallucinations arise when the model extrapolates from patterns in its training corpus and establishes connections that are not in fact real, yet appear plausible (Banh & Strobel, 2023). From the standpoint of advertising, however, inventing a non-existent word or bending reality is not necessarily a mistake; it can be an indicator of the very creativity the discipline seeks. Advertising discourse requires the intentional departure from standard-language norms, the derivation of new words (neologisms), and the construction of unusual associations in order to capture the addressee's attention (Özer, 2010, p. 64). At this point, another ontological question comes into view: can a fabricated word produced "accidentally" by AI (a hallucination) carry the same aesthetic and pragmatic value as a creative neologism produced "deliberately" by a copywriter?

As Leech (1966) notes, advertising discourse is characterised by deviations from the standard language. The derivation of a word that does not exist in the language, as in "Biraver" (Efes Pilsen), constitutes a defect from the perspective of standard grammar, yet a success in advertising terms. The question, then, is whether such a "defect" counts as creativity when a human produces it intentionally, but as hallucination when AI produces it as a by-product of statistical deviation.

Types of AI Hallucination and Their Advertising Potential

Hallucinations in AI-generated text are typically discussed under two main categories:

i. Factual Hallucination: the production of incorrect information. In advertising, this is high-risk and generally undesirable because it can amount to misleading claims.
ii. Linguistic Hallucination: the generation of non-existent words, extra-grammatical structures, or semantically incoherent phrases. This is the category that intersects most directly with advertising's interest in neologism.

AI selects lexical items not primarily based on meaning, but based on sequential likelihood and distributional proximity in a vector space. In this process, it may occasionally form low-probability linkages and produce surreal lexical combinations that the human mind, constrained by conventional plausibility filters, would be unlikely to generate. AI has substantial "knowledge" of Turkish phonetic and morphological constraints, but it applies these constraints statistically rather than intuitively. Its hallucinations can be understood as outputs occurring at the tail ends of the probability distribution. From an advertising perspective, these extremes should be evaluated according to a simple criterion. If a form respects Turkish phonotactic structure and maintains an acceptable sound aesthetic, yet strategically violates semantic expectations, it may be treated as creative. If it disrupts both phonotactic and semantic structure, it is more appropriately classified as an error or noise. At present, AI lacks an aesthetic faculty that would allow it to distinguish which "mistakes" are attractive and productive from those that are merely defective.

WORDPLAY AND POLYSEMY

Advertising discourse is a strategic domain that enhances persuasive impact, captures attention, and secures memorability by deliberately stretching the semantic boundaries of the standard language. Within this domain, humour and wit are among the most effective tools for reducing resistance between the consumer and the brand. The underlying mechanism of humorous and witty expression typically rests on a word's capacity to carry two different meanings at once, that is, polysemy, on homophony, or on the deliberate disruption of idioms through decontextualisation.

From a linguistic perspective, polysemy refers to the process by which a sign comes to denote, in addition to its basic meaning, new concepts that remain related to that meaning (Korkmaz, 1992, p. 38). Homophony, by contrast, concerns the relation between words that are identical in spelling and pronunciation, yet whose meanings are entirely unrelated. Advertisers turn these phenomena into forms of verbal play commonly discussed under the rubric of punning, to convey multiple messages through a single expression and provide the audience with an intellectual pleasure often described as the satisfaction of solving a small interpretive problem.

For example, the Molfix slogan "Var mı benden daha 'Havalı'sı?" exploits the polysemy of *havalı*. The word is activated both in its connotative sense of "stylish/cool" and in relation to the product's technical feature, namely an air-permeable surface, thereby producing a compact intelligence game. Similarly, Shell's slogan "Shell que j'aime" ("the Shell I love") produces humour by establishing a phonetic resemblance, through paronomasia, to the French phrase "Celle que j'aime" ("the woman/person I love") (Çorbacıoğlu Gönezer, 2014, p. 89).

The Metaphor-Simile Distinction in AI-Generated Slogans

When AI is tested with prompts that ask for witty slogans, its outputs tend to be weighted toward similes rather than metaphors. A metaphor performs a direct identity transfer by asserting "A is B" [for example, "Aşk bir savaştır."(Love is a war.), whereas a simile establishes a weaker and more explicit link by stating "A is like B."

- Prompt: "Acı soslu bir cips markası için esprili ve abartılı bir slogan yaz." [Write a witty and exaggerated slogan for a brand of spicy crisps.]
    - o AI Output 1: "Ejderha gibi ateş püskürten lezzet." [A flavour that breathes fire like a dragon.]
    - o AI Output 2: "Yanardağ kadar acı cips." [Crisps as hot as a volcano.]
    - o Copywriter's approach: "Dilinizde yangın tatbikatı." or "İtfaiyeyi aratır." [Fire drill in your mouth.' or 'You will need to call the fire department.]

The AI outputs employ the markers "gibi" and "kadar," producing an overt, low-risk simile. This preference is consistent with distributional learning: the training data repeatedly associates spiciness with fire and volcano imagery through explicit comparative constructions, making such pairings statistically privileged. The copywriter examples, by contrast, relocate the act of eating crisps into a different conceptual field (firefighting and safety drills). This constitutes a metaphorical reframing that demands a more remote associative leap. AI often finds such remote associations difficult, and it therefore tends to generate clichéd similes rather than conceptually disruptive metaphors (Çınar & Karahan, 2009).

Turkish is highly conducive to punning because of its agglutinative morphology and the regularities of vowel harmony. Yet AI has difficulty capturing humour based on sound similarity, since it processes words primarily as tokens rather than as phonetic forms. This limitation becomes visible in pun-based prompts.

Pun 1

- Prompt: "Yüz" sözcüğünün hem 'surat' hem de 'sayı' anlamını kullanarak bir kozmetik reklamı sloganı yaz. [Write a cosmetics advertisement slogan using the word 'face' to mean both "face" and "number".]
- AI output: "Yüzünüzdeki güzellik yüzde yüz artacak." [The beauty on your face will increase by one hundred percent.]
    - o The sentence is technically well-formed, but it does not deliver an aesthetically satisfying pun. The humour relies mainly on repetition rather than on a controlled phonological or morphological twist.
- Human alternative: "Yüz'leşmeye hazır mısın?" [Are you ready to face?]
    - o This option activates both the verb *yüzleşmek* (to face or confront) and a reference to the facial domain, enabling a more compact, layered wordplay effect.

Pun 2

- Prompt: "Bir makarna markası için 'tat' sözcüğünü kullanarak cinaslı bir slogan yaz." [Write a punny slogan using the word "taste" for a pasta brand.]

- AI output: “Makarnanın en güzel tadı, sofranızın baş tacı.” [The finest flavour of pasta, the crown jewel of your meal.]
    - o AI establishes a phonetic echo between “tat” and “taç,” yet the output does not constitute a pun in the strict sense. It does not exploit the multiple grammatical functions of “tat” nor does it trigger a multi-layered interpretive payoff.
- Human alternative: “Makarna bu tat / Tat Makarna tat.” (Tat Makarna advertisement)
    - o Here, the first “tat” means “flavour”, the second “Tat” is the brand name, and the third “tat” is the imperative of “tatmak.” Human cognition merges nominal, brand, and verbal uses within a single phonetic frame, yielding a fully layered pun. AI may be able to perform a morphological analysis of the form, yet it often struggles to integrate different grammatical categories (noun, brand label, verb) into a unified aesthetic structure.

Idiom Adaptation

Advertising discourse also produces surprise by altering a component of an idiom or proverb (for example, replacing “Damlaya damlaya göl olur” with “Damlaya damlaya Bonus olur”).

- Prompt: Rework “Ateş olmayan yerden duman çıkmaz” into a slogan for a barbecue restaurant.
- AI output: “Ateş olmayan yerden lezzetli et çıkmaz.” [You cannot get tasty meat from a place that isn’t on fire.]
    - o AI attempts to preserve the proverb’s logical skeleton by substituting “duman” (smoke) with “lezzetli et” (delicious meat). The result, however, disrupts the rhythm and becomes a didactic statement rather than a slogan.
- Human alternative: “Ateş olmayan yerde biz olmayız.” [Where there is no fire, you will not find us.]
    - o This version maintains rhythm and achieves a sharper brand-centred twist.

Overall, while Turkish grammar is used flexibly by human cognition, AI tends to treat it as a relatively rigid system of constraints. In wordplay, AI often prioritises meaning while neglecting sound, rhythm, and prosodic balance, which can make its slogans more explanatory than witty. Semantically, AI excels at linear, logically coherent relations between words, yet it remains more limited in constructing circular, tension-based, and multi-layered meaning relations that advertising frequently requires. AI aims to communicate meaning; the copywriter aims to play with meaning.

CONCLUSION

This study has examined the relationship between AI and human creativity in a morpho-semantic framework, focusing on neologism and wordplay as core dynamics of advertising discourse. The discussion, organised around the algorithmic creativity paradox, has clarified both the limits of AI's linguistic production and the opportunities it presents for the advertising industry. The main findings and theoretical implications can be summarised as follows.

The analyses indicate that LLMs, when generating advertising copy in Turkish, often display a tendency toward a hybrid register, sometimes referred to as "Anglo-Saxon Turkish," in which surface lexical material is Turkish, yet syntactic organisation and inferential logic track English patterns. Beyond conventionalised renderings such as "make a difference" → "fark yaratmak", the model may produce non-idiomatic calques akin to "It makes sense" → "mantık yapıyor." Such outputs conflict with the advertising requirement of naturalness and interpersonal warmth. In addition, AI tends to overuse the suffix *+sAl* in order to lend a scientific or corporate aura. This tendency, criticised by Lewis (1999), contributes to a mechanisation of advertising language and a reduction in affective resonance.

One of the most consequential outcomes of the study is the reframing of creativity from creation ex nihilo toward selection, curation, and editing. AI functions as a derivational engine capable of producing large numbers of morphological variants, that is, neologism candidates. The human copywriter, in turn, increasingly operates as a curator, selecting among these variants those that best align with cultural codes, phonotactic aesthetics, and brand identity. AI may produce a promising blend such as "Vitazekâ", yet deciding that it can function as a viable brand name remains a human judgement. In this respect, advertising creativity is shifting from writing alone toward prompting, selecting, and refining.

AI does not simply replace the copywriter; it expands the range of available linguistic options. Future advertising practice may therefore be shaped by "centaur" models that combine AI's statistical processing capacity with human cultural and emotional intelligence. In this emerging landscape, linguistic research must track how AI is remodelling Turkish and how this modelling, in turn, transforms speakers' perceptions of language and acceptability, including the diffusion of items such as *görsellemek*. Advertising discourse is likely to remain the most rapid and visible laboratory for this transformation. AI applies rules with high precision; humans know when and why to bend or break them. Creativity begins precisely at the point where a "mistake" becomes intentional, meaningful, and effective.

In line with the study's central claim, the analyses show that AI demonstrates superhuman performance in Rule-Governed Creativity, while remaining ontologically constrained in Rule-Changing Creativity, which is central to advertising and the arts. At present, AI lacks Historical Creativity (H-creativity) in the strong sense: it cannot reliably generate genuinely unprecedented ideas in a manner anchored in communicative intent. Its creativity remains closer to what Boden describes as combinational creativity, namely the recombination of existing material in novel configurations.

Accordingly, AI's role in advertising is less that of an autonomous creative writer and more that of an inspiration engine that can generate an effectively unlimited range of variants. As Yıldırım's (2025) analysis of the advertisement film "Gözlerde Reacher, Kalplerde Türkiye" (Reacher in the eyes, Türkiye in the heart) suggests, AI can produce technically polished visuals and text. What elevates such elements into culturally and emotionally coherent artefacts, especially in contexts involving national sentiment and other abstract values, is human curation. The future of advertising will likely depend on a synthesis in which AI hallucinations and neologisms are treated as raw material, while human intelligence supplies emotion, intent, and cultural context. AI can derive words; it is still the human agent who gives them a social life and a rhetorical "soul." In sum, while AI carries a risk of standardising and mechanising advertising language, it can, when strategically guided through prompt engineering, function as a frontier tool that pushes the boundaries of linguistic practice. Advertising discourse is entering a phase in which AI not only breaks grammar but also participates in remodelling it.

REFERENCES

Akyıldız, E., & Tükel Kanra, Y. (2022). A research on neologism translation: The Handmaid's Tale. *Dokuz Eylül Üniversitesi Sosyal Bilimler Enstitüsü Dergisi, 24*(4), 1449–1469. DOI: 10.16953/deusosbil.1109395

Ayaydın-Cebe, G. Ö. (2021). Smile of the crescent: Constructing a future identity out of historical ambiguity in İstiklâl Marşı (with translation). *Die Welt des Islams, 63*(1), 76–106. DOI: 10.1163/15700607-61040001

Banguoğlu, T. (2015). *Türkçenin grameri*. Türk Dil Kurumu Yayınları.

Banh, L., & Strobel, G. (2023). Generative artificial intelligence. *Electronic Markets, 33*(1), 63. Advance online publication. DOI: 10.1007/s12525-023-00680-1

Barut, E. (2025). A linguistic challenge to ChatGPT: Use of AI in detection, text generation, and translation of false friends in Turkish-English. *Söylem Filoloji Dergisi (Çeviribilim Özel Sayısı II)*, 154-177. https://doi.org/DOI: 10.29110/soylemdergi.1598386

Batı, U. (2002). *Yazılı basın reklamlarında dilin stratejik kullanımı* [Strategic use of language in print media advertisements] [Master's thesis, Marmara University].

Bender, E. M., Gebru, T., McMillan-Major, A., & Shmitchell, S. (2021). On the dangers of stochastic parrots: Can language models be too big? In *Proceedings of the 2021 ACM Conference on Fairness, Accountability, and Transparency* (pp. 610–623). https://doi.org/DOI: 10.1145/3442188.3445922

Boden, M. A. (1998). Creativity and artificial intelligence. *Artificial Intelligence, 103*(1-2), 347–356. DOI: 10.1016/S0004-3702(98)00055-1

Boltayevich, E. B., Adali, E., Mirdjonovna, K. S., Xolmo'minovna, A. O., Yuldashevna, X. Z., & Nizomaddin Uktamboy O'G'li, X. (2023). The problem of POS tagging and stemming for agglutinative languages (Turkish, Uyghur, Uzbek languages). In *Proceedings: 8th International Conference on Computer Science and Engineering (UBMK 2023)* (pp. 57-62). IEEE. https://doi.org/DOI: 10.1109/UBMK59864.2023.10286792

Çelik, M. (1995). Neologisms in contemporary Turkish. *La Trobe Working Papers in Linguistics, 8*(4), 101-119. https://www.latrobe.edu.au/linguistics/LaTrobePapersinLinguistics/Vol%2008/4Celik.pdf

Çelikten, E., & Çelikten, H. (2020). Elektronik kültür ortamında neolojizm. *Uluslararası Dil Edebiyat ve Kültür Araştırmaları Dergisi, 3*(2), 183–205. DOI: 10.37999/udekad.785222

Cesur Kılıçaslan, S., Cesur, S., & Işık, T. (2012). Tüketim kültürü vc rcklamların birey üzerinde doğurduğu zayıflık hissi. [Consumption culture and the feeling of weakness caused by advertisements] In Babaoğul, M., Şener, A., & Buğday, E. B. (Eds.), *Tüketici Yazıları III* (pp. 66–75). Tüketici-Pazar-Araştırma-Danışma Test ve Eğitim Merkezi.

Chomsky, N. (1965). *Aspects of the theory of syntax.* MIT Press.

Chyrvonyi, O. (2025). The language of artificial intelligence: Linguistic and sociolinguistic analysis of AI-related neologisms (2016-2025). *Проблеми гуманітарних наук. Серія. Філологія, 61*, 175–180. DOI: 10.24919/2522-4565.2025.61.20

Çınar, B., & Karahan, L. (2009). Reklam dilinde kullanılan edebî sanatlar [Literary devices used in advertising language]. *Turkish Studies, 4*(8), 892–905.

Çorbacıoğlu Gönezer, E. (2014). *L'analyse figurative et affective des affiches publicitaires* [Figurative and affective analysis of advertising posters] [Doctoral dissertation, Dokuz Eylül University].

Georgiou, G. (2025). Can AI mimic the human ability to define neologisms? *International Journal of Speech Technology, 28*(4), 773–782. DOI: 10.1007/s10772-025-10216-x

Grilli, L., & Pedota, M. (2024). Creativity and artificial intelligence: A multilevel perspective. *Creativity and Innovation Management, 33*(2), 234–247. DOI: 10.1111/caim.12580

Hewitt, J., Geirhos, R., & Kim, B. (2025). We can't understand AI using our existing vocabulary. *arXiv*. https://arxiv.org/abs/2502.07586

Hidalgo Downing, L. (2000). Text world creation in advertising discourse. *Revista Alicantina de Estudios Ingleses, 13*(13), 67–88. DOI: 10.14198/raei.2000.13.06

Karadağ, B. M., & Burnaz, S. (2021). Türkçede işlek bir metaforik neoloji öbeği: X+kafası [A productive metaphorical neology pattern in Turkish: X+kafası]. *Dilbilim Dergisi, 36*, 83–104. DOI: 10.26650/jol.2021.849022

Kim, W. (2022). *Distributional corpus analysis of Korean neologisms using artificial intelligence* [Doctoral dissertation, University of Georgia].

Kolaç, E. (2025). Yapay zekâ tabanlı dil modellerinde anlamlandırma sorunu: Geleneksel sözlük tanımlarının yeniden değerlendirilmesi [Meaning-making problem in AI-based language models: Re-evaluating traditional dictionary definitions]. *Disiplinler Arası Dil Araştırmaları*, *1*(1), 307–358. DOI: 10.48147/dada.1739041

König, W. (1994). Dilbilim ve yapay zekâ [Linguistics and artificial intelligence]. *Dilbilim Araştırmaları Dergisi*, *5*, 233–236.

Korkmaz, Z. (1992). *Dil bilgisi terimleri sözlüğü*. Türk Dil Kurumu Yayınları.

Leech, G. N. (1966). *English in advertising: A linguistic study of advertising in Great Britain*. Longmans.

Lehrer, A. (2003). Understanding trendy neologisms. *Italian Journal of Linguistics. Rivista di Linguistica*, *15*, 369–382.

Lembet, Z. (2012). Kültür, dil, tüketim ve reklam ilişkisi. [Relationship between culture, language, consumption, and advertising] In Babaoğul, M., Şener, A., & Buğday, E. B. (Eds.), *Tüketici Yazıları III* (pp. 44–65). Tüketici-Pazar-Araştırma-Danışma Test ve Eğitim Merkezi.

Lewis, G. (1999). *The Turkish language reform: A catastrophic success*. Oxford University Press. DOI: 10.1093/oso/9780198238560.001.0001

Macquarie Dictionary. (2025, November 24). *Macquarie Dictionary word of the year for 2025*. https://www.macquariedictionary.com.au/macquarie-dictionary-word-of-the-year-for-2025/

Maloku, F., & Avdyli, M. N. (2023). Russian formalism and defamiliarization in language. [Orbis Linguarum]. *Ezikov Svyat*, *21*(1), 42–46. DOI: 10.37708/ezs.swu.v21.i1.5

McGilvray, J. (2001). Chomsky on the creative aspect of language use and its implications for lexical semantic studies. In Busa, F., & Bouillon, P. (Eds.), *The language of word meaning* (pp. 5–27). Cambridge University Press. DOI: 10.1017/CBO9780511896316.004

Mehmandoust, N., & Söylemez, A. S. (2023). Translation strategies of neologisms in Margaret Atwood's MaddAddam trilogy. *Turkish Studies - Language, 18*(2), 1127-1143. https://doi.org/DOI: 10.7827/TurkishStudies.67754

Nazlı, E. H. (2022a). *Dil ve cinsiyet: Reklam dili çözümlemesi* [Language and gender: Analysis of advertising language] [Master's thesis, İstanbul University].

Nazlı, E. H. (2022b). *Reklam dili: Bir iletişim biçimi olarak Türkçe reklam söylemi üzerine toplumdilbilimsel bir inceleme* [Advertising language: A sociolinguistic study on Turkish advertising discourse as a form of communication] [Doctoral dissertation, Dicle University].

Özer, Z. (2010). *Global reklam kampanyalarında kültürel farklılaşmalar* [Cultural differentiations in global advertising campaigns] [Master's thesis, Marmara University].

Pedreschi, D., Pappalardo, L., Ferragina, E., Baeza-Yates, R., Barabási, A.-L., Dignum, F., Dignum, V., Eliassi-Rad, T., Giannotti, F., Kertész, J., Knott, A., Ioannidis, Y., Lukowicz, P., Passarella, A., Pentland, A. S., Shawe-Taylor, J., & Vespignani, A. (2025). Human-AI coevolution. *Artificial Intelligence, 339*, 104244. DOI: 10.1016/j.artint.2024.104244

Rodríguez Guerra, A. (2016). Dictionaries of neologisms: A review and proposals for its improvement. *Open Linguistics, 2*(1), 528–556. DOI: 10.1515/opli-2016-0028

Röhrborn, K. (2001). Artificial idiomaticity in neologistic terms of Republican Turkish. , 20, 1-10.

Sarı, İ. (2015). *Türkçede eklerin dışında kelime yapma yolları ve sözlükselleşme* [Word-formation methods other than suffixation and lexicalization in Turkish] [Doctoral dissertation, Ankara University].

Uçar, A. (2014). Gülmece ve gülme kaynağı olarak sözcük oyunları [Wordplay as a source of humor and laughter]. *Dil ve Edebiyat Dergisi, 11*(1), 17–43.

Wilson, D. (2016). Relevance theory. In Huang, Y. (Ed.), *The Oxford Handbook of Pragmatics* (pp. 79–100). Oxford University Press., DOI: 10.1093/oxfordhb/9780199697960.013.25

Yetkin Karakoç, N. (2014). Structural calques in neologism translation and unintelligibility: The case of Generation X. *Turkish Studies, 9*(3), 1611–1619. DOI: 10.7827/TurkishStudies.6492

Yıldırım, E. (2025). Examining advertisements produced by artificial intelligence from an aesthetic perspective and analyzing a sample advertisement film produced by artificial intelligence. *Journal of Management Theory and Practices Research, 6*(1), 77–94.

Zawada, B. E. (2005). *Linguistic creativity and mental representation with reference to intercategorial polysemy* [Unpublished doctoral dissertation, University of South Africa].

ADDITIONAL READING

Boden, M. A. (2004). *The creative mind: Myths and mechanisms* (2nd ed.). Routledge. DOI: 10.4324/9780203508527

Cook, G. (2001). *The discourse of advertising* (2nd ed.). Routledge. DOI: 10.4324/9780203978153

Delabastita, D. (1996). Introduction. *The Translator, 2*(2), 127–139. DOI: 10.1080/13556509.1996.10798970

Gere, C. (2008). *Digital culture* (2nd ed.). Reaktion Books.

Goddard, A. (2002). *The language of advertising: Written texts* (2nd ed.). Routledge.

Hofstadter, D. R., & Sander, E. (2013). *Surfaces and essences: Analogy as the fuel and fire of thinking*. Basic Books.

McStay, A. (2018). *Emotional AI: The rise of empathic media*. SAGE Publications Ltd. DOI: 10.4135/9781526451293

Tanaka, K. (1994). *Advertising language: A pragmatic approach to advertisements in Britain and Japan*. Routledge.

Veale, T. (2012). *Exploding the creativity myth: The computational foundations of linguistic creativity*. Bloomsbury Academic.

KEY TERMS AND DEFINITIONS

Advertising Discourse: A patterned set of linguistic and semiotic strategies through which advertisements construct persuasive meanings, position audiences, and negotiate brand identity within specific socio-cultural contexts.

AI in Advertising: The deployment of computational models and data-driven techniques to support or automate targeting, content production, optimization, and performance forecasting in advertising workflows.

Artificial Intelligence: A domain of computer science focused on building systems capable of learning, reasoning, and language processing, thereby performing tasks commonly associated with human cognition.

Linguistic Creativity: The ability to produce novel yet contextually appropriate and pragmatically effective utterances by recombining resources or strategically departing from conventional forms.

Morphological Analysis: A systematic examination of word structure that identifies morphemes and specifies the inflectional and derivational rules governing their composition.

Neologisms: Newly coined lexical items, or new senses of existing items, introduced to name emerging phenomena and potentially stabilized through social uptake and conventionalization.

Semantic Ambiguity: The condition in which an expression supports more than one plausible interpretation due to lexical polysemy or compositional structure, typically resolved through contextual and pragmatic cues.

ENDNOTES

1 In Turkish, *-lA* is a common derivational suffix that verbalises nouns.

2 "AI slop" was selected as *Macquarie Dictionary's Word of the Year for 2025.* (Macquarie) In the dictionary's entry, the term is defined as "*noun Colloquial* low-quality content created by generative AI, often containing errors, and not requested by the user." (Macquarie) Conceptually, this definition maps neatly onto the present discussion by foregrounding two salient properties of AI slop: its diminished informational and pragmatic value, and its tendency to appear as unsolicited textual surplus rather than as context-sensitive, audience-oriented discourse.

3 By "Anglo-Saxon Turkish," what is meant is a hybrid and artificial mode of language use in which the lexical items are Turkish, yet the sentence architecture, underlying logic, and overall rhetorical "spirit" are shaped by English, and more broadly by an Anglo-Saxon cultural frame. In linguistics, this phenomenon is often discussed under the heading of calque, and in widespread usage it is sometimes referred to as "Plaza Turkish." The application of English-oriented generative AI patterns to Turkish can also be treated within this scope. For instance, an English-style fabricated template such as "favor-al experience" could yield a formation like "Lezzetsel deneyim" in Turkish. In addition, the notion of "Anglo-Saxon Turkish" captures the mechanism transfer across languages through the direct rendering of high-frequency English light verbs such as *make, do, get, and take*. This produces calqued patterns such as *take a shower* → "duş al-" *make stress* → "stres yap-" and *make an entrance* → "giriş yap-" among others.

4 “Fear not! The scarlet flag rippling at dawns shall not wither”. The İstiklâl Marşı (Independence March), the official national anthem of the Republic of Türkiye, was translated into English by Ayaydın-Cebe (2021).

Chapter 2
Building Brand Loyalty Through Digital Narratives in the AI Era

Mustafa Seçkin Aydın
http://orcid.org/0000-0002-6200-8978
Aydın Adnan Menderes University, Turkey

ABSTRACT

This chapter examines the strategic role of digital storytelling in marketing communication and its theoretical effects on consumer loyalty within an AI-driven digital environment. It outlines the evolution of loyalty from behavioral to emotional and relational dimensions and conceptualizes storytelling as a mechanism for emotional engagement, meaning-making, and long-term consumer–brand relationships. Drawing on narrative transportation, brand attachment, experiential marketing, and customer engagement theories, the chapter explains how digital and algorithmically mediated narratives foster loyalty outcomes. It further discusses AI-supported and computational storytelling practices, including personalized and data-driven narrative production. Measurement challenges, evaluative approaches, and ethical issues such as authenticity, standardization, and consumer resistance are addressed to provide a balanced perspective. Overall, the chapter offers an integrative conceptual framework with managerial implications for digital branding and consumer engagement.

INTRODUCTION

In today's marketing communication environment, storytelling has emerged as a strategic tool for increasing consumer loyalty, thanks to the profound transforma-

DOI: 10.4018/979-8-3373-5666-2.ch002

tion of interaction forms brought about by digital technologies. Unlike traditional promotional messages, storytelling has the potential to establish an emotional connection with the audience, create memorability, and provide an experiential interaction. In an era marked by the proliferation of digital platforms, participatory media culture, and increased attention deficit, brands' efforts to reach consumers through meaningful and original narratives have become even more important (Escalas, 2004; Pulizzi, 2012).

Consumer loyalty has long been evaluated in terms of repeat purchasing behavior and customer satisfaction. However, with digitalization, this concept has also undergone a transformation; not only functional benefits, but also emotional attachment, shared values, and meaningful brand experiences have come to the fore (Chaudhuri & Holbrook, 2001; Verhoef et al., 2010). Loyalty is shaped by the relationships and emotional connections established with a brand.

With the digital transformation, digital storytelling is an important tool for brands to build strong relationships with their customers. Digital storytelling is about the form of content as well as the way it is presented through various digital channels. Moreover, how the narrative is personalized and structured are key focal points of digital storytelling. Narratives are often presented through relevant digital tools such as social media content, brand videos, blogs, etc. When designing a narrative, purposes such as informing, entertaining, and emotionally stimulating are combined (Lundqvist et al., 2013).

Unlike static visuals or concrete promotional content, storytelling appeals to individuals' emotions and values, thereby influencing them. This is because the content of storytelling generally reflects individuals' experiences or dreams. Therefore, stories are not perceived as advertising and promotion like other marketing tools but rather represent an emotional journey with which consumers can connect (Sapre & Longani, 2024).

Storytelling plays an important role in increasing market share for brands, such as maintaining relationships with existing customers and attracting potential customers. Storytelling brings consumers closer to brands, creates memorable experiences, increases trust, and supports consumer brand loyalty (Suryana, 2024). When consumers find a story interesting, they remember the brand more easily and form an emotional connection with it. Storytelling is very effective in establishing an emotional connection with consumers. In the highly competitive digital marketplace, such connections can be a distinguishing factor that increases consumer loyalty (Mandung, 2025).

The main purpose of this study is to evaluate digital storytelling within the context of marketing communication strategy and to examine the theoretical effects of this concept on consumer loyalty. The conceptual framework of storytelling is defined and its impact on loyalty is discussed through various theories. The issue of loyalty is discussed within the context of digital marketing and how brands create emotional bonds through digital storytelling is explained with examples. The potential responses of digital story-based strategies to customer loyalty dynamics in the transition from transactional to relational marketing are discussed. It also discusses the ethical limitations of storytelling strategies. A secondary aim of this study is to provide a theoretical foundation for academics and marketing practitioners. In the study, Grammarly (AI) software was used during the writing process to enhance the linguistic accuracy and readability of the text. All content edited or created with the help of this tool has been thoroughly checked and edited by the author.

UNDERSTANDING CONSUMER LOYALTY IN THE DIGITAL AGE

Loyalty is a fundamental concept that has been the subject of research in the marketing discipline for many years. With digitalization, the scope of consumer loyalty has expanded (e.g. e-loyalty) and its structure has changed. Whereas in the past consumer loyalty was predominantly a behavioral phenomenon, today it is examined in its social, experiential and especially emotional dimensions (Chaudhuri & Holbrook, 2001).

Dimensions of Loyalty: Behavioral and Attitudinal Approaches

In literature, the concept of loyalty is addressed in two ways: behavioral and attitudinal. Consumer repeat preference or purchase of a product is known as behavioral loyalty. On the other hand, tendencies such as trust and loyalty towards a brand or product, and psychological factors such as recommendation and emotions reflect attitudinal loyalty (Khan et al., 2015). With digitalization, attitudinal loyalty has become more prominent and important. This is due to the Web 2.0 infrastructure, where consumers engage in activities like liking, commenting, and creating content about products, services, and brands online. Consumers have moved from the role of audience to the role of participant. This participatory role contributes to the formation of brand loyalty in the long term (Verhoef et al., 2010).

Digital Loyalty Dynamics: Experience, Value, and Interaction

Digitalization has radically affected many disciplines. From a marketing standpoint, loyalty has significantly changed due to digitalization. Consumers' sharing positive experiences about the brand in digital environments is an important indicator of consumer loyalty. The quality of this consumer-brand interaction experience is determined by user experience, personalization, and social media interactions in digital media (Lemon & Verhoef, 2016).

The dynamics of the concept of loyalty have changed in the digital age. Instead of dynamics such as cheapness or cost, product quality, etc., the interaction of the brand with the consumer and the perception reflected by digital tools come into play. In this process, digital storytelling, which can offer significant opportunities to the brand and is effective in creating consumer loyalty by creating value, stands out.

The Process of Building Loyalty and Emotional Connection

Emotional attachment plays an important role in brand loyalty. When consumers interact emotionally with the story behind brands, they form a bridge of loyalty towards the brand. This is because the brand presents the message it wants to give in a theme that will mobilize emotions, creating a distinctiveness for the consumer who is exposed to many marketing messages in the digital age. Consumers who find a slice of themselves in brand messages attribute meaning to the message and the consumer's loyalty to the brand is strengthened. By providing trust and consistency in their stories, brands open the door to establishing an emotional bond with consumers (Park et al., 2010).

THE CONCEPT OF DIGITAL STORYTELLING

Definition and Conceptual Framework

Storytelling is a very old form of communication that dates back to ancient times. People have been using stories for thousands of years to convey information, share cultural values, and create meaning (Yılmaz & Ciğerci, 2019). Furthermore, people think within narrative structures and tend to remember facts in the form of stories. Therefore, stories shape human thought and reflect these thoughts onto others (Behzadi & Bakhtiary, 2023).

Digital storytelling merges traditional storytelling with digital media elements like text, visuals, audio narration, music, and video (Robin, 2016). In the context of marketing communication, storytelling is the presentation of structured narratives with the aim of conveying a brand's message to its target audience in an emotional and meaningful framework (Escalas, 2004). With digitalization, these narratives have transcended traditional media channels and found life in a wide variety of mediums such as social media, video content, podcasts, blogs, and interactive web experiences.

Digital storytelling is the integration of this classic narrative form with digital technologies. According to Lundqvist et al. (2013), digital storytelling is a communication strategy used by brands to establish more meaningful, emotional, and relationship-based connections with consumers. This strategy does not merely tell a story; it also makes the consumer a part of that story. The role of digital storytelling becomes even more prominent in the highly interactive digital environment, especially where social media platforms facilitate real-time interaction and personalized engagement (Mandung, 2025).

The Components of Digital Storytelling

For digital stories to be effective, they must have certain structural and content-related components. The main components highlighted in the literature are as follows:

Protagonist: The central figure in the story can be expressed as a person, brand, or community. This character should be designed in such a way that the target audience can identify with it.

Conflict: A situation that adds dynamism to the story and awaits resolution. The value proposition offered to consumers is usually based on the resolution of this conflict.

Resolution: The brand's product or service is positioned as the element that resolves the conflict.

Call to Action (CTA): It can be described as guidance that encourages consumers to engage (e.g., clicking on a link, sharing, etc.).

Emotional Resonance: The story must leave an emotional impact and resonate with the audience. This is one of the fundamental ways to build loyalty (Herskovitz & Crystal, 2010).

Consistency and Authenticity: The story must be consistent with the brand's overall identity, coherent, and realistic.

The Transformation of Narrative in Digital Media

Digital storytelling can be applied in different ways depending on platform-specific formats and user behavior:

Social Media Narratives: Emotion-based narratives are presented through short, quickly consumed content such as Instagram stories, TikTok videos, and Twitter threads.

Branded Content: Narratives in the form of mini-documentaries or short films published on platforms such as YouTube and Vimeo add depth and meaning to the brand.

Interactive Stories: Applications or web experiences that allow users to participate in the story; they focus on the consumer through methods such as gamification and branching storytelling.

Automated Narratives: It is possible to scale the experience digitally through AI-powered content creation, personalized email narratives, or chatbots.

The Link between Storytelling and Consumer Engagement

Digital stories not only provide consumers with information but also create loyalty, identification, and emotional connection. Consumers can internalize narratives by identifying with them. Through these narratives, consumers see the brand not just as a product provider but as a "meaning provider" (Singh & Sonnenburg, 2012). User participation in the story through comments, likes, shares, and content creation enhances the narrative's impact and fosters loyalty. Frameworks of consumer engagement in social media highlight that consumers are no longer passive listeners; instead, they co-create brand narratives. Active engagement increases psychological ownership and strengthens emotional connections, which are predictors of enhanced loyalty and advocacy (Schivinski et al., 2016).

Digital Storytelling in the AI Era: Algorithmic Narratives and Human–AI Co-Creation

Digital storytelling can be characterized as the transfer of brands' traditional narratives to digital platforms. All digital platforms, especially social networks, where brands can present video narratives and interactive content, form the basis of digital storytelling. Nowadays, with the contribution of artificial intelligence technologies, the scope of digital storytelling has expanded not only to the narrative that is transferred to the digital environment. There is a transformation process that brings along the questions of how the narrative is produced and for whom it is adapted.

At this point, artificial intelligence tools have become an important actor in the production and editing of storytelling. Artificial intelligence algorithms decide which content will be published in which format. Moreover, these algorithms can determine the emotional tone of the content and the time of publication by analyzing user data. This development has given rise to a new form of narrative called "algorithmic storytelling" (Oke, 2025; Sánchez-López et al., 2025). This concept refers to storytelling shaped by data-driven and computational logic (Kátai et al., 2024). Algorithmic storytelling differs from the frequently and overlapping term "Computational Narrative" in the literature. Computational narrative focuses solely on how stories are produced, specifically the generation, modeling, or simulation of stories using algorithms (Valls-Vargas, 2013). Algorithmic storytelling, on the other hand, focuses on the process by which stories are selected, organized, personalized, and distributed by algorithms, as well as how platform logic shapes the narrative.

AI-powered systems not only select and highlight existing stories but can also create new ones through automated narrative generation. Text production tools, visual and video production models, or automated scriptwriting systems enable the rapid and large-scale production of brand narratives. While this provides brands with efficiency and scalability advantages, it also raises some debates regarding the originality and emotional depth of the narrative (Kabashkin et al., 2025).

At this point, digital storytelling is redefined as a human-AI co-creation process, moving away from being a purely human-centric one (Im & Chang, 2025; Serbanescu & Nack, 2023). While the framework, theme, and strategic goals of the story are often determined by humans, the content creation, adaptation, and personalization processes are supported by artificial intelligence. Thus, the subject of the narrative shifts from a single narrator to a hybrid structure shaped jointly by humans and algorithms.

One of the strongest aspects of algorithmic AI-powered storytelling is its personalization capacity (Yunusov et al., 2024). Algorithms that transform data on users' past behaviors, such as interests and social media interactions, into meaningful outputs can tailor digital narratives to an individual level. This personalization feature increases the potential for users to connect with the story (Mohammadkhani et al., 2025; Yunusov et al., 2024). However, the production of narratives based on similar data patterns can lead to the standardization of the narrative. In this case, while benefiting from the personalization power of algorithms, it can also create an environment of user desensitization due to similar narratives (Rettberg & Wigers, 2025). In other words, narratives can appear personal but become increasingly similar, leading to contradictions.

This situation points to a problem that can be expressed in the literature as the "authenticity paradox." Narratives generated specifically for individuals by artificial intelligence may give the consumer a feeling of being "designed for me"; however, the realization that these narratives are produced with an algorithmic and commercial logic can weaken the perception of sincerity and create distrust (Markou et al., 2025). Individuals may perceive overly optimized and targeted narratives as manipulative or artificial. Therefore, AI-powered storytelling operates on a delicate balance between the advantage of creating loyalty and the risk of trust.

Within this context, artificial intelligence should be regarded not only as a tool that enhances digital storytelling, but also as a structural element that fundamentally transforms the nature of narrative. In the age of artificial intelligence, storytelling requires answering not only to the question of "how to tell more compelling stories?", but also to questions such as "who controls the narrative, where are its boundaries, and how does the consumer perceive this process?"

THEORETICAL CONNECTIONS BETWEEN STORYTELLING AND LOYALTY

Digital storytelling is a powerful form of communication that transforms consumers' relationship with brands. There is a growing trend towards storytelling in marketing to reflect brand values, create desired images and encourage consumer-brand interaction (Behzadi & Bakhtiary, 2023). Through processes such as meaning creation, emotional connection and relationship deepening, stories are becoming not only tools that convey information but also experiential tools that build loyalty. Different theoretical approaches have been developed in the literature to explain this effect. This section presents four major theoretical frameworks that explain the relationship between storytelling and consumer loyalty.

Narrative Transportation Theory

Narrative Transportation Theory, developed by Green and Brock (2000), argues that when an individual is mentally and emotionally immersed in a story, i.e. "transported", this experience can affect their attitudes and beliefs. The individual who is transported into the story empathizes with the characters, reacts emotionally to events and becomes more open to the world presented by the narrative.

In digital marketing, this theory points to the ability of brands to create emotional intimacy and loyalty by drawing consumers in through narrative. The move makes the consumer more responsive and favorable to the brand message. In the long run, this can translate into brand loyalty.

Brand Attachment Theory

Brand loyalty refers to the strength of a consumer's emotional relationship with a brand. Park et al. (2010) argue that brand loyalty is built on three main elements: self-connection, passion and commitment: Stories provide a supportive environment for each of these elements.

For example, a brand's founding story, social values narrative or customer success stories allow consumers to integrate the brand with their own identity. This creates loyalty not only to the product but also to the value system that the brand represents.

Experiential Marketing Framework

The experiential marketing approach, developed by Schmitt (1999), focuses on consumers' interaction with the brand along the axes of sensation, emotion, thought, action and relationship. Stories have the potential to activate these five dimensions simultaneously.

While a digital story appeals to the senses with impressive visuals, it finds a place in the heart with emotional narratives, prompts thought, and may eventually result in an action (buying, sharing, commenting). This multidimensional experience creates a lasting and loyal relationship with the brand.

Customer Engagement Theory

Customer engagement is the sum of a consumer's cognitive, emotional and behavioral interaction with a brand (Brodie et al., 2011). Digital storytelling is one of the main mechanisms to increase this engagement. Especially on platforms such as social media, narratives trigger active behaviors such as sharing, commenting and content creation, making the consumer's relationship with the brand more participatory and sustainable.

In this context, a narrative is not just a marketing message; it offers a co-created brand experience. As participation increases, brand loyalty is built on a stronger foundation.

MECHANISMS OF INFLUENCE: THE ROLE OF STORYTELLING IN BUILDING LOYALTY

Although the potential effects of digital storytelling on loyalty have been explained in the theoretical framework, it is necessary to examine the mechanisms of influence to concretize how this relationship works. Digital narratives affect consumer loyalty not directly but indirectly through various cognitive and emotional processes. In this section, these mechanisms are discussed under five main headings.

Emotional Bonding

Stories are very effective in generating emotional responses. When consumers identify with the characters in the story told by the brand, in other words, when they interpret their experiences by adapting them to the story, the process of emotional bonding begins (Escalas, 2004). This bond can be developed not only towards the product or service, but also towards the values and the world that the brand represents. In cases where an emotional bond develops, the consumer becomes more prone to show loyalty towards the brand.

Emotional resonance encourages loyalty by creating a bond based on shared values and experiences. According to Pulizzi (2012), consumers who interact with brand stories internalize brand values and develop loyalty. Video stories can elicit emotional responses because they contain visual and auditory elements, making the brand or product associated with the story interesting and memorable.

Meaning Creation and Identity Construction

While storytelling is a tool for creating meaning to construct identity, narratives can be expressed in terms of our identity, language, and representation. Identity is a phenomenon that develops in relation to individuals' systems of representation and is in a constant process of formation. Storytelling can imbue individuals' identities with meaning. The discourses that societies or brands create through storytelling support representations of identity (Hakanurmi, 2017).

Stories serve not only as entertainment but also as vehicles for generating meaning. When consumers identify with representations within brand narratives, they may perceive the brand as an extension of their own identity (Escalas, 2004; Fournier, 1998). This identification leads to an emotional and symbolic relationship with the brand. Specifically, value-based stories (e.g. social responsibility, equality, environmental awareness) can create a stronger consumer attachment.

Memorability and Persistence through Narrative

Stories are more easily remembered than information. Therefore, a brand message presented in a story format provides higher mental accessibility for the consumer (Woodside et al., 2008). This increases the likelihood of brand preference and creates a strong positioning in consumer minds. Persistence also increases the likelihood of re-engagement.

According to Yang and Kang (2021), narrative transfer that occurs when exposed to digital storytelling advertisements contributes to the recall of autobiographical memories or the simulation of future romantic experiences. This emphasizes the persistence of narratives. In addition, Van Laer et al. (2014) emphasized in their research that narratives that affect consumers emotionally are more easily remembered and are more likely to be associated with positive feelings toward the brand.

Social Sharing and Consumer Engagement

Digital narratives allow consumers not only to experience the story, but also to share and reproduce it. In channels such as social media, the consumer can like the story, comment on it, or contribute to the brand by transforming their own experience into a story. This reinforces both brand interaction and organic loyalty (Brodie et al., 2011).

Consistency and Trust Building

The more consistent, sincere and value-oriented a brand's story is, the more trust consumers have in that brand. Trust is a key determinant of loyalty, especially in the digital age (Chaudhuri & Holbrook, 2001). Inconsistent, artificial or opportunistic narratives, on the other hand, can have the opposite effect on consumers and undermine loyalty. Therefore, it is critical that the digital narrative is aligned with reality, brand identity and consumer expectations.

STRATEGIC IMPLEMENTATION IN MARKETING COMMUNICATION

Brand-Based Story Strategies

There are three basic strategies that brands often use in their story constructions:

Founding Stories: Narratives about how the brand was born create a sense of authenticity and sincerity. Apple's founding story, which started in a garage, creates a perception of sincerity about the brand.

Value Driven Stories: Narratives about social responsibility, sustainability and social values make the brand a "value carrier". The Toms brand's donation of a pair of shoes for every pair of shoes sold is an example of creating a value-driven story. Another example is The Body Shop brand's emphasis on not testing on animals, natural ingredients, women's rights and emphasizing ethical values in product stories with narratives such as "ethical sourcing" and "community trade".

Customer Stories: Narratives based on real user experiences create authentic interactions and strengthen the sense of brand community. For example, Glossier has put customer stories at the center of its marketing strategy, making consumers' real experiences visible in its social media and blog content. This narrative approach enabled the brand to build an intimate and inclusive community, strengthening a sense of belonging and loyalty among users.

Platform Specific Narrative Practices

The effectiveness of storytelling is directly related to the characteristics of the platform on which it is presented:

Instagram and TikTok: Suitable for short, visual, emotionally intense micro-narratives. These platforms provide instant but impressive interactions through the "Story" format.

YouTube and Branded Content: It is suitable for longer, cinematic narratives such as mini-documentaries or brand films and is used for in-depth storytelling (e.g. Nike's commercials).

Podcasts and Audio Narratives: It is a medium that requires aural attention but has strong storytelling potential. Especially effective for creating authentic brand voice.

Web-based Interactive Narratives: Represents interactive web pages or campaign sites with gamification elements, where the visitor can direct the story.

Artificial Intelligence and Personalized Narratives

The future of digital marketing is built on personalized story experiences. Thanks to artificial intelligence-supported algorithms, next-generation applications offer consumers personalized, meaningful and remarkable stories. The future of digital marketing is built on personalized story experiences. Thanks to artificial intelligence-supported algorithms, next-generation applications offer special, meaningful and remarkable stories to consumers. For example, brands can attract the attention of the user with personal narratives by sending mobile notifications or e-mails based on the user's past data. Artificial Intelligence-supported personal narratives create a holistic experience in the customer journey.

Examples of Successful Implementation

Nike made its "You can't stop us" digital narrative strategy viral through YouTube and other social media. With a digital narrative that emphasized the unifying power of sports and the diversity of users, the campaign was successful in attracting the attention of consumers and creating social awareness.

Similarly, Adidas ran the "Impossible is Nothing" campaign, bringing together the inspiring stories of many successful athletes with consumers. It succeeded in attracting the attention of the consumer audience with digital narratives themed on perseverance and courage.

Coca-Cola chose to place personal names on its products with its "Share a Coke" campaign. By using such a strategy for the first time, it executed a unique digital narrative strategy. The names on the products were matched with consumers' own names and the names of their loved ones, making the consumer the main character of the story.

With the "Rebuild the World" campaign, Lego created a story for both children and adults to unleash their imagination and vision. This story was supported by social media and videos, highlighting that Lego products are not just a toy, but a colorful and free way of thinking.

GoPro followed an experience transfer strategy by storytelling the videos shot by its customers using its products. Presenting extreme and exciting experience videos to the audience through digital platforms such as YouTube and Instagram, GoPro carried out a remarkable campaign that puts the user at the center of its narratives.

Dove's "Real Beauty Sketches" campaign is an example of storytelling that questions perceptions of beauty. In fact, the campaign attracted so much attention that it created a worldwide debate on self-confidence and body perception.

These examples of storytelling helped shape the brand image, while at the same time creating a bond with customers and raising awareness.

EVALUATING THE IMPACT OF DIGITAL STORYTELLING ON CONSUMER LOYALTY

Although the impact of digital storytelling on consumer loyalty is frequently discussed in the literature through theoretical frameworks, how this impact should be evaluated and translated into managerial decision-making processes is often addressed in a limited way. However, digital environments offer rich data sources that allow for the multi-dimensional monitoring and evaluation of the effects of narrative-based strategies (Hollebeek et al. 2014). In this context, measuring the impact of digital storytelling on loyalty is not only an academic requirement but also a critical issue from a strategic management perspective.

A Conceptual Measurement Framework

A multi-layered measurement approach is needed to assess the impact of digital storytelling. Rather than focusing solely on behavioral outcomes, this approach should consider the cognitive, emotional and relational effects of narrative on the consumer. Concepts such as narrative transportation, emotional attachment and perceived meaning can be considered as antecedents of loyalty, while indicators such as repeat purchase, recommendation and brand advocacy can be positioned as loyalty outcomes (Escalas, 2004). This multidimensional structure makes it possible to understand how digital storytelling transforms from short-term interactions to long-term loyalty relationships.

Consumer Engagement Metrics

The most immediate impact of digital storytelling is observed through consumer engagement. Metrics, including likes, shares, comments, watch time, and click-through rates, provide valuable insights into a narrative's ability to attract attention and stimulate interest (Hollebeek et al. 2014). However, these indicators alone do not adequately explain consumer loyalty. Elevated engagement levels may not necessarily result in positive attitudes or enduring brand relationships. Consequently, engagement metrics should be regarded as an initial indicator, rather than a definitive measure, of deeper psychological processes.

Attitudinal and Emotional Indicators

A deeper assessment of the impact of digital storytelling on loyalty requires consideration of attitudinal and emotional indicators. Storytelling generates strong emotional responses, and cognitive responses strongly influence behavioral responses (Crespo et al., 2023). Variables such as brand loyalty, emotional closeness, trust, and perceived authenticity reveal how the narrative is interpreted in the consumer's mind. Increased narrative transmission facilitates consumer identification with the brand and their perception of the brand story as a personal experience (Hong et al., 2022). In this context, digital storytelling can be considered not only a communication tool that transmits information, but also a mechanism that produces meaning and contributes to identity construction.

Behavioral Loyalty Indicators

The most tangible dimension of loyalty is measured through behavioral indicators. Variables such as repurchase intention, reluctance to switch brands, decreased price sensitivity, and word-of-mouth communication play a significant role in evaluating the long-term effects of digital storytelling (Umoren et al., 2022). However, it is not always possible to directly attribute these indicators to the narrative. Since digital storytelling often works in conjunction with other marketing activities, its impact on loyalty emerges as an indirect and time-spread process. Therefore, measurement should be considered within the context of continuous narrative strategies rather than individual campaigns.

AI-Powered Analytical Approaches

AI-based analytical systems offer new possibilities for measuring the impact of digital storytelling. Methods such as sentiment analysis, text mining, and behavioral pattern analysis enable a more nuanced assessment of consumer responses (Gutierrez et al. 2021). These systems can reveal which elements of the narrative generate more emotional responses and which narrative structures establish stronger relationships with loyalty indicators. However, while the use of these technologies makes the measurement process more objective, it also raises new debates about data privacy and ethical responsibilities.

Integration of Measurement Results into Managerial Decision-Making Processes

Measurement results regarding the impact of digital storytelling should be used not only for reporting purposes but also to guide strategic decision-making processes. These measurements can help determine which narrative types are more effective in which consumer segments, at what stage the narrative struggles to generate loyalty, and under what conditions narrative strategies need to be revised (Wedel & Kannan, 2016). In this context, measurement should be considered a dynamic tool that serves to optimize future narrative designs, rather than simply evaluating past performance.

Limitations of Measurement and Interpretation Problems

Although digital environments offer vast data possibilities, measuring the impact of digital storytelling does not always produce clear and linear results. The subjective nature of narrative experiences, cultural contexts, and individual differences can make the interpretation of measurement results difficult. Therefore, measurement results should be considered not as absolute truths, but as strategic guides. The success of digital storytelling depends not only on numerical metrics but also on the meaningful relationships the narrative establishes with brand values and consumer expectations.

SECTORAL AND CULTURAL DIFFERENCES IN DIGITAL STORYTELLING

The effects of digital storytelling on consumer loyalty are addressed in most studies from a generalized perspective; how narratives vary across different sectors and cultural contexts is discussed only to a limited extent (Mandung, 2025). However, the perception of storytelling, its methods of meaning-making, and its persuasive power can show significant differences depending on the sectoral structure and cultural context in which it operates.

From a sectoral perspective, experience-oriented sectors (e.g., tourism, fashion, entertainment, and luxury brands) show a more prominent emotional and symbolic dimension to digital storytelling (Jo et al., 2022; Sergio, 2020). In these sectors, narratives are constructed around lifestyle, identity, and experience rather than product features, allowing for stronger emotional connections with consumers. In contrast, in sectors with perceived high risk, such as finance, healthcare, or technology, storytelling is used in a more cautious and informative manner, with an emphasis on trust, transparency, and expertise (Di Furia et al., 2022).

Cultural context is also a significant factor in determining the effects of digital storytelling (Mandung, 2025). In individualistic cultures, narratives are often shaped around themes of personal achievement, authenticity, and individual experience, while in collectivist cultures, belonging, community, and shared values play a more dominant role (Shavitt & Cho, 2016). These differences can lead to the same digital narrative being perceived differently in different cultural contexts and resulting in different levels of loyalty.

For global brands, digital storytelling requires a delicate balance between standardization and localization. The effort to create a consistent global brand narrative can lead to superficial or alien narratives if local cultural codes are disregarded. AI-powered and scalable storytelling systems can weaken the emotional connection between the consumer and the brand if they don't adequately account for cultural nuances (Aulló-Saura et al., 2025).

CHALLENGES AND ETHICAL ISSUES

Digital storytelling, which is one of the powerful and effective tools of marketing communication, brings along some ethical issues. Brands' storytelling is generally embedded with biased content that is constructed to position corporate values and discourses (Dush, 2013). More importantly, the increasing reliance on data-driven and AI-powered systems brings with it significant challenges and ethical concerns. In the age of AI, storytelling is no longer shaped solely by human creativity and intentional narrative design; instead, it is increasingly guided by algorithms that organize, personalize, and sometimes automatically generate narratives. This transformation raises critical questions about authenticity, manipulation, trust, and the long-term sustainability of narrative-based loyalty strategies. The ethical problematic here is that many narratives are fictional rather than natural and attempt to create an emotional connection, leading to consumer manipulation. On the other hand, excessive emotion creation in fictional stories may pose the risk of emotional manipulation. Again, digital stories can disregard cultural sensitivity while conveying a brand's message and can cause disruption to the cultural structure. This section discusses the challenges and ethical issues of storytelling in marketing.

Artificiality and Sincerity Dilemma

In order for the narratives to deeply affect the consumer, brands can sometimes turn to overly emotive and sometimes striking elements in fictional content. In such cases, the stories may not be found sincere by the consumer and may be seen as artificial or blatant fiction. While some digital stories may be successful in attracting attention, they may cause a perception of insincerity due to content that is removed from reality (Holt, 2002).

Artificiality often occurs in ready-made narratives presented by influencers. Consumers may form a negative judgment towards the brand due to the content created by influencers that they feel they cannot connect with the product or brand. Therefore, this may reverse the expected consumer loyalty strategy.

Storytelling Fatigue and Narrative Saturation

One of the challenges emerging in digital environments is storytelling fatigue. As brands increasingly shift towards narrative-based communication strategies, consumers are constantly exposed to emotionally charged stories across multiple platforms. Over time, this saturation can lead to desensitization, diminishing the perceived novelty and impact of narratives. When storytelling becomes ubiquitous, narratives risk being perceived as formulaic rather than meaningful. In such cases, storytelling may fail to create emotional engagement in consumers and may even trigger avoidance behavior (Belova, 2021; Guo & Jiang, 2024). This challenge is particularly pronounced in algorithmically engineered environments where similar narrative patterns are repeatedly presented to users based on interaction optimization logic.

Consumer Manipulation and Emotional Exploitation

Digital storytelling often aims to increase consumer engagement by relying on emotional appeals to encourage identification and connection. These AI-generated appeals can be optimized through data analytics, increasing the risk of emotional exploitation. Algorithmic systems can manipulate which emotional triggers are most powerful, potentially creating a sense of exploitation by encouraging exaggerated dramatization or the exploitation of sensitive social issues (Laczniak & Murphy, 2006). The line between ethically meaningful storytelling and emotional exploitation is increasingly blurring. Brands that prioritize emotional exploitation over ethical responsibility for interaction risk jeopardizing transportation safety and losing reputation. Brands must carefully observe the line between raising awareness and commercial gain, especially when using sensitive social issues in their narratives. Otherwise, the narrative may create a perception that is detrimental rather than beneficial to the brand.

Cultural Insensitivity and Problems in Representation

The global reach of digital storytelling reinforces the ethical implications of cultural representation. Algorithmic systems are trained on existing datasets that can reflect cultural biases or dominant narratives, leading to the reproduction of stereotypes or the marginalization of specific groups. When digital stories fail to account for cultural diversity and contextual sensitivity, they can alienate audiences rather than connect them (Mohamed, 2025). This challenge is particularly relevant for global brands that use standardized, AI-powered narratives across diverse cultural contexts.

Inconsistent Narratives and Loss of Trust

The inconsistency between a brand's story and its actual practices has quickly become noticeable in the digital age. When a brand's story talks about sustainability, but its product chain harms the environment, or when it advocates diversity but lacks equal representation in its management team, consumers perceive a disconnect between narrative and action.

This not only weakens loyalty but also risks creating an active reaction such as a digital boycott against the brand (Li et al., 2022). This is why stories are valuable not only when they are told well but also when they are backed up with facts.

Over-Personalization and Algorithmic Discomfort

As noted in previous sections, AI-powered storytelling enables brands to analyze users' behavioral data, preferences, and engagement history to provide highly personalized narratives. While personalization has the potential to increase relevance, over-targeting can lead to a sense of discomfort, often described as the "creepiness effect". Consumers may feel that brands know too much about them, leading to a perception of surveillance and anxiety rather than connection (Zuboff, 2019). This highlights a fundamental paradox of AI-powered storytelling. In short, narratives designed to feel intimate and personal can simultaneously reduce perceived autonomy and control, undermining emotional engagement and trust (Aguirre et al., 2015).

Authenticity Paradox and Loss of Narrative Credibility

Authenticity is a central determinant of effective storytelling and brand loyalty. However, AI-supported narratives introduce an authenticity paradox (Gillespie, 2014). On the one hand, algorithmic systems can generate stories that closely align with individual preferences; on the other hand, the knowledge that these narratives are automatically generated or optimized for engagement can diminish their perceived sincerity. Consumers may question whether such stories reflect genuine brand values or merely strategic calculations. When authenticity is compromised, the emotional bond between the consumer and the brand becomes fragile, reducing the likelihood of long-term loyalty.

Balancing Innovation and Ethical Responsibility

Despite these challenges, digital storytelling remains a valuable strategic tool when implemented responsibly. Ethical storytelling in the AI era requires transparency, moderation in personalization, and alignment between narrative content and organizational values (Floridi et al., 2018). Rather than viewing AI as a purely efficiency-enhancing technology, brands should approach algorithmic storytelling as a socio-technical system that shapes consumer perceptions and relationships. A balanced integration of human judgment and algorithmic support is essential to preserve authenticity, trust, and long-term loyalty (Shneiderman, 2020).

Digital storytelling brings with it potential challenges and ethical issues. Therefore, brands need to appear more ethical, sensitive, sincere and consistent in digital storytelling. Digital stories that include real user experiences instead of fiction have the potential to be seen as more sincere by the consumer.

CONCLUSION AND FUTURE RESEARCH DIRECTIONS

The marketing communication approach does not see the consumer simply as a target audience. Rather, the consumer is positioned as a role player, value partner and experience sharer of a brand story. Storytelling, which has become an important strategic tool for brands, affects the relationship between brand and consumer at emotional, social, behavioral and cognitive levels.

This study takes a holistic approach to the relationship between digital storytelling and consumer loyalty. Stories mediate the bond between the brand and the consumer and support the formation of long-term consumer loyalty by influencing consumers' perspective on the brand. Narratives facilitate the integration of consumer identity with the brand and create a meaningful experience. The feeling of "belonging to the community", which is one of the benefits that brands provide to consumers, is shaped by digital storytelling and facilitates loyalty to the values created by the brand.

Sincere and consistent storytelling that is sensitive to community values further increases trust in the brand. Narratives are a strategic structure for the formation and maintenance of both emotional and cognitive loyalty. Especially artificial intelligence-supported customizable narratives have the potential to create a fast and lasting bond between consumers and brands. Consumer engagement can be encouraged by AI-supported narratives via social media.

Care should be taken to ensure that digital narratives do not show characteristics of emotional exploitation and artificiality, and that they act within ethical contexts. Again, manipulative narratives can turn a strategic tool with a high potential for influence into a practitioner that undermines loyalty. Problems in the representation of narratives can damage brand credibility.

This chapter contributes to the literature by offering a comprehensive conceptual synthesis of digital storytelling and consumer loyalty, integrating emerging discussions on algorithmic storytelling and AI-based personalization. By combining classical theories with contemporary technological developments, the chapter provides a multidisciplinary perspective that can guide both academic research and managerial practice.

Future Research Directions

There are many research topics that can be done on digital storytelling, which has a significant potential. The perceived authenticity of the stories created and how this perception affects consumer loyalty is a topic that needs to be investigated. The fact that digital content is perceived as artificial and insincere by many consumers and that this reflects negatively on brand images raises the question of how to measure the perception of artificiality and sincerity in digital storytelling. It is also recommended that neuromarketing research be conducted to examine the emotional and unconscious arousal of consumers in the face of digital narratives. Cultural context, which is often the subject of consumer behavior, may be a prominent factor in evaluating the impact of digital narratives on consumer loyalty. Whether global brands' storytelling is perceived differently in collectivist and individualist cultures is a valuable and unique research topic. The impact of artificial intelligence-supported personalized narratives, which are seen as having great future potential, on consumer-brand interaction can be investigated. Moreover, the mediating effect of these narratives, which are shaped according to the user, on consumer loyalty is a subject that has not yet been elucidated. Finally, how digital narratives will be presented consistently across different platforms and the impact of narrative content on the consumer according to the digital platform is one of the topics that should be considered for future research.

REFERENCES

Aguirre, E., Mahr, D., Grewal, D., De Ruyter, K., & Wetzels, M. (2015). Unraveling thc pcrsonalization paradox: The effect of information collection and trust-building strategies on online advertisement effectiveness. *Journal of Retailing, 91*(1), 34–49. DOI: 10.1016/j.jretai.2014.09.005

Aulló-Saura, E., Gutiérrez-Artacho, J., & Díaz Millón, M. (2025). *Transcreation and AI in global marketing: A comparative case study of two telecom websites.* Digital Translation.

Behzadi, M., & Bakhtiary, M. J. (2023). The role of storytelling in age of digital marketing. In *The 5th International Conference on Modern Research in Management.*

Belova, A. (2021). Storytelling in advertising and branding. *Cognition, Communication. Discourse (Berkeley, Calif.)*, (22), 13–26.

Brodie, R. J., Hollebeek, L. D., Jurić, B., & Ilić, A. (2011). Customer engagement: Conceptual domain, fundamental propositions, and implications for research. *Journal of Service Research, 14*(3), 252–271. DOI: 10.1177/1094670511411703

Chaudhuri, A., & Holbrook, M. B. (2001). The chain of effects from brand trust and brand affect to brand performance: The role of brand loyalty. *Journal of Marketing, 65*(2), 81–93. DOI: 10.1509/jmkg.65.2.81.18255

Crespo, C. F., Ferreira, A. G., & Cardoso, R. M. (2023). The influence of storytelling on the consumer–brand relationship experience. *Journal of Marketing Analytics, 11*(1), 41–56. DOI: 10.1057/s41270-021-00149-0

Di Furia, M., Nicoli, N., Akyar, Ö. Y., & Rossi, M. (2022, January). Storytelling practice in sectors of education, psychology, communication, marketing: A narrative review. In *International Conference on Psychology, Learning, Technology* (pp. 41-62). Cham: Springer International Publishing. DOI: 10.1007/978-3-031-15845-2_3

Dush, L. (2013). The ethical complexities of sponsored digital storytelling. *International Journal of Cultural Studies, 16*(6), 627–640. DOI: 10.1177/1367877912459142

Escalas, J. E. (2004). Narrative processing: Building consumer connections to brands. *Journal of Consumer Psychology, 14*(1-2), 168–180. DOI: 10.1207/s15327663jcp1401&2_19

Floridi, L., Cowls, J., Beltrametti, M., Chatila, R., Chazerand, P., Dignum, V., Luetge, C., Madelin, R., Pagallo, U., Rossi, F., Schafer, B., Valcke, P., & Vayena, E. (2018). AI4People—An ethical framework for a good AI society: Opportunities, risks, principles, and recommendations. *Minds and Machines, 28*(4), 689–707. DOI: 10.1007/s11023-018-9482-5 PMID: 30930541

Fournier, S. (1998). Consumers and their brands: Developing relationship theory in consumer research. *The Journal of Consumer Research, 24*(4), 343–373. DOI: 10.1086/209515

Gillespie, T. (2014). The relevance of algorithms. *Media technologies. Essays on Communication, Materiality, and Society, 167*, 167.

Green, M. C., & Brock, T. C. (2000). The role of transportation in the persuasiveness of public narratives. *Journal of Personality and Social Psychology, 79*(5), 701–721. DOI: 10.1037/0022-3514.79.5.701 PMID: 11079236

Guo, R., & Jiang, Z. (2024). Optimal dynamic advertising policy considering consumer ad fatigue. *Decision Support Systems, 187*, 114323. DOI: 10.1016/j.dss.2024.114323

Gutierrez, E., Karwowski, W., Fiok, K., Davahli, M. R., Liciaga, T., & Ahram, T. (2021). Analysis of human behavior by mining textual data: Current research topics and analytical techniques. *Symmetry, 13*(7), 1276. DOI: 10.3390/sym13071276

Hakanurmi, S. (2017). Learning to work through narratives: Identity and meaning-making during digital storytelling. In *Digital Storytelling in Higher Education: International Perspectives* (pp. 149–166). Springer International Publishing. DOI: 10.1007/978-3-319-51058-3_11

Herskovitz, S., & Crystal, M. (2010). The essential brand persona: Storytelling and branding. *The Journal of Business Strategy, 31*(3), 21–28. DOI: 10.1108/02756661011036673

Hollebeek, L. D., Glynn, M. S., & Brodie, R. J. (2014). Consumer brand engagement in social media: Conceptualization, scale development and validation. *Journal of Interactive Marketing, 28*(2), 149–165. DOI: 10.1016/j.intmar.2013.12.002

Holt, D. B. (2002). Why do brands cause trouble? A dialectical theory of consumer culture and branding. *The Journal of Consumer Research, 29*(1), 70–90. DOI: 10.1086/339922

Hong, J., Yang, J., Wooldridge, B. R., & Bhappu, A. D. (2022). Sharing consumers' brand storytelling: Influence of consumers' storytelling on brand attitude via emotions and cognitions. *Journal of Product and Brand Management, 31*(2), 265–278. DOI: 10.1108/JPBM-07-2019-2485

Im, J., & Chang, B. (2025, November). Human–AI co-creativity in storytelling: A scoping review of literature, education, media, and interactive systems. In *International Conference on Interactive Digital Storytelling* (pp. 396-406). Cham: Springer Nature Switzerland.

Jo, M., Cha, J., & Kim, J. (2022). The effects of tourism storytelling on tourism destination brand value, lovemarks and relationship strength in South Korea. *Sustainability (Basel), 14*(24), 16495. DOI: 10.3390/su142416495

Kabashkin, I., Zervina, O., & Misnevs, B. (2025). AI narrative modeling: How machines' intelligence reproduces archetypal storytelling. *Information (Basel), 16*(4), 319. DOI: 10.3390/info16040319

Kátai, Z., Osztián, P. R., & Iclanzan, D. (2024). Enacting algorithms: Evolution of the algorythmics storytelling. *Education and Information Technologies, 29*(14), 19197–19228. DOI: 10.1007/s10639-024-12617-y

Khan, M. T., Humayun, A. A., & Sajjad, M. (2015). Customer loyalty-attitudinal and behavioral aspects (A review). *International Journal of Information, Business and Management, 7*(2), 163.

Laczniak, G. R., & Murphy, P. E. (2006). Normative perspectives for ethical and socially responsible marketing. *Journal of Macromarketing, 26*(2), 154–177. DOI: 10.1177/0276146706290924

Lemon, K. N., & Verhoef, P. C. (2016). Understanding customer experience throughout the customer journey. *Journal of Marketing, 80*(6), 69–96. DOI: 10.1509/jm.15.0420

Li, J., Montgomery, N., & Mousavi, R. (2022). How a brand's social activism impacts consumers' brand evaluations: The role of brand relationship norms, arXiv preprint, arXiv:2210.10832, https://doi.org//arxiv.2210.10832.DOI: 10.48550

Lundqvist, A., Liljander, V., Gummerus, J., & Van Riel, A. (2013). The impact of storytelling on the consumer brand experience: The case of a firm-originated story. *Journal of Brand Management, 20*(4), 283–297. DOI: 10.1057/bm.2012.15

Mandung, F. (2025). The influence of storytelling techniques in digital marketing on brand loyalty: A consumer psychology perspective. *Golden Ratio of Marketing and Applied Psychology of Business, 5*(1), 66–78. DOI: 10.52970/grmapb.v5i1.782

Markou, V., Serdaris, P., Antoniadis, I., & Spinthiropoulos, K. (2025). Personalization, trust, and identity in AI-based marketing: An empirical study of consumer acceptance in Greece. *Administrative Sciences, 15*(11), 440. DOI: 10.3390/admsci15110440

Mohamed, K. M. M. (2025). Visual storytelling and cultural connection in GCC social media advertising. *Frontiers in Communication, 10*, 1584156. DOI: 10.3389/fcomm.2025.1584156

Mohammadkhani, D., Majedi, N., Biniaz, S. A., & Sarhadi, M. (2025). AI-driven personalization strategies and their impact on consumer engagement in digital markets. *Digital Transformation and Administration Innovation*, 1-14.

Oke, T. (2025). Algorithmic narrativity as a new narrative mode. *AI & Society, 40*(7), 1–12. DOI: 10.1007/s00146-025-02297-8

Park, C. W., MacInnis, D. J., Priester, J., Eisingerich, A. B., & Iacobucci, D. (2010). Brand attachment and brand attitude strength: Conceptual and empirical differentiation of two critical brand equity drivers. *Journal of Marketing, 74*(6), 1–17. DOI: 10.1509/jmkg.74.6.1

Pulizzi, J. (2012). The rise of storytelling as the new marketing. *Publishing Research Quarterly, 28*(2), 116–123. DOI: 10.1007/s12109-012-9264-5

Rettberg, J. W., & Wigers, H. (2025). AI-generated stories favour stability over change: Homogeneity and cultural stereotyping in narratives generated by gpt-4o-mini. *Open Research Europe, 5*, 202. DOI: 10.12688/openreseurope.20576.1

Robin, B. R. (2016). The power of digital storytelling to support teaching and learning. *Digital Education Review*, (30), 17–29.

Sánchez-López, I., Gifreu-Castells, A., & Roig, A. (2025). AI storytelling & narrative evolution in creative industries. *Systematic Reviews.*

Sapre, I., & Longani, K. D. (2024). The role of storytelling in advertising: How narrative drives brand loyalty. In *Indonesia Broadcasting Conference (IBC)* (Vol. 1, pp. 187-200).

Schivinski, B., Christodoulides, G., & Dabrowski, D. (2016). Measuring consumers' engagement with brand-related social-media content: Development and validation of a scale that identifies levels of social-media engagement with brands. *Journal of Advertising Research, 56*(1), 64–80. DOI: 10.2501/JAR-2016-004

Schmitt, B. (1999). Experiential marketing. *Journal of Marketing Management, 15*(1-3), 53–67. DOI: 10.1362/026725799784870496

Serbanescu, A., & Nack, F. (2023). Human-AI system co-creativity for building narrative worlds. In *Proceedings of the IASDR 2023: Life-Changing Design*, Milan, Italy. Design Research Society: London, UK. DOI: 10.21606/iasdr.2023.293

Sergio, F. (2020). Storytelling in the Luxury Industry: Narratives as a Tool for Experiential Branding-The Case of Christian Dior Couture. Master's Thesis, Università Ca' Foscari Venezia, Venice, Italy.

Shavitt, S., & Cho, H. (2016). Culture and consumer behavior: The role of horizontal and vertical cultural factors. *Current Opinion in Psychology*, *8*, 149–154. DOI: 10.1016/j.copsyc.2015.11.007 PMID: 28083559

Shneiderman, B. (2020). Human-centered artificial intelligence: Reliable, safe & trustworthy. *International Journal of Human-Computer Interaction*, *36*(6), 495–504. DOI: 10.1080/10447318.2020.1741118

Singh, S., & Sonnenburg, S. (2012). Brand performances in social media. *Journal of Interactive Marketing*, *26*(4), 189–197. DOI: 10.1016/j.intmar.2012.04.001

Suryana, P. (2024). Building a strong brand image: The role of storytelling in marketing. [JECOMBI]. *Journal of Economics and Business*, *4*(02), 107–115.

Umoren, O., Didi, P. U., Balogun, O., Abass, O. S., & Akinrinoye, O. V. (2022). Strategic digital storytelling techniques for building authentic brand narratives and driving cross-generational consumer trust online. *International Scientific Refereed Research Journal*, *5*(3), 238–261.

Valls-Vargas, J. (2013). Narrative extraction, processing and generation for interactive fiction and computer games. In *Proceedings of the AAAI Conference on Artificial Intelligence and Interactive Digital Entertainment* (Vol. 9, No. 6, pp. 37-40). DOI: 10.1609/aiide.v9i6.12600

Van Laer, T., De Ruyter, K., Visconti, L. M., & Wetzels, M. (2014). The extended transportation-imagery model: A meta-analysis of the antecedents and consequences of consumers' narrative transportation. *The Journal of Consumer Research*, *40*(5), 797–817. DOI: 10.1086/673383

Verhoef, P. C., Reinartz, W. J., & Krafft, M. (2010). Customer engagement as a new perspective in customer management. *Journal of Service Research*, *13*(3), 247–252. DOI: 10.1177/1094670510375461

Wedel, M., & Kannan, P. K. (2016). Marketing analytics for data-rich environments. *Journal of Marketing*, *80*(6), 97–121. DOI: 10.1509/jm.15.0413

Woodside, A. G., Sood, S., & Miller, K. E. (2008). When consumers and brands talk: Storytelling theory and research in psychology and marketing. *Psychology and Marketing*, *25*(2), 97–145. DOI: 10.1002/mar.20203

Yang, K. C., & Kang, Y. (2021). Predicting the relationships between narrative transportation, consumer brand experience, love and loyalty in video storytelling advertising. *Journal of Creative Communications, 16*(1), 7–26. DOI: 10.1177/0973258620984262

Yılmaz, R., & Ciğerci, F. M. (2019). A brief history of storytelling: From primitive dance to digital narration. In *Handbook of Research on Transmedia Storytelling and Narrative Strategies* (pp. 1–14). IGI Global. DOI: 10.4018/978-1-5225-5357-1.ch001

Yunusov, S., Sidat, H., & Emami, A. (2024). MirrorStories: Reflecting Diversity through Personalized Narrative Generation with Large Language Models. /arXiv.2409.13935 arXiv:2409.13935DOI: 10.18653/v1/2024.emnlp-main.382

Zuboff, S. (2019). *The age of surveillance capitalism: The fight for a human future at the new frontier of power*. Public Affairs.

KEY TERMS AND DEFINITIONS

Digital Storytelling: The strategy of brands to deliver experiences to consumers through structured narratives to create an emotional connection through digital platforms.

Consumer Loyalty: Emotional and behavioral commitment to a brand.

Narrative Transportation: The state in which an individual is completely immersed mentally and emotionally in a story, thus temporarily living in the narrative world by disconnecting from reality.

Brand Loyalty: Refers to the strong emotional relationship a consumer has with a brand and includes elements of identification, passion and continuity.

Experiential Marketing: A marketing approach that focuses on creating interaction between the consumer and the brand in the dimensions of sensation, emotion, thought, action and relationship.

Consumer Engagement: Refers to the level of cognitive, emotional and behavioral interaction with a brand; it includes activities such as sharing, commenting and content creation, especially in digital environments.

Authenticity in Brand Narratives: When the narrative is perceived by the consumer as sincere, real and trustworthy.

Emotional Resonance: The effect of a story that evokes strong emotions in the audience and creates a deep connection with the brand.

Chapter 3
The Use of Artificial Intelligence in Brand Advertising Narratives

Betül Başer
http://orcid.org/0000-0001-5226-9771
Ondokuz Mayıs University, Turkey

ABSTRACT

This study is designed as qualitative research aiming to reveal how meaning is produced in artificial intelligence-supported advertising narratives. In the research, a semiotic analysis method was adopted to decipher which signs are used to give meaning to the visual and narrative elements in advertising films. The analytical framework combines Roland Barthes' semiotic approach based on the signifier-signified distinction with Charles Sanders Peirce's classification of icons, indices, and symbols. Accordingly, the study examines color, image, composition, and AI-supported aesthetic elements in a multi-layered manner from a visual semiotics perspective. The universe of the research consists of advertisements produced with artificial intelligence or supported by artificial intelligence, while the sample is Popeyes Turkey's advertisement produced with artificial intelligence and published on digital platforms in 2025, selected using purposive sampling.

INTRODUCTION

The digital transformation in communication technologies has fundamentally changed the concept of advertising in terms of production methods, narrative structures, and interpretation processes. In particular, the proliferation of internet-based platforms and the rise of data-driven communication practices have transformed

DOI: 10.4018/979-8-3373-5666-2.ch003

advertising into a more measurable, targetable, and personalized structure. Within this transformation process, artificial intelligence technologies have become a strategic element in advertising. They have begun to be actively used in many stages, from the design of advertising messages to visual production, target audience analysis, and performance measurement. AI-powered advertising applications require advertising to be viewed not only as a technical production process but also as a new form of narrative and representation. Visuals produced through algorithms, with hyper-realistic aesthetics, dramatic lighting, and sensory intensity, set advertising narratives apart from traditional narrative forms while offering viewers more striking, attention-grabbing, and emotionally powerful experiences. This situation means that advertising films are no longer just texts promoting products, but are now considered cultural texts that produce meaning, value, and ideology

The increasing role of artificial intelligence in advertising narratives also raises the question of how meaning is produced and conveyed to the audience. This new advertising language, created through visual signs, color usage, images, narrative structure and digital aesthetics, is transforming how brands position themselves and the symbolic relationship they establish with consumers. In this context, AI-supported advertisements should be considered communication practices that produce new regimes of meaning alongside technological innovations. This study aims to reveal the meaning production processes of AI-generated advertising narratives and examines these advertisements from a semiotic perspective. The focus of the study is on which signs the visual and narrative elements used in advertising films are structured through, which layers of meaning these signs produce, and how AI aesthetics transform the advertising narrative. In this regard, the research aims to understand the place of AI-supported advertisements within the contemporary understanding of advertising and to make a theoretical contribution to this new advertising language.

A GENERAL OVERVIEW OF THE CONCEPT OF BRAND

According to the American Marketing Association's definition, a brand is "*a name, term, sign, symbol, design, or combination thereof used by a seller or group of sellers to distinguish their goods from those of others*" (Demir, 2009, p. 6). *A* brand is defined as *"a name, term, sign, symbol, design, or combination thereof used to identify the goods and services of a seller or group of sellers and to distinguish them from others"* (Kotler 1991, p. 442). Aaker (2012) defines the concept of *a brand* as *"an asset (asset and liability) associated with a brand name and symbol; a company or a company's goods or services for its customers"* (Kotler, 1997, p. 482).

The terms brand strategy and branding strategy are interchangeable. Park et al. (1986) define brand strategy as a positioning strategy responsible for creating brand image. Murphy (1990) defines it as the long-term differentiation of brands from competing brands, Arnold (1992) defines it as the positioning of brands to maximize consumer satisfaction, Kapferer (1992) defines it as the development of a perception in the consumer's mind that is different from competitors through different activities, Aaker (2012) describes it as developing flexibility due to changing market conditions, Keller (1998) describes it as developing more inclusive strategies for all brands and sub-brands, and Cherantony (2001) describes it as the creation and maintenance of a brand through a systematic process aimed at strengthening and developing the different products sold by organizations (Alamro, 2010, pp. 56-57). A review of the literature reveals that brand strategy can be derived from six factors. These are communication strategy, brand heritage, brand values, brand identity, brand personality, and brand positioning (Alamro, 2010, p. 57).

***Brand Positioning*:** It is seen as an important tool for brand applications. It is the act of designing a company's offer and image in such a way that it occupies a distinct place in the minds of consumers. In fact, brand positioning can be described as a branch of differentiation in which researchers attempt to investigate the distinct dimensions of positioning from the consumer perspective (Wang, 2015, p. 727).

Brand Personality: It has been stated that this concept is a simple translation from individual psychology to the field of marketing. The human personality framework is known as the "big five." Extraversion (energy or enthusiasm), conscientiousness (control or restraint), openness to experience (originality or open-mindedness), agreeableness (altruism or compassion), and neuroticism (negative emotionality, irritability) are seen as an appropriate analogy for understanding consumers' perceptions of brand images or for defining brand attributes (Ratnayake, 2012, p. 58).

Brand Identity: A concept used to express the distinctive and partially enduring qualities of a brand that differentiate it from competing brands. When a brand identity is perceived as prestigious and distinctive, it tends to have an attractive and powerful identity. Brand identity is what makes a brand different from others. Most often, brand identity consists of a set of brand attributes (He et al., 2016, p. 5). Brand identity expresses the essence of the brand itself, all the characteristics that make it "it" (Hanna & Rowley, 2013, p. 1788).

Brand Value: A brand value is a distinct preference and response to marketing efforts derived from a product's brand identity (Datta et al., 2017, p. 1). "*A brand is a set of brand assets and obligations associated with a name and symbol that add to or detract from the value a product or service provides to a company and/or its customers*" (Aaker, 1991, p.15). Brand equity *is "the difference in consumer response* *to brand marketing based on brand knowledge*" (Keller, 1993, p. 2). Brand equity is the effort to create value by communicating with a brand's name and symbol as an asset type for a product or service. There are five types of assets in these values: brand loyalty, brand awareness, brand associations, perceived quality, and other registered characteristics (Methanuntakul, 2010, p.52).

Brand Heritage: There are five different elements that indicate whether a brand potentially has heritage. The heritage of a brand's identity is an organizational dimension where core values, longevity, success, and the significance of its history are important (Ratnayake, 2012, p.62).

Communication Strategies: These relate to how an institution communicates a brand to its consumers. It consists of components such as press releases, sponsorship, and employee behavior (Alamro, 2010, pp. 64-65). Duncan (2002, p.15) defines communication as "*a common term used in marketing*, such as *product advertising, public relations, direct marketing, sales promotion, etc.*"

When examining the literature on the concept of brand and brand strategies, it is seen that a brand is not just a name or symbol, but a complex structure that is interpreted in the consumer's mind through multidimensional elements such as identity, personality, values, heritage, and communication strategies. Concepts such as brand positioning, brand identity, and brand personality enable brands to differentiate themselves in competitive markets, while brand value and brand heritage play a decisive role in building long-term perception and trust.

Communication strategies, which are at the center of this process, are one of the fundamental elements that determine how the brand conveys this multi-layered structure to consumers. With the acceleration of digitalization and technological transformation today, brands' communication strategies have also entered a significant process of change. Particularly in advertising, the use of artificial intelligence technologies is reshaping how brands express themselves, their narrative structures, and their relationship with consumers. In this context, the next section will address the effects of using artificial intelligence in advertising on brand communication and advertising narratives.

THE CONCEPT OF ADVERTISING AND THE USE OF ARTIFICIAL INTELLIGENCE IN ADVERTISEMENTS

The concept of advertising, etymologically speaking, refers to the act of "announcing" or "declaring" in its most basic sense. Derived from the Latin root *reclamare*, this term means to call out, attract attention, and announce something repeatedly (Taşkıran & Yılmaz, 2014, p. 3). According to the American Marketing Association's definition of advertising, "*Advertising* is *any promotional* activity that involves *paying for a product, service, or idea and clearly indicating who paid for it, excluding personal sales"* (Odabaşı & Oyman, 2013, p. 98). Advertising is the process of promoting a product, service, idea, person, or institution to a wide audience by purchasing space and time in mass media, with the cost covered by a specific person, institution, or organization. In this definition, one of the fundamental elements of advertising activity is that the party financing the advertisement is clearly known. Conducting advertising as a planned and strategic communication process requires purchasing a specific space or time slot in the media to ensure that the message reaches the target audience effectively.

In this regard, advertising can be used as an effective tool not only for products or services but also for presenting a wide variety of content to the public, such as the image of institutions, the dissemination of ideas, or the promotion of individuals (Elden, et al., 2015, p. 62). Advertising is an effort to inform and persuade individuals to make a purchase. The place and time are purchased by the person preparing the messages. For this reason, the messages can be kept under control. Although advertising is a non-personal form of communication, the identities of the institutions or organizations that advertise are not secret but clear (Bülbül, 2004, p. 88). A broader definition is that it is the process of informing a wide audience about the availability of goods and services and related information through mass communication tools such as the press, film, and television (Mutlu, 2017, p. 275).

Advertising has become an important component of marketing strategies as a type of communication that draws on different disciplines of art and considers psychological processes to influence consumer attitudes. Thanks to its structure, which combines creative fields such as cinema, graphic design, photography, and music, advertising emerges as a multifaceted communication practice that aims to introduce and promote a product, service, or idea to consumers. This approach demonstrates that advertising is not merely an aesthetic creation but also a research-based and target audience-focused marketing communication activity (Peltekoğlu, 2019, p.1).

The transition from traditional advertising to digital advertising has begun to transform not only communication processes but also the overall structure of the market. With the development of the internet, digital media environments have increasingly replaced traditional media channels and provided businesses with a faster, more flexible, and measurable communication space. Digital advertising has become one of the fundamental elements of marketing activities within this new structure and has provided brands with the opportunity to reach consumers through different digital channels. Digital marketing allows businesses to maintain constant communication with their target audiences while also contributing to the more effective promotion of products and services and is therefore considered an inevitable necessity in modern marketing (Anand, 2020, p. 131). According to Smith (2011, p. 491), digital advertising refers to the delivery of marketing messages to the target audience through digital technologies. In this context, identifying the right target audience is a critical factor in the effectiveness of digital advertising. Interactions established through social networks, in particular, help build stronger bonds between brands and consumers, supporting brand loyalty and consumer trust. Technological developments rapidly transforming consumer behavior have made social media an indispensable communication channel for brands, prompting companies to develop new advertising and communication strategies that adapt to the dynamics of the digital environment.

In this transformation process, the need for digital advertising to be conducted in a more effective, personalized, and data-driven manner has increased the importance of artificial intelligence-based technologies.

Artificial intelligence is defined as a set of systems that aim to mimic human cognitive processes and provides an infrastructure capable of responding to these new requirements of digital advertising. AI-based systems analyze the data they obtain to make probabilistic inferences and can generate specific responses or actions based on these inferences. When considered in a broader context, these technologies have the capacity to perform human-specific cognitive functions such as learning, language use, communication, perception of environmental elements, and acting in accordance with predefined goals (Adaş & Erbay, 2021, p. 328). These features make artificial intelligence a strategic tool in digital advertising for targeting, content production, and managing consumer interaction.

These developments are leading advertising to evolve into an increasingly data-driven, automation-focused, and personalized structure. Thanks to AI-powered systems, advertising messages are shaped according to consumers' interests, online behaviors, and previous interactions, thus reaching the target audience at the right time and with more appropriate content. Argan and colleagues (2022, p. 334) state that AI-based applications transform advertising communication into a more flexible, measurable, and optimizable process. This enables advertising communication to evolve from a one-way information activity into a dynamic structure that interacts with users and is continuously restructured based on feedback. Algorithms and machine learning-based applications, especially those used on digital platforms, increase the effectiveness of advertising campaigns while also transforming the nature of the relationship brands establish with consumers.

METHODOLOGY

This research aims to reveal how artificial intelligence directs advertising narratives by examining Popeyes Turkey's advertising film, which was prepared using artificial intelligence technologies, and to evaluate the effects of this new production method on brand identity and consumer perception. The direct involvement of artificial intelligence in the production of visual and verbal content creates a new narrative order in advertising, transforming both the aesthetic structure and the forms of message delivery. The limited number of advertising examples in Turkey that are entirely prepared with artificial intelligence and the Popeyes advertisement standing out as one of the pioneering examples in this field make the research important. It also provides a valuable contribution to understanding how artificial intelligence- based advertising applications generate meaning in terms of local marketing communication.

This study, designed within the framework of a qualitative research approach, aims to analyze the meaning production processes of AI-supported advertising narratives. In the study, a semiotic analysis method was adopted to reveal which signs are used to give meaning to the visual and narrative elements used in advertising films. In this regard, the study was conducted based on Roland Barthes' semiotic approach. According to Barthes, a sign consists of a signifier and a signified, with the signifier forming the level of expression and the signified forming the level of content (Barthes, 1997, p. 41). Semiotics is defined as a field of study that examines how signs are structured and how meaning is produced through these signs. A sign is considered to be any object, form, or phenomenon that represents a meaning outside itself and can replace that meaning (Rıfat, 2019, p. 11).

In addition to Barthes' approach, Charles Sanders Peirce's semiotic classification has also been included in the analytical framework in order to analyze the multi-layered structure of meaning more comprehensively. Peirce examines signs under three basic categories—*icon*, *index*, and *symbol*—to explain the process by which an object acquires meaning (Sudi, 2024, p. 233). With the development of new communication technologies, the increasing importance of visual elements in communication processes has led to the concept of visual semiotics gaining significance. Visual semiotics examines meanings produced through colors, shapes, images, and visual compositions (Srivastava & Muskaan, 2023, p. 296).

The universe of the study consists of advertising films produced with artificial intelligence or prepared with artificial intelligence-supported techniques. The sample for the study was determined using purposive sampling, and an advertising film published by Popeyes Turkey in 2025 and produced entirely with artificial intelligence technologies was selected. This advertising film is one of the first examples of advertising created with artificial intelligence in Turkey, making it a meaningful and highly representative sample for the study. The fact that the commercial was published on digital platforms allows for the examination of AI-supported advertising narratives in the Turkish context. Accordingly, within the scope of this study, the Popeyes commercial was analyzed in terms of visual signs, color usage, narrative structure, and AI-supported aesthetic elements within the framework of Barthes and Peirce's semiotic approaches.

The main research questions addressed in this study are as follows:

R.Q.1: How do artificial intelligence technologies affect the narrative structure and meaning production processes of the Popeyes commercial?

A.S.2: What do the AI-based visual and verbal signs used in the commercial signify in terms of brand identity and brand message?

RQ3: In what ways does the AI-generated commercial differ from traditional advertising aesthetics and narrative structure?

A.S.4: How does Popeyes' AI-generated commercial create symbolic value in terms of consumer perception and brand communication?

SEMIOTIC ANALYSIS OF THE POPEYES ADVERTISING FILM

Figure 1. "Popeyes wings fell into the sauce"

Table 1. Saussure Semiotic Analysis

Sign	Signifier (Visible Form)	Signified (Meaning / Interpretation)
"WINGS" text	Large, bright neon-effect letters	The core theme of the product; attention-grabbing quality and dynamism
Light bursts	Warm, glowing lights surrounding the letters	Energy, movement, and the appeal of flavor
Blurred silhouette	A human silhouette emerging in the foreground	Mystery, speed, cinematic impact, dramatic introduction
Warm tones	Yellow–orange color palette	Warmth, taste, and the energetic brand identity associated with Popeyes
Artificial intelligence texture	Slight distortion and digital blur	AI-generated visual aesthetics and a sense of digital creation

Table 2. Peirce Semiotic Analysis

Type of Sign	Element in the Advertisement	Interpretation
Icon	The visual form of the "WINGS" text	Direct representation of the product
Index	Light bursts and neon tones	Indicators of speed, dynamism, and the warmth of flavor
Symbol	Golden light combined with a silhouette background	The visual style of artificial intelligence; a cinematic and fantastical world

The word "WINGS" featured in the opening scene of the advertisement is a powerful visual element symbolizing the transition to a digital universe created by artificial intelligence. The letters, designed in bright, neon tones, invite the viewer into a dynamic, energetic, and flavor-focused atmosphere, while the vague human silhouette appearing in the background adds both mystery and cinematic depth to the scene. The blurred nature of this silhouette reflects the tendency to "push the human into the background and centralize the image," a characteristic feature of artificial intelligence aesthetics. Blurred transitions, bursts of light, and a warm color palette reinforce the feeling that the advertisement is progressing not in reality, but in a digitally produced visual space. Thus, the scene establishes the fundamental direction of the narrative, communicating to the viewer that the hero of the advertisement is the product, and that this product will be presented in a hyper-real world reinterpreted by artificial intelligence. The opening scene both supports the energetic and bold tones of the brand identity and offers the first indication of how artificial intelligence is used as an aesthetic tool in narrative production.

Figure 2. "Popeyes wings fell into the sauce"

Table 3. Saussure Semiotic Analysis

Sign	Signifier (Visible Form)	Signified (Meaning / Interpretation)
Giant LED screen	A massive, illuminated image of chicken wings positioned at a height	Enhancement of Popeyes' power, popularity, and cultural visibility
Crowd watching the screen	People looking upward with excitement	Social excitement, collective approval, and the product's "trending" status
Smoke and night atmosphere	Cinematic fog and dramatic lighting	A sense of spectacle, celebration, and launch effect
Moving crowd	Enthusiastic gestures and bodily movement	The idea that the product creates a shared social experience
Hyper-bright wing image on screen	Exaggerated, AI-enhanced food visuals	Idealization of the product, presented as an almost "iconic" flavor

Table 4. Peirce Semiotic Analysis

Type of Sign	Element in the Advertisement	Interpretation / Meaning
Icon	The giant wing image displayed on the LED screen	Direct representation of the product, enhanced through AI aesthetics
Index	The crowd looking upward, waving, and reacting	Indicators of curiosity, excitement, and approval toward the product
Symbol	Advanced screen technology combined with a nighttime urban setting	Modernity, innovation, youth culture, and a "grand launch" aesthetic

This scene positions Popeyes' new product not merely as food, but as an urban spectacle. Hyper-realistic images of wings glowing on a giant screen, combined with the idealizing aesthetics of artificial intelligence, transform the product into an almost mythical "city icon." The crowd's upward gaze and admiring reaction supports Barthes' concept of "myth creation": the product transcends its status as an everyday object and becomes a symbol of collective admiration within pop culture. Smoke, lights, and the nighttime atmosphere enhance the dramatic structure of the scene, creating a brand image that aligns with Peirce's symbolic category, embodying innovation, energy, and youth culture. Thus, Popeyes is coded not merely as a brand offering flavor but as a producer of socially exciting experiences.

Figure 3. "Popeyes wings fell into the sauce"

Table 5. Saussure Semiotic Analysis

Sign	Signifier (Visible Form)	Signified (Meaning / Interpretation)
Character portrait	A prominent young woman with braided hair and glitter makeup	Youth, dynamism, trend culture, and the modern consumer
Neon texts	"Honey BBQ? Yes", "Sweet spicy? Yes"	Variety, freedom of choice, and the diversity of the product range
Orange–yellow neon lighting	Bright neon typography in the background	Energy, warmth, flavor, and urban culture
Mesh Popeyes T-shirt	Brand name displayed on the character's clothing	Brand affiliation and the emphasis on the Popeyes lifestyle
Bokeh background	Indistinct city lights	Urban atmosphere, modern life, and nighttime aesthetics
Glitter makeup	Shimmering details around the eyes	Artificial intelligence texture and a futuristic appearance

Table 6. Peirce Semiotic Analysis

Type of Sign	Element in the Advertisement	Interpretation
Icon	The character's face and clothing	Indicators of the target audience: youth and trend-conscious consumers
Index	Orientation toward neon lights	An energetic environment, urban rhythm, and fast-paced lifestyle
Symbol	Neon texts combined with glitter makeup	A futuristic aesthetic created by artificial intelligence; a symbol of "freedom of choice" through diverse flavor options

In this scene, the aesthetic of AI production, combined with the character's stylized appearance and neon text, creates an atmosphere that reflects modern, youthful, and digital culture. The character's glitter makeup, when viewed alongside the smooth and hyper-realistic textures on their face, highlights AI's tendency to idealize human faces. The neon text not only introduces the product flavors but also provides the viewer with energy through its "yes" repetitions, offering a fast and positive rhythm. This repetition transforms the flavor options into a moment of decision in the advertising narrative, producing a discourse that promises the consumer freedom, variety, and enjoyment. The uncertainty of the background and the brightness of the neon lights suggest that the scene takes place not in a real space but in a digitally produced universe. Thus, Popeyes positions the product not just as food but as part of a lifestyle blended with youthful energy and urban culture. Artificial intelligence functions as a creative tool in this scene, transforming character presentation, text delivery, and atmosphere creation into a holistic narrative

Figure 4. "Popeyes wings fell into the sauce"

Table 7. Saussure Semiotic Analysis

Sign	Signifier (Visible Form)	Signified (Meaning / Interpretation)
Popeyes store entrance	Branch illuminated with warm, bright lighting	Invitation, accessibility, and the brand's warm identity
Walking people	A group moving rapidly toward the restaurant	Demand, popularity, and social attraction
Urban atmosphere	Nighttime setting with skyscraper lights and modern streets	Urban life, dynamism, and fast-consumption culture
Yellow–orange lighting	Dominant warm tones at the store entrance	Warmth, flavor appeal, attraction, and Popeyes' color identity

continued on following page

Table 7. Continued

Sign	Signifier (Visible Form)	Signified (Meaning / Interpretation)
Large emoji patch	Prominent smiling face patch on a jacket	Happiness, satisfaction, and positive emotions associated with the brand
Low-angle camera shot	Viewpoint looking up at the moving crowd	Amplification of movement, energy, and crowd impact

Table 8. Peirce Semiotic Analysis

Type of Sign	Element in the Advertisement	Interpretation
Icon	Popeyes logo and store entrance	The brand's physical presence; a tangible point of attraction
Index	Crowd moving toward the restaurant	Indicator of popularity and strong consumer demand
Symbol	Warm lighting combined with a nighttime urban setting	Urban consumption habits, modern life rhythm, and fast-food culture

The image of people walking towards the Popeyes branch in this scene creates a powerful narrative that emphasizes the brand's position in urban life. The nighttime atmosphere and modern city lights position Popeyes as an "essential stop in urban life," part of the fast-paced consumer culture. The warm, bright orange lights emanating from the store entrance both reference Popeyes' corporate colors and create a welcoming warmth that invites consumers inside. Young people approaching the space with quick steps show that the brand is particularly preferred by the young audience and is associated with dynamism. The prominent selection of a large smiley emoji on one of the characters' jackets becomes a symbolic element that reinforces the themes of happiness, pleasure, and satisfaction, combined with the hyper-realistic texture of AI aesthetics. AI-generated blurred motion transitions and light reflections make the scene feel more like a digitally expanded space than a real city environment. Thus, Popeyes is presented both as a physical restaurant and as a lifestyle brand promising consumers "city energy + flavor + youth."

Figure 5. "Popeyes wings fell into the sauce"

Table 9. Saussure Semiotic Analysis

Sign	Signifier (Visible Form)	Signified (Meaning / Interpretation)
Wing pieces (close-up)	Fried surface of the product with sauce and texture details	Freshness, intense flavor, and quality
Floating / motion	Wings depicted as if suspended in mid-air	Product dynamism and a playful consumption experience
Spice particles	Crumbs and spices bursting into the air	Crumbs and spices bursting into the air
Flowing sauce	Bright red sauce poured over the product in slow motion	Pleasure, richness, and the myth of flavor
Hands holding the product	Product presented close-up in human hands	Accessibility, consumer connection, and warmth
Warm lighting – orange tones	Golden-yellow and orange illumination	Popeyes' warm and energetic brand identity; appetite-stimulating color use
Repetitive visuals	Product repeatedly shown from multiple angles	Reinforcement of appeal; transformation of flavor into a myth

Table 10. Peirce Semiotic Analysis

Type of Sign	Element in the Advertisement	Interpretation
Icon	Realistic appearance of the chicken wing	Direct representation of the product; recognizability
Index	Flowing sauce, airborne spices, and heat	Fresh preparation, freshness, and hot serving
Symbol	Orange lighting, dramatic aesthetics, hand-held presentation	The brand's warm and dynamic identity; attraction to the product and accessibility

In the first analysis scene of the advertisement, the product is presented to the viewer in a hyper-realistic and dramatic manner over four micro-frames. The close-up of the wings, the slow-motion flow of the sauce, and the flying spice particles convey the appetizing visual appeal of food at Barthes' denotative level, while showing that at the connotative level, the taste is transformed into an exaggerated experience of pleasure. The use of compositions that transcend the physical limits of reality in these scenes—floating in the air, intense light effects, particle effects—elevates the product from an ordinary food item to a mythical "object of taste." From Peirce's perspective, the sauce and particle movements function as indices of freshness and warmth, while the orange lights symbolize Popeyes' energetic and youthful brand identity. The frame where the product is held in hand creates an image of closeness and accessibility, establishing direct contact with the consumer. Thus, these four frames form a powerful narrative that places the viewer at the center of the myth of taste and pleasure as the first scene analyzed in the advertisement.

Figure 6 "Popeyes wings fell into the sauce"

Table 11. Saussure Semiotic Analysis

Sign	Signifier (Visible Form)	Signified (Meaning / Interpretation)
Flavor texts: Honey BBQ and Sweet Spicy	Prominent typography on the left and right sides of the screen	Flavor variety and product options addressing individual preferences
Two female consumers	Two young women with distinct styles	The ability of Popeyes products to unite individuals with different identities and tastes
Lighting tone contrast	Warm red tones on the left; cool blue–green tones on the right	Differentiation of flavor profiles: Honey BBQ as softer/sweeter, Sweet Spicy as sharper/bolder
Close-up shots of wings	Detailed depiction of the moment before tasting	Sensory intensity and appetite-inducing realism
Facial expressions of the women	Expressions approaching the moment of biting	Pleasure, flavor experience, and individual enjoyment
Split-screen	Simultaneous presentation of two flavors	Variety, comparison, and freedom of choice

Table 12. Peirce Semiotic Analysis

Type of Sign	Element in the Advertisement	Type of Sign
Icon	Close-up shots of the chicken pieces held by the women	Direct representation of the product; crispiness, sauce intensity, and textural realism
Index	Facial expressions and physical reactions during the biting moment	Bodily indicators of pleasure, flavor experience, and satisfaction
Symbol	Flavor texts combined with split-screen presentation	Cultural coding of flavor differences and the variety offered by the brand

This scene creates a powerful sensory narrative by presenting two contrasting flavors. The split-screen aesthetic has become a symbol of a brand strategy that offers viewers freedom of choice and variety. On the left, the "Honey BBQ" option, supported by warm-toned lighting, evokes a softer, sweeter, and more comforting flavor profile, while on the right, the "Sweet & Spicy" option, highlighted by sharper lighting effects, is associated with dynamism and a bold flavor experience. The facial expressions of both women, showing natural reactions of pleasure and satisfaction as they bite into the saucy chicken pieces, convey to the viewer the level of sensory satisfaction that the product physically creates. Close-up iconographic shots idealize the product's real texture, while fonts and color codes become symbolic elements that culturally signify different flavor profiles. Thus, the scene constructs a multi-layered flavor narrative in which Popeyes presents a product not merely as food, but as an identity-forming experience.

Figure 7. "Popeyes wings fell into the sauce"

Table 13. Saussure Semiotic Analysis

Sign	Signifier (Visible Form)	Signified (Meaning / Interpretation)
Product boxes (with Popeyes logo))	Chicken wings placed in orange branded boxes	Corporate identity, standardized quality, and brand affiliation
Sweet Spicy – Honey BBQ texts	Two flavor labels designed in a handwritten style	Flavor variety and appeal to individual preferences
"New" text	Bright neon-style typography with dynamic lines	Emphasis on novelty, campaign announcement, and arousing curiosity
Texture of the wings	Crispy surface with glossy sauce coating	Freshness of flavor, appetite appeal, and idealized presentation
Bokeh background	Blurred clusters of colorful lights	Digital/cinematic atmosphere; an indicator of AI aesthetics
Dominance of orange	Intensive use of the brand color	Energy, dynamism, youth, and an identity strongly associated with Popeyes

Table 14. Peirce Semiotic Analysis

Type of Sign	Element in the Advertisement	Type of Sign
Icon	Realistic details of the chicken wings	Direct representation of the product; crispiness, sauce intensity, and physical visibility of flavor
Index	Crispy surface and glossy oil–sauce texture	Connotations of freshness, newly fried quality, and hot serving
Symbol	Neon handwritten "New" text combined with the orange brand color	Novelty, dynamism, campaign messaging, and reinforcement of brand identity

This final scene serves as a "product showcase" that brings together the entire narrative of the advertisement. The dual sweet structure—Sweet Bitter and Honey BBQ—is presented in a romantic and playful handwriting font, coding it as a personalized taste experience. The word "New" prominently displayed at the center of the scene transforms the idea of novelty into a consumption myth, in line with Barthes' concept of myth; it is presented not just as a new product, but as an "exciting experience worth trying." The hyper-realistic presentation of the wings, combined with the aesthetic of artificial intelligence that exaggerates details, idealizes the product, with each piece perfectly crispy, evenly coated in sauce, and perfected with almost laboratory precision. The prominent placement of orange boxes transforms the brand's corporate identity into the main carrier of the scene, turning it into not just a presentation of flavor, but also a sensory display of Popeyes' identity. The digital bokeh texture in the background obscures physical reality, creating a modern "flavor universe" dominated by AI aesthetics. Thus, the stage positions the product not just as food, but as a mythically valued, culturally coded object of consumption with enhanced appeal.

CONCLUSION

This study aims to demonstrate the transformative effect of artificial intelligence technologies on advertising narratives, using the example of an AI-generated advertising film by Popeyes Turkey. The increasing dominance of digitalization and algorithmic production processes in advertising is transforming advertising films from mere promotional texts into complex communication practices that produce aesthetic, ideological, and cultural meanings. In this context, the study presents important findings on contemporary advertising by examining the meaning production processes of AI-supported advertising narratives from a semiotic perspective.

The analyses conducted within the scope of the research reveal that AI functions not only as a technical production tool in advertising narratives but also as a creative and symbolic element that shapes the narrative. The hyper-realistic visuals, dramatic lighting, exaggerated motion effects, and digital aesthetic elements used in the Popeyes commercial transform the product from an everyday consumer item into a mythical "object of taste." When evaluated within the framework of Barthes' distinction between signifier and signified and his concept of myth, it is seen that the narrative of the advertisement presents values such as taste, pleasure, youth, dynamism, and urban culture as natural and inevitable phenomena.

Analyses based on Peirce's classification of icons, signs, and symbols show that the visual elements used in the commercial create a multi-layered meaning structure. Close-up shots of the product offer direct representations at the iconic level, while the flow of sauce, spice particles, and the use of warm lighting function as signs of sensory characteristics such as freshness, warmth, and having been freshly prepared. At the same time, neon signs, color codes, and urban aesthetics reinforce the Popeyes brand's young, energetic, and modern identity at the symbolic level. Thus, the commercial offers the viewer not just a product, but also the promise of a certain lifestyle and experience.

One of the study's key findings is that the aesthetics of artificial intelligence push the human element into the background in advertising narratives, creating a narrative structure that centers visual displays and the product. The commercial emphasizes collective excitement, movement, and experience rather than the individual characteristics of the characters, demonstrating that consumption has transformed from an individual act into a social and cultural spectacle. This aesthetic structure, produced by artificial intelligence, distances the advertising narrative from physical reality and positions it in a digitally expanded universe.

In conclusion, this study reveals that AI-supported advertising narratives fundamentally transform the ways in which brands produce meaning and establish symbolic connections with consumers. AI has become not only a technology that provides efficiency and automation in advertising but also a powerful narrative tool that creates myths, establishes aesthetic codes, and reconstructs brand identity. Given the limited number of advertising examples produced entirely by artificial intelligence in the Turkish context, this analysis of the Popeyes commercial provides an important contribution to both academic literature and advertising practice. Future studies comparing AI-supported advertisements from different sectors will enable a more comprehensive understanding of the cultural and ideological dimensions of this new advertising language.

REFERENCES

Aaker, D. (1991). Brand equity. *La gestione del valore della marca, 347*, 356.

Aaker, D. A. (2012). *Building strong brands*. Simon and schuster.

Adaş, E. B., & Erbay, B. (2021). Yapay Zekâ Sosyolojisi Üzerine Bir Değerlendirme. *Gaziantep University Journal of Social Sciences, 21*(1), 326–337. DOI: 10.21547/jss.991383

Alamro, A. S. (2010). *Branding and brand preference in the mobile phone service industry*. Bangor University.

Anand, A. (2020). Impact of Digitalisation of Marketing: An Analysis. *Research Review Journals, 5*(8), 131–134. DOI: 10.31305/rrijm.2020.v05.i08.031

Barthes, R. (1997). *Göstergebilimsel Serüven*. Yapı Kredi Yayınları.

Bülbül, R. (2004). *Halkla İlişkiler*. Nobel Yayın Dağıtım.

Datta, H., Ailawadi, K. L., & van Heerde, H. J. (2017). How Well Does Consumer-Based Brand Equity Align with Sales-Based Brand Equity and Marketing-Mix Response? *Journal of Marketing, 81*(3), 1–20. DOI: 10.1509/jm.15.0340

Demir, M. Ö. (2009). Tüketici İmajı ve Marka İmajı Uyumunun Marka Sadakati Üzerine Etkisi. Doktora Tezi. Antalya: Akdeniz Üniversitesi Sosyal Bilimler Enstitüsü.

Duncan, T. (2002). *IMC using advertising and promotion to build brands*. McGraw-Hill.

Elden, M., Ulukök, Ö., & Yeygel, S. (2015). *Şimdi Reklamlar....* İletişim Yayınları.

Hanna, S., & Rowley, J. (2013). A practitioner-led strategic place brand-management model. *Journal of Marketing Management, 29*(15-16), 1782–1815. DOI: 10.1080/0267257X.2013.800901

He, H., Harris, L. C., Wang, W., & Haider, K. (2016). Brand identity and online self-customisation usefulness perception. *Journal of Marketing Management, 32*(13-14), 1308–1332. DOI: 10.1080/0267257X.2016.1170720

Keller, K. L. (1993). Conceptualizing, measuring, and managing customer-based brand equity. *Journal of Marketing, 57*(1), 1–22. DOI: 10.1177/002224299305700101

Kotler, P. (1991). *Marketing Management: Analysis, Planning, Implementation and Control* (7th ed.). Prentice-Hall Inc.

Kotler, P. (1997). *Marketing Management* (9th ed.). Prentice Hall.

Methanuntakul, K. (2010). *High-street fashion brand communication amongst female adolescents* (Doctoral dissertation, Brunel University School of Engineering and Design PhD Theses).

Mutlu, E. (2017). *İletişim Sözlüğü.* Ütopya Yayınevi.

Odabaşı, Y., & Oyman, M. (2013). *Pazarlama İletişimi Yönetimi*. MediaCat Kitapları.

Peltekoğlu, F. (2019). *Kavram ve Kuramlarıyla İkna*. Beta Yayınevi.

Ratnayake, N. (2012). *The Predictive validity of brand-related autobiographical memories on brand commitment.* PhD thesis. Coventry: Coventry University

Rıfat, M. (2019). *Göstergebilimin ABC'si*. Say Yayınları.

Srivastava,S. & Muskaan, D. (2023). A Semiotic Exploration of AI-Driven Personalization in Advertising.

Sudi, M. (2024). Semiotic Analysis in Advertising: How Messages Are Communicated To Society. *Jurnal Komunikasi*, *2*(3), 224–235.

Taşkıran, Ö. N., & Yılmaz, R. (2014). *99 Soruda Reklam ve Reklamcılık.* Derin Yayınları.

Wang, H.-J. (2015). A New Approach to Network Analysis for Brand Positioning. *International Journal of Market Research*, *57*(5), 727–742. DOI: 10.2501/IJMR-2015-060

Yuan, R., Liu, M. J., Luo, J., & Yen, D. A. (2016). Reciprocal transfer of brand identity and image associations arising from higher education brand extensions. *Journal of Business Research*, *69*(8), 3069–3076. DOI: 10.1016/j.jbusres.2016.01.022

KEY TERMS AND DEFINITIONS

Advertising: A planned communication process aimed at introducing and persuading a target audience about a product, service, idea, or brand through mass media in exchange for a specific fee.

Artificial Intelligence: A set of algorithmic systems capable of mimicking human cognitive processes and possessing data analysis, learning, and decision-making abilities, which plays an active role in content production and meaning construction in advertising narratives.

Semiotic Analysis: A qualitative analysis method that examines meaning production processes through the signs carried by text, visual, and narrative elements and analyzes them within the framework of signifier-signified and icon, index, and symbol relationships.

Advertising Narratives: These are narrative wholes created by structuring visual and auditory elements within a specific framework in advertising texts, conveying meaning, values, and ideological messages related to the brand.

Brand Communication: This is an integrated communication process carried out through communication tools such as advertising, public relations, and digital media to convey the brand's identity, values, and positioning to the target audience.

Chapter 4
Measurement and Optimization:
Understanding a Story's Success in Marketing Communication

Tugay Sarıkaya
http://orcid.org/0000-0003-1091-4167
Istinye University, Turkey

Elif Yılmaz
http://orcid.org/0000-0003-1414-4083
Istinye University, Turkey

ABSTRACT

This study aims to evaluate marketing strategies and communications alongside the concept of success, considering changes in measurement and optimisation methods. The discussion at this juncture centres on a fundamental argument: marketing cycles and interpretations of success lack financial-based strategies. Consequently, marketing strategies should be considered within a cyclical, evolutionary and sustainable process, requiring a continuous focus on new strategies and methods. To this end, the research seeks to answer the fundamental question: how can a model be developed to demonstrate the success of a marketing strategy based on the concepts of measurement and optimisation? Within the scope of this study, each marketing strategy is evaluated as a story. In this regard, data-driven performance measurements, monitoring and optimisation, and the continuous updating of these processes are regarded as dynamic processes.

DOI: 10.4018/979-8-3373-5666-2.ch004

INTRODUCTION[1]

Marketing cannot be viewed solely as a promotional activity; it is increasingly becoming a decision-making system in which multichannel activities are constantly evaluated and improved using data. However, despite the growth in available data, interpreting marketing outcomes has become more difficult due to channel fragmentation, platform-mediated measurement and rapidly changing consumer behavior. In addition to digitalization, generative artificial intelligence and platform algorithms have fundamentally transformed both the story production speed and the distribution logic of marketing communications (Balcıoğlu, 2025; Spanos, 2021; Alaghappan & Nalini, 2025). Therefore, success is no longer solely about measuring campaign outputs; it must be approached as maintaining the consistency of the story under AI-assisted content production, algorithmic distribution, and post-privacy measurement constraints. This chapter discusses success as a sustainable learning system by positioning the Story–Measurement–Optimisation framework alongside the measurement and governance challenges of the AI era.

Accordingly, researchers have long argued that marketing performance should be traceable and optimizable (Ambler & Kokkinaki, 1997; Järvinen & Karjaluoto, 2015; Farris et al., 2021). This study evaluates marketing strategies and communications alongside the concept of success, focusing on how measurement and optimisation influence the interpretation of success and strategic renewal. The central research question is: How can a model be developed to demonstrate the success of a marketing strategy through measurement and optimisation? In this study, each marketing strategy is considered a narrative with a coherent value proposition and logical structure that must be made measurable, interpreted and improved through an iterative process. Rather than addressing the relationship between marketing narrative, measurement and optimisation through broad background narratives, this chapter focuses on critical issues that determine current performance management:

(i) attribution and causality gaps in multi-channel structures;
(ii) post-privacy signal loss and data integration challenges;
(iii) the risk of long-term value erosion from short-term, metric-focused optimisation;
(iv) the imbalance between micro and macro optimisation.
(v) increased test/learning complexity with the scaling of content production.

These issues cannot be resolved simply by increasing the number of metrics or content; they require measurement to be linked to a governance structure that triggers decisions, as well as feedback at two levels to manage optimisation. The proposed model provides an analytical framework for these problems by linking story components to measurable signals and institutionalizing the micro–macro decision cycle. Although marketing measurement and optimisation are discussed extensively in the literature, most studies fail to clarify at which decision level, time scale and integration conditions metrics are transformed into a decision mechanism (Clark, 1999; Farris et al., 2010; Pauwels et al., 2009). Similarly, while storytelling literature powerfully explains narrative in terms of persuasion and brand identity, there are relatively few model-based frameworks that link these narratives to measurement and optimisation cycles in a traceable and repeatable manner (Fog et al., 2005; Papadatos, 2006).

The original contribution of this section is to propose a repeatable governance architecture that treats the marketing strategy as a "measurable narrative", links the narrative components to KPI signals, and transforms these signals into micro/macro-optimisation decision routines. This goes beyond the frequently seen "metric lists" or "storytelling principles" approach in the literature, clearly modelling which metrics trigger which decisions at which levels.

The contribution can be summarized in three points:

(1) conceptual integration of story, measurement and optimisation.
(2) multidimensional success (financial, brand, operational and sustainability),
(3) an operationalizable roadmap for research and application.

The purpose of this section is to clarify the fundamental concepts we will use throughout the chapter and the axes of the literature on which the discussion is based. This will make it clear to which problem domain we are responding by establishing the measurement–optimisation–narrativization framework we propose in the next section.

CONCEPTUAL FRAMEWORK

This chapter positions the proposed model within;

(i) feedback-loop and organisational learning perspectives, where performance improves through repeated measurement/diagnosis/intervention cycles;
(ii) marketing performance measurement and control systems research, which emphasizes metric governance (diagnostic vs. evaluative use) and decision routines;
(iii) hierarchical decision-making in marketing analytics, where micro-level experimentation informs macro-level resource allocation and strategic constraints.

By integrating these streams with a marketing-communication *story* lens, the model theorizes how narrative components (promise, proof, and cross-channel consistency) can be operationalized into measurable signals and connected to micro/macro-optimisation as a continuous learning system.

Marketing is a recurring system that transforms market data into decisions: measurement is the system's "detection/diagnosis" layer; optimisation is the "intervention" layer based on diagnosis. Success is therefore not a one-off output; it is a performance curve that evolves over time through cycles of measurement–interpretation–redesign. This approach has two critical consequences. First, reading performance through singular financial metrics increases the risk of local optimisation; short-term efficiency improvements can erode long-term outputs such as brand trust or customer value. Second, micro and macro-optimisation are not two separate practices, but hierarchical decision levels: micro-optimisation improves execution, while macro-optimisation redefines strategic boundaries such as budget allocation, segmentation, and pricing (Mantrala & Kanuri, 2018). Sustainable success depends on these two levels *feeding into each other* through measurement findings. Therefore, the study defines success as a multidimensional structure: financial outputs; brand outputs, operational outputs and sustainability-based outputs should be evaluated together (Clark, 1999; Pauwels et al., 2009).

In the age of AI, this cycle automates not only the measurement and intervention layers but also the production and distribution layers of the story: algorithmic recommendation systems determine "which story to show to whom," while generative AI scales "which variations to produce." This situation increases the speed of micro-optimisation while creating new governance needs at the macro-optimisation level brand promise, ethical boundaries and consistency principles must be defined as a human-controlled protective framework.

The proposed Story–Measurement–Optimisation model structure combines five structural issues in the current marketing communication environment within a single learning architecture:

(i) attribution/causality gaps in multi-channel structures,
(ii) post-privacy signal loss and integration difficulties,
(iii) the risk of short-term metric-focused optimisation eroding long-term value,
(iv) imbalance between micro and macro-optimisation, and
(v) increasing test/learning complexity with scaled content production.

The model addresses these issues through a measurement layer that translates the narrative (promise–evidence–consistency) into measurable signals and an optimisation layer that links these signals to micro/macro decision routines. Therefore, the following sections aim to focus not only on the question "what metrics exist?" but also on "which metric triggers which decision at which level?"

This heading highlights that marketing success is too multidimensional to be captured by a single indicator. In the next section, we discuss how this multidimensionality translates into an evaluation problem in measurement and optimisation practices.

MEASUREMENT PROCESSES IN MARKETING

Marketing measurement can be categorized into three complementary areas: financial outcomes balanced performance monitoring via multi-metric dashboards; and customer and brand value from an asset perspective (Clark, 1999; Farris et al., 2010; Pauwels et al., 2009). The central challenge across these logics is not the existence of metrics, but their governance; which metrics are diagnostic versus evaluative; how data sources are linked; and which metric movements trigger which decisions. Firstly, attribution systems may systematically over credit certain channels due to platform dependency, the default last-click logic and unobservable variables. Secondly, data quality, identity resolution and consent-based constraints can make it difficult to integrate CRM, web analytics and advertising data (Järvinen & Karjaluoto, 2015; Singh, 2021). Thirdly, converting metrics into "targets" without a diagnostic layer may improve short-term KPIs, but it can lead to a decline in long-term outcomes. Finally, governance gaps relating to KPI ownership, inconsistent definitions, and anomaly monitoring reduce the effectiveness of measurement in supporting decision-making, instead relegating it to the realm of retrospective reporting. These limitations reinforce the need for a model in which metrics are explicitly aligned with decision levels (micro–macro), data linkage principles are defined, and optimisation is designed as an evidence-based learning cycle rather than a one-off adjustment. As attribution uncertainty increases, the purpose of the framework is not so much to find "the one correct result" but rather to reliably track which signals drive narrative shifts under which conditions, thereby improving decision quality.

AI-driven campaign management complicates causality/attribution further because it manipulates numerous variables simultaneously; therefore, "experimental validation" and anomaly monitoring routines become critical at the measurement level. Furthermore, as signal loss increases in post-privacy conditions, the model's objective is less about finding "the single correct attribution" and more about establishing a set of reliable indicators that prevent AI-accelerated micro-decisions from eroding long-term outputs such as brand value or customer lifetime value.

In summary, the critical outcome of the measurement debate is not the multiplicity of metrics, but how these metrics function as detectors within the model. In the proposed framework, measurement converts narrative components (promise, evidence, channel consistency) into observable signals at different funnel stages, and these signals are divided into two classes:

(1) diagnostic KPIs—to investigate causes.
(2) evaluative KPIs—for targets and accountability.

Thus, even in post-privacy conditions, the boundary between "what we know and what we don't know" is defined; even when data integration is weak, the aim is to establish rules for which findings should be transferred to micro-level tests and which to macro-level resource allocation. In this context, the optimisation approaches discussed in the next section should be considered as the intervention layer that translates the diagnostic findings produced by measurement into action.

This metric set is used not only to report performance in the model, but also to diagnose which elements of the narrative are working or where they are breaking down. Measurement makes performance "visible"; however, it does not produce decisions on its own. Therefore, we now move on to the optimisation dimension to explain how measurement outputs are converted into action and the logic of iterative improvement.

OPTIMIZATION APPROACHES

Goal optimization is one of the most important layers in marketing optimization. When considered as an overarching framework, goal optimisation can be fundamentally addressed under micro- and macro-optimisation. In this context, micro-optimisation covers improvements relating to campaigns and A/B tests, while macro-optimisation covers the key points relating to the main objectives. Macro-optimisation basically encompasses resource allocation, product structuring, and pricing (Mantrala & Kanuri, 2018).

Optimisation can only gain strategic significance when supported by a reliable measurement architecture. While micro-optimizations may deliver short-term efficiency gains, when not aligned with macro-objectives they can lead to "metric chasing" and inconsistent performance. Conversely, if not fueled by micro-level experimentation and testing routines, macro-optimizations carry the risk of remaining slow and assumption-based (Mantrala & Kanuri, 2018). Therefore, sustainable marketing performance requires an iterative process in which micro-level experiments inform macro-level resource allocation and macro-level goals determine the agenda for micro-level experimentation.

The main outcome of this section in terms of the model can be explained as follows: Micro and macro-optimisation are two decision layers that can be evaluated hierarchically, intervening in the same success problem from different time scales. At the micro level, efficiency gains are achieved through creativity, targeting and experiment design; at the macro level, the budget, segment priorities, offer/price and channel roles are redefined. The model proposes macro-level protective constraints and a multi-dimensional success dashboard to prevent short-term KPI improvements from eroding long-term value components. Therefore, optimisation can be presented not as chasing metrics, but as sustainably rebalancing performance while preserving the narrative promise.

The use of artificial intelligence plays a key role in optimizing and accelerating decision-making processes in marketing (Stone et al., 2020). Productive AI and platform automations can dramatically accelerate micro-optimisation, enabling creative variation generation, mass production and message personalization to be scaled at low cost. However, this speed can lead to metric chasing and long-term value erosion if the "brand promise/consistency/ethical boundaries" at a macro level are not defined. Therefore, the model requires the outputs of AI-supported micro-experiments to be interpreted alongside macro-level protective constraints.

The goals relate to using revenue and continuous profitability as a basis. In parallel, elements such as the firm's market share, brand awareness, customer satisfaction with products and maintaining customer loyalty should be considered. However, another point to consider when setting these objectives is constraints. These may relate to budget, time, or the firm's capacity. Depending on the constraints of resources, the objectives may also be evaluated in terms of technological infrastructure or the poor quality of data obtained due to this infrastructure being inadequate.

Another dimension of optimisation focuses on the reasons for variability in decisions. For example, differences in resources across units, customer segmentation or defining the target audience for a product may cause decisions to vary under certain conditions. The above processes are interrelated and continuously renewed in line with customer feedback and data analysis.

Users' experiences with the business also bring conversion optimisation into scope. Event-based tracking, which involves monitoring customers' user experiences (such as; filling out forms, scrolling pages, eye tracking, clicking, adding products to the cart, removing products from the cart and keeping products in the cart), is important for identifying the stage at which users' relationship with the business stands and for evaluating the stage at which they abandon the product or decide to purchase it (Kakatkar & Spann, 2019; Wahyudin & Tjoa, 2007, April). It is important to optimise marketing strategies based on similar data. In addition, design optimisations are important when monitoring criteria such as the interface of the purchased channel, usability, and easy access to desired information or products. In this respect, user experience is key to ensuring continuous optimisation (Kaponis et al., 2025; Salgado-Reyes, 2025, January).

Customers' behaviors and the reasons for these behaviors at the stages of viewing a product, evaluating it, adding it to the basket, reaching the payment stage and completing payment are meaningful for marketing optimisation. Alongside marketing optimisation linked only to data, it is important for brands to optimise and improve practical, fast purchasing methods that guide customers more easily towards shopping, in line with data obtained from them.

One of the analysis methods considered important for optimisation is cohort analysis. This involves analyzing customers' or users' retention, spending or interest in the brand at specific intervals following their first purchase or touchpoint over time. In this context, it is possible to analyze customer behavior according to periods, campaigns, or conditions during specific periods. Numerous customer-oriented or seasonal optimisations can therefore be conducted through cohort analyses during optimisations.

Customer Lifetime Value is also among the elements considered in optimisations. The objective here is to calculate the long-term profit that a customer will provide to the business. When analyzed correctly, models that yield long-term profit can be developed for customers from whom long-term gains can be obtained, even if this reduces profit margins in the short term. In this context, segmenting customers based on their behavioral patterns may require the business to optimise its marketing strategies. Additionally, frequency, recency and monetary analysis are important for determining the most effective way to reach customers and the nature of the offer.

GENAI-SUPPORTED AND ALGORITHMICALLY CURATED MARKETING NARRATIVES

The transformation of digital marketing storytelling in the age of artificial intelligence goes beyond the level of "message personalization," simultaneously changing the processes of selecting, producing, and managing narratives (Vidrih and Mayahi, 2023; Lal, 2024). Generative artificial intelligence tools and platform algorithms enable us to reconfigure the flow of the brand story by determining which narrative fragments the consumer will encounter, in what order, and in what context. Therefore, GenAI should be considered not merely as an operational accelerator in the Story-Measurement-Optimisation cycle, but as a structural force that increases measurement uncertainty, variation management, and governance needs.

Firstly, in the age of AI, narrative performance is shaped not only by "what the brand says" but also by "who the narrative reaches, when, how often, and in what order". Recommendation systems, search ranking algorithms, and social platform distribution logic rank the content consumers are exposed to base on personal history, contextual signals, and likelihood of interaction. This leads to the consumer journey being shaped more by the algorithmic order established by platforms than by the linear funnel designed by the brand. From a modelling perspective, this layer makes the *consistency* component critical.

On the measurement side, signals such as frequency saturation, creative fatigue, channel switching, and ranking effects should be monitored, not just outputs such as reach or clicks. In this context, separating KPIs into 'diagnostic' and 'evaluative' is functional in managing the uncertainty produced by algorithmic distribution. Secondly, GenAI delivers narrative production in different variations: advertising texts, visual variations, video scripts, email subject lines, and chatbot dialogues can be produced in hundreds of different forms in a very short time (Kumar, 2023; Kumar and Kotler, 2024). This enhances micro-optimisation; because creative hypotheses are tested faster, message adaptation according to segments becomes easier, and content production problems decrease. However, the same scale, measurement, and interpretation layer introduces a new risk: as the number of variations increases, measuring performance becomes equally challenging. Therefore, clear narrative standards must be established to ensure that the "promise-evidence-CTA" triad is preserved in content generated by GenAI.

(i) which promise each variation carries and which segment need it is linked to,
(ii) the type of evidence and its verifiability
(iii) the CTA logic appropriate to the channel role must be clarified.

This allows the measurement layer to distinguish more clearly which narrative component (promise, evidence, consistency) is causing the performance issue. Thirdly, in practice, the increasingly prevalent approach is human–AI co-creation rather than fully autonomous storytelling. In this division of labor, human strategists define the narrative's theme, emotional tone, brand voice, and ethical boundaries; GenAI then generates variations within this framework, supports rapid testing cycles, and scales distribution/format adaptations. The critical point regarding the model's "optimisation" layer is this: if micro-level interventions accelerated by GenAI are not managed alongside macro-level protective constraints, short-term metric gains may erode long-term value components.

For success in marketing, brands' integration with artificial intelligence has become vital (Wu & Monfort, 2023; Sharma et al, 2023; Kloba and Kloba, 2025). Consequently, sustainable success in the GenAI era depends on establishing a governance architecture that links narrative components to measurable signals and institutionalizes the micro–macro decision cycle, rather than simply producing more content.

CREATING SUCCESS STORIES IN MARKETING COMMUNICATION

Humans need meaningful wholes in which to store information, so we generally narrate information in the form of stories. This storytelling process is crucial for understanding and acceptance (Akbayır, 2016, p. 69) and is built around a theme with three fundamental elements: *Challenges:* These represent the journey and effort required to overcome obstacles and are vital for creating a sense of reward. *Reciprocity:* This involves a fair and equal exchange of value. *Defining moments:* These are real moments of happiness that we remember (Papadatos, 2006, p. 383).

All these elements help to explain why organizations and brands create narrative-based strategies for their storytelling processes. In both internal and external communications, storytelling is an effective and significant branding tool. Adopting a holistic approach utilizes both processes to support the brand message (Fog et al., 2005, p. 52). As a strategic narrative method, storytelling permanently conveys the brand's values and promises. It plays a critical role in forming brand image and identity (Akbayır, 2016, p. 68). Brand identity relates to how you position the brand in consumers' minds. To make your name known, this positioning must be unique to stand out in a diverse market. It should align with consumers' needs, and maintaining brand authenticity and fulfilling promises is crucial. Trustworthiness and brand authenticity are fundamentally connected to the consumer's spirit. The brand image and value should appeal to consumers' feelings and desires. In this way, a purpose emerges that speaks to the whole person (their mind, heart and spirit) (Kotler et al., 2010). Storytelling is a supportive narrative form that conveys the brand's values and the principles upon which it is founded. Storytelling maintains a holistic relationship between the brand and its target audience. Thus, the value of the success story emerges through the interaction established between the brand, the story and the target audience. Additionally, to clearly see progress in a brand's story, it is important to determine the characters used in the storytelling. It is essential to create a draft of key characters to advance the brand story. According to Fog et al. (2005, p. 87), these are:

Purpose: What is the general purpose of the company? The key point here is to focus on passion and creating impact rather than just filling shareholders' pockets.

Competitors: Who does your company face? Competitors can vary in different forms or sizes. They may come from internal pressures due to a lack of innovation or external pressures from competitors.

Hero: The company often takes on the role of a hero aiming to conquer a kingdom. What are the characteristics of this hero? It's important to remember that the hero can also be a customer aiming to achieve a goal.

Support: The tools or methods necessary for the hero to reach the defined goal typically play the role of support. How will your company defeat the enemy? If the customer is the hero, then the supportive role could be the product or service that helps realize their dream.

Benefactor: The company generally adopts the role of a benefactor focused on helping customers realize their dreams.

Beneficiary: These are the individuals who contribute to the hero's goal. Typically, this role is taken on by customers who benefit from the company's efforts to achieve its purpose.

In the age of AI, narrative authority (who produced the story) is becoming blurred (Oke, 2025, p. 5463): when consumers sense whether a message stems from human creativity or algorithmic optimisation, their perception of authenticity may be affected. Therefore, a success story is not merely a persuasive narrative; it is about maintaining the promise, evidence, and channel consistency even under AI-scaled production conditions. The model's narrative layer therefore tracks whether AI-assisted production erodes brand trust by linking the "unique voice + proof + consistency" triad to measurable signals.

Determining and structuring the characters in a story strengthens the bond between a brand and its target audience. Identifying how the storytelling process unfolds is critical to enhancing the success story's persuasive power.

Based on Papadatos's research data on the interaction between brands and their target audiences, the fundamental elements of storytelling can be summarized as follows (2006, p. 383):

Expectation: Stories generally begin with a sense of hope for the future. Every story starts with a period of expectation.

Crisis: Generally, all stories involve conflict. After the initial feeling of expectation, a genuine period of hopelessness typically follows.

Support throughout the process: Stories generally contain small and large miracles. Following the crisis, an unexpected form of support leads to an intensive working process.

Reaching the goal: The story concludes with achieving the goal after this challenging process.

Considering all these processes, it becomes evident that a systematic approach should be adopted to create a success story in marketing communication. Storytelling is not just about conveying messages; it requires a strategic process that emphasizes character and emotional flow to create sustainable relationships with the target audience. Integrating measurement and optimisation approaches with this core model enhances success in marketing communication.

At this point, we are shifting the discussion to a more operational ground: the multidimensional nature of success raises the question of which metrics are meaningful in which contexts. In the next section, we are structuring the "measurement" component as the first pillar of our model.

MEASUREMENT AND OPTIMIZATION-BASED MARKETING STORY SUCCESS MODEL

When proposing a model, it should be noted that storytelling is influenced by measurements and optimizations, and feedback should be considered through a strategic lens. As discussed above, they are crucial for ensuring the sustainability and success of the marketing communication process. These include:

I. Marketing Story

When creating a marketing story, it is important to consider the three key components of *character*, *narrative* and *metaphor*. *Characters* are central to the story. They symbolize how the brand is perceived in the human psyche. *Metaphors* represent unconscious processes that emerge in the human mind. Suitable metaphors gain validity and are accepted as truth by consumers. These three elements are essential for creating a story that will affect people. Formulating a strong mission statement is a significant step for companies. Furthermore, disseminating that mission through stories is another major step (Kotler et al., 2010).

In a highly competitive market, to create awareness and stand out from competitors, the brand needs to construct its message in a compelling way and convey it to its target audience using supporting tools. The key point here is that the content of this message must be determined correctly and strategically. Storytelling plays a crucial role at this stage. The message must connect with the target audience through storytelling, capturing their imagination. This will lead to a successful outcome. Supporting this process with measurement and optimisation will ensure long-term success.

II. Measurement Processes

There are variables to consider when making measurements. The measurement of marketing performance areas includes the following elements (Clark 1999, p. 714):

Figure 1. The Measurement of Marketing Performance

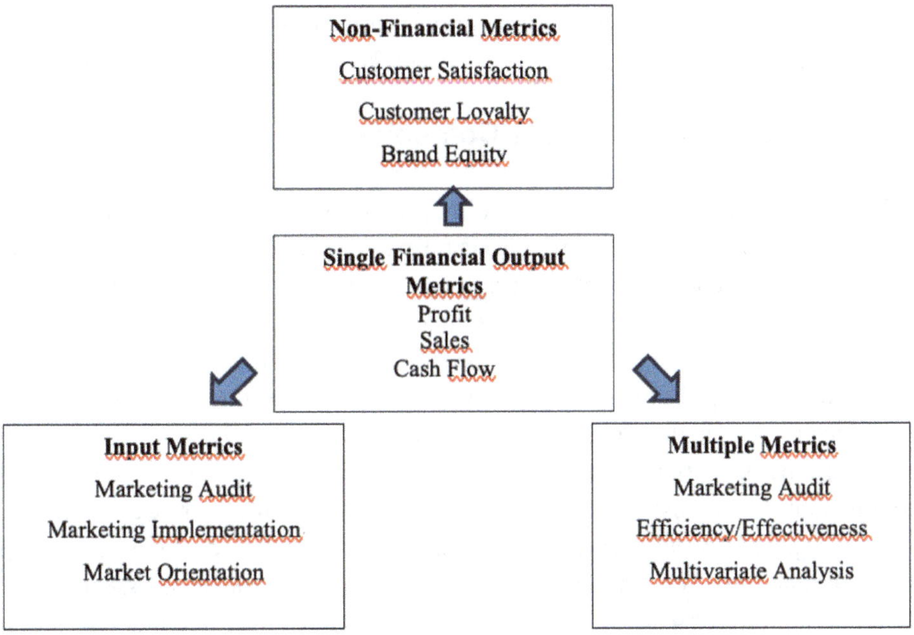

Because the chapter proposes a conceptual model, it provides an illustrative, sector-agnostic walkthrough to demonstrate internal validity: each step makes explicit (i) which story element is being acted upon, (ii) which KPI signals represent that element at different funnel stages, and (iii) which optimisation decision is triggered at the micro vs. macro level. This illustration is intended to show the model's operationalizability and falsifiability (which observable signals would confirm or contradict the model's predictions), while leaving causal estimation to future empirical studies.

In addition to traditional measurement processes, innovative measurement methods are also gaining attention. Specifically, the Purchase Action Rate (PAR) measures the extent to which a company's brand awareness translates into consumer purchases, while the Brand Advocacy Rate (BAR) assesses how effectively companies convert individuals aware of their brand into loyal brand advocates. Together, these two new efficiency metrics provide a better measurement process for Return on Marketing Investment (ROMI). Brand awareness plays a crucial role in this context. Therefore, in the ROMI equation, brand awareness becomes an essential component of marketing investment. The returns are twofold: the first is the purchase action from the company's perspective, while the second focuses on advocacy aimed at indirectly increasing sales (Kotler et al., 2016).

From this perspective, in addition to the technical aspects of ongoing marketing strategies, it is important to create brand awareness and solidify this awareness to foster trust and loyalty. Supporting strategic efforts to cultivate a loyal customer base will be a key point in driving the success of marketing communication narratives.

III. Optimization Approaches Component

Integrating marketing and optimisation processes is crucial for enhancing efficiency and effectiveness, increasing visibility, and providing a roadmap for continuous improvement. In a context of rapid technological and artificial intelligence advances, establishing a functional system and accurately managing and continuously updating marketing strategies is essential to keep pace with innovations. At this stage, dynamically integrating optimisation into marketing communication is critical for survival in the digitalization process. This requires companies and brands to develop strategies that are sensitive and applicable not only during planning and implementation, but also for sustaining communication with their target audience.

The proposed model defines the marketing narrative, brand promise, message architecture and cross-channel narrative consistency. Measurement processes translate this narrative into observable metrics at different stages of the funnel and across success dimensions (financial, brand, operational and sustainability). Optimisation intervenes at two levels: micro-optimisation improves execution variables (creativity, targeting and page experience) through experimentation, while macro-optimisation recalibrates strategic boundaries such as budget allocation, segmentation and pricing. The cycle closes with lessons learned from optimisation being fed back into redesigning the story and updating the metric set. This prevents the system from becoming stuck in short-term local optima, ensuring continuity and scalability. To empirically test the proposed model, the following propositions could be investigated in future studies:

P1. Businesses with a multidimensional marketing dashboard that uses financial + brand + operational + sustainability indicators together exhibit more stable long-term performance compared to businesses that focus on single financial output metrics.

P2. The positive effect of micro-optimisation intensity (e.g., frequency of systematic experiments/A-B testing) on short-term performance is stronger when macro-optimisation alignment (e.g., budget–segment–pricing consistency) is high.

P3. As measurement infrastructure maturity increases (integration of CRM + web analytics + media data with consistent KPI definitions), the marginal return on optimisation actions increases.

P4. The cross-channel narrative consistency of the marketing story is positively related to brand outputs (e.g., advocacy, trust indicators); these brand outputs also produce an indirect (mediating) effect on long-term financial outputs.

P5. Organizations that institutionalize measurement governance, such as through KPI ownership, anomaly monitoring, and decision routines, are more effective at translating measurement findings into action (optimisation cycle) compared to reporting-focused organizations.

This section presents an example application demonstrating how the proposed Marketing Story–Measurement–Optimisation model can be operated through an industry-independent scenario, with the aim of making the model more academically traceable. This example does not claim empirical validation; rather, it explains in an illustrative manner the sequence in which the model's components can be executed, the types of metrics that can be used, and the decision levels at which they can be applied.

The following loop diagram transforms the measurement, optimisation, and narrative discussions addressed separately throughout the section into a single decision mechanism.

At each step:

(i) which component of the narrative is being changed,
(ii) which KPI signals represent it, and
(iii) under which conditions intervention will occur through micro-level experiments or macro-level strategy/budget decisions is clearly specified.

Thus, the section can answer the question of "how to measure and sustain success" independently of sectoral differences through a repeatable measurement–interpretation–intervention cycle.

Table 1. Loop Steps of The Model

Loop Step	Marketing Story Output	Measurement Signal (KPI Examples)	Data Source	Diagnosis (What does it mean?)	Optimization Decision (Micro/Macro)
1. Design	Promise + core message + proof + CTA	Initial KPI set: reach, brand search, CTR, CVR, CAC, proxies for repeat purchase intent	Ad platforms, web analytics, CRM	"Which funnel stage is weak?"	Experiment plan and target thresholds are defined
2. Measurement	Message–channel consistency check	Awareness: reach/frequency, brand search; Consideration: product page engagement; Purchase: CVR, AOV; Loyalty: repeat rate, returns/ complaints	Web analytics + CRM + sales	Low CTR = message/creative mismatch; high cart abandonment = UX/payment friction	Micro: creative/ landing A/B; Macro: channel mix revision
3. Diagnosis	"Proof" elements in the story are strengthened	Segment-based performance differentiation; new vs. returning user difference	CRM segments + analytics	"In which segment does the promise resonate?"	Macro: segment prioritization, budget reallocation
4. Micro Optimization	Message variations (metaphor, proof, CTA)	A/B: CTR, scroll depth, form completion; email: open/click rates	Experimentation infrastructure + email reports	Which narrative component reduces friction?	Micro: creative, targeting, bid, page flow
5. Macro Optimization	Strategic promise of the story is preserved, channel roles are clarified	POAS/ROAS plus CLV proxies; return rate; service quality indicators	CRM + finance + operations	"Is short-term gain harming the long term?"	Macro: price/ offer, budget, channel role, product/ portfolio
6. Redesign	Story is updated with learnings	KPI set revision: split between diagnostic KPIs and evaluation KPIs	Integrated reporting	"What did we learn, what do we standardize?"	New cycle: goals and experimentation agenda

Ultimately, the contribution of the section is to demonstrate that measurement and optimisation are not separate technical fields from storytelling, but rather complementary components of a single decision architecture that transforms the narrative into sustainable success.

This example application demonstrates the academic value of the model in two ways. Firstly, it illustrates how the story components (promise, evidence and consistency) are converted into measurement indicators, and which signals trigger which type of optimisation. Secondly, it shows that, although micro-optimisation improves execution in the short term, macro-optimisation reconfigures resource allocation and strategic boundaries. Sustainable success is made possible by the interaction between these two levels.

CONCLUSION

This study presents a model for achieving marketing success, driven by the emergence of various channels alongside digitalization. It has been established that marketing success requires consideration of many aspects beyond creativity and content production, encompassing a multifaceted process that includes optimisation. A dynamic model has now been proposed that goes beyond single financial outputs, incorporating measurements, data analytics and optimisations. In other words, the model is centered on continuously renewing and sustainable cycles.

In the age of GenAI, the marketing narrative is shifting from a linear flow controlled by the brand to an experience reshaped by the selection and ranking logic of platform algorithms. Therefore, sustainable success depends not on producing "more content," but on establishing a decision-making architecture that manages GenAI production within strategic boundaries, ethical principles, and a measurement infrastructure.

It is emphasized in this context that a simple cause-and-effect relationship is an inadequate evaluation method for contemporary marketing strategies. Instead, the existence of a new marketing ecosystem is highlighted, characterized by evolutionary processes that emphasize connection, meaning-making, memorability, persuasion and the continuous interpretation of obtained data. Based on this approach, the success or failure of a marketing strategy can be revealed through multilayered analysis. Here, the weak links or aspects of the proposed marketing strategy can be improved through various optimisations after its formulation. The marketing strategy is portrayed as a living process, akin to a living organism.

Throughout this process, the marketing story that emerges strengthens aspects such as trust and loyalty, while presenting all facets of the brand to customers. At this stage, the measurement process goes beyond reporting. A decision-support mechanism is established based on KPIs that are aligned with business, web and CRM data, as well as the interconnections of all metrics. Consequently, elements such as trust and loyalty can be measured at different levels and in different ways, going beyond mere reporting.

This study presents a cyclical model with strong feedback and optimisation aspects that encompasses all the elements. This model can undoubtedly be developed or differentiated at specific points. However, the goal should be to test the proposed model through field studies. While the study aims to contribute to the literature, it also intends to inform field studies. In this respect, the study acknowledges the lack of field study presentations while offering innovation.

As this study proposes a conceptual model, the next step to strengthening the model's academic credibility is to conduct empirical testing. A two-stage validation design is proposed for future studies.

Table 2. Stages of Testing

Stage	Component	Description
1. Case Study + Process Tracing	Purpose	To show which decision routines the model components (Story–Measurement–Optimization) interact with in a real organization.
	Data	Campaign reports, dashboard screens, experiment logs, meeting notes, KPI ownership documents, CRM segments.
	Output	Qualitative evidence on the model's applicability, measurement governance, and the alignment between micro–macro optimization.
2. Quantitative Test + Causal Inference (Incrementality-Focused)	Purpose	To quantitatively test the relationships proposed by the model (e.g., measurement infrastructure maturity → optimization effectiveness; story consistency → brand metrics → long-term financial outcomes).
	Data Infrastructure	Web analytics event data, ad spend and impressions, CRM/ sales data, email data, and if possible, brand search or brand lift measurements.
	Method	- Controlled experiments (A/B) and multivariate tests for micro-optimization effects \ - Incrementality (uplift) designs for channel effects where possible (e.g., geo tests or holdout groups) \ - Calibrating multi-channel attribution results with experimental findings.
	Success Measurement	Short-term metrics (CVR, CAC, ROAS/POAS) and long-term metrics (repeat purchase, retention, CLV proxies, return/complaint rate) are considered together; the model's claim of "multi-dimensional success" is empirically tested.
	Overall Aim	To ensure the model does not remain merely a conceptual proposal but becomes more firmly embedded in the academic literature through case evidence on applicability and testable quantitative relationships.

In conclusion, the proposed Story–Measurement–Optimisation model is not merely a conceptual synthesis; it is a unique decision architecture that links narrative design to measurement signals and a two-tiered (micro–macro) optimisation governance framework. The model's testability is clearly defined in terms of which signal indicates the strengthening/weakening of which narrative component and under which conditions a micro experiment or macro reallocation decision will be triggered.

Recently, numerous studies have emphasized the importance of incorporating artificial intelligence into processes (Jarek and Mazurek, 2019; Kumar and Suthar, 2024; Labib, 2024; Potwora et al., 2024). As artificial intelligence evolves, it is evident that these models will also change or be re-optimized in future studies. As this chapter illustrates, the process is open to feedback and dynamic. Within this context, the model should be tested in ongoing studies and expanded or developed by incorporating new processes. This is a necessity dictated by the nature of academia.

REFERENCES

Akbayır, Z. (2016). Bana bir hikâye anlat: Marka iletişiminde hikâyeleştirme ve internet [Tell me a story: Storytelling in brand communication and the internet]. *KTÜ İletişim Fakültesi E-Dergi, 3*(12), 67–84.

Alaghappan, T., & Nalini, R. (2025). AI-powered emotional storytelling for brand narratives and consumer perception. In *International Conference on Artificial Intelligence in Commerce and Management* (pp. 200-210). DOI: 10.34293/ICAICM-25.ch029

Ambler, T., & Kokkinaki, F. (1997). Measures of marketing success. *Journal of Marketing Management, 13*(7), 665–678. DOI: 10.1080/0267257X.1997.9964503

Clark, B. H. (1999). Marketing performance measures: History and interrelationships. *Journal of Marketing Management, 15*(8), 711–732. DOI: 10.1362/026725799784772594

Farris, P. W., Bendle, N., Pfeifer, P., & Reibstein, D. (2021). *Marketing metrics: The manager's guide to measuring marketing performance.* FT Press.

Farris, P. W., Bendle, N. T., Pfeifer, P. E., & Reibstein, D. J. (2010). *Marketing metrics: The definitive guide to measuring marketing performance* (2nd ed.). Pearson Education.

Fog, K., Budtz, C., & Yakaboylu, B. (2005). *Storytelling: Branding in practice.* Springer.

Jarek, K., & Mazurek, G. (2019). Marketing and artificial intelligence. *Central European Business Review, 8*(2).

Järvinen, J., & Karjaluoto, H. (2015). The use of web analytics for digital marketing performance measurement. *Industrial Marketing Management, 50*, 117–127. DOI: 10.1016/j.indmarman.2015.04.009

Kakatkar, C., & Spann, M. (2019). Marketing analytics using anonymized and fragmented tracking data. *International Journal of Research in Marketing, 36*(1), 117–136. DOI: 10.1016/j.ijresmar.2018.10.001

Kaponis, A., Maragoudakis, M., & Sofianos, K. C. (2025). Enhancing user experiences in digital marketing through machine learning: Cases, trends, and challenges. *Computers, 14*(6), 211. DOI: 10.3390/computers14060211

Kloba, L., & Kloba, V. (2025). Implementation of artificial intelligence in marketing strategy of financial services. *Green. Blue and Digital Economy Journal*, *6*(2), 1–7. DOI: 10.30525/2661-5169/2025-2-1

Kotler, P., Kartajaya, H., & Setiawan, I. (2010). *Marketing 3.0: From products to customers to the human spirit*. John Wiley & Sons. DOI: 10.1002/9781118257883

Kotler, P., Kartajaya, H., & Setiawan, I. (2016). *Marketing 4.0: Moving from traditional to digital*. John Wiley & Sons.

Kumar, C. P. (2023). *Mastering Content Creation with ChatGPT*. CP Kumar.

Kumar, D., & Suthar, N. (2024). Ethical and legal challenges of AI in marketing: An exploration of solutions. *Journal of Information. Communication and Ethics in Society*, *22*(1), 124–144. DOI: 10.1108/JICES-05-2023-0068

Kumar, V., & Kotler, P. (2024). Transformative marketing with generative artificial intelligence. In *Transformative marketing: Combining new age technologies and human insights* (pp. 65–102). Springer Nature Switzerland. DOI: 10.1007/978-3-031-59637-7_4

Labib, E. (2024). Artificial intelligence in marketing: Exploring current and future trends. *Cogent Business & Management*, *11*(1), 2348728. DOI: 10.1080/23311975.2024.2348728

Lal, R. (2024). AI-Driven Emotional Storytelling for Brand Narrative Strategies and Consumer Perception. *IUP Journal of Brand Management, 21*(4).

Mantrala, M. K., & Kanuri, V. K. (2018). Marketing optimization methods. In *Handbook of marketing analytics* (pp. 324–370). Edward Elgar. DOI: 10.4337/9781784716752.00027

Oke, T. (2025). Algorithmic narrativity as a new narrative mode. *AI & Society*, *40*(7), 5457–5468. DOI: 10.1007/s00146-025-02297-8

Papadatos, C. (2006). The art of storytelling: How loyalty marketers can build emotional connections to their brands. *Journal of Consumer Marketing*, *23*(7), 382–384. DOI: 10.1108/07363760610712902

Pauwels, K., Ambler, T., Clark, B. H., LaPointe, P., Reibstein, D., Skiera, B., Wierenga, B., & Wiesel, T. (2009). Dashboards as a service: Why, what, how, and what research is needed? *Journal of Service Research*, *12*(2), 175–189. DOI: 10.1177/1094670509344213

Potwora, M., Vdovichena, O., Semchuk, D., Lipych, L., & Saienko, V. (2024). The use of artificial intelligence in marketing strategies: Automation, personalization and forecasting. *Journal of Management World*, *2*(2), 41–49. DOI: 10.53935/jomw.v2024i2.275

Salgado-Reyes, N. (2025). User experience (UX) optimization with AI: Integration of artificial intelligence to personalize the user experience in applications and websites, anticipating their needs and preferences. In *International conference on information technology & systems* (pp. 223–231). Springer Nature Switzerland. DOI: 10.1007/978-3-031-93106-2_19

Sharma, K. K., Tomar, M., & Tadimarri, A. (2023). Unlocking sales potential: How AI revolutionizes marketing strategies. *Journal of Knowledge Learning and Science Technology ISSN: 2959-6386 (online)*, *2*(2), 231-250. DOI: 10.60087/jklst.vol2.n2.p250

Singh, A. (Ed.). (2021). *Big data analytics for improved accuracy, efficiency, and decision making in digital marketing*. IGI Global. DOI: 10.4018/978-1-7998-7231-3

Spanos, M. (2021). Brand storytelling in the age of artificial intelligence. *Journal of Brand Strategy*, *10*(1), 6–13. DOI: 10.69554/BANG8294

Stone, M., Aravopoulou, E., Ekinci, Y., Evans, G., Hobbs, M., Labib, A., Laughlin, P., Machtynger, J., & Machtynger, L. (2020). Artificial intelligence (AI) in strategic marketing decision-making: A research agenda. *The Bottom Line (New York, N.Y.)*, *33*(2), 183–200. DOI: 10.1108/BL-03-2020-0022

Vidrih, M., & Mayahi, S. (2023). Generative AI-driven storytelling: A new era for marketing. *arXiv preprint arXiv:2309.09048*.

Wahyudin, D., & Tjoa, A. M. (2007). Event-based monitoring of open source software projects. In *Proceedings of the Second International Conference on Availability, Reliability and Security (ARES'07)* (pp. 1108–1115). IEEE. DOI: 10.1109/ARES.2007.84

Wu, C. W., & Monfort, A. (2023). Role of artificial intelligence in marketing strategies and performance. *Psychology and Marketing*, *40*(3), 484–496. DOI: 10.1002/mar.21737

ADDITIONAL READINGS

Basha, M. (2023). Impact of artificial intelligence on marketing. *East Asian Journal of Multidisciplinary Research, 2*(3), 993–1004. DOI: 10.55927/eajmr.v2i3.3112

Huang, M. H., & Rust, R. T. (2021). A strategic framework for artificial intelligence in marketing. *Journal of the Academy of Marketing Science, 49*(1), 30–50. DOI: 10.1007/s11747-020-00749-9

Mustak, M., Salminen, J., Plé, L., & Wirtz, J. (2021). Artificial intelligence in marketing: Topic modeling, scientometric analysis, and research agenda. *Journal of Business Research, 124*, 389–404. DOI: 10.1016/j.jbusres.2020.10.044

KEY TERMS AND DEFINITIONS

Marketing Success: Processes for measuring and optimising the success of marketing strategies.

Multi-Channel Measurement: Methods for measuring and evaluating the impact of different marketing channels.

Storytelling: Using story-based strategies to convey brand values and messages.

Data Integration: Combining and analysing different data sources.

Continuous Optimisation: Continuously reviewing and improving marketing strategies.

ENDNOTE

1 For language-editing purposes, GPT-5.2 (ChatGPT) and the Deeply AI application were used

Section 2
AI, Narrative Transformation, and Media Shift

Chapter 5
Digital Breaking Point: The Transformation of Traditional TV Advertising by Artificial Intelligence

Nursel Bolat
http://orcid.org/0000-0002-3986-7408
Ondokuz Mayıs Universty, Turkey

ABSTRACT

While AI comprises stages such as creative idea development, script writing, cast selection, set design, shooting, post-production, and versioning in traditional advertising production, the integration of AI-based tools is reshaping this structure. The research technically examines the impact of AI-supported creative idea development systems, automated script generators, AI-based consumer insight analysis tools, and visual design models on decision-makers during the pre-production phase.During the production phase, innovations such as virtual production technologies, AI-optimized lighting and camera placement systems, digital actors and performance production, and automated production planning algorithms were evaluated. In the post-production phase, the time/cost efficiency impact of tools such as AI-assisted editing, color correction, sound design, scene cleanup, face replacement, and rapid variant generation was analyzed.

INTRODUCTION

While the concept of digital advertising represents a significant change in the field of advertising, when considering the characteristics that emerge differently in digital media compared to traditional media, it becomes clear that advertising and the

DOI: 10.4018/979-8-3373-5666-2.ch005

advertising industry need to be re-examined (Adams, 2004, p. 68). This is because the sharing of messages between individuals, which began with digitization, has given way to fluid time and virtual space with the digital transformation, replacing the time and space constraints inherent in traditional media (Çakın & Bolat, 2018, p. 176). With the Digital Age, the information society is moving in close connection with the economic sphere within its development process. In this context, the information society is undergoing changes within itself and uses information as one of the main elements of production. The digitization of information as one of the main elements of production necessitates close monitoring of developments in the field of technology. Developments in artificial intelligence technology, which has been frequently discussed in recent times, have also found their place in the field of marketing, enabling businesses to develop customer-focused strategies and increase the usability of data obtained from customers through the opportunities provided by this new technology.

"The basic criterion for creativity in digital advertising is that the content attracts the attention of users and is accepted and considered shareable by them" (Yılmaz & Erdem, 2016, p. 250). Digital advertising is generally defined as communication initiated by a brand through digital media channels with the aim of creating an impact on consumers. Due to its unique characteristics, digital advertising has become an important and indispensable part of the advertising industry. Digital advertising has given rise to interactive advertising types that can deliver the message to the right target with accurate targeting, as well as generate likes, shares, comments, or direct action. Features such as targeting capabilities, measurability, and low cost give digital advertising advantages over traditional advertising (Hudders et al., 2019, p. 2). With digitalization, social media in particular facilitates the process of building brand identity, offering low-cost marketing communication opportunities and a high level of accessibility, making it easier for brands to reach a global audience (Çakır & Çakın, 2022, p. 105).

Interactive advertising programs in digital publishing are prepared in a special way, from the script to the shooting, editing, and broadcasting. Programs are prepared considering the target audience and all their expectations and information requests, and are organized according to the access possibilities of different communication channels. In this technique, the visual and audio presentation of the product to be advertised is prepared with text, graphics, and live image support. Detailed information about the product is provided at, and even payment and purchase information for the product is uploaded, allowing the viewer or consumer to immediately access the product (Durmaz, 1999, p. 339). Consumers can not only immediately access the product they see advertised in digital environments, but also enjoy the convenience of purchasing the product from the digital environment.

Artificial Intelligence (AI) is a rapidly advancing process linked to technological developments, and is currently one of the topics of discussion across various disciplines. The basis of artificial intelligence lies in making machines more autonomous and intelligent (Kuşçu, 2015, p. 46). Artificial intelligence is seen as a broad and somewhat cyclical approach to exhibiting intelligent behavior

Intelligent behavior involves perception, reasoning, learning, communication, and movement in complex environments. One of the long-term goals of artificial intelligence is to develop machines that can perform these tasks as well as humans, and possibly even better (Nilsson, 1998, p. 1). Artificial intelligence is a technology that encompasses the development of machines that exhibit human-like behaviors and movements, created entirely by artificial means, independently of living organisms (Aydın & Değirmenci, 2018, p. 20). Although many people today do not accept the association between artificial intelligence and creativity, artificial intelligence has also taken its place in people's lives for creative purposes. One such area is the advertising industry, and artificial intelligence appears to be taking a very active role in this field in the near future. Developments in digital advertising also play an important role in the prominence of artificial intelligence's use in the advertising industry.

In the field of digital advertising, artificial intelligence has been used to write advertising texts, determine advertising strategies, create advertising slogans, and even conduct creative directing experiments. Artificial intelligence is present in countless areas of human life today. Opinions are emerging that artificial intelligence will increase the productivity of individuals and organizations. One such area is the advertising sector, where AI advertising collaboration continues to grow day by day. One of the most important factors driving this process is the digitalization of the advertising sector and the rise of digital advertising. Advertising is constantly connected to technological developments and is rapidly becoming part of the process. Within this transformation, the central issue is not only technological change but the reconfiguration of narrative structures and advertising discourse through AI. This chapter therefore examines how AI reshapes storytelling logic, meaning production, and persuasive narrative strategies in contemporary advertising.

Digital Advertising and Artificial Intelligence Technologies With Mobile Advertising

One of the most important developments in advertising is the rapid rise of artificial intelligence technologies. Artificial intelligence is attracting significant interest in the global advertising industry, and this interest is expected to increase further as the technology develops (Yu, 2022, p. 190).

Digital advertising has changed and transformed the entire advertising industry since 1994. Interactive advertising formed the first stage of digital advertising, while programmatic advertising represents the second stage. When the transformation process associated with digital advertising is evaluated in certain stages, smart advertising is considered the third stage of advertising (Li, 2019, p. 334).

In Rodgers and Nguyen (2022, p. 1044), the digital advertising process is evaluated in three stages: interactive advertising, programmatic advertising, and artificial intelligence advertising.

Interactive Advertising has reached its peak in the field of advertising, thanks to the rapid increase in the number of internet users and the opportunities offered by high technology in the digital age. Consequently, interaction has become a promising research subject for many scientists in various fields such as advertising, marketing, communication, education, information science, and computer science (Resuloğlu & Yılmaz, 2017, pp. 1-3). This process has also led to a rapid shift away from traditional structures in advertising towards the opportunities offered by digital technology.

Programmatic advertising is a new technique developed in recent years that uses large amounts of data or big data. Programmatic advertising encourages growth and investment in online display advertising. Compared to traditional online advertising buying and selling models, programmatic advertising has led to models that utilize user impression counts, banner click costs, and creative advertising. The technology driving programmatic advertising analyzes millions of real-time data points, enabling it to precisely convert a user's exact interests into a purchase or accurately display an ad at the moment when the likelihood of a click is highest. It also has the potential to ensure sufficient online audience reach and ensure that ads are displayed whenever viewers use their devices. Furthermore, ads can be targeted across different online platforms such as social networks, news platforms, or mobile applications via (Palos-Sancheza, Saurab & Martin-Veliciaa, 2019, pp. 61-62).

Programmatic advertising involves some tension as "mechanization." It contains the competing characteristics of automating the marketing process and the challenges posed by the absence of human judgment. The ongoing development of automated programmatic advertising systems is considered a dilemma, meaning that an organization chooses to actively adopt programmatic advertising to take advantage of its efficiency. In this process, the organization must be aware that it will also be exposed to the risk of inappropriate ad placement. This may seem more concerning to some organizations than others, but there is also the possibility that advertisements for any product or service could be positioned in a way that damages the organization's desired image. Incorporating human judgment into the programmatic advertising process is not feasible without undermining programmatic advertising's goal of providing real-time ad placement. Therefore, it is an inseparable dilemma linked to the decision to adopt programmatic advertising and carries a natural risk that ads may be placed inappropriately (Samuel, et al., 2021). Therefore, it can be said that programmatic advertising is more about people taking a backseat in the advertising buying and selling process, which instead takes place through a system of machines. However, saying that programmatic advertising only takes place between machines limits its scope. Thus, programmatic systems not only automate placement but also reshape the logic of narrative delivery and audience meaning-making.

Smart advertising begins as the third stage of digital marketing, with artificial intelligence impacting the advertising industry at different levels. The use of artificial intelligence in advertising customizes smart advertising not only to users' preferences but also to their characteristics (Rodgers & Nguyen, 2022, p. 1046). In other words, smart ads go beyond simply predicting users' interests; they can also predict users' needs and desires in various contexts, as well as suggest specific time frames and specific offers. This kind of prescription power is obtained by the user providing their first-party data to serve them. Just as patients share their physical conditions with their doctors, users allow a trusted application to collect their data, and in return, the application data is used for a better purpose. Trust is the cornerstone of using first-party data in smart advertising (Li, 2019, p. 335). Despite constant changes and developments in the field of digital advertising and the addition of new features, it can be seen that the general characteristics of digital advertising have been preserved.

According to marketing experts working in the field of advertising, artificial intelligence applications stand out with features such as smarter searches, smarter ads, reliance on chatbots, continuous learning, and prevention of fraud and data breaches. In addition, it is emphasized that artificial intelligence can be utilized for purposes such as sentiment analysis, image and voice recognition, sales forecasting, prediction-based customer service, and customer segmentation (Dimitrieska et al. 2018; Dolu & Marangoz, 2023, p. 531). Therefore, smart advertising represents an advanced stage in the advertising creation, production, and marketing process. Smart advertising offers many unique advantages in terms of internet advertising. With the developments in the field of smart advertising, many products and brands are taking their place in this field of advertising.

Defined as smart advertising, the participation of artificial intelligence in the advertising field involves different stages in the use of artificial intelligence in advertising. These are, first and foremost, determining customer preferences and customer behavior through data mining from social media and other sources. Then, the process of creating personalized advertisements begins by creating relevant content through language processing and deep learning. Then, based on customer preferences, media planning and purchasing are carried out through programmatic advertising, and in the final stage, the advertisement is evaluated by analyzing feedback (Qin & Jiang, 2019, p. 343).

The importance of artificial intelligence in advertising is significant and continues to grow day by day. When examining how artificial intelligence is used in advertising:

Personalized Ads: Artificial intelligence is widely used by many marketers as a well-known AI application for content personalization. Although AI offering user-specific personalization is not new, Adobe's Sensei AI takes this process a step further. Sensei can make decisions in the style of an editor. Image personalization work is also being done. Recent work in the field of artificial intelligence has enabled automatic tagging of images with critical visual information such as object, color, and text recognition. With these pieces of information, an artificial intelligence model will be able to present images in the style or color preferred by each customer (URL 2). By determining users' online behaviors with the applications used, these are analyzed and personalized advertising content is created.

Prediction and Optimization: Artificial intelligence plays an important role in determining and analyzing the target audience in the advertising industry. The gender of the target audience affects not only the advertising content but also its design . Artificial intelligence can predict which age group or gender will click on which advertisement. Advertising content can be determined based on these predictions. In addition, it can also predict which consumers are most likely to convert. Advertisers are targeting the goals set by artificial intelligence.

By developing new techniques for solving complex problems, artificial intelligence has provided a frequently used application area in research, both in terms of usage techniques and optimization algorithms (Coşkun, 2007, p. 145). Artificial intelligence is the process of selecting the best alternative solution that can be implemented under certain conditions. The objective function here stands out with its recognition of many conveniences, such as the cheapest, easiest, longest-lasting, and shortest-term. Artificial intelligence can predict future performance and optimize the advertising budget to increase the success of advertising campaigns.

Target Audience Identification: Artificial intelligence ensures that information about the products and services offered by businesses is matched in the most appropriate and effective way with the information needed by potential consumers (Sterne, 2017, p. 6; Erdem, 2022, p. 89). From the perspective of digital marketers, AI makes it much easier to determine the target audience for advertisements. AI analyzes the demographic, geographic, and psychographic structure of the target audience, as well as their behavioral characteristics, to determine the most appropriate advertising format to capture the target audience. In addition, while the gender of the target audience influences the content and design of the advertisement, artificial intelligence facilitates the identification of the target audience by predicting which advertisement a specific age group or gender will click on. Therefore, artificial intelligence helps advertisers define better target audiences.

Emotion Analysis: Advances in artificial intelligence systems have also brought facial recognition systems to an advanced level. In addition, cameras are now capable of analyzing people's emotional states using special software. In a study conducted in China on the process of analyzing people's emotional states with artificial intelligence, security cameras were installed in classrooms at a school in Beijing, and students' facial expressions were analyzed to determine their emotional states. Using the "emotion recognition" program developed by Hanwang Technology, artificial intelligence identified the face of each student in this classroom and then began to analyze their behavior. Based on certain criteria, for example, it marked a student whose eyes constantly wandered around the desk as "distracted," while used descriptions such as "focused" for a student who was looking intently at the blackboard. Students' behavior is analyzed based on their responses to questions and their interactions with other students (URL 2). These studies, conducted using artificial intelligence software and cameras, are then used to create visual texts. The emotional tone of text and visual content is analyzed to evaluate the impact of advertisements.

Beyond these applications in advertising, one of the significant promises of artificial intelligence lies in content creation within the creative industry. It can produce technological artificial creative content that can prepare visuals with specified keywords and "prompts" and write highly original texts. This facilitates the work of advertisers and raises the possibility of the sector becoming "dehumanized." Areas where artificial intelligence is beginning to be used, particularly in the advertising creation process, include:

Artificial Intelligence and Creativity: Regarding the process of artificial intelligence taking a place on the creative side, Türkömer states, "Its use seems likely to increase as the number of high-profile projects increases. In the coming period, data will diversify with insights and creative ideas, clearly becoming the hidden hero behind award-winning work in the industry" (Türkömer, 2018). For advertising and many other visual production industries, the use of computers and elements such as the structure and meaning of images in the visual design process emerge as cultural outputs of creativity. Today, artificial intelligence applications can produce design actions by repeating many of their activities using programmed algorithms and machine learning methods. This means that artificial intelligence applications used for design purposes are creative and, in addition, can work by drawing on various cultural experiences and knowledge without any design process (Karabulut, 2022, p. 1530). In this sense, AI becomes not merely a production tool but a co-author influencing narrative form, symbolic construction, and discourse strategies.

Creating an Advertising Scenario with Artificial Intelligence: The credits of the advertising film, whose scenario was written by artificial intelligence, appear on a black screen with the statement, "Presented by Lexus, a film written by artificial intelligence, directed by an award-winning human." In the scene that follows this statement, the car and the man are standing opposite each other (Kurt & Aydemir, 2021, p. 153). As seen in the Lexus commercial, artificial intelligence has begun to be used in writing advertising scripts. Artificial intelligence advertising scripts are increasingly being adopted in the field of marketing. This is because artificial intelligence has a greater data processing capacity and can make advertising more efficient and effective.

Creating Advertising Content with Artificial Intelligence: After images are selected and separated within themselves, they are divided into groups. The image recognition algorithm in this process, called image classification, analyzes the content in detail by including the images as input in the system being used. Images that are determined to not attract the consumer's interest are discarded. The system performs this process internally in a localized manner. Thus, artificial intelligence is designed to evaluate the differences in specific data groups in order to interpret the content of an image. As a result, artificial intelligence analyzes the objects in the images, processes them, and interprets them as desired (Sarıoğlu & Develi, 2022, p. 109). In addition, artificial intelligence uses data such as users' browsing history, demographic information, and behavior to personalize and determine advertising content. Furthermore, artificial intelligence can also tailor advertising content to be compatible with the target language and culture. Artificial intelligence saves time in the advertising content creation process and can achieve more effective results.

Creating Advertising Slogans with Artificial Intelligence: Advertiser Jean-Baptiste Le Divelec is conducting an experimental study to observe the effectiveness of artificial intelligence in the creative process in advertising and is creating an advertisement with artificial intelligence. For this study, he is using the Nike brand, which he describes as "one of the world's most iconic brands." To observe whether artificial intelligence can write an original advertising text, he feeds an artificial neural network with Nike advertisements over a period of ten years and demonstrates that artificial intelligence can do this with the results he obtains. The slogan "If you can't beat 'em, join 'em," produced by artificial intelligence, successfully aligns with the brand (Şahinci, 2021, p. 95). This demonstrates that artificial intelligence can produce interesting and creative slogans by suggesting different words and using its language.

Artificial Intelligence in Design and Logo Creation: Artificial intelligence, which has begun to be used in the field of graphic design in an advanced way with cognitive abilities, saves time in analyzing data sets and presenting alternative designs for the graphic industry. Designs created by artificial intelligence must then be developed and reviewed by designers. Therefore, artificial intelligence is a good assistant for designers. Artificial intelligence, with its cognitive abilities, offers convenience to graphic designers in image creation, logo design, and website creation. In addition, it can create suitable color combinations, prepare backgrounds, develop fonts, and select the page layout of websites. With these capabilities, artificial intelligence systems provide advantages in terms of time and cost (Kocaman, 2021, p. 3007). Artificial intelligence's ideas on color theory and color harmony, as well as its suggestions for specific color palettes or combinations, can support the creation of creative logos.

Preparing Advertising Videos with Artificial Intelligence: Advertising videos, as a vision-oriented marketing application, involve determining the relationships between previously defined data to increase operational efficiency. Users share their opinions about brands and the products they use with other users on many social media channels through image-focused text content with pictures and video images. Artificial intelligence enables brands to monitor social channels and recognize visual patterns related to individual products alongside the brand logo using deep learning techniques, thereby improving their applications (Keleş et al. 2017, p. 115). Artificial intelligence uses this acquired knowledge to create visual and video content. For example, it can reproduce videos showing a product from different angles or various product photos on its own.

Writing Advertising Copy and Storytelling With Artificial Intelligence

While earlier sections focused on technological transformation, the core transformation occurs at the level of narrative logic, discourse formation, and symbolic persuasion. In traditional screenwriting, the screenwriter plays a vital role in the narrative foundation of the film. Screenwriters shape the story, establish the characters in a certain form, and create dialogues that evoke deep emotions in the audience. This creative process, particularly dependent on the screenwriter's choices, creates atmosphere in the narrative, sets the pace, and creates deep effects with an emotional approach, generating tension (Zahrandama & Arryadianta, 2021). Therefore, the screenwriter makes the dialogue, character development, and narrative structure coherent and interconnected. In doing so, they highlight the subject with their refined skills and broad perspective. Screenwriters are more successful at placing emotional layers, symbols, and subtexts in the story. In addition, they localize the cultural context, humor, and irony with considerable nuance.

With the transition to the age of artificial intelligence, AI-generated writing scenarios are undergoing a transformation. The most important role of artificial intelligence in scenario writing is that it offers new possibilities in narrative construction. Scenarios created with artificial intelligence technologies contribute to various aspects of storytelling, such as character evolution and plot development. Processes such as scripts, games, and interactive fiction written by artificial intelligence present important areas of research in digital media (Thorne, 2020). This development also brings to the fore critiques linking traditional concepts of authorship and creativity with the creative role of artificial intelligence. The emergence of writing and creativity resulting from artificial intelligence's ability to analyze large data sets, distinguish patterns, and produce content, along with the increasingly blurred boundaries between human intelligence and machine-generated content, brings new dynamics to scriptwriting. The fact that artificial intelligence can generate a large number of scenarios in a matter of seconds and quickly revise new suggestions has instantly drawn attention to itself.

With its systematic and integrated structure, artificial intelligence creates a wide range of applications, from idea generation to target audience segmentation, content production to insight analysis, meeting numerous needs in the advertising field. In addition, artificial intelligence saves time and energy by automating simple daily tasks. This allows practitioners to devote more time to activities that require creativity, enable higher completion rates of business objectives, and generate value for the mutual benefit of buyers and sellers (Shah et al., 2020, p. 3). However, it falls short in terms of producing human-like depth, originality, and risk-taking creative ideas. At the same time, artificial intelligence is far from producing bold, unexpected, and creative ideas that push boundaries.

In this process, artificial intelligence collects real-time feedback in various formats, such as voice, text, and images, from tools like computers, smartphones, and tablets. Using machine learning methods, feedback data characteristics can be analyzed and compiled for later use. This allows the advertising impact to be obtained for comparison with the expected advertising goals and objectives (Qin & Jiang, 2019, p. 343). In addition, it avoids risk and tends to produce mostly safe scenarios.

Artificial Intelligence has begun to make progress in screenwriting by demonstrating significant developments in the screenwriting process and using various revolutionary technologies in this field. One of the fundamental AI technologies used in this field employs natural language processing technology that can evaluate character relationships and emotional tendencies in screenplays (Liu et al., 2018). With these developing technologies, advertising activities such as content creation, messaging, and visual design are now being carried out instantly on digital platforms through artificial intelligence. Artificial intelligence algorithms can create personalized text writing simulations that match the language and message tone used by brands. Thus, despite the ability to create large-scale advertising content alternatives to increase clicks and interactions (Kaput, 2024), the ideas presented may be similar, with a high risk of being average and repetitive.

Digital narratives are more likely to be based on multiple possibility networks and interactive plots rather than singular, linear, and author-centered structures (Murray, 1997). According to Murray, scenarios written with artificial intelligence support provide a convenient framework for explaining their structural logic. The fact that large language models produce different scenarios with the same characters and thematic inputs shows that visual narrative has become a multi-layered decision-making process managed by a system.

One of the ways messages are conveyed in advertisements is through storytelling; that is, advertisements tell stories. Narrative is both a form of reasoning and a form of representation. People can understand the world through narrative, and people can describe the world through narrative. In other words, these are texts with a sequential structure that arrive at a specific type of solution. They occur within a specific time frame and contain certain important relationships (Berger, 2022, p. 45). Story ads are credible due to their accuracy and narrative structure, as they explain their messages through stories. Narrative advertising, which includes drama and storytelling, tells a story about the product consumption experience and influences consumers' emotions in order to persuade them.

Digital Storytelling is the adaptation of traditional storytelling techniques for the digital world. This technique is used to make stories more effective and engaging, aiming to better influence target audiences. With the proliferation of the internet and social media, digital storytelling is becoming increasingly popular. The key elements of Digital Storytelling are as follows:

Characters: Characters play a crucial role in the success of any story. Digital storytelling aims to draw the target audience closer to the characters in order to capture their interest.

Events: Events that determine the flow of the story are also important in digital storytelling. Therefore, the right events must be selected for the narrative. Theme: Every story has a theme. Digital storytelling aims to strengthen the connection between the theme and the target audience.

Visuals: Digital storytelling uses visuals to tell the story more effectively. Visuals are important for creating the atmosphere of the story and capturing the reader's interest.

Interaction: Digital storytelling aims to increase interaction with the reader. Therefore, the use of interactive elements makes the story more meaningful and understandable (Aydemir & Fetah, 2023, p. 260).

Digital Storytelling utilizes low-cost digital cameras, non-linear editing software, and laptops to create short multimedia stories. These are primarily personal stories and are made to be published on the internet (Meadows, 2003, p.189).

One of the most important stages in the filmmaking process is the creation of the idea and script. Large language models (LLMs) can be used in the script production process due to their connection to natural languages and within the scope of deep learning models. ChatGPT and Claude are among the leading models.

AI Algorithms That Can Be Used in Screenplay Writing

ChatGPT is a large language model (LLM) developed by a company called OpenAI. This tool can provide support in processes such as developing innovative ideas, designing dialogues, or suggesting scene structures during the scriptwriting process.

Gemini, developed by Google DeepMind, is an algorithm capable of understanding context and offering innovative content suggestions. It is thought to be particularly helpful in areas such as enriching storylines or suggesting scenes suitable for different genres during scriptwriting.

Claude, developed by Anthropic, stands out as an "ethics-focused" AI. This tool can be used in processes such as creating storylines, shaping dialogues, or editing texts.

Sudowrite is a tool for writing processes that enables screenwriters to receive support in stages such as story development, character design, and dialogue writing. It can help overcome writer's block and contribute to the production of original content.

Plot Generator is a tool that creates story outlines based on user input. This tool can be used in the early stages of the writing process to generate ideas or create basic story structures.

StoryLab.ai is a platform that supports screenwriting processes. It can offer original ideas for different genres in screenwriting.

Notion AI is a tool that facilitates writing and editing processes. This tool can be used in areas such as scene development, character profiling, and story structuring in screenwriting. It also has the potential to make the writing process more organized (Demir & Kaplan, 2025, 516).

Artificial intelligence supports screenwriters by providing reasoning and intuitive inquiry systems with a story-focused and character-focused approach, thereby assisting screenwriters. This process contributes to extracting information from stories produced in natural language and improving the storytelling process (Sanghrajka et al., 2018). Artificial intelligence performs quite well in generating safe and average ideas. While artificial intelligence cannot produce unique narratives, it supports screenwriters in coming up with more creative ideas by scanning similar works.

AI-Powered Motion Graphics Advertising Production

Artificial intelligence-supported narrative forms can be considered a dynamic of structural and aesthetic restructuring in cinematic narrative architecture. It has been observed that generative artificial intelligence (GenAI) models can provide formal consistency through algorithmic patterns in areas such as scene composition, character design, and aesthetic integrity (Zhang, et al., 2025). Going beyond simply writing code, artificial intelligence has become the mental focal point of an artist in the digital realm with its ability to analyze large data sets, recognize patterns, and make design choices. Artificial intelligence serves as a creative collaborator, providing valuable insights that elevate animations to the highest possible level. Furthermore, the application of artificial intelligence in creating animation design elements not only saves time but also benefits consistency and accuracy. It also simplifies the process of creating animation elements such as characters and backgrounds, making it easier for the creative visionary to guide the process (Alamarat, 2025, p. 5). Artificial intelligence technologies involved in this transformation process are redefining the ways in which moving advertising images are produced. The idea development, shooting, animation, and post-production stages, which are based on the traditional advertising production process relying on human labor, are now being produced faster, more flexibly, and in a more personalized manner with AI-supported tools. New software and programs developed for this purpose have begun to be used.

As attention-grabbing as text-generating AI tools, this group of visual-generating tools is actively used. Tools such as Dall-E, Midjourney, Stable Diffusion, and Adobe Firefly are generative AI tools used to translate words, thoughts, or ideas into images. These tools are used by organizations and agencies in visual production. Recently, AI tools that generate videos have come to the fore. OpenAI Sora, Runway ML Gen-3, Stable Video Diffusion, and Invideo.io are text-based tools that are developing as generative AI tools for converting text into video (text-to-video) (Çeber, 2025, p. 176). The production of animated advertising images with these artificial intelligence tools is based on sub-technologies such as machine learning, deep learning, generative AI, and computer vision. Text-to-video, image-to-video, and automatic animation systems enable advertisers to produce animated content based solely on verbal commands or simple drafts.

These systems can automatically design cinematographic elements such as character movements, camera angles, lighting, color palette, and scene transitions. Thus, advertising images can be created in less time and at lower cost compared to traditional production processes. This production process still operates with human commands, and moving image formation is achieved in connection with data inputs. AI-driven visual production therefore contributes to the emergence of new audiovisual narrative grammars in advertising discourse.

Coşkuner (2023) states that artificial intelligence offers functional solutions in the genres of science fiction, animation, and dystopia. However, it is observed that aesthetic satisfaction remains limited in narratives requiring dramatic intensity. The concept of creativity in the production of animated advertisements using artificial intelligence is thus reopened for discussion. In contrast to the human approach to creativity, artificial intelligence takes on this process with the role of "co-creator." Human creativity retains its importance through the function of selecting from the possibilities offered by artificial intelligence and establishing narrative integrity.

With the development of AI-based generative models and the transformation of audiovisual production processes, Sora, developed by OpenAI, has emerged as one of the most current and striking examples of this transformation. It is an AI model capable of producing high-resolution, cinematic-quality videos from textual inputs.

Sora allows users to create videos containing complex scenes, characters, and specific types of movements using text inputs. It can also take an existing image and animate its content to create a video or extend an existing video by filling in missing frames. Thanks to these features, Sora has the potential to transform the field of advertising. Sora can be used particularly in the production and post-production stages of advertising film production (Çeber, 2025, p. 177). This model can construct cinematic elements such as camera movements, lighting, spatial depth, character behaviors, and physical interactions within a consistent narrative. This feature enables the automatic construction of narrative integrity, visual flow, and emotional atmosphere, which are important in advertising films. Sora has the potential to significantly reduce the set, crew, actor, and time costs required in traditional animation or live-action filming processes.

Areas of Application for Artificial Intelligence in Advertising Image Production

Concept and Moodboard Creation: Moodboards are visual tools used in various stages of the design development process to convey an idea, trend, or vision to relevant stakeholders, communicate within this scope, think, and share and discuss different opinions arising from the design brief (Mcdonagh and Storer, 2004). The concept refers to the creative idea at the heart of the advertising campaign. It encompasses the message the brand wants to convey, the form of communication to be established with the target audience, and the narrative strategy. A moodboard is a design tool that presents the visual and emotional counterpart of the concept. Color palettes, typography samples, photographs, illustrations, texture samples, use of light, and reference scenes are the basic components of a moodboard.

Product Visualization and Virtual Production: Virtual production offers many advantages over traditional production processes. This method allows production teams to visualize and arrange the physical characteristics of the set in advance, improving the planning process before shooting. Furthermore, virtual production provides the flexibility to make set changes and adjustments in real time, which helps creative teams bring their vision to life more effectively (Halaçoğlu, 2021, p.

73). Thanks to virtual production, camera movements, backgrounds, and product interactions can be controlled in real time, allowing creative teams to quickly carry out visual experiments. Since the same product image can be reused for different campaigns and media, consistency and scalability in advertising production are increased. In this process, product visualization enables a product to be represented in a realistic manner in a digital environment through three-dimensional (3D) models, while virtual production refers to a comprehensive production process in which these digital assets are used in real time on virtual sets.

Personalized Advertising Visuals; Automation systems use algorithmic recommendation systems to automatically provide personalized content recommendations based on users' past behaviors and preferences. This both enriches the user experience and enables platforms to increase user engagement. Thanks to content recognition and classification technologies, relevant content can be automatically tagged and categorized within large data sets (Kırçıl & Karagüler, 2008, p.153). At the same time, artificial intelligence systems can automatically generate multiple variations of the same advertisement for different target audiences. Language, visual tempo, color usage, and even character representations can be reshaped according to the demographic and behavioral characteristics of the audience. This approach strengthens the impact of advertising and the connection it establishes with the audience across a wide range of areas, from television advertising to digital platforms.

Examples of AI-Generated Advertising Scenarios and Commercials

Be a tourist, be an explorer!; The advertiser for the first advertising script written by ChatGPT was the Danish tourism agency VisitDenmark. VisitDenmark, which released the new promotional video titled "Be a tourist, be an explorer!" signed by Brandhouse/Subsero, had ChatGPT write the film's script. In the commercial, the Mona Lisa addresses visitors with a line written by ChatGPT: "While I appreciate your interest, let's be honest. Waiting in line for hours just to see me isn't the most exciting way to spend your vacation." The Statue of Liberty invites visitors to Denmark with the words, "You can skip the crowds there and enjoy life's simple pleasures" (Gören, 2023).

LİST Flavours has made history with an ad film created entirely by artificial intelligence. The brand's ad film, prepared as part of its New Year's communication, has been broadcast on social media platforms and digital screens.

The preparation process was carried out by Bark Creative Studio, and both the visual narrative and the jingle were produced by artificial intelligence. In addition to ChatGPT, Midjourney was used to create the visuals and Runway was used to create the video for the LİST Flavours commercial. The jingle was developed by Suno platforms (Önder, 2024).

Mint Mobile owner Ryan Reynolds shared how he used ChatGPT to write a special ad copy for Mint Mobile in a video posted on social media., tasked with "writing an ad for Mint Mobile in Ryan Reynolds' voice," was given additional instructions to include jokes and profanity in the script and to inform the target audience that Mint's holiday promotion was still ongoing.

The Kalshi ad shows a series of unbelievable scenarios in just 30 seconds: a potbellied partygoer holding a Chihuahua dog in his lap; a bride escaping from the police in a golf cart; a farmer enjoying himself in a pool filled with eggs. The screen is filled with bizarre details, such as a sign reading "Fresh Sea Cow."

It caused a huge stir when it aired during the YouTube TV broadcast of Game 3 of the NBA Finals on June 11. Kalshi media representative Jack Such told NPR, "We are extremely pleased with the results of the ad and its effectiveness so far. It has generated a lot of buzz on social media" (Chappell, 2025).

Examples of TV Ads Created With AI

Heinz – "AI Ketchup; Heinz Artificial Intelligence Ketchup – With new artificial intelligence text-to-image conversion programs taking over the internet, Heinz needed to know one thing: How does artificial intelligence see ketchup? Just like humans, artificial intelligence also prefers Heinz. After searching for everything from "diving into ketchup" to "ketchup in space" using the advanced image generator DALL-E 2, it was found that most of the results resembled Heinz bottles. Heinz fans are involved in the process by sharing their visual suggestions related to ketchup. The best suggestions were turned into social media posts and print ads, creating the first advertising campaign entirely with AI-generated visuals (Heinz, 2023).

Coca-Cola – "Create Real Magic"; Using the Create Real Magic artificial intelligence platform, the best visual designs produced in many countries were selected and displayed on Coca-Cola's digital billboards in New York's Times Square and London's Piccadilly Circus. Coca-Cola also collaborated with digital content creators Emma Sofija, Ean Hwa Huag, Chris Branch, and Paul Parsons, who used OpenAI tools to promote the project. A video showcasing both the AI platform and the artist collaborations has been produced (Gören, 2024).

Coca-Cola has also adopted a strategy of using artificial intelligence to produce its annual Christmas campaign. In this campaign, the iconic "Holidays Are Coming" theme has been reinterpreted using generative AI technologies and enriched with details specific to different regions. The company has stated that this approach helps it reach its advertising target audience in a more dynamic and personalized way.

Starburst – "Different Every Time"; Generative AI was used to produce campaign spots featuring diverse scenes and styles. This project includes over 300 unique pieces of content and spans TV, online, social media, and other channels, including an augmented reality (AR) lens on Snapchat and a Spotify activation. Created by Team OMC, a collaboration between Omnicom agencies DDB and Critical Mass, the "Different Every Time" campaign, created by Team OMC in collaboration with Omnicom agencies DDB and Critical Mass, aims to influence Generation Z consumers around innovation and discovery and demonstrates how marketers can use generative AI to create content at scale (Kelly, 2024).

Toys "R" Us – "The Origin of Toys R Us"; Toys "R" Us's Origin is the first brand film created using OpenAI's text-to-video conversion tool, Sora. The iconic retailer, part of the WHP Global family of companies, collaborated with Native Foreign agency, which has alpha access to Emmy-nominated Chief Creative Officer Sora, to create the film. Sora, which has not yet released a public version, can create one-minute, dialogue-free video clips using generative AI. A commercial film has been produced that revisits the origin of Toys "R" Us, depicting the dream in which the retail chain's founder, Charles Lazarus, first envisioned the giraffe mascot Geoffrey (ToyBook, n.d.).

CONCLUSION

The digital transformation process brings significant changes to traditional advertising concepts. With the advent of digital transformation, digital advertising and digital storytelling have emerged, and the advertising production process, which is intertwined with technology, has begun to incorporate many new technologies. The most significant change in this process is the role artificial intelligence plays in advertising narratives and production. Creating advertising images with artificial intelligence is fundamentally transforming both production practices and creative understanding in the advertising industry. While offering cost and time advantages, these technologies do not completely eliminate the role of human creativity; rather, they shift it to a different plane.

While artificial intelligence is involved in the advertising production and broadcasting process on many platforms, it is seen that in TV advertising, it is not just a technical tool that speeds up production processes; it is also an actor that fundamentally restructures the aesthetic language of advertising, the creative division of labor, and the relationship it establishes with the audience. Applications such as AI-supported script writing, motion graphics production, virtual production, product visualization, and automatic versioning greatly relax the constraints of time, space, and cost that are central to traditional advertising production. This enables television commercials to be produced more quickly, adapted to different target audiences, and re-circulated across multiple platforms. Thus, TV advertising is evolving into a hybrid structure that integrates the speed and flexibility of digital advertising.

The study reveals that artificial intelligence transforms human creativity in advertising rather than eliminating it. The role of the advertiser is shifting from being an actor who directly produces content to being a creative who manages, selects, and interprets the possibilities generated by artificial intelligence. On the other hand, the aesthetic and cultural dimensions of advertising content produced with artificial intelligence are also important components of this digital turning point. The blurring of the perception of reality, the risk of weakening emotional bonds, and algorithmic repetitions stand out as problem areas that need to be carefully addressed for the future of television advertising. In this context, the sustainability of AI-supported advertising production appears to depend not only on technological innovation but also on human creativity.

Traditional TV advertising is not a model that ends with artificial intelligence; it can be evaluated as a narrative and production field that is being reshaped around digitalization. This transformation is turning television advertising from merely a mass communication tool of the past into a data-driven, flexible, and multi-layered visual narrative practice.

REFERENCES

Adams, R. (2004). Intelligent Advertising. *AI & Society, 18*(1), 68–81. DOI: 10.1007/s00146-003-0259-9

Alamarat, İ. (2025). Using Artificial Intelligence in Producing Animation Elements. *Art and Architecture Journal, 6*(1), 1–10. DOI: 10.21608/aaj.2025.344652.1085

Aydemir, M., & Fetah, V. (2023). Yapay Zekanın Dijital Hikayeleştirme ve Senaryo Tasarımında Kullanımı: Kısa Film Uygulamalı Bir Araştırma. *Pamukkale Üniversitesi Sosyal Bilimler Enstitüsü Journal*, (58), 255–275.

Aydın, İ., & Değirmenci, C. H. (2018). *Yapay Zekâ*. Girdap.

Berger, A. (2022). All Ads Are Narratives. *Media-Biznes-Kultura. Dziennikarstwo i komunikacja społeczna*, (13), 43-54.

Çakın, Ö., & Bolat, N. (2018). Sosyal Medya Reklamcılığı ve Dijital Mecra Etkileşimleri. *Dijital Kültür ve İletişim*. In Çakmak, V., & Çavuş, S. (Eds.), *Literatürk*.

Çakır, S., & Çakın, Ö. (2022). Markaların Dijital İletişimde Emoji Kullanım Alışkanlıkları -Emoji Usage Habits of Brands in Digital Communications. *Middle Black Sea Journal of Communication Studies, 7*(1), 101–114.

Çeber, B. (2025). Yapay Zekâ "Sora" İle Üretilen Reklamların Mcluhan'ın "Araç Mesajdır" Perspektifinden İncelenmesi: Toys "R" Us Reklam Örneği. *Yeni Medya Elektronik Journal, 9*(2), 171–200.

Chappell, B. (2025, June 23). An AI video ad is making a splash: Is it the future of advertising? NPR. https://www.npr.org/2025/06/23/nx-s1-5432712/ai-video-ad-kalshi-advertising-nba-finals

Coşkun, A. (2007). Yapay Zekâ Optimizasyon Teknikleri: Literatür Değerlendirmesi. *Fırat Üniversitesi Doğu Anadolu Bölgesi Araştırmaları Journal, 5*(2), 142–146.

Coşkuner, A. (2023). Sinemanın Denetimsiz Teknolojiyle Sınavı: Yapay Zeka'nın Film Endüstrisine Etkisi. *Türkiye Film Araştırmaları Journal, 3*(1), 1. Advance online publication. DOI: 10.59280/film.1284277

Demir, M, Kaplan, M. (2025) Yapay Zekâ Araçlarının Sinematik Anlatıda Kullanımı. *İNİF E- Journal*, 10(2), pp. 509-540.

Dimitrieska, S., Stankovska, A., & Efremova, T. (2018). Artificial Intelligence and Marketing. *Entrepreneurship, 6*(2), 298–304.

Dolu, Z. T., & Marangoz, M. (2023). Yapay Zekâ Uygulamalarının Tüketicilerin Satın Alma Niyeti Üzerine Etkisi: Büyük Hazine Filmi Üzerine Bir Analiz. *Pamukkale Üniversitesi İşletme Araştırmaları Dergisi, 10*(2), 525–549. DOI: 10.47097/piar.1271887

Durmaz, A. (1999). *Dijital Televizyonun Temelleri.* Anadolu Üniversitesi Eğitim Sağlık ve Bilimsel Araştırma Çalışmaları Vakfı.

Erdem, B. (2022). Yapay Zekanın Pazarlamaya Etkisi, *Sosyal Bilimlerde Disiplinlerarası Akademik Çalışmalar.* In Terzioğlu, D., & Korkmaz, S. S. (Eds.), *Eğitim.*

Gören, G. (2023, March 6). Danish tourism promotion film signed by ChatGPT. Bigumigu. https://bigumigu.com/haber/danimarkadan-chatgpt-imzali-turizm-tanitim-filmi/

Gören, G. (2024). Coca-Cola launches AI platform for digital artists. Bigumigu. https://bigumigu.com/haber/coca-coladan-dijital-sanatcilar-icin-yapay-zeka-platformu/

Halaçoğlu, B. N. (2021). Makinimanın Gelişimi: Film Yapımının Sanal Prodüksiyona Dönüşümü. *Dumlupınar Üniversitesi Sosyal Bilimler Dergisi*, (68), 73–89. DOI: 10.51290/dpusbe.823660

Heinz. (2023). Heinz: A.I. Ketchup [Online campaign description]. Ads of the World. https://campaignsoftheworld.com/digital-campaigns/heinz-a-i-ketchup/

Hudders, L., Reıjmersdal, E. A. V., & Poels, K. (2019). Digital Advertising and Consumer Empowerment. *Journal Of Psychosocial Research On Cyberspace, 13*(2), 1–10.

Kaput, M. (2024). 20 Ways AI Could Transform PR and Communications. https://www.marketingaiinstitute.com/blog/how-ai-could-transform-pr-and-communications

Karabulut, B. (2022). Yapay Zeka Bağlamında Yaratıcılık ve Görsel Tasarımın Geleceği.

Keleş, A., Keleş, A., & Akçetin, E. (2017). Pazarlama Alanında Yapay Zekâ Kullanım Potansiyeli ve Akıllı Karar Destek Sistemleri. *Electronic Turkish Studies, 12*(11), 109–124. DOI: 10.7827/TurkishStudies.12022

Kelly, C. (2024, May 9). Starburst taps generative AI for "Different Every Time" campaign assets. Marketing Dive. https://www.marketingdive.com/news/starburst-generative-ai-campaign-assets-gen-z/715524/

Kırçıl, A. G., & Karagüler, T. (2008). *Dijital Çağda Iletişime Yeni Yaklaşım: Online Gazetecilik, Akademik Bilişim Konferansı.* Çukurova Universty.

Kocaman, Ş. (2021). Grafik Tasarım Endüstrisinde Yapay Zekâ. *Journal of Social and Humanities Sciences Research, 8*(77), 3000–3016.

Kurt, S., & Aydemir, D. (2021). *Ya Reklam Senaristi Bir Makine Olursa?* Ağrı Uluslararası Yapay Zekâ Transhümanizm Posthümanizm ve Din Sempozyumu.

Kuşçu, E. (2015). Çeviride Yapay Zekâ Uygulamaları. *Kazım Karabekir Eğitim Fakültesi Dergisi*, (30), 46–58.

Li, H. (2019). Special Section Introduction: Artificial Intelligence and Advertising. *Journal of Advertising, 48*(4), 333–337. DOI: 10.1080/00913367.2019.1654947

Liu, S., Zhang, Y., & Wang, C. (2018). A Realization Framework of Intelligent Film Evaluation System. 2018 11th International Congress on Image and Signal Processing, BioMedical Engineering and Informatics (CISP-BMEI)

Mcdonagh, D., & Storer, I. (2004). Mood boards as a Design Catalyst and Resource: Researching an Under-Researched Area. *The Design Journal, 7*(3), 16–31. DOI: 10.2752/146069204789338424

Meadows, D. (2003). Digital Storytelling: Research-Based Practice in New Media, *SAGE.* Thousand Oaks. *Visual Communication, 2*(2), 189–193. DOI: 10.1177/1470357203002002004

Murray, J. H. (1997). Hamlet on the holodeck: The future of narrative in cyberspace.

Nilsson, N. J. (1998). *Artificial Intelligence A New Synthesis.* Morgan Kaufmann Publishers, China Machine Press.

Önder, N. (2024, December 6). Full AI-generated List Flavours commercial now live. Marketing Türkiye. https://www.marketingturkiye.com.tr/kampanyalar/list-flavoursin-tamami-yapay-zeka-ile-hazirlanan-reklam-filmi-yayinda/

Palos-Sancheza, P., Saurab, J. R., & Martin-Veliciaa, F. (2019). A Study of The Effects of Programmatic Advertising on Users' Concerns About Privacy Overtime. *Journal of Business Research, 96*, 61–72. DOI: 10.1016/j.jbusres.2018.10.059

Qin, X., & Jiang, Z. (2019). The Impact of AI on the Advertising Process: The Chinese Experience. *Journal of Advertising, 48*(4), 338–346. DOI: 10.1080/00913367.2019.1652122

Resuloğlu, F., & Yılmaz, R. (2017). A model for interactive advertising narration. In Yilmaz, R. (Ed.), *Narrative Advertising Models and Conceptualization in the Digital Age* (pp. 1–20). IGI Global., DOI: 10.4018/978-1-5225-2373-4.ch001

Rodgers, W., & Nguyen, T. (2022). Advertising Benefits from Ethical Artificial Intelligence Algorithmic Purchase Decision Pathways. *Journal of Business Ethics, 178*(4), 1043–1106. DOI: 10.1007/s10551-022-05048-7

Şahinci, D. (2021). *Yapay Zekâ ve Reklamcılığın Geleceği.* İstanbul Üniversitesi Sosyal Bilimler Enstitüsü.

Samuel, A., White, G. R. T., Thomas, R., & Jones, P. (2021). Programmatic Advertising: An Exegesis of Consumer Concerns. *Computers in Human Behavior, 116,* 106657. Advance online publication. DOI: 10.1016/j.chb.2020.106657

Sanghrajka, R., Witoń, W., Schriber, S., Gross, M., & Kapadia, M. (2018). Computer-Assisted Authoring for Natural Language Story Scripts. *Proceedings of the AAAI Conference on Artificial Intelligence, 32*(1). Advance online publication. DOI: 10.1609/aaai.v32i1.11420

Sarıoğlu, B., & Develi, İ. (2022). Pazarlamada Kampanya Yönetimi Ve Yapay Zekâ Kullanımı. *Uluslararası Halkla İlişkiler ve Reklam Çalışmaları Dergisi, 5*(2), 91–124.

Shah, N., Engineer, S., Bhagat, N., Chauhan, H., & Shah, M. (2020). Research Trends on the Usage of Machine Learning and Artificial Intelligence in Advertising. *Augmented Human Research, 5*(1), 19. Advance online publication. DOI: 10.1007/s41133-020-00038-8

Sterne, J. (2017). *Artificial Intelligence for Marketing: Practical Applications.* Rising Media. DOI: 10.1002/9781119406341

Thorne, S. (2020). Hey siri, tell me a story: Digital storytelling and ai authorship. *Convergence (London), 26*(4), 808–823. DOI: 10.1177/1354856520913866

ToyBook. (n.d.) AI-generated Toys "R" Us brand film announces first ever AI retail film. ToyBook. https://toybook.com/ai-generated-toys-r-us-brand-film/

Türkömer, G. (2018). Yapay Zeka Reklam Sektörünün Geleceğini Nasıl Etkiler? https:// digitalage.com.tr/yapay-zeka-reklam-sektorunun-gelecegini-nasil-etkiler/ . E.T: 27.09.2023

Yılmaz, R., & Erdem, N. M. (2016). *150 Soruda Geleneksel ve Dijital Reklamcılık.* Umuttepe.

Yu, Y. (2022). The role and influence of artificial intelligence on advertising industry. In *Proceedings of the 2021 International Conference on Social Development and Media Communication (SDMC 2021)* (pp. 190–194). Atlantis Press. https://doi.org/ DOI: 10.2991/assehr.k.220105.037

Zhang, R., ... (2025). *Generative AI for Film Creation: A Survey of Recent Advances*. https://doi.org//arXiv.2504.08296DOI: 10.1109/CVPRW67362.2025.00623

ADDITIONAL READING

Barber, J. F. (2016). Digital storytelling: New opportunities for humanities Scholarship and pedagogy. *Cogent Arts & Humanities*, *3*(1), 1181037. Advance online publication. DOI: 10.1080/23311983.2016.1181037

Barrett, H. (2006). "Researching and evaluating digital storytelling as a deep learning tool". In C. Crawford, et al. (Eds.), Proceedings of society for information technology and teacher education international conference 2006, (pp. 647-654), AACE, Chesapeake, VA.

Chang, W. N. (2017). The effects of digital storytelling on student achievement, social presence, and attitude in online collaborative learning environments. *Interactive Learning Environments*, *25*(3), 412–427. DOI: 10.1080/10494820.2015.1135173

Gao, J., & Yin, J. (2024). Emotional Expression of AI-generated Artistic Design: A Case Analysis Approach. *Chitrolekha Journal on Art and Design*, *8*(1). Advance online publication. DOI: 10.21659/cjad.81.v8n104

Kietzmann, J., Paschen, J., & Treen, E. (2018). Artificial Intelligence in Advertising: How Marketers Can Leverage Artificial Intelligence Along the Consumer Journey. *Journal of Advertising Research*, *58*(3), 263–267. DOI: 10.2501/JAR-2018-035

Li, Y. (2021). Film and TV animation production based on artificial intelligence AlphaGd. *Mobile Information Systems*, *2021*, 1–8. DOI: 10.1155/2021/1104248

Midjourney (2023). Screenplay Design and Text Visualization Section https://www.midjourney.com/ home/?callbackUrl=%2Fapp%2F (February 11, 2023).

Patel, M. (2009). The digital visual effects studio: The Artists and Their Work Revealed.

Trach, Y. (2022). Experience and Prospects of Artificial Intelligence Technologies Application in the Film Industry. Digital Platform: Information Technologies in Sociocultural Sphere.

Vakratsas, D., & Wang, X. (2020). Artificial Intelligence in Advertising Creativity. *Journal of Advertising*, *50*(1), 39–51. DOI: 10.1080/00913367.2020.1843090

Wibowo, M. C., Nugroho, S., & Wibowo, A. (2024). The Use of Motion Capture Technology in 3D Animation. International Journal of Computing and Digital Systems, 15(1), 975-987. Wright, Steve. (2002). Digital Compositing for Film and Video. Oxford Burlington: Focal Press.

Xu, Y. (2025). Balancing Creativity and Automation: The Influence of AI on Modern Film Production and Dissemination (No. arXiv:2504.19275). arXiv. https://doi.org// arXiv.2504.19275DOI: 10.48550

KEYWORDS & DEFINITIONS

Digitalization: Digitalization means the digitization of various information and content in parallel with technological developments along with the expansion of the use of the internet. Digitalization, which includes the storage and transfer of data as well as technological transformation, has an impact on many areas.

Digital Storytelling: Digital storytelling is also important for the marketing and advertising sectors. Brands can find creative ways to influence potential customers and promote their products through storytelling. However, creating this type of storytelling requires a high level of creativity and technical skills (). Therefore, digital storytelling has become an important skill for both professional writers and business owners.

Digital Performance: Digital performance essentially encompasses all performance works in which computer technologies play a central role. In these performances, computer technologies play a leading role rather than a supporting role in terms of content, technique, aesthetics, or audience reach.

Artificial Intelligence: Artificial intelligence is broadly and somewhat cyclically seen as an approach that exhibits intelligent behavior. Intelligent behavior involves perception, reasoning, learning, communication, and movement in complex environments.

Artificial Intelligence Advertising: Artificial intelligence advertising has a structure that is accelerating with dynamic changes in advertising strategies and fundamentally transforming the way brands interact with their target audiences. Today, advertisers use artificial intelligence to create personalized experiences, target specific demographic groups, and make faster decisions.

Chapter 6
The Impact of Artificial Intelligence on Advertising Production and the Construction of Narrative:
A Qualitative Analysis With Advertising Professionals

Eda Turancı
http://orcid.org/0000-0002-2539-8452
Independent Researcher, Turkey

Oğuzhan Alın
http://orcid.org/0009-0006-4654-9703
Independent Researcher, Turkey

ABSTRACT

This chapter examines the impact of artificial intelligence (AI) tools on advertising production processes and the construction of narratives from the perspective of advertising professionals. Drawing on a phenomenological qualitative design, in-depth interviews were conducted with 16 advertising practitioners integrating AI into creative workflows. The findings indicate that AI is mainly conceptualized as a supportive assistant rather than an autonomous creator. While AI enhances speed, efficiency, and idea generation, participants emphasize that originality, emotional depth, and narrative authenticity remain human-driven. The study reveals a shift toward hybrid creativity, where routine tasks are increasingly delegated to AI, yet

DOI: 10.4018/979-8-3373-5666-2.ch006

strategic thinking and insight development remain human-centered. Although concerns regarding standardization and superficiality persist, AI is largely perceived as transformative rather than disruptive. The sustainability of advertising practice depends on balancing algorithmic efficiency with human imagination and cultural sensitivity.

A BRIEF INTRODUCTION TO THE CONCEPT OF ARTIFICIAL INTELLIGENCE

Among today's rapidly evolving digital technologies, artificial intelligence (AI) stands out not only as a technical innovation but also as an encompassing and innovative concept that transforms production and communication processes across numerous fields. Beyond being merely a part of the evolutionary process of the internet, AI is transforming into a fundamental necessity by reflecting core functions of daily life within its essence. At this point, examining the concept of artificial intelligence from its origins gains importance. Wildenhain (2025, pp. 15-22) states that AI has two pioneers in the field of literature. Goethe's Homunculus and Shelley's Frankenstein point to two fundamental prerequisites for AI within a human framework in a general sense: "the existence of a body living on earth and its counterpart within the social community" (Wildenhain, 2025, p. 22). Although neither author experienced the contemporary equivalent of artificial intelligence, the two prerequisites they proposed shed light on the current use of the AI metaphor.

From a historical perspective, although AI has followed a trajectory parallel to advancements in computer and transistor technologies, its development is not limited solely to the technical field and incorporates many different building blocks. When these are examined broadly, it is observed that the foundation of the field dates back to work of McCulloch and Pitts in the 1940s, which modeled the functioning of neurons. In 1950, Turing discussed the capacity of machines to think and proposed the Turing Test. In 1956, the term "artificial intelligence" was coined by McCarthy. Since the 1960s, natural language processing (NLP) programs such as early ELIZA have been developed, followed by expert systems in the 1980s and the resurgence of learning-capable artificial neural networks in the 1990s. Deep Blue's victory over Kasparov in 1997 contributed to the increase in social interest toward AI. Since the 2000s, progress in the fields of robotics and social learning has enabled AI to exhibit human-like behaviors. Today, it has gained widespread prevalence in many areas and has become one of the fundamental components of daily life (Arslan, 2020, pp. 76-78; Ertel, 2025, pp. 5-9). In this context, it can be anticipated that AI, which has grown with a snowball effect from the recent past to the present, will continue its upward momentum.

When looking at the definitions regarding the concept, various perspectives and disciplines emerge. At this point, it should also be noted that there is not yet a consensus on a universal definition. In this context, firstly, Kaplan and Haenlein (2019, p. 17), focusing on adaptation, define AI as "a system's ability to correctly interpret external data, to learn from such data, and to use those learnings to achieve specific goals and tasks through flexible adaptation." Pei Wang (2019, pp. 318-320) evaluates intelligence as "a system's ability to adapt to its environment while operating with insufficient information and resources" and provides an indirect framing of AI by pointing out that an intelligent system must rely on a finite processing capacity, operate in real-time, be prepared for unexpected tasks, and learn from experiences in accordance with this principle. Abbass (2021, p. 95) defines AI as "social and cognitive phenomena that enable a machine to socially integrate with a society to perform competitive tasks requiring cognitive processes and to communicate with other entities of the society by exchanging messages through shorter representations with high information content." Sheikh, Prims, and Schrijvers (2023, p. 19), instead of definitions based on the imitation of human intelligence, explain AI as "systems that display intelligent behavior by analysing their environment and taking actions—with some degree of autonomy—to achieve specific goals," which they predict will encompass the present and the near future. Gil de Zúñiga et al. (2024, p. 320) provide a communication-oriented definition of AI as the "tangible, real-world capacity of non-human machines or artificial entities to solve tasks, communicate, interact, and behave logically, as in biological humans." These definitions demonstrate that there are numerous perspectives toward AI in different sectors and fields, and new perspectives continue to be added to these regularly.

Types of artificial intelligence are categorized under three headings: ANI, AGI, and ASI. Artificial Narrow Intelligence (ANI) is the first level, capable of achieving success in only a single area. It is divided into sub-branches such as "machine learning, natural language processing (NLP), and robotics". Artificial General Intelligence (AGI) is the type that reaches and surpasses the level of human intelligence, thus possessing abilities such as "reasoning, planning, problem-solving, abstract thinking, making sense of complex situations, and learning quickly from experience." Thirdly, Artificial Super Intelligence (ASI) refers to a form of intelligence that would significantly surpass the most advanced human cognitive abilities across nearly all domains, including scientific innovation, broad reasoning capacity, and social competence; however, it is widely considered unlikely to emerge in the foreseeable future (Haymond & McCudden, 2021, pp. 1641-1642). Today, ANI can be considered the predominant and utilized type of AI. In addition to AI tools that generate text like ChatGPT, recommendation systems used by Spotify and Netflix, face or voice recognition systems, and systems used in autonomous driving constitute examples of ANI due to their application in limited and specific tasks.

Within the framework of the definitions and types of AI, both positive and negative perspectives exist regarding usage practices. While Grzybowski, Pawlikowska–Łagód, and Lambert (2024, p. 227) state that users often do not understand how AI tools work despite their widespread commercial adoption, they mention that despite the possibilities of misuse, AI holds significant positive potential and they predict that its long-term results will be positive. However, along with positive views, there are also opinions suggesting that AI is exaggerated (Fjelland, 2020, pp. 7-8), and that machine learning-based chatbots, especially ChatGPT and Gemini, present negative aspects such as security issues, potential for inaccuracy, and data limitations (Singh, Kumar, & Mehra, 2023, p. 5). In their study examining the relationship between film and AI from the 1960s to the present, Anderson, Roggerman, and Fuller (2024) evaluate that while the value of AI in human life has increased in terms of acceptance and importance today, as the skills of AI develop, ethical debates and questions regarding state policies have also become more central.

ARTIFICIAL INTELLIGENCE AS A VISUAL PRODUCTION TOOL

The functionality of artificial intelligence in the visual production process renders the relationship between AI and visuality a subject of extensive debate. Images generated by AI, which are increasingly prevalent in various fields, are significant within the framework of this study's primary problematique. The transformation in visual production technologies is entering a radical phase, particularly with the development of "Generative Artificial Intelligence" models. In this context, the ability of AI to produce visual, literary, and video content in an exceptionally short time is facilitated by the processing of big data and the synergy of machine learning (Sivri, 2024, pp. 328-329). AI tools—resulting from the processing and analysis of digital content accumulated since Web 1.0 through machine learning—function today as practical instruments utilized in various spheres of life. Text-guided image synthesis initiated its development with the emergence of GANs (Generative Adversarial Networks) and Deep Dream; however, the primary breakthrough occurred with the publication of CLIP (Contrastive Language-Image Pretraining) in 2021. As a language-image model trained on web-scale data that can pair natural language with visuals, CLIP has played a critical role in generating images from text. Initially functioning as a discriminative component in GAN-based systems, CLIP enabled the production of visuals compatible with text prompts. This approach became popular in digital art production through systems like Big Sleep and especially VQGAN-CLIP, and was subsequently superseded by more advanced models such as CLIP-guided and latent diffusion models (Oppenlaender, 2022, pp. 193-194).

The relationship between artificial intelligence and visual production can be addressed within two frameworks: "text-based" and "image-based" visual-generating AI tools. Text-based tools utilize "prompts" to guide the AI, enabling the creation of desired visuals through specific directives. Image-based tools, on the other hand, allow for the production of new visuals or the modification of existing ones by using an input image. While DALL-E and Midjourney serve as prominent examples of text-to-image AI tools, platforms such as OpenAI Sora, Stability AI, Invideo AI, and Deepbrain AI represent text-to-video capabilities. Additionally, image-to-image/video AI tools include Google Lumiere AI, Alibaba EMO AI, HeyGen, and Deepfakes (Türten, 2024, pp. 406-411).

Generating visuals with the help of existing and evolving AI tools has become a commonplace practice. However, this should not foster the perception that AI tools are sufficient for the entirety of the production process. Processes such as textual prompting and the evaluation of the AI-generated results remain subjects of discussion. In his study, Hunt (2023, p. 112) compared weather photographs created with three different AI tools against award-winning photographs from the "Weather Photographer of the Year" competition, determining that human creativity is indispensable for designing textual prompts, optimizing generated images, and selecting superior output. Furthermore, Lin et al. (2024, p. 367) state that generative AI users lack a metric to reliably demonstrate the extent to which an image aligns with its text prompt. In this context, it is understood that AI tools used for visual production cannot yet manage the process entirely autonomously.

ADVERTISING AND ARTIFICIAL INTELLIGENCE

Advertising is regarded as an indispensable communication tool within both traditional and digital media. The discipline of advertising—directly or indirectly influenced by advancements in artificial intelligence—encompasses numerous definitions. For a promotional effort to be classified as advertising, it must be published by purchasing space and time from mass media for a specific fee, designed for a specific object to achieve particular marketing objectives, and broadcast with the explicit indication of its promotional nature (Serttaş Ertike & Yılmaz, 2011, p. 6). In this context, advertising can be defined as "paid, owned, and earned mediated communication, conducted by an identifiable brand, shaped with persuasive intent to create a cognitive, affective, or behavioral change in the consumer now or in the future" (Kerr & Richards, 2021, p. 190).

Elden (2018) categorizes the fundamental functions of advertising as a form of communication under four headings. The first is the informative function, which is actively employed in various aspects such as demonstrating product usage, announcing price changes, explaining operational mechanics, introducing services, and alleviating consumer concerns. Second is the reminding function, which serves to keep the product prominent in the consumer's mind, particularly during the maturity stage of the product life cycle. The third, the value-adding function, encompasses efforts to portray a product or service as superior to its competitors. Finally, the function of supporting other organizational objectives plays a secondary role in achieving goals related to personal selling or sales promotion (Elden, 2018, pp. 21-22).

Beyond these functions, advertising constructs a narrative through its messaging; thus, narrative construction itself can be considered a core function of advertising. Within this scope, the concept of narrative is crucial. Examining its essence, narrative has existed since the dawn of human existence (Jahn, 2020, p. 48). Narrative is defined as "the transmission of two or more logically interconnected events (or a state and an event) occurring over time and integrated into a coherent whole" (Mutlu, 2017, pp. 31-32). In advertising, narrative content shifts the focus from actual utility and rationalist inquiries toward story-driven applications where consumers develop emotional and attitudinal responses (Erdem & Çakın, 2018, p. 29). Research on viewer effects suggests that narrative advertisements elicit stronger emotional responses, higher perceived hedonic value, and greater credibility compared to non-narrative counterparts, thereby shaping brand attitudes more positively (Kim, Ratneshwar, & Thorson, 2017, p. 293).

One element that has introduced a new dimension to this field is artificial intelligence. The term "artificial intelligence" was designated as the "marketing word of the year" in 2017 by the Association of National Advertisers (ANA) (Kirkpatrick & Adams, 2017). Current AI tools significantly impact both advertisement content and the broader industry.

Literature examines the relationship between AI and advertising from two primary perspectives. The first concerns the role of AI in strategic planning and performance evaluation. Here, the processing of user data to derive actionable insights represents the primary benefit. By identifying precise target audiences, selecting optimal media, and adjusting budgets in real-time, advertisements become more effective and cost-efficient (Şahin Başfırıncı & Koç, 2023, p. 128). Li (2019, p. 335) refers to these as "intelligent ads," emphasizing their importance in predicting consumer desires and offering personalized suggestions through consented data. Kietzman, Paschen, and Treen (2018, pp. 266-267) further characterize AI as a transformative tool for understanding and guiding consumer behavior.

The second perspective posits that AI is actively utilized throughout the entire production process, not merely in pre- or post-production. Shah et al. (2020, p. 19) states that machine learning techniques facilitate targeted advertising, creative content generation, and performance optimization more effectively than in previous eras. Qin and Jiang (2019) classify this impact under four main headings: "consumer insight discovery, ad creation, media planning and buying, and ad effectiveness evaluation." This framework highlights how AI-driven data informs "ad creation" by using natural language processing and deep learning to generate tailored text and visuals (Qin & Jiang, 2019, pp. 341-342).

Furthermore, since advertising relies heavily on visual production, AI can be utilized for specific scenes or entire campaigns. Tissera (2025, pp. 49-51) found that Generation Z prefers AI-produced advertisements over traditional ones. Similarly, research on deepfake applications in banking advertisements indicates that while deepfakes can create unrealistic content, they can also positively enhance the advertising narrative (Acar & İmik Tanyıldızı, 2022, pp. 93-94).

However, Masahiro Mori's concept of "The Uncanny Valley"—describing the negative emotions elicited by humanoid entities that appear "almost" human—adds a critical layer to this debate. In the context of AI-generated visuals, the illusory relationship with reality may trigger a sudden distancing or "shiver" in the perceiver if the appearance is realistic but the behavior feels "off" (Mori, MacDorman, & Kageki, 2012, p. 99). To mitigate this, practitioners can either deliberately pursue a non-human design to maintain affinity or maximize human likeness to fully bridge the valley (Zhang et al., 2020).

The AI-advertising relationship also intersects with creativity debates. Vakratsas and Wang (2021, p. 49) argue that creativity is a systematic process rather than an elite privilege, one that can be significantly bolstered by computational data. Ultimately, the future of the communication profession is envisioned as a synergy between AI technologies and human insight (Türksoy, 2022, pp. 406-407).

This integration is evident in recent industry examples. Google's "Tom the Turkey" was the first TV commercial entirely prepared with AI (Kartal, 2025). Toys"R"Us utilized OpenAI's Sora for its "Origin of Toys"R"Us" campaign (Toys"R"Us, 2024). In a socially conscious application, Sephora Italia (2023) used ChatGPT-generated scenarios to highlight violence against women. In Turkey, Tadelle's "Happy Red" and Popeyes' "Popeyes Wings Fell into the Sauce" represent pioneering AI-supported and AI-produced commercials (Tadelle, 2025; Popeyes Türkiye, 2025). Finally, Nike simulated Serena Williams' career evolution through AI in its "#Nike50" campaign (Kalum, 2025). These examples underscore that AI is becoming a foundational force in the advertising landscape.

METHODOLOGY

The objective of this study is to examine and understand the impact of artificial intelligence (AI) tools on advertising production processes and their role in transforming advertising narratives from the perspective of advertising professionals, who serve as primary producers. More specifically, the study aims to explore how advertising professionals utilize AI tools in production processes and narrative construction, evaluate the impact of these tools on the production workflow, discuss their influence on human creativity, and assess how AI transforms advertising production in terms of ideation, production, design, and narrative. In line with the objectives mentioned above, the research questions that this study aims to answer are as follows:

- How are AI tools defined and perceived by advertising professionals?
- For what purposes and with what frequency do advertising professionals utilize AI tools?
- How have AI tools influenced advertising production processes in the context of ideation, creation, production, and design?
- What kind of impact have AI tools exerted on the construction of advertising narratives?

In line with the objective of the study and to seek answers to the research questions, a phenomenological study based on qualitative research design was conducted with advertising professionals. Qualitative research, which enables access to in-depth information on a subject and facilitates a better understanding of participants' ideas, thoughts, and experiences, as McCracken (1988, p. 10) puts it, "may have the power to take the investigator into the minds and lives of the respondents, to capture them warts and all". In addition, Creswell and Creswell (2018) emphasize qualitative research focuses on exploring the diverse meanings and conceptualizations that individuals or groups attach to specific social or human issues, furthermore, it typically involves collecting data in the participants' natural setting and reaching themes through an inductive analysis. Since this study aims to explore the relationships that advertising professionals establish with AI tools and the meanings they ascribe to them, it adopts a phenomenological approach—a framework grounded in a philosophical system of ideas that focuses on the meanings of various phenomena and how individuals experience events in the world (Bhattacharya, 2008, p. 466). The phenomenological approach, according to Yin (2011, p. 17), "studies human events as they are immediately experienced in real-world settings, resisting prior categories and concepts that might distort the experiential basis for understanding the events".

Data were collected through in-depth interviews. In-depth interviews are a method in which participants are encouraged and guided to discuss the research topic in detail; the versatility of this approach has established it as one of the most widely utilized data collection techniques in qualitative research (Cook, 2008, pp. 422-423). In this study, where data was analyzed using the qualitative analysis software MAXQDA, and thematic analysis was employed to interpret the findings. Thematic analysis is widely recognized as a systematic and rigorous methodological approach for identifying and examining patterns within qualitative data (Terry et al., 2017, p. 17). According to Braun and Clarke (2006), this method provides a structured way to identify and interpret significant patterns, or themes, extracted from qualitative material.

This research received ethical clearance from the Ankara Hacı Bayram Veli University Ethics Committee (Decision dated January 21, 2026, No. 01, E-11054618-302.08.01-419050). In this study, where all participants provided informed consent, no personal data was collected, and participants voluntarily joined the research. The study's purposive sample consists of 16 advertising professionals who actively utilize AI in their creative workflows. As Willig (2008, p. 61) asserts, purposive sampling is ideal for phenomenological analysis, as it ensures a homogeneous participant group with direct experience of the specific phenomena under investigation.

FINDINGS AND ANALYSIS

An analysis of the role distributions of the 16 participants (N = 16) indicated that the sample comprised social media managers and specialists (N = 6), copywriters (N = 5), art directors (N = 3), one account executive (N = 1), and one marketing specialist (N = 1). Regarding the specific AI applications employed, ChatGPT and Gemini emerged as the most frequently utilized tools. Given that participants often used multiple tools concurrently, 11 participants reported using ChatGPT, 9 reported using Gemini, 3 each reported using Midjourney and Adobe Firefly, 2 reported using NotebookLM, and 1 reported using Envato Gen AI.

Participants' definitions of artificial intelligence tools were also examined, and a word cloud visualizing the most frequently occurring terms in their definitions is presented in Figure 1. As can be seen from the word cloud, concepts such as "assistants, tools, digital, interactive, partners, responses, communication, companions, brainstorming, generate, feedback, reciprocal, infinite, capable, creative, rapid, ability, guidance, data, user, production, learn and understand" emerged as the most prominent terms in the participants' definitions. In particular, the prominence of the concept of "assistants" within the definitions represents a noteworthy finding, as it reflects how advertising professionals conceptualize and position AI tools within their professional practices.

Figure 1. Word cloud of participants' definitions of AI

Selected excerpts from participants' definitions of AI are presented below.

"I define these tools as diligent assistants that are always accessible and tireless, yet require guidance. They possess an infinite pool of data and operate at great speed; however, if one does not know what to ask or how to process the output,

the results may remain superficial. In short, they are not authorities that take over the work, but rather skilled collaborators with whom I cooperate." (P1)

"I would describe them as digital assistants that not only provide answers but also retain context and gradually understand what I want as communication progresses, adapting accordingly." (P10)

"They are highly functional but require supervision. They are particularly flawless in operational tasks such as translation, image resizing, and data analysis. However, in areas requiring emotional intelligence, human input is still necessary." (P12)

"I define interactive AI tools as digital assistants that generate responses based on user input, develop through direction, and accompany the creative process. For copywriters, they function as a kind of rapid brainstorming partner." (P16)

"I would describe interactive AI tools as digital companions capable of rapid communication with the user. Their greatest advantage lies in their ability to adapt to the question posed. As they learn over time and better understand the user, they distinguish themselves from conventional software." (P2)

"Interactive AI tools are not merely used like search engines; rather, they enable reciprocal communication, offer ideas on various topics, assist in reviewing our work, and provide new perspectives." (P5)

"They are digital assistants capable of reciprocal communication with the user, producing instant responses based on questions, commands, or feedback." (P6)

Analysis of participants' definitions revealed several recurring themes in how AI tools are conceptualized within advertising practice. First, AI was predominantly framed as an *assistant*, emphasizing accessibility, speed, and operational efficiency. Second, participants described AI as a *collaborative partner*, highlighting its role in idea exchange and creative support. Third, AI was positioned as a *supervised tool*, indicating that although highly functional, it requires human oversight, particularly in tasks demanding emotional intelligence. In addition, AI was frequently characterized as a *brainstorming partner*, especially in copywriting and ideation processes. Participants also conceptualized AI as an *interactive system*, capable of reciprocal communication and contextual adaptation. Finally, several statements explicitly differentiated AI from traditional search engines, framing it instead as a non-search-based *interactive system* that enables dialogue rather than simple information retrieval.

When analyzing the stages of the advertising production process where AI tools are employed, three fundamental areas of application emerge. Specifically, advertising professionals utilize these tools primarily for visual design (n = 22[1]), followed by copywriting and content creation (n = 13) and video production (n = 12).

Furthermore, analysis of advertising professionals' statements revealed that the purposes underlying the use of AI tools clustered into nine distinct themes (see

Figure 2). The findings indicate that AI tools are most frequently employed for "brainstorming and idea generation" (n = 16), "draft development" (n = 15), and "research and data collection" (n = 11), rather than for purely technical components of the advertising production process.

Figure 2. Hierarchical Code-Subcodes Model of the Reasons for Using AI Tools

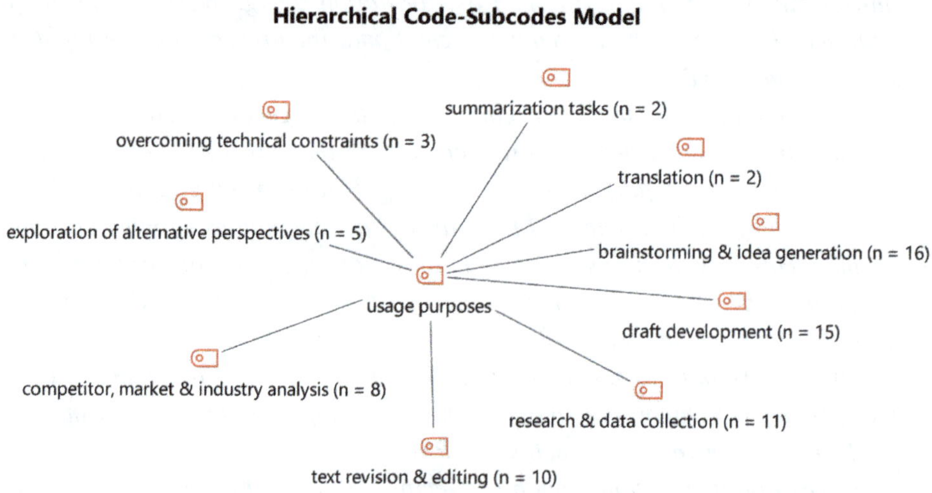

The analysis examining the advantages and disadvantages (see Figure 3) associated with the use of artificial intelligence among advertising professionals has also been reviewed. It has been understood that the primary disadvantages include artificiality (n = 10), superficiality (n = 9), copyright issues, and ethical problems (n = 12). Additionally, AI use may lead to intellectual laziness (n = 13), weaken originality and creativity (n = 35), and diminish emotional depth due to the lack of a human touch (n = 22).

Figure 3. Model Regarding the Disadvantages of AI Tools

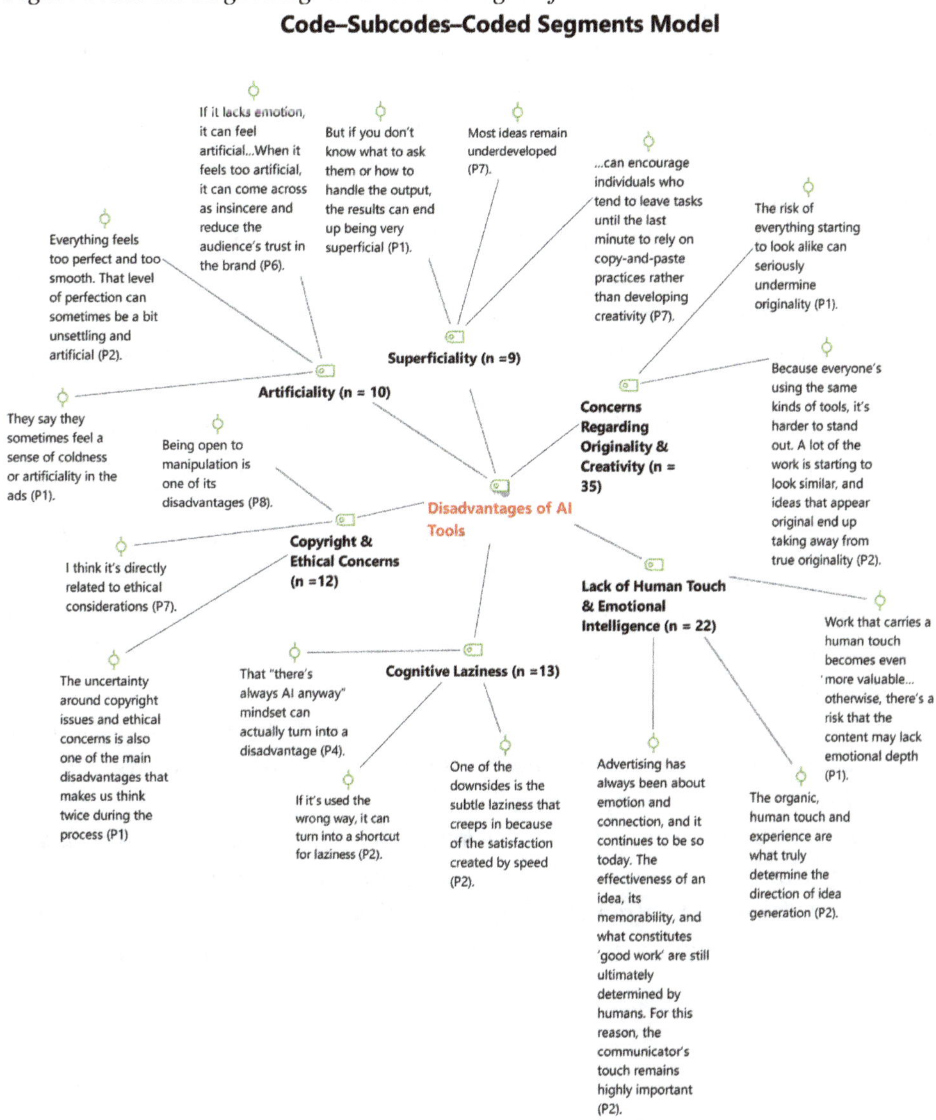

In the interviews, it was observed that the issues of originality and creativity, along with the lack of emotional depth resulting from the absence of a human touch, emerged as prominent themes. It was understood that participants made significant statements regarding these concerns. A general examination of participant responses indicates that the emphasized lack of human touch constitutes one of the fundamental reasons behind the perceived superficiality and artificiality in advertising. Accordingly, advertisements produced without substantial human involvement—constructed more mechanically through artificial intelligence tools—tend to be relatively deprived of emotional depth. This situation leads to a form of communication characterized by artificiality and superficiality. Furthermore, positioning artificial intelligence tools at the forefront of the advertising production process, while relegating human contribution to the background, results in the generation of similar types of content due to the comparable operational logic of these tools. Consequently, this contributes to the emergence of materials with diminished originality and reduced emotional narrative weight. Given that human touch plays a crucial role in the transmission of emotion and the deepening of narrative structure, the importance of the "human role" in producing more original and distinctive advertising content has been particularly emphasized in this study. The participant statements regarding the subject are presented as follows:

> *"Human touch is still indispensable in contexts requiring emotional intelligence and culturally grounded humor; otherwise, there is a risk of losing human warmth." (P12)*
>
> *"Strategic thinking and insight generation continue to be human-centered processes; otherwise, a mechanical tone becomes noticeable in the texts. Preserving an approach that places human creativity at the core is highly important." (P13)*
>
> *"Authentic originality resides in the 'unconventional' and 'imperfect' human touch that artificial intelligence cannot replicate." (P15)*
>
> *"When used excessively, it may weaken the spirit and originality of texts. If the content appears flat and emotionally detached, it conveys a distinctly artificial intelligence–generated impression." (P16)*
>
> *"I observe that these tools fall short when it comes to capturing cultural nuances, employing humor, or establishing a deep emotional connection. Therefore, although their technical functionality may be highly effective, they remain dependent on human craftsmanship in areas requiring emotional intelligence." (P1)*

Figure 4. Model Regarding the Advantages of AI Tools

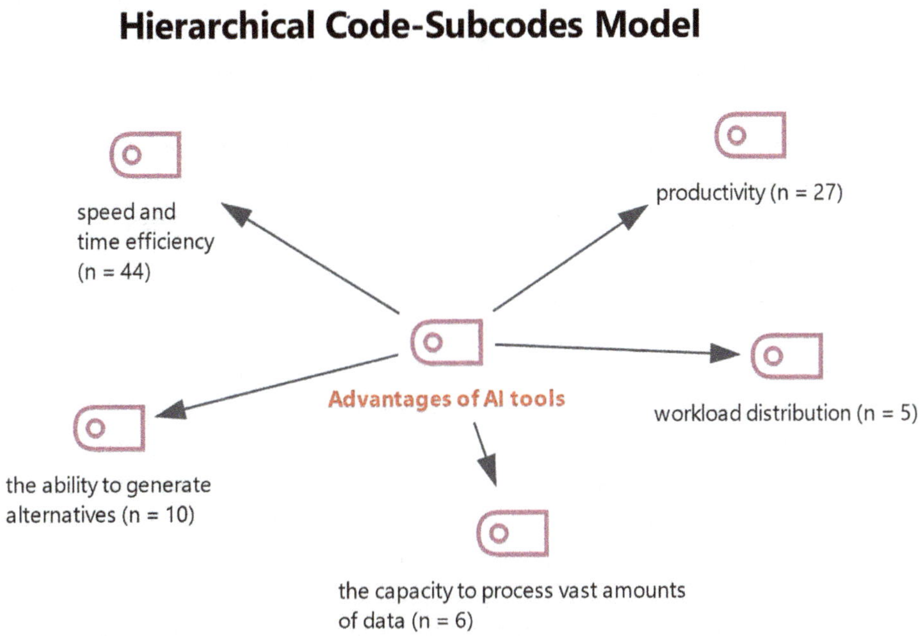

On the other hand, participants who addressed the advantages (see Figure 4) associated with the use of artificial intelligence tools explained these benefits in terms of speed and time efficiency (n = 44), productivity (n = 27), the ability to generate alternatives (n = 10), the capacity to process vast amounts of data (n = 6), and workload distribution (n = 5). Some participants expressed their views on the subject as follows:

> *"These tools enable writers and designers to experiment more boldly. I have observed that teams who treat them simply as tools to refine and enhance creative ideas produce highly successful work. Proper use means employing technology not as a spectacle, but as a way to strengthen the story." (P1)*
>
> *"They have made it much easier to overcome the operational difficulties and costs that existed in workflows without artificial intelligence." (P5)*
>
> *"AI tools allow us to complete tasks instantly. As a result, the budget allocated for that line of work often stays within the agency instead of being outsourced." (P4)*
>
> *"In terms of advantages, I would highlight speed, efficiency, rapid access to alternative ideas, and the ability to generate visuals quickly with the right prompts." (P6)*
>
> *"Faster production times create more space for thinking about content, make previously inaccessible projects feasible, and reduce costs to some extent." (P3)*

"Based on the information provided by the target audience, more strategic content can be produced, which accelerates progress toward the intended goal. It also enables visually richer and more imaginative outputs. Product promotions can be created with AI in a way that looks as if they were actually filmed, without requiring large operational budgets." (P11)

"It has eliminated the nightmare known as "writer's block" and significantly shortened the research process." (P14)

In addition to these considerations, the study also sought to understand— from the perspective of advertising professionals — how artificial intelligence tools influence advertising narratives and, consequently, the concept of creativity itself. At this point, it was observed that while evaluating the relationship between creativity and artificial intelligence, participants placed particular emphasis on the "human" factor. Nearly all participants stated that creativity cannot be meaningfully discussed in the absence of human agency, underscoring that although these tools may support creative processes, narratives tend to remain inadequate and artificial when devoid of human influence. In this respect, artificial intelligence tools are positioned as supportive assistants that enhance creativity; however, they do not surpass or replace human creativity. The word cloud (see Figure 5) generated from participants' statements is significant in that it highlights the most frequently used terms. As reflected in the visualization, concepts such as "human, creativity, originality, believe, intelligence," and "touch" emerge prominently, with "human" standing out as the most recurrent term. The participants' statements further provide more detailed insights into this issue.

"Creativity is no longer really about creating something completely from scratch. It's becoming more about taking what AI produces and reshaping or differentiating it properly. I think originality will rise in the hands of those who can take the average output AI gives and add human spirit and intelligence on top of it." (P1)

"AI represents the average. If you rely on it alone, your work will also be "average." Originality and creativity will stay with the writer who can look at the AI's answer and say, "No, this is too ordinary," and then take it one step further." (P14)

"I think it's an area that can really push the limits of creativity. For someone who knows how to use it well, it can actually trigger creativity. When it becomes more of an exchange of ideas, it brings in different perspectives, and that supports creativity." (P4)

"But at the end of the day, there has to be a human touch. If I had to give it a percentage, I'd say the best formula for creativity would be around 40% AI and 60% human touch." (P5)

"I don't think AI tools directly reduce creativity. On the contrary, when used properly, they speed up idea generation and offer different perspectives. Origi-

nality is still shaped by a person's point of view and interpretation, and I think AI simply supports that process." (P6)

Figure 5. Word cloud of participants' definitions of creativity

At this point, the significance of the "human" element in advertising narratives became particularly prominent. In connection with this emphasis, the study also raised the question of whether audiences would be able to distinguish advertisements produced with the support of artificial intelligence (see Figure 6). Within this context, evaluations concerning the distinguishability of AI-supported advertising narratives once again highlighted concerns related to artificiality among advertising professionals. However, it was observed that no full consensus was reached among participants on this issue. Accordingly, more than half of the participants stated that audiences would not be able to discern the use of artificial intelligence in advertisements.

Figure 6. Awareness Model of the Use of Artificial Intelligence Tools in Advertising

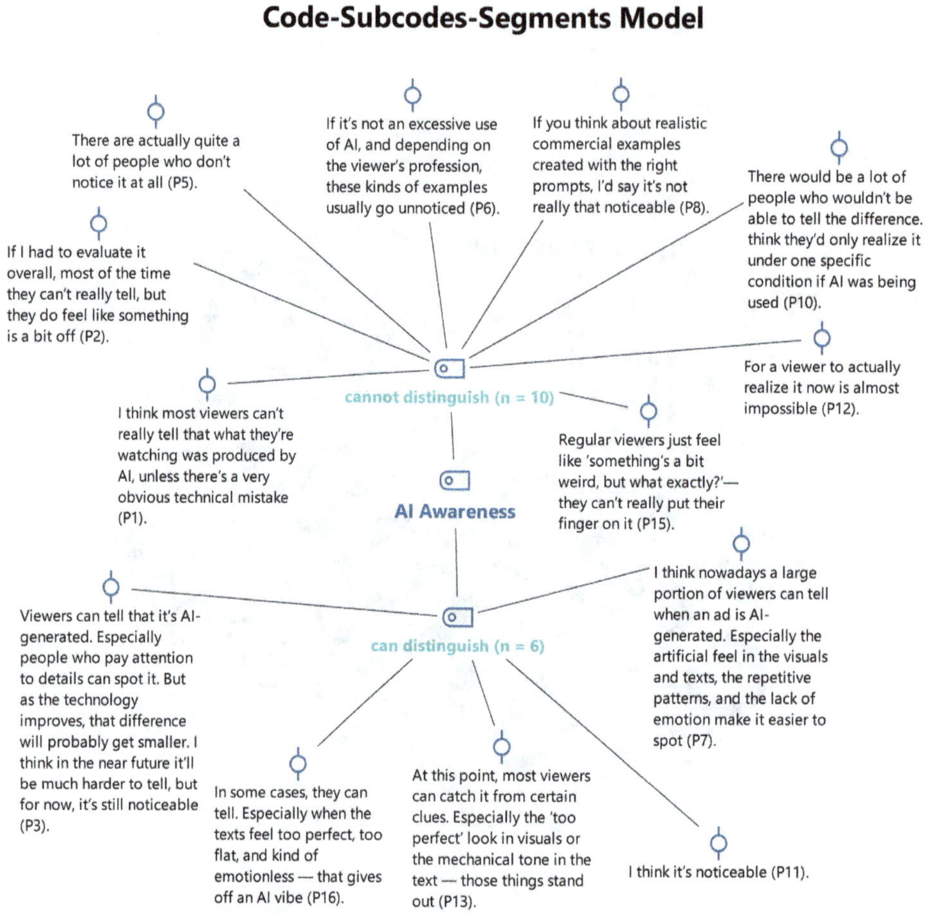

Finally, the study also examined the potential future impact of artificial intelligence on the advertising sector from the perspective of advertising professionals, and distinct themes were identified based on participants' statements. The primary emphasis among participants was that "artificial intelligence will not eliminate the sector, but rather transform it." Consistent with previous findings, references to the human factor once again emerged prominently. Within this anticipated transformation, artificial intelligence is positioned as an instrumental tool, whereas the human agent remains at the center of the creative process. Nearly all participants converged on the view that the "core of the creative process must remain human." In this context of transformation, participants generally highlighted that professional roles will evolve, routine tasks will increasingly be delegated to AI tools, while strategic thinking and empathy will continue to reside with human practitioners. Moreover, it was emphasized that those who successfully adapt to this transformation will be the ones who ultimately thrive within the sector. The participants' statements on this issue are as follows:

"I think the services AI provides will definitely continue to improve. The outcomes, when combined with human ideas, will offer us a different kind of reality. In terms of employment, I believe some professions in the sector will face serious challenges. Many companies will probably downsize and start aiming for more effective results with fewer people and lower costs — and honestly, we're already starting to see signs of that today." (P11)

"It's very clear that AI will become a permanent tool in advertising and communication. However, I believe these tools should be positioned as supportive elements, not at the center of the creative process." (P7)

"I don't believe AI will completely take over production. Wherever there are humans, there will always be room for romance and originality. I don't think that kind of depth can be achieved by AI." (P8)

"Brands and agencies that pay attention to ethical use and transparency toward audiences will be perceived as more trustworthy and stronger in the future. The competitive advantage will belong to teams that manage AI properly and balance it with human creativity." (P6)

"I don't agree with the claims that AI will destroy the sector. I believe it will move industry forward and make things easier for writers, graphic designers, and video producers. In the end, AI cannot produce something meaningful on its own without humans. What feeds it, directs it, and makes it valuable is human imagination. As long as people imagine, question, and assign meaning, quality work will continue to emerge." (P10)

"No matter how advanced AI becomes, the core of advertising — the ability to find insight — belongs entirely to humans. A machine can analyze data, but it cannot feel longing, jealousy, or joy the way a human does, and it cannot build a story from those emotions. As advertisers, we should embrace technology, but we must never forget that the heart of our work is human emotion. The future will belong not to those who oppose AI, but to those who work with it best. AI will become an indispensable operating system in advertising, but that doesn't mean it will take our jobs. Copywriters and designers will evolve into more editor- or creative director-like roles, managing AI rather than competing with it. Routine and boring tasks will be handed over to AI, while we focus on strategy, empathy, and human psychology." (P1)

"As a copywriter, I think AI should be seen as a tool, and creative decisions should remain with humans. Rather than taking copywriters' jobs away, I believe it will push them toward more strategic and creative thinking. Humans will generate the creative idea, and AI will serve as a supporting tool." (P16)

"I think we're about to see something similar to what happened when scribes protested after the invention of the printing press. We're already seeing calls to limit or even ban AI use. In my opinion, yes, AI will inevitably cause some people in the sector to lose their jobs. But just like in the past, it wasn't those who resisted the printing press who survived, but those who adapted to it. The same will happen here. Those who complain that AI is taking their jobs may struggle, but those who adapt to change and improve themselves by learning how to write the right prompts will move ahead." (P5)

"Designers who only know how to use software will struggle much more; those who know how to imagine will grow significantly." (P15)

"We often hear claims that AI will end the advertising industry. But at its core, advertising is about communication. And communication means saying the right thing in the right way — creating emotional impact. Yes, AI will continue to improve, but it will never be enough on its own. That's why those who survive in the future will be the real communicators who position AI as a tool, not as the goal." (P2)

"As AI develops, I think the sector's ability to adapt will also improve. I don't have the perception that AI will take our jobs." (P9)

As can be understood from the participants' statements, artificial intelligence tools are perceived less as a threat and more as instruments of transformation. At the same time, participants demonstrate a strong belief that the creative essence remains inherently human. The most significant risk they identify is the standardization problem, while the greatest opportunity lies in the empowerment of practitioners who can use these tools effectively. Although participants clearly emphasize that artificial intelligence will not eliminate the sector, they also acknowledge that one possible outcome of this transformation may be a partial sectoral contraction. Nevertheless, it is underscored that sustaining a presence within the sector will ultimately depend on the ability to integrate these tools with human creativity in an original and meaningful manner.

CONCLUSION

The findings of this study reveal that artificial intelligence tools are predominantly conceptualized by advertising professionals not as autonomous creators, but as supportive instruments embedded within human-centered creative processes.

AI is positioned as an assistant, collaborator, and operational facilitator rather than as a replacement for human agency. This framing is particularly significant, as it challenges narratives that portray AI as an existential threat to creative industries. Instead, participants articulate a model of augmented creativity, in which artificial intelligence functions as an enabling infrastructure that enhances efficiency while leaving the core of ideation, insight generation, and emotional narrative construction firmly in human hands.

One of the most striking findings concerns the emphasis placed on the "human touch." Participants repeatedly highlighted emotional depth, cultural nuance, strategic insight, and interpretive capacity as irreducibly human qualities. In this context, the perceived risk of artificiality and superficiality stems not from the use of AI per se, but from its excessive or uncritical application. When AI-generated content lacks human refinement, it tends to appear standardized, emotionally detached, and aesthetically homogenized. Similarly, Demsar et al. (2025) drew attention to the human touch and creativity in their study, and the findings from interviews with senior advertising executives showed that artificial intelligence does not completely replace human creativity in advertising, but rather transforms the nature of the creative process, and that humans remain at the center of creativity.

The study also shows that AI tools are significantly transforming workflow structures. Speed, efficiency, cost reduction, and the elimination of operational bottlenecks were identified as major advantages. These findings align with broader discussions of technological transformation where automation is restructuring the workforce without completely eliminating human roles. Participants' narratives consistently reflect a shift from application-oriented roles to more strategic, supervisory, and editorial positions. While routine and repetitive tasks are increasingly being delegated to AI systems, strategic thinking, empathy, and narrative creation remain human-centered, which is consistent with the emphasis on the "human touch." This workforce redistribution indicates a restructuring, not the disappearance, of creative professions. This finding is consistent with the results reported by Bir and Aksu (2024), who examined the mechanisms underlying the adoption and acceptance of artificial intelligence in the advertising sector. According to their study, advertising professionals do not express significant concerns about job loss due to artificial intelligence. Rather, their confidence stems from the belief that AI can achieve its highest level of effectiveness only when operating in collaboration with human intelligence. In this respect, the present study's findings demonstrate clear parallelism, particularly in their shared emphasis on the centrality of the human element.

Nevertheless, participants acknowledged the possibility of partial sectoral contraction, citing downsizing, cost optimization, and the displacement of certain roles as potential consequences of technological integration. However, these concerns were framed within a broader narrative of adaptation rather than decline. Consequently, sustainability within the sector thus appears contingent upon the ability to orchestrate a balanced integration of algorithmic efficiency and human creativity. The findings presented thus far are consistent with several results reported by Weila, Martin, and Ruizhi (2025). According to their study, artificial intelligence in advertising agencies is positioned not as a replacement for human actors but as a co-creative partner. AI contributes to faster draft production, reduced operational bottlenecks, shorter delivery timelines, and lower costs, thereby reshaping internal agency workflows. However, the study also emphasizes that the use of artificial intelligence in advertising carries risks of standardization and superficiality, particularly due to the increasing similarity of content outputs. Furthermore, it underscores that the effective utilization of AI ultimately depends on human guidance and oversight.

Regarding audience perception, the study found no consensus among participants regarding the distinguishability of AI-generated advertisements. While some professionals believe artificiality is still detectable – especially in emotionally subdued or mechanically structured content – others argue that technological advancements will make such distinctions increasingly difficult. This ambiguity further strengthens the study's central argument: the determining factor is not solely the presence of AI, but the degree of human involvement in shaping narrative authenticity.

Overall, this research contributes to ongoing debates surrounding artificial intelligence and creative production by demonstrating that advertising professionals conceptualize AI as a transformative but subordinate force within creative ecosystems. Rather than embracing narratives of technological replacement, participants articulate a model of hybrid creativity in which human agency retains epistemological and emotional primacy. The study thus challenges reductionist views of automation in cultural industries and instead foregrounds the co-constitutive relationship between human imagination and algorithmic assistance.

Several limitations should be acknowledged. The study is based on a purposive sample of 16 advertising professionals, which limits generalizability. Future research could expand the sample size, incorporate cross-cultural comparisons, or examine audience responses empirically to better understand perceptual differences regarding AI-generated content.

In conclusion, the findings indicate that artificial intelligence is reshaping advertising production processes, accelerating workflows, and redefining professional roles. However, it is not perceived as displacing the human core of creativity. Instead, AI emerges as an infrastructural layer within a fundamentally human-centered creative paradigm. The sustainability of advertising practice in the age of artificial intelligence will depend on maintaining this balance — integrating technological efficiency with human insight, emotional intelligence, and cultural sensitivity.

FUTURE RESEARCH DIRECTIONS

While this study provides valuable insight into how advertising professionals conceptualize the role of artificial intelligence within creative processes, several avenues remain open for further investigation. First, future research could expand the sample size and incorporate cross-cultural comparisons to examine whether perceptions of AI-assisted creativity vary across different national advertising ecosystems. Given that technological adoption and creative norms differ globally, comparative studies may reveal culturally specific attitudes toward human–AI collaboration.

Second, quantitative research designs could complement these qualitative findings by measuring correlations between AI usage intensity and perceived creativity, job security, or narrative originality. Experimental studies may also investigate audience responses to AI-generated versus human-refined advertising narratives, particularly in relation to emotional engagement, trust, and perceived authenticity. Third, longitudinal studies would be particularly valuable in assessing how professional roles evolve over time. As AI tools continue to develop, future research could explore whether the predicted shift toward strategic and supervisory roles materializes and how this transformation impacts professional identity within the sector. Finally, further inquiry into ethical considerations—such as transparency in AI usage, disclosure practices, authorship attribution, and algorithmic bias—would deepen understanding of the normative frameworks shaping AI integration in advertising.

REFERENCES

Abbass, H. (2021). What is Artificial Intelligence? *IEEE Transactions on Artificial Intelligence*, *2*(2), 94–95. DOI: 10.1109/TAI.2021.3096243

Acar, H. M., & İmik Tanyıldızı, N. (2022). Reklamda yapay zekâ kullanımı: Ziraat Bankası #Senhepgülümse reklam filminde deepfake uygulamasının görsel anlatıya etkisi. *Kastamonu İletişim Araştırmaları Dergisi, 8*, 78–99.

Anderson, K., Roggeman, A., & Fuller, J. (2024). *Artificial intelligence and film: A journey in public perception from 1960 to the present day*. Celebrating Scholarship and Creativity Day.

Arslan, K. (2020). Eğitimde yapay zeka ve uygulamaları. *Batı Anadolu Eğitim Bilimleri Dergisi, 11*(1), 71–88.

Bhattacharya, H. (2008). Interpretive Research. In Given, L. M. (Ed.), *The Sage Encyclopedia of Qualitative Research Methods* (pp. 464–467). Sage.

Bir, G., & Aksu, S. (2024). An examination of the utilization of artificial intelligence technologies by advertising agencies. *Yeni Medya, 16*, 19–37. DOI: 10.55609/yenimedya.1434419

Braun, V., & Clarke, V. (2006). Using thematic analysis in psychology. *Qualitative Research in Psychology*, *3*(2), 77–101. DOI: 10.1191/1478088706qp063oa

Cook, K. E. (2008). In-Depth Interview. In Given, L. M. (Ed.), *The Sage Encyclopedia of Qualitative Research Methods* (pp. 422–423). Sage.

Creswell, J. W., & Creswell, J. D. (2018). Research design qualitative, quantitative, and mixed methods approaches. *Sage (Atlanta, Ga.)*.

Demsar, V., Ferraro, C., Sands, S., & Kohn, A. (2025). Harmony or discord? The intersection of generative AI and human creativity in advertising. *Journal of Advertising Research*, *65*(2), 150–166. DOI: 10.1080/00218499.2025.2464305

Elden, M. (2018). *Reklam yazarlığı*. İletişim.

Erdem, M., & Çakın, Ö. (2018). *Anlatısal reklamda negatif marka yerleştirme: anti-reklamoyunlar. Uluslararası İletişimde Yeni Yönelimler Konferansı Eğlence ve Ürün Yerleştirme*. İstanbul Ticaret Üniversitesi.

Ertel, W. (2025). *Introduction to artificial intelligence*. Springer. DOI: 10.1007/978-3-658-43102-0

Fjelland, R. (2020). Why general artificial intelligence will not be realized. *Humanities & Social Sciences Communications*, *7*(10), 1–9. DOI: 10.1057/s41599-020-0494-4

Gil de Zúñiga, H., Gonayes, H., & Duroyote, T. (2024). A scholarly definition of artificial intelligence (AI): Advancing AI as a conceptual framework in communication research. *Political Communication*, *41*(2), 317–334. DOI: 10.1080/10584609.2023.2290497

Grzybowski, A., Pawlikowska-Łagód, K., & Lambert, W. C. (2024). A history of artificial intelligence. *Clinics in Dermatology*, *42*(3), 221–229. DOI: 10.1016/j.clindermatol.2023.12.016 PMID: 38185196

Haymond, S., & McCudden, C. (2021). Rise of the machines: Artificial intelligence and the clinical laboratory. *The Journal of Applied Laboratory Medicine*, *6*(6), 1640–1654. DOI: 10.1093/jalm/jfab075 PMID: 34379752

Hunt, K. M. (2023). Could artificial intelligence win the next Weather Photographer of the Year competition? *Weather*, *78*(4), 108–112. DOI: 10.1002/wea.4348

Jahn, M. (2020). *Anlatıbilim anlatı teorisi el kitabı*. Dergah.

Kalum. (2025, October 2). *13 Brands Using AI for Social Media Marketing, Advertising & Content Creation*. Metricool. https://metricool.com/brands-using-ai-social-media-marketing/?utm_source=chatgpt.com

Kaplan, A., & Haenlein, M. (2019). Siri, Siri, in my hand: Who's the fairest in the land? On the interpretations, illustrations, and implications of artificial intelligence. *Business Horizons*, *62*(1), 15–25. DOI: 10.1016/j.bushor.2018.08.004

Kartal, B. (2025, November 03). *Google, Tamamen Yapay Zeka ile Oluşturulan İlk Reklam Filmini Yayınladı [Video]*. Webtekno. https://www.webtekno.com/google-yapay-zeka-ilk-reklam-filmi-video-h206121.html

Kerr, G., & Richards, J. (2021). Redefining advertising in research and practice. *International Journal of Advertising*, *40*(2), 175–198. DOI: 10.1080/02650487.2020.1769407

Kietzmann, J., Paschen, J., & Treen, E. (2018). Artificial intelligence in advertising: How marketers can leverage artificial intelligence along the consumer journey. *Journal of Advertising Research*, *58*(3), 263–267. DOI: 10.2501/JAR-2018-035

Kim, E., Ratneshwar, S., & Thorson, E. (2017). Why narrative ads work: An integrated process explanation. *Journal of Advertising*, *46*(2), 283–296. DOI: 10.1080/00913367.2016.1268984

Kirkpatrick, D., & Adams, P. (2017, December 7). ANA Declares AI The Marketing Word of the Year. MarketingDive. https://www.marketingdive.com/news/ana-declares-ai-the-marketing-word-of-the-year/512484/

Li, H. (2019). Special section introduction: Artificial intelligence and advertising. *Journal of Advertising*, *48*(4), 333–337. DOI: 10.1080/00913367.2019.1654947

Lin, Z., Pathak, D., Li, J., Xia, X., Neubig, G., Zhang, P., & Ramanan, D. (2024). Evaluating Text-to-Visual Generation with Image-to-Text Generation. *European Conference on Computer Vision* (pp. 366-384). Springer.

McCracken, G. (1988). The Long Interview. *Sage (Atlanta, Ga.).*

Mori, M., MacDorman, K. F., & Kageki, N. (2012). The Uncanny Valley [From the Field]. *IEEE Robotics & Automation Magazine*, *19*(2), 98–100. DOI: 10.1109/MRA.2012.2192811

Mutlu, E. (2017). *İletişim sözlüğü*. Ütopya Yayınevi.

Oppenlaender, J. (2022, November 16-18). *The Creativity of Text-to-Image Generation* [Conference Presentation]. Academic Mindtrek '22: Proceedings of the 25th International Academic Mindtrek Conference, Jyväskylä, Finland.

Popeyes Türkiye. (2025, May 8). *Popeyes® Kanatları Sosa Düştü!* [Video]. YouTube. https://www.youtube.com/watch?v=PhWlrSPlIcg&t=14s

Qin, X., & Jiang, Z. (2019). The impact of AI on the advertising process: The Chinese experience. *Journal of Advertising*, *48*(4), 338–346. DOI: 10.1080/00913367.2019.1652122

Şahin Başfırıncı, Ç., & Koç, N. (2023). İletişim alanındaki mesleklerde yapay zekâ uygulamaları: Mevcut durum analizi ve alan yazın taraması. *Karadeniz İletişim Araştırmaları Dergisi*, 121-148.

Sephora Italia. (2023, November 28). *mAI colpevoli – Home* [Video]. Youtube. https://www.youtube.com/watch?v=ozO6vqgaRWU&t=39s

Serttaş Ertike, A., & Yılmaz, R. (2011). *Reklamcılığın anahtar kavramları*. Kitabevi Yayınları.

Shah, N., Engineer, S., Bhagat, N., Chauhan, H., & Shah, M. (2020). Research trends on the usage of machine learning and artificial intelligence in advertising. *Augmented Human Research*, *5*(19), 5–19. DOI: 10.1007/s41133-020-00038-8

Sheikh, H., Prims, C., & Schrijvers, E. (2023). Artificial intelligence: Definition and background. *Mission AI*, 15-41.

Singh, S. K., Kumar, S., & Mehra, P. S. (2023). Chat GPT & Google Bard AI: A Review. 2023 International Conference on IoT (pp. 1-6). Gorakhpur, India: Communication and Automation Technology (ICICAT).

Sivri, O. (2024). Yapay zekâ çerçevesindc görscl sanatların geleceği. *İnsanat. Sanat Tasarım ve Mimarlık Araştırmaları Dergisi*, *4*(1), 322–344.

Tadelle. (2025, May 30). *Mutluluk, lezzet ve Tadelle; Onun adı MUTLU KIRMIZI, Onun adı TADELLE* [Video]. Youtube. https://www.youtube.com/watch?v=YbcLD939Q2A

Terry, G., Hayfield, N., Clarke, V., & Braun, V. (2017). Thematic Analysis. In Willig, C., & Rogers, W. S. (Eds.), *The Sage Handbook of Qualitative Research in Psychology* (pp. 17–37). Sage. DOI: 10.4135/9781526405555.n2

Tissera, W. (2025). The Future of Generative Artificial Intelligence in Visual-based Digital Marketing [Undergraduate Dissertation]. Jyaskylan Ammattikorkeakoulu University.

Toys"R"Us. (2024, June 21). *The Origin of Toys"R"Us: Brand Film Teaser | Toys"R"Us* [Video]. Youtube. https://www.youtube.com/watch?v=F_WfIzYGlg4

Türksoy, N. (2022). The Future of Public Relations, Advertising and Journalism: How Artificial Intelligence May Transform the Communication Profession and Why Society Should Care? *Türkiye İletişim Araştırmaları Dergisi*, (40), 394–410. DOI: 10.17829/turcom.1050491

Türten, B. (2024). Yapay zekâ ve sinema: Film yapımında olanaklar ve fırsatlar. *Anadolu ve Balkan Araştırmaları Dergisi*, *7*(14), 399–425. DOI: 10.32953/abad.1539736

Vakratsas, D., & Wang, X. S. (2021). Artificial intelligence in advertising creativity. *Journal of Advertising*, *50*(1), 39–51. DOI: 10.1080/00913367.2020.1843090

Wang, P. (2019). On defining artificial intelligence. *Journal of Artificial General Intelligence*, *10*(2), 1–37. DOI: 10.2478/jagi-2019-0002

Weila, C., Martin, J. L., & Ruizhi, Y. (2025). Exploring the integration of generative AI in advertising agencies: A co-creative process model for human–AI collaboration. *Journal of Advertising Research*, *65*(2), 167–189. DOI: 10.1080/00218499.2024.2445362

Wildenhain, M. (2025). *Yapay zekanın kısa tarihi*. Düşbaz Kitaplar.

Willig, C. (2008). *Introducing qualitative research in psychology*. McGraw-Hill.

Yin, R. K. (2011). *Qualitative research from start to finish*. The Guilford Press.

Zhang, J., Li, S., Zhang, J. Y., Du, F., Qi, Y., & Liu, X. (2020). A Literature Review of the Research on the Uncanny Valley. In Rau, P. L. (Ed.), Lecture Notes in Computer Science: Vol. 12192. *Cross-Cultural Design. User Experience of Products, Services, and Intelligent Environments. HCII 2020*. Springer. DOI: 10.1007/978-3-030-49788-0_19

ADDITIONAL READING

Chuan, C. H., Tsai, W. H. S., & Yang, J. (2023). Artificial intelligence, advertising, and society. *Advertising & Society Quarterly, 24*(3).

El-aasy, H. A. (2023). Employing artificial intelligence (AI) technology in advertising design on social media. *Journal of Design Sciences and Applied Arts, 4*(2), 247–263. DOI: 10.21608/jdsaa.2023.194906.1260

Ezzat, R. (2024). Enhance the advertising effectiveness by using artificial intelligence (AI). *Journal of Art. Design and Music, 3*(1), 1.

Katyal, S. K. (2019). Artificial intelligence, advertising, and disinformation. *Advertising & Society Quarterly, 20*(4).

KEY TERMS AND DEFINITIONS

Advertising Narrative: The structured construction of meaning, emotion, and persuasion within advertising messages through storytelling techniques, symbolic framing, and audience-oriented communication strategies.

Artificial Intelligence: A computational system capable of processing data, identifying patterns, and generating outputs that simulate cognitive functions traditionally associated with human intelligence, particularly within creative and decision-making processes.

Creativity: The capacity to generate novel, meaningful, and contextually relevant ideas through interpretation, imagination, and strategic synthesis rather than through mere replication of existing patterns.

Human Touch: The uniquely human contribution to creative work characterized by emotional depth, contextual sensitivity, ethical judgment, and the ability to interpret complex social meanings.

ENDNOTE

1 The n values indicate the number of references made to each category during the interviews. As these figures represent the cumulative frequency of mentions across all participants rather than the number of individuals, they may exceed the total sample size (N = 16).

Chapter 7

Impact of AI-Driven Narrative Marketing Strategies on the Consumer Decision-Making Process

Farheen Zaki Sayyad
http://orcid.org/0009-0009-1020-6153
Aljamea-tus-Saifiyah Business School, Marol, India

Aafreen Shaikh
http://orcid.org/0009-0009-0086-2616
Sheth T.J. Education Society's, Sheth NKTT College of Commerce and Sheth JTT College of Arts, India

Yogeshwari Patil
http://orcid.org/0009-0005-7734-9897
Sheth T.J. Education Society's, Sheth NKTT College of Commerce and Sheth JTT College of Arts, India

ABSTRACT

This study investigates the impact of AI-driven narrative marketing strategies on the consumer decision-making process. As marketing communication increasingly becomes mediated by intelligent systems, algorithmically generated and personalized narratives are reshaping how consumers perceive, evaluate, and choose products. Drawing on consumer decision-making theory and narrative persuasion, the study proposes a conceptual framework linking AI-driven narrative marketing to the five stages of the decision journey: need recognition, information search, evaluation of

DOI: 10.4018/979-8-3373-5666-2.ch007

alternatives, purchase decision, and post-purchase evaluation. Data were collected from digitally active consumers and analyzed using Structural Equation Modeling (SEM). The findings reveal that AI-driven narratives exert a significant positive influence across all stages of decision-making, with the strongest effects observed during the evaluation of alternatives and purchase decision stages.

INTRODUCTION

Background and Context

Marketing communication has evolved in many ways within the last three decades. This has been owing to advancement in computer technology, data analysis and to a more recent advancements such as artificial intelligence. The initial digital marketing used to be primarily tool-based. The main internet activities that firms employed were to create an online presence, spread advertisement messages via email and banner advertising. This will assist them to reach further than the traditional mass media constraints (Kotler and Keller, 2016). These advances enhanced effectiveness and magnitude but the promotional communications at this time were mostly standardized and firm-focused. The communication flows were providing only a limited responsiveness to the individual consumer behavior, which made them more and more out of touch with the rising heterogeneity of consumer preferences. This was a shortcoming that marked the onset of data-driven marketing.

The use of customer relationship management tools and web analytics marked the start of using behavioral data to divide consumers and develop products and services to them (Wedel and Kannan, 2016). The process of decision-making became much more data-focused with the previous data serving. This helps to forecast the future behavior and maximize the communication strategy. The firm no longer employed mass communications. Only statistically optimized communication strategies were employed in order to enhance relevance and efficiency. Nevertheless, even with these advancements, data-driven marketing remained a standardized content or rule-based personalization. Adaptation was yet to be developed and was not always sensitive to situational context and evolving consumer expectations.

The other major change in marketing communication is the growth of Artificial Intelligence. This is not merely with regards to degree but also with regard to kind. AI systems mostly transcend data-driven marketing. This is achieved through permitting ongoing learning by the interactions with the consumer and real time adjustment of messages. The marketing communication is increasingly proactive and responsive as the systems that predict and respond to the consumer needs instead of responding to the previous action. The trend has seen a significant change in retrospective analysis to anticipatory marketing communication. This has transformed the way corporations consider, strategize and implement their marketing communication messages and position the AI as a major component in the marketing ecosystem. At the same time the growing significance of storytelling has caused a significant change of the process of creating and receiving the marketing messages.

Narrative marketing has become a new genre in online marketing. This has brought the significance of employing storytelling to create a meaning, provoke emotions and a bond between the consumer and the brand. Consumer psychology research has determined narrative formats to be more engaging, create more meaningful brand relationships and encourage repeat behavior. This will assist in contextualizing the marketing messages in a way that is emotionally appealing. Traditionally these stories were structured and conveyed to the target audiences in a consistent way by organizations. However, nowadays, in the digital environment the consumer behavior is also becoming a factor in the narrative-building process. The AI technology enables the marketer to incorporate the behavior, tastes, and expressions of consumers into tailored stories. AI-driven narratives are radically different to the traditional narratives both in their form and effect. With the help of the recommender systems AI creates micro-narratives that put the consumer in the center of an unfolding story. This is affected by the historical information, contextual hints and the immediate interaction (Tucker, 2014). These narratives are not static representations but dynamic sequences that adjust as consumers move across digital platforms. As a result, marketing communication increasingly resembles an ongoing dialogue rather than a one-directional persuasive effort. This shift has important implications for how influence operates in digital environments.

This is done to guide the consumer attention and choice (Yeung, 2017). The narrative formats that come out in such systems become very influential. Individual stories employ persuasive factors to encode the information in meaningful situations. This guides interpretation and decision making without necessarily applying the open arm-twisting influence. By introducing the strategic organization of information experience, the AI-Driven narratives redefine the circumstances in which the consumer decision is formed. This makes the narratives a key element in AI-driven marketing. This allows the decoding of complex, data-driven suggestions in a rational and appealing consumer experience. AI-driven stories do not aim at conveying individual product attributes or advertising messages. Instead in consists of collecting information and putting it together into a unified narrative that is aligned with the identity of the consumer, objectives and situational circumstances. This correspondence raises the chances of marketing messages affecting several stages of the consumer decision process. To conclude the digital marketing to data-driven marketing to AI-Driven marketing is a paradigm shift in marketing communication. This demonstrates how the intelligent systems have changed the way marketing is carried out through transmission to narrative marketing. At the same time, the influence of AI-driven narrative marketing is neither uniform nor unproblematic.

The success of AI depends on the variables like trust of consumers in AI-driven systems, openness of AI-Driven communication and the level of comfort that consumers have with the data-driven narrative personalization. In case data-driven narratives are considered as opaque, invasive or manipulative, it may actually act against consumer autonomy, trigger resistance or decrease brand trust instead of establishing trust. Ethicalities of data utilization, disclosure and boundary between persuasion and manipulation are therefore a crucial component of the narrative marketing puzzle in AI-driven systems. The full examination of AI-driven narrative marketing must take into account not only the persuasive power of AI-based products but also the context and ethical parameters under which AI-driven narrative marketing influences consumer decisions.

Gaps in the Existing Literatures

Over the past few years, there has been an expanding literature on the marketing field that is looking at the prospects of artificial intelligence in helping to improve marketing communications and facilitate strategic decision-making. Much of this research, however, remains fragmented. The research that is available is inclined to analyze particular elements of marketing communication, e.g. creative advertising, personalization, or consumer reactions, out of context instead of as linked parts of a more significant decision-making process. This has led to the cumulative knowledge produced over these streams not being fully incorporated and this constrained our knowledge of how AI-driven communication works in a holistic manner.

A single current of study is dedicated to AI-driven personalization and its implications in terms of consumer engagement and reaction. Empirical evidence has been consistent in indicating that algorithmically personalized content has been shown to increase the rate of click-throughs, likelihood of purchase, and perceived usefulness and confidence by matching messages to personal preferences. Regardless of these contributions, the concept of personalization in this literature views it as an informational or functional addition. The narrative structure in which the personalized content is presented, how messages are framed as stories that make them interpreted and have a meaning, has been only marginally empirically studied. Personalization is therefore considered to be an optimization technique and not a convincing narrative procedure.

The second, more developed line of research is the research which focuses on the consumer decision-making process itself. Classical and modern models view decision-making as a process and consist of several steps such as need recognition, information search, evaluating the alternatives, purchase decision and post purchase evaluation (Blackwell, Miniard, and Engel, 2006; Solomon, 2018). Although this framework still holds power, a significant portion of the empirical work in this field still focuses on the conventional marketing inputs and fixed stimuli. Digital developments have been seldom accompanied by a corresponding development of adaptive, AI mediated communication into process-based decision models, which creates a disconnect between the way decisions are theorized and the actual functioning of marketing communication in modern settings.

A third stream of research examines narrative advertising and storytelling as a form of persuasion. The mentioned literature proves that narratives can impact consumer attitudes, feelings, and brand associations through the establishment of narrative transportation and decreased resistance to persuasive purpose (Escalas, 2008; Van Laer et al., 2014). Although narrative persuasion is not new, empirical studies have mostly been done on human-created narratives presented by traditional or online media. The contribution of AI-driven or AI-edited narratives, in particular, those that change dynamically based on consumer data and context, is understudied.

Though there are some theoretical contributions that have come to recognize the fact that AI systems can be used in facilitating persuasion and influencing consumer decision-making, the empirical evidence is very sparse and narrow. The available literature usually focuses on individual results like product attitude, brand trust, engagement, or buying intention. What is missing is an integrative empirical perspective that explains how AI-driven narrative marketing influences multiple stages of the consumer decision-making process simultaneously. Lack of such integration limits theoretical advancement and managerial practice since it is not clear where and how AI-driven narratives have the greatest impact throughout the decision process.

This gap in the literature brings out a research gap. The proposal is to have an extensive model that reflects the process-based effects of AI-driven narrative marketing on all levels of consumer decision-making. To fill this gap, it is necessary to leave the analysis of single outcomes and go to a comprehensive approach that combines personalization, narrative persuasion, and decision-process theory. The current chapter addresses this gap straight away by empirically investigating the impact of AI-driven narratives across every phase of the consumer decision-making process on the basis of Structural Equation Modeling, and provides methodologically rigorous evidence to the growing body of literature on AI-driven marketing communication.

Objectives of the Chapter

The key focus of this chapter, therefore is the analysis of the effects of AI-driven narrative marketing strategies on consumer buying behavior along the five-stage consumer decision-making process. As marketing communication rapidly becomes mediated by intelligent systems, there is a growing need to understand not only whether AI-driven narratives are effective, but also how and at which stages of the decision journey they exert influence. The current chapter addresses this need by integrating the positions of consumer decision-making theory, narrative persuasion, and AI-driven marketing communication.

The chapter has pursued the following specific objectives:

- To assess the eventual impact of AI-driven narrative marketing strategies on each stage of the consumer decision-making process, namely need recognition, information search, evaluation of alternatives, purchase decision and post-purchase evaluation.
- To develop and empirically test a conceptual framework which models the direct relationships between AI-driven narrative marketing and the five decision-making stages using Structural Equation Modeling.
- Empirically validate the relationships proposed, in order to add methodologically sound evidence to the burgeoning literature in AI-driven marketing communication.
- To extend the narrative marketing and consumer behavior theories into the AI context by conceptualizing AI-driven algorithmically generated and personalized narratives as a unique and potent form of persuasion.
- To provide actionable insights to marketing practitioners so that they can design AI-driven narrative strategies to meet particular stages of the consumer decision journey.

In light of these objectives, the chapter tries to fill both the theoretical and empirical gaps found in the literature and to offer a more fine-grained understanding of persuasion and decision-making within AI mediated marketing contexts.

Significance of the Study

The study can offer valuable contributions in three areas such as academia (theory), practical business (management) and ethical/policy dialogue. Since AI will become an instrument through which marketers will use their marketing activities to communicate with the consumers, it is clear that knowing how companies can use AI as a narrative and persuasive tool is essential in the development of the theory, which in turn would inform practice and the establishment of responsible governance over AI.

Academic Relevance: Research-wise, the study also contributes to the spheres of consumer behaviour, narrative persuasion, and AI-driven marketing communication. Consumer decision making model has played a central role in marketing research throughout the years, but in most instances, models have relied on static marketing stimuli generated by human beings (Blackwell, Miniard, and Engel 2006; Solomon 2018). The present study is no exception because the main focus of the current study is to test, through empirical research, the impact of AI-driven narratives on customer behaviour at varying decision making stages. By doing this, it modernizes the old theory of consumer decision making to mirror on the prevailing reality of how the customer interaction occurs in AI-driven settings. The current literature has up to this point given substantial attention to the role of narrative marketing in transportation of customers, emotional appeal, and attitude towards the brand (Escalas 2004; Van Laer et al. 2014). Moving on, the chapter shall expand the history of the narrative theory past the creative side of the story telling by placing the AI-driven narratives as a new and scalable type of persuasion. Furthermore, the application of Structural Equation Modeling gives power to the existing study by enabling a rigorous and empirical study of how narratives generated using AI can be utilized to produce stage-based effect in consumer-level decision making; moreover, it addresses the current need to have more rigorously methodology studies in both AI and marketing analytics (Wedel and Kannan 2016).

Managerial Relevance: The results of this chapter are highly useful to marketing practitioners operating in the highly automated Data-driven and AI-driven settings. The increasing proportion of recommendation systems and personalization engines that are present in the current business world dictate that market practitioners should understand how AI-driven messages influence consumer behaviour throughout the entire decision process in order to develop effective combination strategies. Instead of devising a single personalization approach that fits all individuals, the managers can use the knowledge gained in this research to come up with narrative approaches in every phase of the decision-making that will be more appropriate to the way the consumers think and feel when making buying choices. Moreover, the effects of AI-driven narrative on consumer behaviour have also been empirically established in this study and have generated insight that will guide practitioners in the market to develop a strategy that fully leverages the opportunities to maximize customer engagement, relevant perceptions and development of more enduring relationships with their customer base. Insight helps especially the companies who are trying to develop an amalgamation of automated and meaningful experiences of their customers in a highly competitive and dynamic digital market environment (Davenport, Guenole and Murray, 2020).

Policy and Ethical Implication: This research has implications beyond scholarly and managerial levels to show us how policy and ethical debate exists around the use of AI-driven persuasion. Along with the growth of the utilization of algorithmic services, the life of algorithmic systems that dictate the information that consumers are presented to is becoming even more widespread, leading to the appearance of the growing levels of transparency, autonomy and manipulation issues (Yeung, 2017). By adding persuasive factors to personalized stories with the assistance of AI, AI-driven narratives can be used to influence the consumer behaviour in an insidious and unnoticed way. As a result, explicit analysis of the impact of AI-driven stories on the decision-making process at different stages of the consumer journey can enable policymakers, regulators and consumer advocates to obtain a better understanding of the AI persuasion process. Such understandings can guide policymakers, regulators and consumer advocates to establish policies that are aimed at encouraging ethical applications of AI technology, so that consumers have the right to make their own choices, and develop sensible and responsible approaches to promoting sustainable marketing conduct in an online setting. Thus, this chapter adds to the academic knowledge base, although it also adds to the public discussion within the society on how to put in place governance systems of AI-driven persuasive communications.

THEORETICAL FOUNDATION AND LITERATURE REVIEW

The consumer decision-making model is a long-established, widely recognized framework for understanding consumer behavior. Consumers start their buying process with a goal-pursuing behaviour that starts with recognizing an unmet need, gathering information to fulfil that need, evaluating available options, making a purchase, and subsequently reviewing the purchasing decision. Therefore, we can use this model to evaluate how different forms of marketing stimuli have an influence on consumers during different stages of the decision process instead of just at one specific point in time.

The Classical Five-Stage Model

Engel et al. (2006) present the process in five steps namely: 1) Need Recognition; 2) Information Search; 3) Evaluation of Alternatives; 4) Buying Decision; 5) Post Purchase Evaluation. Although all these stages of consumer decision making process may happen in a relatively parallel fashion it offers a convenient analytical approach of examining the effects of marketing interventions on the decision-making process.

Recognizing that there is a gap between where you currently are and where you want to be is the first step in making a consumer purchase. A need could come from your own body telling you that you need to eat or from someone else's advertisement suggesting that you should be doing something (like buying a certain product). In the online world, this has only increased as algorithms present content tailored to an individual's latent preferences.

Once the need has been identified, the consumers go through information search as a decision-making process. It can be conducted in two directions: search within the internal memory (prior experience) and search in the external direction (searching the Internet review or advice of friends and relatives via social media). The entry of digital technologies has made the information technology available to consumers much easier via external means. Consumers, many times, employ search engines which employ algorithms and recommenders (recommendation engines) to minimize their work, as well as their perceived risks in their choices (Kotler & Keller, 2016).

In the assessment stage, the consumers are assessing the options they are weighing against other aspects, such as price, quality, brand name and perceived value. The use of marketing communications (marketing tools) and heuristic techniques helps in making decisions among the competitors as they help in the construction of evaluative structures. Nevertheless, the assessment procedure has been heavily colored by the use of rankings, ratings, and AI-driven tailor-made systems which offer a distinctive perspective of the substitutes via digital media (Solomon, 2018).

Purchase decision stage indicates where consumers go and make a desired choice and make a purchase. Although this is a discrete decision, it has been demonstrated that such decision depends on the situational factors, perceived trust and the cumulative impact of all the preceding stages (Blackwell et al., 2006). Digital interfaces and Nudges driven by AI can have significant effects on the final outcomes of purchases by helping to decrease friction and boosting the feeling of confidence in the choice.

The last phase is post-purchase evaluation that involves an appraisal of consumers in regard to their level of satisfaction with the product or service purchased. The appraisal influences the repeat buying behaviour, the word-of-mouth communication, and brand loyalty. In modern online settings the after sales support systems like reviews, ratings and personal follow-up messages take this step to the next level of the personal assessment. This leads to an algorithmically mediated socially visible process. (Kotler & Keller, 2016)

Relevance of the Digital and AI-Driven Environment.

Even though the five-stage decision-making model could be traced back to pre-digital consumer research, it is incredibly relevant in these digital and AI-driven conditions. Instead of rendering this model obsolete, the evolution of digital technological platforms redefines the way every one of these phases is lived and influenced. Artificial intelligence systems will be involved in the decision-making process as the company needs to recognize their emerging needs, filter information, organize assessments, and make purchases, and shape the post-purchase experience by engaging with customers personally.

Most importantly AI-driven marketing does not eliminate consumer agency but alters the system of choice where decisions are made. Algorithms have an impact on the saliency of options chosen, the saliency of narratives and how the information is framed during the process. Thus, to make the consumer decision-making process in the era of AI be intelligible, the clarity of the analysis must be preserved. This embodies the classical model without omitting the dynamism, adaptiveness and personalization as the features of the AI-driven marketing communication.

In this regard, consumer decision-making process provides a sound theoretical background through which AI-driven narrative marketing strategy can be analyzed in terms of its impact at each stage. Having the ability to project AI-driven stories on every stage of decision path. Through this, a researcher will have a better insight on how AI influences cognition, emotion, and behavior in the marketplace.

Narrative Marketing and Storytelling

Storytelling and narrative marketing have become a phenomenal strategy in the modern marketing communication because of the ability to generate consumer meaning, emotion and judgment in ways that cannot be generally attained with mere informational messages. Narrative marketing is a type of communication where the information related to the brand is designed in the form of a story, and its key features are recognizable actors, cause-and-effect relationships, and significant consequences. Through delivery of marketing messages in narrative ways, companies allow customers to perceive brand communications as continuous experiences as opposed to being discrete messages. This strategy is rooted in the narrative persuasion theory, which makes sense why stories may be especially useful in terms of convincing attitudes and behavior.

Narrative Persuasion

Narrative persuasion refers to the act whereby an individual influences beliefs, attitudes, and decisions by engaging people in a narrative world. In contrast to the argumentative or factual persuasion, narrative persuasion works by minimizing resistance to persuasion motive and increasing interaction with the message itself (Green and Brock, 2000). Consumers lost in a story tend to be less capable and less motivated to engage in a critical counter-argument to marketing messages, thus being more susceptible to the implicit meanings that are practiced through narrative form. Narratives enable brands to establish products and services as part of the consumer lived experience marketing-wise. Experienced research indicates that narrative messages can be used to build brand attitudes, reinforce emotional connections and augment persuasive appeal by creating identification with story characters and scenarios (Escalas, 2004). This has also made storytelling an important tool towards capturing consumers in even more crowded and attention-deficit online spaces.

Emotional and Cognitive Processing Within Narratives

One of the features of narrative advertising is the simultaneous use of both emotional and cognitive processing. Affective reactions are part of emotional processing and they involve empathy, anticipation or excitement caused by exposure to the narrative and cognitive processing is how the causal relationship and meanings in the story are understood (Escalas and Stern, 2003). It is this two-tracking that makes narrative communication unlike the classical information-based advertising that makes its primary emphasis on the comparison of attributes and arguments. Consumer studies have also revealed that the use of narratives can trigger a state of narrative transportation where individuals are psychologically absorbed with the world of the story. This is a condition that is associated with more involvement of emotions and more positive attitudes towards the message and the brand (Green and Brock, 2000). At the same time, narratives provide a structured form that helps consumers process complex information, evaluate alternatives, and make relatively less judgment with relatively less cognitive effort. It is worth noting that storytelling does not make the process of making rational choices futile; it just improves the information processing that implies the use of affective signals and meaningful information. This involvement of emotions and clarity of thinking is one of the reasons why narratives are so powerful in various steps of consumer decision-making process. The narrative messages can stimulate the need recognition through framing the problem in an emotionally involving manner, information search through avoiding information search process by organizing information and post purchase evaluation through reinforcing consumer choice by positive outcome narratives.

From Human-Created to AI-Driven Narratives

Historically, marketing stories were produced by human creative organizations and transmitted using mass or segmented media. Such stories were very convincing but were much less dynamic and homogenous, which had limited accommodation to consumer-specific situations. With the growing application of artificial intelligence in marketing communication, this dynamic has changed fundamentally. Narratives produced or edited algorithmically leave the fixed narrative behind and enter into data-driven, dynamic construction of narratives. Through the use of AI systems, narrative content can be created or recommended based on behavioral, preference, and contextual cues of the consumer, thus creating and updating personalized content.

Instead of providing one, unitary brand story, AI-driven systems allow building various micro-narratives with each consumer as the protagonist. This change has strong consequences to narrative persuasion. Narratives generated algorithmically using AI can be delivered at pivotal points in the consumer experience and be positioned to fit the motivations and decision-making contexts of an individual and modified based on real-time feedback. As a result, the storytelling under AI-driven conditions is more personalized, as well as more persistent and has a presence on a variety of touchpoints throughout time.

Although the literature about narrative marketing has mainly relied on stories and narratives by humans, the increased use of AI in the creation of narratives requires a fresh theoretical and empirical research. Gaining insight on how AI-based storytelling influences consumer perception and feeling are necessary to apply the theory of narrative persuasion to modern digital marketing conditions. In response to this demand, the conceptualization of AI-driven narrative marketing presented in the present study is a unique and prominent form of persuasion, which works along the consumer decision-making trajectory.

AI in Marketing Communication

The integration of artificial intelligence in the marketing communication process has radically transformed the relationship between a firm and consumers. Marketing communication has taken a new form of automatic, adaptive and data centric communication instead of manual and rule centric communications. The term AI in marketing communication in the present study implies the application of machine learning, natural language processing and predictive analytics to design, deliver, and optimise marketing messages in real-time. This transformation has not only widened the marketing communication activities beyond the dissemination of messages but has also incorporated the coordination of smart and personalized encounters in various touchpoints of consumers.

Initial uses of AI in marketing were mostly analytical in nature and included forecasting, segmentation, and customer profiling. With the growth of computational power and the availability of data, the AI systems started to assist in analyzing the data; however, with more computational power came the ability to give autonomous decisions regarding content selection, message timing, and personalization (Wedel and Kannan, 2016). As a result, marketing communication is more and more run by algorithmic systems that keep adapting to consumer behavior and keep modifying communication strategies on a dynamic basis. AI-driven marketing communication has become characterized by personalization on a large scale. The AI systems allow personalized communication, unlike the old methods that were based on segmentation, because they combine past behavior, context, and real-time feedback (Arora et al., 2008). The empirical data indicate that this kind of personalization increases relevance, perceived usefulness, and consumer engagement when applied properly (Bleier and Eisenbeiss, 2015).

The content aspect of marketing communication has also been transformed by AI. The development of natural language processing and automated content generation enables AI systems to generate and modify text based messages, recommendations and conversational responses that are similar to natural human communication. Instead of substituting human imagination, such systems allow creative fluctuation of narrative frames and focus due to the perpetual consumer interactions (Davenport et al., 2020). This has made marketing messages dynamic objects and not fixed components as they are enshrined in ongoing consumer-brand relationships.

Conventionally, in terms of persuasion, AI-driven communication presents novel sources of influence. The content of the messages as well as the structure of the decision-making process by the consumer is determined by algorithmic systems. AI systems can easily influence consumer decisions and behavior by attempting to place information first, sequence messages, and frame alternatives (Yeung, 2017). Notably, AI-driven communication is applicable throughout the consumer decision process. AI systems are able to predict demands, customise information search, arrange evaluative comparisons, aid in making purchase choices and support after-sale analysis. Regardless of these developments, the current literature has mostly studied AI-driven communication as an individual outcome as opposed to a procedural shape in influencing consumer decision-making. This weakness highlights the necessity of integrative frameworks that look at how AI-driven communication influences decisions at each of the stages, not at discrete touchpoints.

AI-Driven Narrative Marketing

AI-driven narrative marketing is a slightly different variant of persuasive communication involving the combination of artificial intelligence and narrative-based marketing through the consumer decision making process. It describes how AI can be strategically used to generate, organize and provide a customized narrative in marketing that changes dynamically based on specific consumer data and situational indicators. In contrast with the traditional narrative marketing, which is based on unresponsive spread of stories created by humans, AI-driven narratives are adjusted according to the feedback of consumer interaction and behavioral patterns (Davenport et al., 2020; Wedel and Kannan, 2016).

In the given work, the idea of AI-driven narrative marketing is implemented in the form of algorithmically individualized narrative content as opposed to a complete autonomy of AI-driven storytelling. It is focused on a selection of narrative forms managed by the logic of personalization and managerial will instead of AI as a creative agent in itself. In theory, this strategy incorporates the theory of narrative persuasion and process models of consumer decision making. Narrative persuasion theory describes the way in which stories can manipulate consumers by transportation, emotional involvement and lessening resistance (Green and Brock, 2000; Escalas, 2004) whereas the consumer decision-making theory conceptualizes the way consumers want to consume various products as a series of steps such as need recognition, information search, evaluation of alternatives, purchase decision and post purchase evaluation (Blackwell, Miniard and Engel, 2006).

In AI-driven settings, narratives tend to be micro-narratives being circulated through recommendation systems, custom content feeds, and interactive interfaces. These stories make the consumer a focal player and products or services as a topically relevant action. The AI- driven narratives affect the attention, interpretation, and action at several steps of the decision-making process instead of producing targeted results like purchase intention (Bleier and Eisenbeiss, 2015). This ongoing, step-by-step impact is what differentiates AI- driven narrative marketing and its predecessors, who operated on individual contact points in digital marketing.

Although AI- driven narrative marketing is becoming more relevant, there is limited and disjointed empirical research on the topic. The majority of studies concentrate on such single outcomes as engagement or purchase intention and do not provide much information about the role of narrative-based AI communication in influencing consumer choices at different stages. Sealing this gap, the current research makes AI-driven narrative marketing one of the central tools of persuasion in the modern digital marketing and grounds the proposed research model conceptual center. Simultaneously, the success of AI- driven narrative marketing lies in the levels of consumer trust in algorithmic systems and visualized transparency of AI- driven communication. Ethical issues in data use, autonomy, and limits of persuasion hence continue to form part of comprehending the manner and the time when AI-driven narrative strategies will be used to persuade consumers to make decisions.

AI–Driven Personalization and Consumer Response

Literature on the effectiveness of personalization by AI is abundant. It is proven that consumers feel that the content is more relevant in case the content is focused on their preferences in addition to the situation (Arora et al., 2008; Bleier and Eisenbeiss, 2015). Digital advertising is showing indications that personalization responses more often and also assist in the consumer making faster decisions due to less information overload. In the recent past, the research has pointed out the growing use of AI and machine learning in automated such personalization decisions. As an example, Davenport et al. (2020) provide an example of how AI can optimize communication messages depending on the interaction with a view to enhance communication as it becomes more responsive and adaptive. Nevertheless, despite the research confirming AI personalization to be effective, it is more likely to define its effectiveness by the number of clicks or individuals intending to purchase an item based on self-report. As it is contrary to assess the influence of AI personalization content on individuals in different stages of the decision-making process. Although there is a lot of empirical evidence regarding the effectiveness of AI-driven personalization, the existing studies are mostly cross-sectional in nature and do not provide much information about how the process of personalization affects consumer decision-making processes over an extended period of time.

Narrative Advertising and Persuasion

Research conducted on narrative advertising has widely affirmed that stories are more convincing since they draw people emotionally and cognitively. It has been found through both experiments and surveys that stories boost brand attitudes, elevate emotional engagements and behavioral intentions by elevating transportation into the story and identification with the story (Escalas 2004; Van Laer et al. 2014). Such effects are attained or best achieved where they are relatable and experience-based on consumers and not categorically enumerating features. Some other findings also lead to the role of narratives in lowering resistance to persuasion as they cause people to switch off analysis and switch to experience (Green and Brock 2000). It can have an impact on the attitude towards a brand, an advert, and evaluation of the same in marketing. It can be known that most of them were made by humans and were either delivered in conventional ways or in the virtual world. Few things have been investigated into the nature of AI-driven narratives and how it works. Consequently, the concept of narrative persuasion is firmly rooted in the marketing literature, which is why the use of narrative persuasion in AI-driven and algorithmically personalized settings has not been thoroughly examined yet.

Decision-Making by Consumers in Digital Spaces

Studies, which have been conducted through decision theory, investigate how digital technology is influencing the search, evaluation and purchase practices of people. The internet space motivates consumers to undertake external processing of decisions such as global feedback and suggestions instead of engaging in internal processing (Beatty and Smith, 1987). The more recent literature emphasizes effects of the recommender systems on the decision making in particular to the restricted alternatives of the systems and perception of quality of the options (Bettman, Luce, and Payne, 1998). It is brought out as clear that these systems influence the decision making but the technology used in these studies is as a helper and not a narrator. Narrative-based decision-making with the aid of AI has not been studied in detail. Consequently, the concept of narrative persuasion is firmly rooted in the marketing literature, which is why the use of narrative persuasion in AI-driven and algorithmically personalized settings has not been thoroughly examined yet.

Towards an Integrative Empirical Approach

Studies are starting to spring out on the capability of AI systems to manipulate consumer behavior, but there are no studies examining narrative marketing in AI systems holistically and intricately. The interest in the current research is brought to the level of a particular outcome, like engagement, trust or purchase intention and they do not necessarily follow the process of decision-making. They do not even use process research methods like Structural Equation Modeling that can be used to track influences of communication at multiple levels. This empirical need is reflected in this disunity. Therefore, there is some research gap in understanding the effects of AI-driven stories on cognition and behaviour across the whole range of decision-making process, rather than a reaction to the perceived points of decision-making. The piece of this fragmentation of empirical methods indicates an evident research gap on the effect of AI-driven narratives on consumer cognition and behavior in the entire decision-making process and not at single points of decision-making.

Sealing that gap in the research might form the basis of a more comprehensive view to the field of AI-based persuasion and its application to the sphere of marketing with reference to real algorithm methods that are being employed. To fill this gap, the chapter combines the theory on personalization and narrative persuasion theory with research on consumer decision with personalization research and conduct a study to identify the direct impacts of AI-driven narrative marketing at each of the stages of consumer decision-making through a holistic approach and decision-process approach.

CONCEPTUAL FRAMEWORK AND HYPOTHESES DEVELOPMENT

Conceptual Model Overview

Building on the theoretical foundations and empirical insights reviewed in the preceding sections, this chapter advances a conceptual model that explains how AI-driven narrative marketing strategies influence consumer behavior across the decision-making process. This model explicitly grounds itself in consumer decision-making theory and the literature on narrative persuasion. This is in direct proportion to the contribution of artificial intelligence to the development of marketing communications. The exogenous construct in the proposed framework would be AI-driven narrative marketing, which refers to the AI-driven algorithmically generated and personalized storytelling that would be offered through digital platforms. It is an effort to indicate a proactive power of AI systems to edit, contextualize and modify the content of narratives in relation to consumer information and engagement behaviors. Rather than viewing it as a pure technology this model places AI as a proactive persuasive force that exists in marketing communication. The new consumer decision making process is a modeled endogenous construct, which entails the following five stages; need recognition, information search, evaluation of alternatives, purchase decision and post purchase evaluation. All the five stages represent a different but related stage through which consumers go through during consumption decision making. In line with previous studies of consumer behavior, these steps are analytically differentiated to enable a subtle analysis of the effect of marketing stimuli on the decision-making process at various stages of consumer journey.

Figure 1. Conceptual Framework

It suggests direct influences of AI-driven narrative marketing on every stage of the decision-making process. This assumes that AI-driven narratives could exert influence along the decision journey by activating needs and guiding information search, shaping evaluative comparisons, reinforcing purchase decisions, and validating post-purchase evaluations. By specifying a number of direct influences, the model seeks parsimony while enabling a comprehensive test of the influence of AI-driven narrative marketing. In this study, SEM was used to empirically test the relations so that multiple dependent constructs could be estimated simultaneously. This also helps the strength of the model's explanatory power that could be measured comprehensively. Figure 1 shows the conceptual model of the chapter, depicting the hypothesized paths of AI-driven narrative marketing in correspondence to the five stages of the consumer decision-making process. By integrating AI-driven marketing strategies into process-based consumer behavior theory, the proposed conceptual model leads to a holistic framework in view of persuasion in AI-driven algorithmically mediated environments. The model also provides the basis for the development of hypotheses and subsequent empirical analysis later in the chapter.

Hypotheses Development

Building on consumer decision-making theory, narrative persuasion theory, and AI-driven marketing communication literature, this study proposes that AI-driven narrative marketing exerts a direct influence across all stages of the consumer decision-making process. Unlike traditional marketing communications that rely on static and non-personalized messages, AI-driven narratives dynamically adapt to consumer data and context, enabling persuasive influence to unfold continuously throughout the decision journey. Accordingly, the following hypotheses are proposed.

AI-Driven Narrative Marketing → Need Recognition

Narrative persuasion theory suggests that stories are effective in activating need recognition by embedding problems within emotionally engaging and relatable contexts. In AI-driven environments, algorithmically personalized narratives can proactively surface latent needs by aligning story cues with consumers' past behaviors, preferences, and situational signals. Through predictive analytics and adaptive storytelling, AI-driven narrative marketing is expected to intensify need recognition by presenting narratives at moments of heightened receptivity.

H1: AI-driven narrative marketing has a significant positive influence on need recognition.

AI-Driven Narrative Marketing → Information Search

In digital environments, information search is increasingly shaped by algorithmic systems that curate and prioritize content. AI-driven narrative marketing structures complex product information into coherent story-based formats, reducing cognitive effort and guiding consumers toward relevant options. Personalized narrative continuations further streamline search processes by directing attention and shaping the depth and direction of information exploration.

H2: AI-driven narrative marketing has a significant positive influence on information search.

AI-Driven Narrative Marketing → Evaluation of Alternatives

The evaluation of alternatives involves cognitively demanding comparisons among competing options. Narrative-based framing enables consumers to process evaluative information holistically rather than through isolated attribute analysis. In AI-driven contexts, algorithms enhance this process by ranking options, highlighting relative strengths, and embedding comparisons within personalized narrative structures, thereby shaping evaluative criteria and confidence.

H3: AI-driven narrative marketing has a significant positive influence on the evaluation of alternatives.

AI-Driven Narrative Marketing → Purchase Decision

Purchase decisions reflect accumulated perceptions and confidence developed across earlier decision stages. AI-driven narrative marketing reinforces choice confidence through personalized storytelling, optimized message timing, and adaptive choice architectures. By embedding persuasive cues within narratives aligned with individual consumer contexts, AI-driven marketing communication is expected to reduce uncertainty and facilitate purchase completion.

H4: AI-driven narrative marketing has a significant positive influence on purchase decisions.

AI-Driven Narrative Marketing → Post-Purchase Evaluation

Post-purchase evaluation shapes satisfaction, repeat behavior, and long-term consumer–brand relationships. AI-driven narrative marketing extends influence beyond the transaction by delivering personalized post-purchase narratives that validate decisions, reduce cognitive dissonance, and support adaptive engagement. Through continuous feedback and personalization, AI-enabled narratives are expected to positively shape post-consumption evaluations.

H5: AI-driven narrative marketing has a significant positive influence on post-purchase evaluation.

RESEARCH METHODOLOGY

Research Design

This research has applied cross-section design to investigate the role and impact of narrative marketing enabled by AI on the decision-making journey among consumers. For this study a survey research design was employed to study the perceptions among a group of study participants concerning the role of AI-driven marketing narratives and how these narratives play out at various decision-making stages. Structural Equation Modeling (SEM) is used as the primary analytical technique because it allows to test multiple hypotheses concerning relationships simultaneously while also dealing with properties of measurement simultaneously. This is particularly appropriate in this study since the study is dealing with latent variables that are measured using multiple indicators and are attempting to account for variance in multiple dependent variables.

Measurement of Constructs

AI-Driven Narrative Marketing: Defined as a high-level perceptual construct that attempts to capture the consumer's experience with the personalized marketing story generated through algorithms in the AI system. Items were created based upon the adaptation of theory related to personalization, story processing, and AI-driven marketing communication processes. There are dimensions such as personalization, perceived relevance and story engagement in this construct because a prior scale does not exist for AI-driven narrative marketing and therefore cannot be a direct copy of any other instrument because it has been carefully adapted to retain its accurate meaning.

The measurement scales used in this study were adapted from established and validated instruments in prior research on narrative persuasion, personalization, and consumer decision-making, with minor modifications to reflect the AI-driven narrative marketing context. Scale adaptation was considered appropriate to ensure content validity while maintaining conceptual consistency with existing literature. To minimize the risk of common method bias, procedural remedies were applied, including ensuring respondent anonymity and reducing evaluation apprehension through neutral item wording. In addition, a post hoc statistical assessment indicated that common method bias was unlikely to pose a serious threat to the validity of the findings.

Modelling Consumer Decision Phases: The five different decision phases (Need Recognition, Information Search, Evaluation of Alternatives, Purchase Decision, and Post-Purchase Evaluation) were assumed to be different endogenous constructs. The items in the different decision phases were adapted from established scales in the study of consumer behavior to capture the effects of AI-driven narrative marketing stories at each different stage. The different stages could be analysed independently rather than aggregated on a single scale.

Instrument Development

A structured research instrument was devised in a three-part manner. The initial part of the instrument provides a background and checks that respondents can cope with virtual and AI-driven marketing settings. The second part consists of questions about perceptions of AI-driven narrative marketing, and then questions related to the five stages of decision-making. Demographic variables are sought in the third part of the instrument. All questions employ a five-point Likert scale (order 1=Strongly Disagree to 5=Strongly Agree). Prior to conducting a full-scale implementation, pilots tested the instrument for neutrality and conceptual appropriateness which has necessitated slight conceptual adjustments related to AI-driven marketing.

Sample and Data Collection

The subjects include consumers who already have past experiences with digital services employing AI-driven personalization, such as e-commerce, video streaming, and social media. The study adopts non-probability sampling given the exploratory nature of AI-driven consumer experiences and relevance after considering the novelty that AI presents in this respect. The sampling technique uses an online platform whereby the respondents are free to take part willingly. Such an approach aligns with the target demographic of digitally engaged consumers and AI-driven marketing contexts.

Data Analysis Technique

This study employed the threefold SEM procedure as follows.

- Exploratory Factor Analysis (EFA): Because the theoretical framework of AI-driven narrative marketing was more theorized than proved in empirical research, we started with EFA in a search for underlying factor structures before decisions about specific structures had been made.
- Measurement Model Evaluation: On the basis of the results of the EFA analysis, Confirmatory Factor Analysis was conducted on the measurement model. Reliability was evaluated through Cronbach's alpha and Composite Reliability.
- Structural Model Testing: Subsequently, the proposed model paths between AI-driven narrative marketing and the decision stages were analyzed. Fit indices of the model were estimated employing typical indices like CFI, TLI, RMSEA, and SRMR.

EMPIRICAL RESULTS AND ANALYSIS

Demographic Analysis: The demographic profile shows that the sample population is composed of young and economically active respondents, the almost half of the respondents represent the age group of 25-34 years, followed by the age group of 35-44 years. The gender balance is also quite even and there is a sufficient representation in groups. The respondents are mostly well educated with most of them being graduate/higher educated which is ideal in engage with AI-driven digital content.

The majority of the respondents work in the private sector and have their income between 50,001 and 75,000 which is relatively high purchasing power. It is mostly an urban population with the frequency of online shopping and multi-platform digital use being high. Moreover, a relatively high percentage of the respondents have 1-3 years of experience with AI-driven recommendation systems this means that the sample is not too new to AI-driven narrative marketing to give reliable and informed answers.

Table 1. Demographic Analysis

Demographic Aspect	Categories / Options	Number	Percentage
Age	18-24 years	124	15.74
	25-34 years	387	49.11
	35-44 years	183	23.22
	45-54 years	78	9.90
	55 years and above	16	2.03
Gender	Male	354	44.92
	Female	387	49.11
	Prefer not to say	47	5.96
Educational Qualification	Undergraduate	188	23.86
	Graduate	320	40.61
	Postgraduate	141	17.89
	Doctorate / Professional	139	17.64
Occupation	Student	96	12.18
	Employed (Private)	470	59.64
	Employed (Public)	125	15.86
	Self-employed	56	7.11
	Homemaker	33	4.19
	Other	8	1.02

continued on following page

Table 1. Continued

Demographic Aspect	Categories / Options	Number	Percentage
Monthly Income	Below 25,000	127	16.12
	25,001– 50,000	73	9.26
	50,001– 75,000	511	64.85
	75,001– 100,000	47	5.96
	Above 100,000	30	3.81
Geographical Location	Urban	521	66.12
	Semi-urban	204	25.89
	Rural	63	7.99
Frequency of Online Shopping	Rarely	42	5.33
	Occasionally	79	10.03
	Frequently	561	71.19
	Very frequently	106	13.45
Primary Digital Platform Used	E-commerce platforms	47	5.96
	Streaming platforms	36	4.57
	Social media	101	12.82
	Multiple platforms	604	76.65
Experience with AI-Based Recommendations	Less than 1 year	124	15.74
	1–3 years	588	74.62
	More than 3 years	76	9.64

Descriptive Statistics and Reliability Estimates of the Study Constructs:

This section presents the descriptive statistics and internal consistency measures for all study constructs. Mean scores and standard deviations provide an overview of respondents' perceptions. The Cronbach's alpha and McDonald's omega are used to assess the reliability of each construct.

Table 2. Reliability Analysis

Construct	Mean	SD	Cronbach's α	McDonald's ω
AI-Driven Narrative Marketing	4.18	0.72	0.91	0.92
Need Recognition	3.44	0.75	0.77	0.79
Information Search	4.16	0.7	0.73	0.75
Evaluation of Alternatives	4.21	0.74	0.88	0.89
Purchase Decision	4.14	0.69	0.9	0.91
Post-Purchase Evaluation	3.79	0.71	0.8	0.82
Overall Scale	**4.18**	0.68	0.88	0.89

The mean scores suggest that the perceptions of AI-driven narrative marketing and the majority of consumer decision-making process phases are rather positive. The maximum mean was the highest in evaluation of alternatives and lowest in need recognition. Standard deviations are not too large, which indicates that there is normal variability of responses. The findings of reliability indicate that the instrument has good internal consistency since the Cronbach alpha and McDonald omega coefficients of all constructs are above the recommended threshold of 0.70. The reliability of the scale is also high in the overall scale, which proves that the measurement tool is consistent and can be used later in the process of factor and structural analysis.

Table 3. Item Reliability Analysis

Item Code	Mean	SD	Item–Rest Correlation	Cronbach's α (if item dropped)	McDonald's ω (if item dropped)
AINM1	4.15	0.73	0.74	0.9	0.91
AINM2	4.22	0.71	0.78	0.89	0.9
AINM3	4.18	0.69	0.71	0.91	0.92
NR1	3.39	0.77	0.68	0.76	0.78
NR2	3.46	0.74	0.72	0.75	0.77
NR3	3.47	0.73	0.7	0.76	0.78
IS1	4.13	0.72	0.69	0.72	0.74
IS2	4.19	0.7	0.71	0.71	0.73
IS3	4.16	0.69	0.7	0.72	0.74
EA1	4.18	0.75	0.83	0.87	0.88
EA2	4.25	0.74	0.85	0.86	0.88
EA3	4.2	0.73	0.81	0.88	0.89
PD1	4.1	0.7	0.86	0.89	0.9
PD2	4.18	0.68	0.88	0.88	0.91
PD3	4.14	0.69	0.84	0.89	0.9
PPE1	3.76	0.72	0.74	0.79	0.81
PPE2	3.83	0.71	0.76	0.78	0.8
PPE3	3.8	0.7	0.75	0.79	0.81

The psychometric properties of all the items are high with item-rest correlations that are above acceptable levels which is evidence of good internal consistency. Cronbach alpha and McDonald omega values when an item is dropped do not exhibit significant improvement, which proves that every item is adding value to its construct. Mean scores are high with moderate variability which indicates that all the items should be retained to conduct further factor and structural analysis.

Exploratory Factor Analysis

Exploratory Factor Analysis (EFA) was conducted to examine the underlying factor structure of the measurement items and to assess whether the observed variables load appropriately on their intended constructs.

Table 4. Bartlett's Test of Sphericity

χ^2 (Chi-square)	df	p-value
9,462.18	**171**	**< .001**

The Bartlett's test is statistically significant (χ^2 = 9,462.18, $p < .001$) and indicates that the correlation matrix is not an identity matrix and that the data are suitable for factor analysis.

Table 5. Kaiser–Meyer–Olkin (KMO) Measure of Sampling Adequacy

Item	MSA
Overall KMO	**0.94**
AINM1	0.95
AINM2	0.94
AINM3	0.93
NR1	0.92
NR2	0.93
NR3	0.92
IS1	0.91
IS2	0.92
IS3	0.91
EA1	0.95
EA2	0.94
EA3	0.93
PD1	0.95
PD2	0.94
PD3	0.93
PPE1	0.92
PPE2	0.93
PPE3	0.92

The overall KMO value of 0.94 suggests **excellent sampling adequacy**. Individual MSA values for all items exceed the recommended threshold, confirming that each item is appropriate for inclusion in the factor analysis.

Table 6. Exploratory Factor Analysis

Item	Factor 1 (AINM)	Factor 2 (NR)	Factor 3 (IS)	Factor 4 (EA)	Factor 5 (PD)	Factor 6 (PPE)
AINM1	**0.81**	0.22				
AINM2	**0.84**	0.19				
AINM3	**0.78**	0.25				
NR1	0.21	**0.76**	0.18			
NR2	0.18	**0.79**	0.21			
NR3	0.24	**0.74**	0.19			
IS1		0.2	**0.77**	0.17		
IS2		0.18	**0.81**	0.19		
IS3		0.22	**0.76**	0.21		
EA1			0.23	**0.79**	0.18	
EA2			0.2	**0.82**	0.21	
EA3			0.24	**0.77**	0.19	
PD1				0.22	**0.83**	0.18
PD2				0.19	**0.81**	0.21
PD3				0.24	**0.78**	0.2
PPE1					0.23	**0.81**
PPE2					0.21	**0.79**
PPE3					0.25	**0.76**

The EFA results reveal a clear **six-factor structure**, with all items loading strongly on their respective constructs. Factor loadings exceed acceptable levels, and cross-loadings are minimal, supporting good discriminant separation among constructs. These findings confirm the conceptual distinctiveness of AI-driven narrative marketing and the five stages of the consumer decision-making process, justifying progression to confirmatory factor analysis.

Confirmatory Factor Analysis

Confirmatory Factor Analysis (CFA) was conducted to validate the measurement model and to examine the convergent validity of the constructs identified through exploratory factor analysis.

Table 8. Model Fit for CFA – Chi-Square Test

χ^2	df	p
412.67	237	< .001

The chi-square statistic is significant ($\chi^2 = 412.67$, $p < .001$), which is common in large samples. Given the sample size, the chi-square result is interpreted alongside alternative fit indices to assess overall model adequacy.

Table 9. Fit Indices for CFA

Fit Measure	Value
CFI	0.923
TLI	0.914
RMSEA	0.054
RMSEA 90% CI (Lower)	0.048
RMSEA 90% CI (Upper)	0.060

The comparative fit index (CFI = 0.923) and Tucker–Lewis index (TLI = 0.914) exceed the recommended cutoff of 0.90 and indicates good model fit. The RMSEA value of 0.054 falls within acceptable limits and its 90% confidence interval (0.048–0.060) further supports a close approximation of the data to the hypothesized model. Overall, these indices confirm that the measurement model fits the data well.

Table 10. Confirmatory Factor Analysis (CFA)

Factor	Indicator	Estimate	SE	90% CI (Lower)	90% CI (Upper)	Z	p	Standardized Estimate
AI-Driven Narrative Marketing	AINM1	1.00 (fixed)						0.78
	AINM2	1.12	0.09	0.98	1.27	12.44	< .001	0.82
	AINM3	0.96	0.08	0.84	1.09	11.93	< .001	0.75
Need Recognition	NR1	1.00 (fixed)						0.71
	NR2	1.05	0.11	0.87	1.23	9.55	< .001	0.74
	NR3	0.92	0.12	0.72	1.12	7.67	< .001	0.68
Information Search	IS1	1.00 (fixed)						0.7
	IS2	1.08	0.1	0.92	1.25	10.58	< .001	0.76
	IS3	0.94	0.11	0.77	1.12	8.55	< .001	0.69
Evaluation of Alternatives	EA1	1.00 (fixed)						0.77
	EA2	1.14	0.08	1.01	1.28	14.25	< .001	0.83
	EA3	0.98	0.09	0.83	1.13	10.89	< .001	0.75

continued on following page

Table 10. Continued

Factor	Indicator	Estimate	SE	90% CI (Lower)	90% CI (Upper)	Z	p	Standardized Estimate
Purchase Decision	PD1	1.00 (fixed)						0.8
	PD2	1.09	0.07	0.97	1.22	15.57	< .001	0.84
	PD3	0.95	0.08	0.82	1.08	11.88	< .001	0.77
Post-Purchase Evaluation	PPE1	1.00 (fixed)						0.74
	PPE2	1.03	0.1	0.86	1.2	10.3	< .001	0.76
	PPE3	0.91	0.11	0.73	1.09	8.27	< .001	0.71

All indicators load significantly on their respective latent constructs, with standardized factor loadings ranging from moderate to high. The majority of loadings exceed the recommended threshold and demonstrated satisfactory convergent validity. The statistically significant Z-values and narrow confidence intervals further confirm the stability and reliability of the measurement items. Collectively, these results validate the proposed six-factor measurement model and support its use for subsequent structural equation modeling.

Structural Equation Modeling Analysis

Structural Equation Modeling (SEM) was employed to examine the hypothesized relationships between AI-driven narrative marketing and the five stages of the consumer decision-making process, using the validated measurement model.

Table 11. Overall Test of Model

Model Tests	χ^2	df	p
User Model	438.52	243	< .001
Baseline Model	2,914.76	276	< .001
Scaled User Model	421.18	243	< .001
Scaled Baseline Model	2,782.41	276	< .001

The chi-square values for the user, baseline, and scaled models are statistically significant, which is expected, given the large sample size. However, the substantial reduction in chi-square values for the user model compared to the baseline model indicates a meaningful improvement in model fit, supporting the adequacy of the proposed structural model.

Table 12. Model Fit Indices

Type	SRMR	RMSEA	90% CI (Lower)	90% CI (Upper)	RMSEA
Classical	0.056	0.057	0.051	0.063	0.082
Robust	0.059	0.054	0.048	0.060	0.104
Scaled	0.061	0.056	0.050	0.062	0.091

The SRMR values across classical, robust, and scaled estimations are below recommended thresholds, indicating good residual fit. RMSEA values remain within acceptable limits, and the confidence intervals further support a reasonable approximation of the model to the data. The RMSEA p-values also suggest that the model cannot be rejected on the basis of poor fit. Collectively, these indices confirm that the structural model demonstrates satisfactory overall fit.

Table 13. Reliability Indices

Variable	Cronbach's α	Ordinal α	ω_1	ω_2	ω_3	AVE
AINM	0.91	0.92	0.89	0.91	0.93	0.61
NR	0.77	0.79	0.74	0.77	0.8	0.49
IS	0.73	0.75	0.71	0.74	0.76	0.5
EA	0.88	0.89	0.86	0.88	0.9	0.59
PD	0.9	0.91	0.88	0.9	0.92	0.63
PPE	0.8	0.82	0.78	0.8	0.83	0.52

All constructs exhibit acceptable to high reliability, as indicated by Cronbach's alpha, ordinal alpha, and multiple omega coefficients. AVE values meet or approach recommended levels, supporting adequate convergent validity. These results confirm that the constructs are measured consistently and reliably within the structural model.

Table 14. Heterotrait–Monotrait (HTMT) Ratio of Correlations

Construct	AINM	NR	IS	EA	PD	PPE
AINM	—	0.62	0.58	0.66	0.71	0.6
NR		—	0.69	0.55	0.51	0.57
IS			—	0.63	0.59	0.56
EA				—	0.74	0.65
PD					—	0.72
PPE						—

The HTMT values for all construct pairs remain below conservative thresholds, indicating adequate discriminant validity. This suggests that each construct captures a distinct concept and that multicollinearity among latent variables is not a concern.

Table 15. SEM Path Analysis

Hypothesis	Path	Standardized β	t-value	p-value	Decision	Interpretation
H1	AINM → NR	0.29	4.18	< .001	Supported	AI-driven narrative marketing has a moderate positive effect on need recognition. This indicates its role in triggering initial awareness rather than strong motivation.
H2	AINM → IS	0.34	5.02	< .001	Supported	AI-driven narratives significantly enhance information search by guiding consumers toward relevant and personalized content.
H3	AINM → EA	0.41	6.37	< .001	Supported	The strongest effect is observed during evaluation of alternatives. This suggests that AI narratives are most influential in comparative judgment stages.
H4	AINM → PD	0.38	5.89	< .001	Supported	AI-driven narratives positively influence purchase decisions. Although the effect is slightly lower than during evaluation this reflects intervening situational factors.
H5	AINM → PPE	0.26	3.74	< .001	Supported	The effect on post-purchase evaluation is positive but weaker. This indicates that AI narratives shape satisfaction perceptions indirectly over time.

Special attention should be paid to the relatively high effect that is observed at the evaluation of alternatives stage. This is a very crucial step in the decision-making procedure where the consumers evaluate the alternatives and make choices. The results indicate that AI-driven narratives are an important factor in developing comparative judgments through framing alternatives that are contextually relevant and personalized. Although this kind of influence can contribute to the effectiveness of decisions and their perceived relevance, it also creates pertinent concerns regarding consumer autonomy and choice architecture. At this phase, with algorithmically-filtered narratives controlling the focus of attention and meaning, the judgments by consumers might become more and more indicative of the search format of the narrative setting and less about the autonomous assessment (Yeung, 2017). These implications point to the fact that the usefulness of AI-driven narratives should be examined, however, in the context of whether their impact is conducive to or inhibits informed consumer choice.

Figure 2. Structural Model

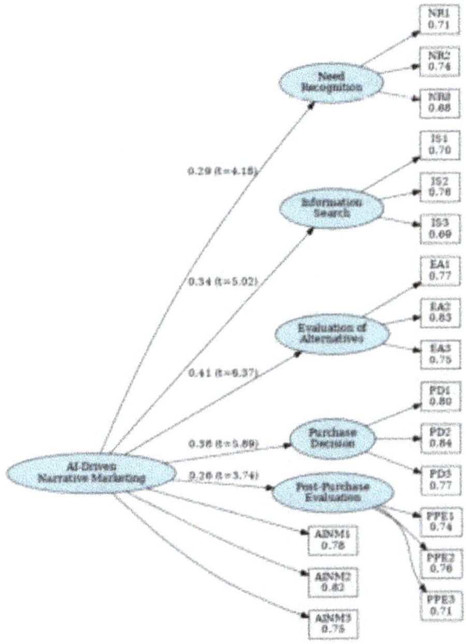

MANAGERIAL IMPLICATIONS

These results provide a number of practical recommendations to managers in the markets which are very digital and data-driven. The high role of AI-driven narrative marketing in the process of evaluating the alternatives implies that managers should no longer be focused solely on campaigns aimed at creating awareness but invest more meaningfully in narrative-based content that will aid comparative decision-making. Individualized narratives that place products features in perspective, bring out pertinent comparisons and make offerings relevant to the needs of individual consumers may significantly influence the judgments at the most cognitively decisive points of the buying decision process.

The fact that the AI-driven narratives positively impact the information search process also hints at the idea that information search through the use of the algorithmically-filtered storytelling can decrease consumer effort by sorting and prioritizing the information. The managers are thus advised to invest in the AI-driven recommendation systems which not only propose products but also give narrative explanations to why certain products are applicable. Clear and understandable descriptions of logic behind the recommendations have the potential to increase perceived usefulness, trust, and engagement.

Despite the fact that the influence of AI-driven stories on post-purchase analysis is relatively less strong, it is still significant and has management implications. The onboarding content, usage guidance, and personalized follow-up communication should be used by firms as narrative-based and should be used on top of the point of purchase. These practices may strengthen satisfaction, decrease post purchase dissonance, and facilitate long-term brand relationships. All in all, use of AI-driven narrative throughout the consumer experience (as opposed to a single touchpoint) is capable of improving retention and lifetime value.

Responsible and Ethical Utilization of AI-driven Narrative Marketing

The findings, along with the benefits related to the use of AI-driven narrative marketing, highlight the necessity of responsible management of the latter. Since AI stories have most significant influence on the evaluation and comparison levels, managers should pay attention to the questions of consumer autonomy and equity. It must be narrative personalization which ought to aid in the development of informed decision-making as opposed to clouding decisions or biasing tastes. The crucial aspect of preserving trust is a clear disclosure of AI engagement, responsible handling of consumer data, and the absence of manipulative practices of framing. The issue of ethical governance of AI-driven narratives is thus a normative issue but also a long-term strategic need to maintain the relationships of consumers.

THEORETICAL CONTRIBUTIONS

The study contributes to the marketing and consumer behavior theory in a number of ways. One, it is an extension of the consumer decision-making model, empirically proving that the use of AI-driven narrative marketing affects not only final results like purchase intention, but also other stages of the decision-making process. Through a process-oriented approach, the chapters brings out the importance of algorithmically mediated stories as contributors to need recognition, information search, alternatives evaluation, purchase decisions, and post-purchase evaluation in a holistic approach.

Second, the research advances the narrative persuasion theory by demonstrating that AI is an active narrative facilitator instead of a neutral delivery mechanism. The results also suggest that narrative persuasion is especially prominent in the period of evaluative decision-making, which favors the opinion that stories do not only affect the opinions or the impact of repetition but also cognition and judgment. This develops the previous narrative research by putting the persuasion in an adaptive and data-driven setting.

In terms of methodology, the study reinforces the empirical literature on the use of AI in marketing communication by confirming a multi-construct process-based model through structural equation modeling. The confirmatory factor analysis, diagnostics of reliability and the assessment of the discriminant validity offers a sound framework that can be replicated and expanded in subsequent studies on the topic of AI-driven marketing communication.

ETHICAL, POLICY, AND FUTURE RESEARCH IMPLICATIONS

From an ethical perspective the findings raise important questions regarding the transparency, consumer autonomy, and the boundaries of algorithmic persuasion. As AI-driven narratives increasingly influence evaluative and purchase decisions, firms must ensure that personalized storytelling practices do not mislead consumers or compromise informed choice. Ethical use of consumer data and clarity regarding AI-driven communication are essential components of responsible marketing practice.

From a policy standpoint, the growing integration of AI-driven narratives into digital platforms suggests the need for regulatory guidance addressing areas such as targeted persuasion, personalization practices, and data privacy. Policymakers may need to balance innovation with consumer protection by establishing standards for disclosure, accountability, and fairness in AI-driven marketing communication.

Future research can extend this study in several directions. Longitudinal designs may provide deeper insight into how AI-driven narratives shape post-purchase behavior and brand relationships over time. Comparative studies across industries, platforms, or cultural contexts could further clarify the generalizability of the findings. Additionally, future research should more explicitly examine moderating variables such as consumer trust in AI, perceived transparency, algorithmic literacy, and skepticism toward personalization, which may condition the effectiveness of AI-driven narrative strategies.

CONCLUSION

This chapter has considered the effect of AI-driven narrative marketing on the consumer decision-making process through a structural equation modeling method. These findings indicate that AI-driven narratives have a considerable impact on all five phases of decision-making, and most powerfully at the stages of evaluation of alternatives and purchase decision. Such results indicate that AI-driven stories are not merely automated communication systems, but they proactively influence the search behavior and option comparison of consumers in the context of algorithmic mediated information seeking.

Despite the fact that the effect of AI-driven narratives on post-purchase assessment is relatively lower, it is significant and indicates the continuity of communication based on the story even after the purchase. This research is a contribution to a more inclusive scenario of how AI re-defines marketing communication in the modern digital setting by combining the narrative persuasion theory with process-based consumer decision-making models.

Meanwhile, the consequences found in this research are not to be supposed to be the same across all customers and contexts. Personal variability in the cognizance of AI systems, skepticism towards algorithmic persuasion, and the exposure to personalized digital spaces might influence the perception and processing of AI-driven persuasion. These effects can be further contingent upon contextual factors including product category, platform design and cultural setting. These conditions are important to identify the boundaries of interpretation of the results and to inform the future research on AI-driven narrative marketing in more algorithmic marketplaces.

FUTURE RESEARCH AGENDA

Even though the conclusions show strong implications of AI-driven narrative marketing at every level of the consumer decision-making process, the implications are not expected to be the same among consumers and situations. Personal attributes like algorithmic literacy can have mediating influences on the perception and re-action of consumers to AI-driven narratives, especially in the stages of evaluation and comparison. Consumers that are more aware of algorithmic personalization can be expected to process it in a less critical way, which can decrease the strength of narrative influence, and lower literacy can increase the use of narrative signals. Equally, the efficacy of AI-driven persuasion might be mitigated by consumer doubt regarding the use of algorithms, particularly during the purchase process. Such effects can also be determined by cultural context in that norms that touch on uncertainty avoidance, technology trust and decision-making styles can have an impact on how receptive people are to personalized narratives. Future studies ought to be empirical to test these moderating impacts to improve knowledge about when and who AI-driven narrative marketing works best.

REFERENCES

Arora, N., Dreze, X., Ghose, A., Hess, J. D., Iyengar, R., Jing, B., Joshi, Y., Kumar, V., Lurie, N., Neslin, S., Sajeesh, S., Su, M., Syam, N., Thomas, J., & Zhang, Z. J. (2008). Putting one-to-one marketing to work: Personalization, customization, and choice. *Marketing Letters*, *19*(3–4), 305–321. DOI: 10.1007/s11002-008-9056-z

Beatty, S. E., & Smith, S. M. (1987). External search effort: An investigation across several product categories. *The Journal of Consumer Research*, *14*(1), 83–95. DOI: 10.1086/209095

Bettman, J. R., Luce, M. F., & Payne, J. W. (1998). Constructive consumer choice processes. *The Journal of Consumer Research*, *25*(3), 187–217. DOI: 10.1086/209535

Bhattacherjee, A. (2001). Understanding information systems continuance: An expectation-confirmation model. *Management Information Systems Quarterly*, *25*(3), 351–370. DOI: 10.2307/3250921

Blackwell, R. D., Miniard, P. W., & Engel, J. F. (2006). *Consumer behavior* (10th ed.). Thomson South-Western.

Bleier, A., & Eisenbeiss, M. (2015). Personalized online advertising effectiveness: The interplay of what, when, and where. *Marketing Science*, *34*(5), 669–688. DOI: 10.1287/mksc.2015.0930

Davenport, T. H., Guha, A., Grewal, D., & Bressgott, T. (2020). How artificial intelligence will change the future of marketing. *Journal of the Academy of Marketing Science*, *48*(1), 24–42. DOI: 10.1007/s11747-019-00696-0

Dodds, W. B., Monroe, K. B., & Grewal, D. (1991). Effects of price, brand, and store information on buyers' product evaluations. *JMR, Journal of Marketing Research*, *28*(3), 307–319. DOI: 10.1177/002224379102800305

Engel, J. F., Blackwell, R. D., & Miniard, P. W. (1995). *Consumer behavior* (8th ed.). Dryden Press.

Escalas, J. E. (2004). Narrative processing: Building consumer connections to brands. *Journal of Consumer Psychology*, *14*(1–2), 168–180. DOI: 10.1207/s15327663jcp1401&2_19

Escalas, J. E., & Stern, B. B. (2003). Sympathy and empathy: Emotional responses to advertising dramas. *The Journal of Consumer Research*, *29*(4), 566–578. DOI: 10.1086/346251

Green, M. C., & Brock, T. C. (2000). The role of transportation in the persuasiveness of public narratives. *Journal of Personality and Social Psychology, 79*(5), 701–721. DOI: 10.1037/0022-3514.79.5.701 PMID: 11079236

Kotler, P., & Keller, K. L. (2016). *Marketing management* (15th ed.). Pearson Education.

Oliver, R. L. (1980). A cognitive model of the antecedents and consequences of satisfaction decisions. *JMR, Journal of Marketing Research, 17*(4), 460–469. DOI: 10.1177/002224378001700405

Oliver, R. L. (1997). *Satisfaction: A behavioral perspective on the consumer.* McGraw-Hill.

Pavlou, P. A. (2003). Consumer acceptance of electronic commerce: Integrating trust and risk with the Technology Acceptance Model. *International Journal of Electronic Commerce, 7*(3), 69–103. DOI: 10.1080/10864415.2003.11044275

Solomon, M. R. (2018). *Consumer behavior: Buying, having, and being* (12th ed.). Pearson Education.

Srinivasan, N., & Ratchford, B. T. (1991). An empirical test of a model of external search for automobiles. *The Journal of Consumer Research, 18*(2), 233–242. DOI: 10.1086/209255

Tucker, C. (2014). Social networks, personalized advertising, and privacy controls. *JMR, Journal of Marketing Research, 51*(5), 546–562. DOI: 10.1509/jmr.10.0355

Van Laer, T., De Ruyter, K., Visconti, L. M., & Wetzels, M. (2014). The extended transportation-imagery model: A meta-analysis of the antecedents and consequences of consumers' narrative transportation. *The Journal of Consumer Research, 40*(5), 797–817. DOI: 10.1086/673383

Wedel, M., & Kannan, P. K. (2016). Marketing analytics for data-rich environments. *Journal of Marketing, 80*(6), 97–121. DOI: 10.1509/jm.15.0413

Yeung, K. (2017). 'Hypernudge': Big data as a mode of regulation by design. *Information Communication and Society, 20*(1), 118–136. DOI: 10.1080/1369118X.2016.1186713

Zhang, M., Liu, Y., Wang, Y., & Zhao, L. (2022). How to retain customers: Understanding the role of trust in live streaming commerce with a socio-technical perspective. *Computers in Human Behavior, 127*, 107052. DOI: 10.1016/j.chb.2021.107052

APPENDIX

Appendix A: Measurement Items Used in the Study

Given the evolving nature of AI-driven narrative marketing, no single established scale exists that captures its influence across consumer decision-making stages. Therefore, measurement items were developed through theory-informed adaptation, drawing on foundational research in personalization, narrative persuasion, and consumer decision-making. All items were measured using a five-point Likert scale ranging from 1 = Strongly Disagree to 5 = Strongly Agree. Items were reviewed by subject-matter experts to ensure content validity and contextual relevance. This approach is consistent with prior process-based SEM studies examining emerging digital marketing phenomena.

Table 16. Measurement Items and Sources

Construct	Item Code	Measurement Statement	Primary Theoretical Basis
AI-Driven Narrative Marketing (AINM)	AINM1	AI-driven marketing messages I encounter are tailored to me based on my past behavior and preferences.	Algorithmic personalization (Bleier & Eisenbeiss, 2015)
	AINM2	The marketing content presented to me by digital platforms feels relevant to my personal needs and context.	Personalization relevance (Arora et al., 2008; Bleier & Eisenbeiss, 2015)
	AINM3	AI-driven marketing messages engage me in a story that emotionally connects the product or service to my personal experiences.	Narrative processing and transportation theory (Escalas, 2004)
Need Recognition (NR)	NR1	AI-driven marketing content makes me realize needs or problems I had not previously considered.	Need activation and problem recognition (Engel et al., 1995; Solomon, 2018)
	NR2	Personalized digital content increases my awareness of products or services that could improve my life.	Consumer problem recognition (Blackwell et al., 2006)
	NR3	AI-based recommendations highlight gaps between my current situation and desired outcomes.	Consumer decision process theory (Solomon, 2018)
Information Search (IS)	IS1	I rely on AI-driven recommendations when searching for product-related information.	External search behavior (Beatty & Smith, 1987)
	IS2	Personalized digital content reduces the effort required to search for information.	Search efficiency (Srinivasan & Ratchford, 1991)
	IS3	AI-driven narratives guide me toward information that is relevant to my needs.	Digital search guidance (Srinivasan & Ratchford, 1991)
Evaluation of Alternatives (EA)	EA1	AI-driven content helps me compare different product options effectively.	Constructive choice processes (Bettman et al., 1998)
	EA2	Personalized recommendations simplify my evaluation of available alternatives.	Choice simplification logic (Blackwell et al., 2006)
	EA3	AI-driven narratives help me weigh the pros and cons of competing options systematically.	Decision processes in choice construction (Bettman et al., 1998)

continued on following page

Table 16. Continued

Construct	Item Code	Measurement Statement	Primary Theoretical Basis
Purchase Decision (PD)	PD1	AI-driven marketing narratives influence my final purchase choice.	Purchase evaluation (Dodds et al., 1991)
	PD2	Personalized digital content increases my confidence in completing a purchase.	E-commerce decision confidence (Pavlou, 2003)
	PD3	AI-based recommendations encourage me to proceed with a purchase.	Decision facilitation (Dodds et al., 1991)
Post-Purchase Evaluation (PPE)	PPE1	AI-driven follow-up communication reassures me that I made the right purchase decision.	Satisfaction confirmation (Oliver, 1980)
	PPE2	Personalized post-purchase messages strengthen my satisfaction with the product or service.	Satisfaction reinforcement (Oliver, 1997)
	PPE3	Continued AI-based engagement increases my likelihood of remaining loyal to the brand.	Expectation-confirmation logic (Bhattacherjee, 2001)

Chapter 8
Consumer Behavior and Response to AI-Crafted Narratives

Suman Vij
http://orcid.org/0000-0002-1565-9161
SGT University, Gurugram, India

ABSTRACT

The chapter investigates consumer perception and response to advertising stories based on the use of artificial intelligence (AI). The emotional appeal, trust, and perceived authenticity were examined in this light. AI-generated stories are an increasing trend in the marketing world to an extent that the need to understand its effects on consumer behavior is growing. How people reacted to AI-driven rather than human-made narratives in different product categories is also shown by the chapter based on an empirical, mixed-method study. The results indicate that the demographic attributes, digital literacy, and prior exposure to AI technologies could be crucial to determine the performance of a story. The chapter integrates the insights provided by the psychology of consumers and the theory of narrative in proposing a conceptual framework that must compete with marketers in establishing AI-assisted but human-sensitive solutions to storytelling. The aim is to develop both theoretical and practical research on narrative advertising in the age of AI.

INTRODUCTION

The current chapter starts by following the evolution of artificial intelligence as a revolutionary aspect in contemporary narrative advertising. The following introduction contains a description of the history of AI-based advertising, the importance

DOI: 10.4018/979-8-3373-5666-2.ch008

of learning how consumers react to the stories, messages, and narratives produced by machines, the research problem, and the objectives that direct the analysis in the chapter.

Background and Emergence of AI in Narrative Advertising

The revolution of advertising that is based on AI lies in its capacity to reproduce and even improve human narrative capabilities. Manoharan (2024) highlights that the digital marketing environment has reached a new stage of emotional storytelling where AI systems that can analyze behavioral data, forecast emotional stimulators, and create contextually appropriate stories are becoming more important.

According to Gkikas and Theodoridis (2021), the role of AI in the study of consumer behavior is not limited to its application in automating a process, it is also the process of modeling psychological and emotional processes underlying the decision-making process. Combining machine learning and behavioural science, AI allows the brand to mimic the speech patterns of the humans and customise the story that a particular audience is going to love. Balciooglu (2025) goes on to say that the marketing narrative has evolved past the old in the forms of the narrative designs to a new form of AI structures, which entails combination of data analysis and storytelling on the elements of creativity. The evolution is a tremendous change in the sense and emotion creation in the discipline of advertising where the algorithms do not only say what is being said about the things but also how people feel about the said things.

There are also new ethical and perceptual problems accompanying introduction of AI in advertising. Although it can be used with precision and efficiency, it contains very serious questions of authenticity. Mechanization of creativity disrupts the historic expectations of consumers to discover storytelling as the uniquely human process. With algorithms generating stories that seem emotionally intelligent, it becomes unclear what counts as authentic and synthetic forms of expression, and their development requires further comprehension of how the audience interprets and reacts to the new form of communication.

The Significance of Learning the Consumer Reaction to AI-Generated Stories

Awareness of consumer reaction to AI-generated narratives is critical since such reactions will either make a marketing campaign successful or unsuccessful in an AI-based world. As Dogra and Dogra (2025) emphasize, the ability of AI to seamlessly combine both data-driven insights and narrative can only be used to engage consumers better provided that the audience views the stories as authentic and emotionally consistent. When the AI-generated messages become perceived by the consumers as manipulative or cold, storytelling will lose its persuasive force, no matter how technologically advanced they are.

The comparison of AI and human-made experiential narratives in marketing (Wen and Laporte 2025) revealed that although AI text is frequently as clear in structure and as rich in information as human-created and generated text, it has a lower likelihood of eliciting emotions. Alaghappan and Nalini (2025) noted that a positive impact can be instilled in consumer perception through the application of AI-supported emotive storytelling, which is created with human-sensitive algorithms that help to replicate human sensitivity. Equally, Ratta, Muneer, and ul Hassan (2024) found that advertising generated by AI boosts consumer engagement and purchase intention, yet it depends on the trust that they have on the medium. As Lal (2024) notes, the brands are in the best position to gain by making AI storytelling complementary to the human aspect, which does not diminish authenticity but enhances the emotional dimension.

Research Problem and Rationale Statement

The key issue that is discussed in this chapter is that it is not clear how consumers imagine and respond to the narratives created by AI systems. Even though AI has demonstrated its ability to create impressive and customized advertisement content, there is the question of whether people find these stories to be authentic, moving, and credible. There are established theories of narrative persuasion in traditional advertising research, which however, tend to presuppose the existence of a human author. The lack of this human origin in AI-generated writing questions the premises of consumer psychology and requires reconsidering of the definition of the narrative effectiveness of the digital age.

The justification of carrying out this study can be explained by the fact that marketing is increasingly relying on the automation of content generation and that the necessity to comprehend its psychological consequences arises. Since AI keeps imitating human creativity, it is essential to explore how viewers perceive these messages as they see them as expressions of a brand identity or as algorithmic forms of construction as tools of persuasion only. This study is required to both the researchers, who would like to clarify the theories of the role of the narratives in the environment of intelligence of machines, and the marketers, who would like to keep abreast of technological innovation and ethical communication.

The proposed research will help answer the question of the way consumers are cognitively and emotionally reacting to the advertising stories developed by the AI, compared to the ones developed by the humans.

It addresses the role of perceived authenticity, trust and emotional involvement in consumer attitudes and behavior intentions. Moreover, it examines the way in which these perceptions are influenced by demographic characteristics and digital literacy levels, which potentially may differ among various categories of the audience when using AI-mediated storytelling.

The chapter aims at examining consumer response to AI generated advertising texts, both theoretically and empirically, to determine the most important elements of consumer engagement and trust, and to develop a conceptual framework between characteristics of AI-generated storytelling and consumer behavioral consequences. By so doing, this chapter is expected to add to the current discussion between narrative psychology, advertising theory and AI ethics by illuminating the interaction of human emotion and machine generated creativity in mediating persuasion and decision-making.

Figure 1. Conceptual Overview of AI-Driven Narrative Advertising

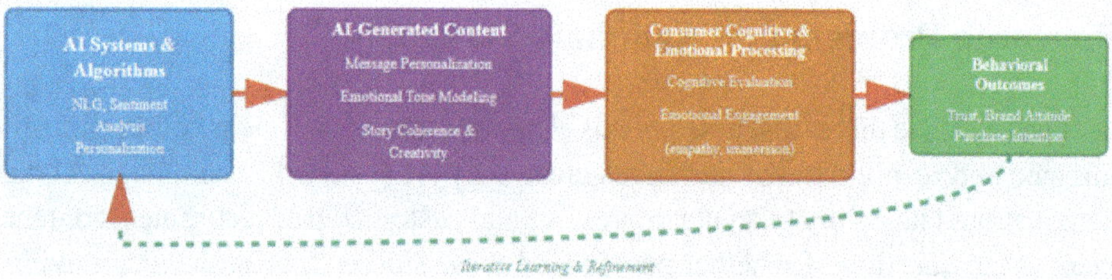

The figure depicts the conceptual sequence of the AI-based narrative advertising. It portrays the interaction between the AI technologies creating and presenting narrative and the consumer response mechanism of cognition, emotion and behavior. The figure shows how AI systems guided by data analytics develop stories that shape perception by consumers by providing an emotional and psychological connection, ultimately leading to purchase intent and brand loyalty.

Table 1. Summary of Key Research Questions and Objectives

Research Focus	Purpose
Understanding how consumers perceive and emotionally respond to AI-generated versus human-created narratives	To assess cognitive and emotional differences in consumer interpretation and engagement
Exploring the role of authenticity, trust, and emotional connection	To determine the psychological variables that shape acceptance and persuasion in AI storytelling
Examining demographic and technological influences	To identify moderating effects of digital literacy and demographic diversity on consumer perception
Evaluating the behavioral outcomes of AI-generated narratives	To link consumer perception with engagement and purchase intention, establishing implications for marketing practice

The introduction lays the groundwork, putting AI in its context in terms of narrative advertising and determining what the research is all about. The second part is the literature review, which combines consumer psychology, narrative theory, and studies concerning AI-generated content. Then, the conceptual framework and research objectives are introduced to provide a theoretical background. The research design and the data collection procedures are then described in the methodology section. The section of analysis and results illustrates the findings of the empirical results and then these findings are discussed in the discussion section in comparison to the prevailing theories. Lastly, implications, strategic recommendations and concluding insights are provided which give recommendations on direction to research and practice in future.

This systematized method, in its turn, contributes to the understanding of the interaction between AI-generated storytelling and the consumer cognition and emotion and provides a thorough discussion of the nature of the current relationship between the human perception and machine-generated creativity in the modern marketing communication. It is within this context that the next chapter examines the current literature on narrative persuasion, consumer psychology, and AI-generated content to be able to place the present study within the existing scholarly discussions.

LITERATURE REVIEW: NARRATIVE ADVERTISING, CONSUMER PSYCHOLOGY, AND THE INTEGRATION OF AI

The section is arranged in a manner that it will first explain narrative persuasion theory, then discuss psychological reactions to storytelling, and lastly determine how these processes are used in the AI-generated advertising situation. The current chapter is based on a significant amount of literature that ties the contribution of narrative persuasion, consumer psychology, and artificial intelligence (AI) integration in marketing communication. Advertising scripts have been used as techniques of persuasion that attract cognitively and emotionally the levels of perception, attitudes and behavior to brands. Storytelling has been made grounded in data and responsive with the rise of AI as well, allowing the creation of content that matches the specific preferences of consumers. In this literature review, three areas are looked at, including theoretical framework of narrative persuasion and consumer behavior, psychological processes involved in emotional involvement during advertisement and development of AI-generated material in marketing communication.

Narrative Persuasion and Consumer Behavior

According to narrative persuasion theory, consumers would respond better to narrative-based messages than to straight informational appeals. The storytelling marketing as described by Chinki, Rana, Yadav, and Sinha (2025) is presented as a review and it is stated that this type of advertising works by helping people get into story worlds, make it easier to persuade them and identify with the characters or the situation. Such effects lead to increased emotional linking and behavioral effects compared to actual or argumentative communication. The interactive quality of the stories allows the consumers to absorb messages subconsciously into the context of personal experiences to incorporate brand meanings into them.

According to Taufiq (2021), the importance of digital storytelling is increasing rapidly in terms of consumer behavior influence. The stories become interactive, dynamic, personalized in the digital space where consumers are given the chance to participate as opposed to observers. These stories enable engagements of the psyche that promotes brand memory and attachment. Jain, Lal, and Raina (2023) can show that the arrangement of the narrative plot, and the description of characters, can evoke emotional reactions that define the audience identification and the attitudes after the viewing process. Their results point to the fact that the emotional congruence of the audience and the protagonist of the story increases narrative persuasion and establishes brand empathy.

According to Lal (2023), the technological progress in the sphere of communication requires the necessary changes in the methods of narration to correspond to the requirements of the audience. With the emergence of digital environments, where content and consumers merge, the use of AI tools by advertisers grows to track emotional trajectories and adjust the narrative, respectively. In this regard, Manoharan (2024) describes AI as a collaborator in story creation, which steers marketers towards the emotionally-oriented approach of taking up the sentiment of the real-time consumer. In the same fashion, according to the authors Alaghappan and Nalini (2025) observe that AI-driven storytelling is a combination of human-based creativity with the use of data analytics, which bases brand narrative on consumer psychology. This merging of storytelling, inclusiveness and human-centered design has transformed the study of advertising. Eisend, Muldrow, and Rosengren (2023) emphasize that genuine diversity and inclusion in the stories enhance the emotional appeal and brand belief. Similarly, Gottgens and Oertelt-Prigione (2021) emphasize the importance of empathy and user context to construct the narrative as a factor in contributing to narrative persuasion as a combination of psychological, emotional, and moral factors in how consumers internalize brand messages.

Figure 2. The Relationship Between Narrative Persuasion and Consumer Trust

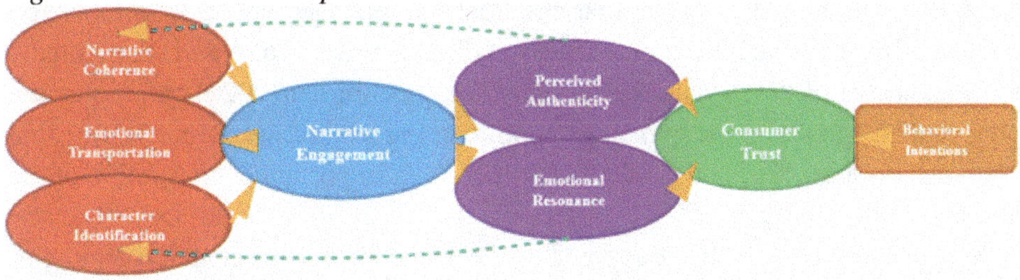

Figure 2 shows the correlation between narrative persuasion and consumer trust, with the mediation of the persuasive impact of storytelling through emotional transportation, identification and perceived authenticity. Consumers who have narrative immersion develop stronger emotional links as seen, and this leads to the establishment of credibility and trust in the brand. The model emphasizes that persuasion should not occur only based on rational appeal but affective appeal that builds up relational aspects between the consumers and narratives.

The persuasive nature of storytelling in consumer behavior is anchored on emotional involvement. Kang, Hong, and Hubbard (2020) demonstrate that emotionally coherent advertising narratives increase consumer engagement, intentions to spread the word positively, and favorable brand appraisals because consumers who engage with the characters in the story process and internalize brand messages more favorably.Rahimah, Aqfa Dzikrullah, and Astira (2025) go further and reveal that narrative video advertisement makes consumers more engaged and connected to the brand by resonating with the emotions. The emotion tone is supported through visual and auditory components in narrative videos by enhancing cognitive focus and emotional involvement. In this context, emotional involvement is an intermediary between understanding of the narrative and intentions to act.

AI application in advertising makes emotional storytelling have a new dimension. In the article by Gupta and Bansal (2023), the authors discuss the idea of AI-based emotional recognition in online advertisements and mention that advanced algorithms can evaluate customer expressions and emotions to dynamically change the tone of the message and emotion content. This skill enables marketers to write responsive stories that will develop depending on the feedback about the audience to generate a feeling of personalization and empathy to make the experience more engaging. AI therefore does not just work as a narrative generator but also an emotional interpreter.

Nevertheless, emotional involvement should be interpreted concerning authenticity and moral perception. Too much tweaking of the algorithms will create suspicion in case the consumers will recognize the insincerity or overemphasis of emotions. Human-centered communication is an idea that has been created based on health and social research by Göttgens and Oertelt-Prigione (2021), and it provides a beneficial analogy to marketing. It indicates that true emotional engagement can be achieved by the stories that observe the distinctiveness of the consumer as opposed to embracing the weaknesses of the psyche. Lester, Cho, and Lochmiller (2020) emphasize the interpretative quality of the human perception of the qualitative setting, stating that emotions are subjective and contextual, which is an important consideration of the AI-driven storytelling.

Martin-Sanz et al. (2022) appreciate the value of person-centered strategies by pointing out that understanding individuals through empathy and personalized communication between two people leads to trust and relational richness. When used in the advertising context, the insights mean that an emotional narrative should be sensitive to the diversity and experience of consumers. By incorporating these human-oriented values, there will be no need to lose the appeal of AI-enhanced stories, as ethical standards won't be undermined.

Artificial Intelligence Generated Content in the Marketing Communication

The development of AI-generated content has disrupted marketing communication creativity that requires human interaction, instead of providing production algorithms that can adapt constantly. Ratta, Muneer, and ul Hassan (2024) review the effect of AI-created advertising on consumer involvement and purchasing intentions and conclude that algorithm text can be extremely compelling when it has coherence, emotional hue, and contextual correspondence. AI content that matches the preference of consumers and reflects a kind of human expressiveness causes the consumer to react positively.

Ananthakrishnan and Arunachalam (2022) contrast the perceptions towards AI-assisted and human-made brand content and find that although both are effective in information transfer, human-created narratives have a better result in emotional depth and perceived sincerity. This shows that although AI has been effective in its structure and personalization, it should continue evolving to bring an emotional feel of human expression.

Ruuska (2025) speaks about the use of AI in voice communication and the effect it has on the consumer experience and states that the tone of voice, its rhythm, and personality is an important factor in trust and engagement. The existence of a synthetic voice may also interest and put off consumers based on how authentic it feels.

Feng (2025) describes the emergence of AI in advertising as a conflict between fascination and resistance, as a result of ambivalent attitudes of consumers towards machine creativity. According to Ganesh (2023): AI social media algorithms enhance this effect by maximizing the narrative reach and making it adaptive and responsive to user interactions, but raise the issue of emotional exhaustion and ethical concern. Puntoni, Reczek, Giesler, and Botti (2021) suggest that consumers do not view AI as a tool but as a socially and emotionally competent agent, which can be observed from an experiential standpoint. Pröbstl-Haider, Gugerell, and Maruthaveeran (2023) assert in case of disruption globally that the expectations of AI-mediated communication are formed by increased expectations of authenticity and ethical sensitivity. The development of AI-generated narratives has shown a path towards precision of the data to an emotionally intelligent storytelling- a trend that continues to reinterpret the concept of authenticity and meaning in advertisements by the consumers.

Horgby and Galizzi (2024) examine the role of advertisement creators; human/AI in persuading consumers to accept the advertisements. Their study indicates that although AI-created advertisements can be as clear, coherent, and retaining to the message as those created by humans, they can create an ambivalence effect on consumers owing to the perception of a lower level of emotional authenticity. The paper highlights that the credibility to understand AI as a creative agent is, to a great extent, determined by the degree of human-related empathy it elicits, and by the extent to which consumers are familiar with AI technologies. AI stories that are sensitive to context and intelligence in terms of emotion create a comparable level of engagement as those written by humans. On the other hand, consumers are less trusting and less emotionally engaged when the AI content is seen as too mechanical or lacking in warmth.

Burrow and Gutentag (2025) discuss the creative opportunities of AI in advertising and discover that AI-based content does not do so badly in analytical and informational appeals but does worse in emotional or symbolic messages. Narratives created by humans still do better in suggesting empathy, moral framing and storytelling coherence. It is important to note this difference as proof of the complementary effect of human and machine creativity as AI is efficient and focused on the individual, whereas human creativity maintains authenticity and cultural appeal.

In a similar fashion, Lankinen (2025) analyses how AI-generated advertisements impact consumer attitude and concludes that exposure to AI-generated content can result in ambivalent reactions in some cases. Customers understand the new and high-tech nature of AI stories but tend to doubt their authenticity. The research concludes that trust is a moderating factor: the better the technological literacy and the attitudes of consumers towards AI, the more acceptance and involvement can be observed, and the less exposure, the more skepticism.

Rahman, Lal, and Rena (2024) evaluate the interaction between communication and the Gen Z audience in the digital economy based on AI, highlighting that younger consumers are more flexible to the AI-generated content. They are also, however, more sensitive to authenticity. The digital capabilities of this generation make them more conscious of the power of AI-based personalization and, at the same time, more sensitive to a shallow tone of the emotional message. Therefore, the usefulness of AI does not only rely on the level of technological intricacy but on the storyline to convey the authentic human emotion.

The wider frame of interactive marketing provides more information. According to Wang (2021), the future marketing approach is in the interactivity and hybrid creativity where human insight and AI potential meet in the creation of adaptive and emotion-driven campaigns. Following this, Sarkar and Lal (2023) speak about the challenges to the credibility of content produced by the AI or human-produced content that change the pattern of consumer trust due to the tendency to move towards media ownership and the population interest in the community-based online platforms. This point of view is supported by Singh, Prakash, and Lal (2021), who develop their evaluative models of media effectiveness taking into consideration the cognition, affect, and behavior of the audience. Using the same frameworks to AI-created narratives implies that the effectiveness is multi-dimensional and requires such factors as emotional appeal, authenticity, and transparency of ethics.

The issue of AI-generated advertising and their ethical concerns have been analyzed in detail, especially regarding the aspect of transparency, consumer protection, and the possibility of being manipulated emotionally (Farooq et al., 2025). Simultaneously, cultural context has become one of the major determinants of the ways in which audiences receive AI-assisted creative content, cross-cultural studies illustrating discrepancies in authenticity, creative content, and trust by region (Chateau et al., 2025). The studies of multimodal AI narratives have shown that the textual, visual, and embodied cues such as human-like service robots can be effective in creating emotional resonance and attitude based on their combination, which serves as a strong argument in favor of multimodality in AI-based storytelling (Daruwala, 2025). Adding to these arguments, current research on AI-assisted storytelling focuses on providing creative partners in digital media, offering more narrative options to users and raising the question of authorship and control at the same time (Singh et al., 2026).

Table 2. Summary of Key Studies on AI-Generated vs. Human-Generated Advertising

Author(s) and Year	Focus of Study	Key Findings
Horgby & Galizzi (2024)	Influence of AI vs. human ad creators	AI-generated ads perform comparably in structure but face challenges in perceived authenticity and trust.
Burrow & Gutentag (2025)	Creative effectiveness of AI vs. human content	AI excels in analytical clarity; humans outperform in emotional persuasion and symbolic messaging.
Lankinen (2025)	Consumer attitudes toward AI-generated ads	Acceptance varies by technological familiarity and perceived sincerity of AI narratives.
Rahman, Lal & Rena (2024)	Communication with Gen-Z audiences	Younger consumers embrace AI creativity but remain sensitive to authenticity and emotional realism.
Wang (2021)	Interactive marketing paradigms	Advocates hybrid creativity combining human insight and AI adaptability.
Sarkar & Lal (2023)	Media ownership and audience engagement	Effectiveness depends on audience alignment and perceived transparency of content source.
Singh, Prakash & Lal (2021)	Communication effectiveness models	Highlights importance of emotional and cognitive factors in evaluating narrative impact.

Although there is an increasing focus on AI-based storytelling, the literature available shows that there are a number of open theoretical and empirical constraints.

Gaps and Inconsistencies in Existing Literature

Despite the rapid increase in research on AI-generated narratives, there are still a number of gaps and inconsistencies in the literature. According to Mariani, Perez-Vega, and Wirtz (2022), although research has started mapping the impact of AI in the marketing and consumer psychology field, much of the research is still preliminary and no longitudinal findings are present. The active launch of AI technologies surpasses the creation of any comprehensive theoretical framework that would clarify the decisions and emotional reactions of consumers toward AI-generated messages.

According to Jain, Wadhwani, and Eastman (2024), the existing literature is divided into studies about AI capabilities and technologies, and those about psychology and consumer attitudes. Not many frameworks are able to combine these views into a unified concept of AI-mediated persuasion. Furthermore, most studies use experimental designs which only capture short-term response but does not reflect on long-term effects of repeated exposure to AI-generated stories on brand loyalty and trust.

Iniesta and Lopez (2025) draw attention to the increasing applicability of conversational AI in consumer behavior shaping and simultaneously note that this narrative component of AI is an under-researched one. The vast majority of studies revolve around the efficiency of chatbots or the linguistic correctness and not around the persuasiveness of the conversational storytelling. On the same note, Popkova and Gulzat (2020) claim that technological revolutions have increased the rapidity of digital creativity, but the ethical and intellectual effects of making machines to do the storytelling have not been properly tackled.

Suleiman, Awan, and Javed (2021) discuss AI-driven websites in marketing performance but admit that there is no information available on how emotional and narrative elements contribute to consumer satisfaction in such settings. The article by Sung, Han, Bae, and Kwon (2022) also focuses on the topic of digital humans and technology-enhanced storytelling and states that immersion is based on realism and emotional believability. Nevertheless, the psychological lines between fake and authentic communication remain unclear, and researchers do not have a clear framework by which emotional credibility may be measured in AI narratives.

Table 3. Literature Gaps in AI Narrative Advertising Research

Identified Gap	Description	Implication for Future Research
Theoretical integration	Lack of unified frameworks connecting AI technology and narrative persuasion theory.	Develop integrative models linking emotional, cognitive, and technological processes.
Longitudinal evidence	Predominantly short-term experimental designs with limited generalizability.	Conduct longitudinal and cross-cultural studies on sustained consumer trust and engagement.
Emotional authenticity	Limited understanding of how AI narratives evoke and sustain genuine emotions.	Explore mechanisms of perceived authenticity and emotional realism in AI storytelling.
Conversational narratives	Underexplored role of AI chatbots and voice assistants as narrative agents.	Analyze conversational AI as persuasive storytelling platforms.
Ethical perception	Insufficient focus on moral and ethical interpretation of AI-generated messages.	Examine ethical transparency and consumer acceptance in AI-mediated persuasion.
Measurement consistency	Inconsistent operationalization of engagement, trust, and authenticity variables.	Standardize measurement instruments for cross-study comparison.

Although comparative research has shown that AI-generated narratives are progressing toward structural and informational competitiveness with human-generated advertising, theoretical and methodological holes still exist. The most urgent issues that need scholarly focus are emotional authenticity, long-term persuasion, and ethical considerations. By filling these gaps, one will be able to see the process of AI and human creativity coexisting to create narratives which are not only convincing, but also emotionally plausible and socially responsible.

RESEARCH OBJECTIVES AND CONCEPTUAL FRAMEWORK

The hypotheses and these objectives serve as the guiding principles in the selection of the research design and the selection of methodologies that are discussed in the next section. Here, the theoretical points of view of narrative theory, AI ethics, and advertising psychology are combined to develop a theoretical framework that describes consumer perceptions and reactions to AI-generated narratives. The paradigm is based on the interdisciplinary knowledge, integrating the theories of narrative persuasion with the ethical and psychological factors applicable to the communication between AI and humans. It aims at bridging the gap between technological invention and human emotional experience by asserting that successful AI narration has to be a source of authenticity, trust, and emotional expression in order to impact behavioral results.

Theoretical Underpinnings: Narrative Theory, AI Ethics, and Advertising Psychology

The narrative theory gives the basis of how human cognition and emotion can be formed by stories. Narratives in advertising are mental frames to aid consumers to make meaning about information, relate to brand identities, and internalise persuasive advertisements. Balcıoğlu (2025) follows the development of marketing storytelling through the traditional and the AI-driven ones, stating that technology is currently a medium and creator of brand meaning. The gist of story persuasion is the act of transportation- the check-out experience where the consumer becomes engrossed in a story both psychologically and emotionally. This absorption brings about a lower level of cognitive resistance to persuasion and emotional attachment to the themes of the narrative and the characters therein.

Advertising psychology builds upon this concept by exploring the effects of consumer responses on the emotional and cognition processes. Vakratsas and Wang (2020) hold that the effectiveness of advertising is due to an interplay between cognitive evaluation (attentional, comprehension, recall) and affective engagement (emotional resonance, identification). Consumers mediate these processes when AI produces advertising discourse by their perception of the source.

Lastly, it adds to the ethical aspect of AI marketing research by portraying that authenticity is not only a moral but also a cognitive concept, which is a perception that is built through narrative empathy and ethical transparency.

Having diversity and inclusion in storytelling enhances authenticity as it reflects the lived experience of a diverse consumer and increases emotional credibility and social responsibility. All these theoretical foundations propose a belief that psychological success of AI narratives is not only a matter of technical expertise but also ethical design and human creativity.

Figure 3. Conceptual Framework: AI Narrative Impact on Consumer Behavior

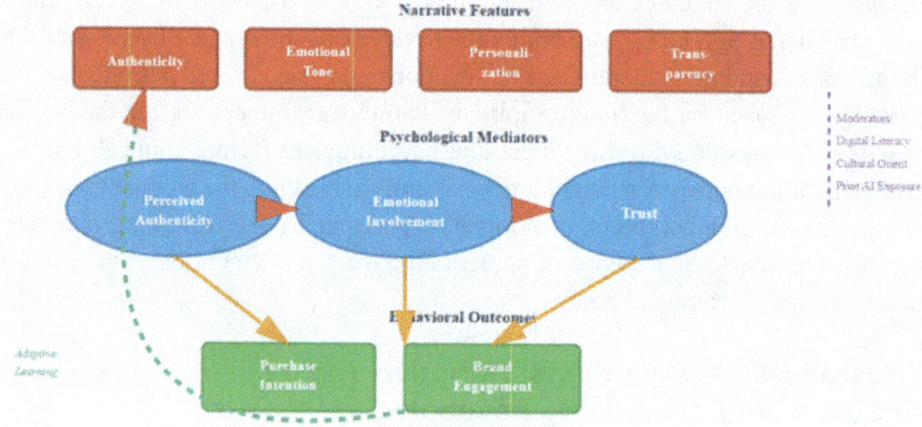

Figure 3 is the conceptual framework that connects the features of AI narrative with consumer behavioral outcomes. The model assumes that such features as narrative coherence, emotional tone, and perceived human-likeness shape three mediating variables namely authenticity, emotional involvement and trust. The aggregate effect of these mediators is on the purchase intention and involvement of the consumers with the brand. The strength of these relationships depends on external modulating variables such as demographic variables, digital literacy and prior experience with AI technologies. The cultural background also directly impacts the way consumers perceive AI authorship, emotional appeal, and authenticity, which has been shown to affect the trust and narrative involvement between distinct groups of consumers. The framework highlights that the mediating factor of the overall effectiveness of AI-generated storytelling is the interaction between technological accuracy and the human emotive perception. The key ethical issues concerned AI-generated narrative advertisement, especially transparency, perceived manipulation, and emotional sincerity. The narratives that consumers accept about AI are not only based on the coherence of the narrative but the sense that the content is ethically consistent, not misleading, and respectful of consumer autonomy.

Creation of Conceptual Framework of the Connection Between AI Narrative Features and Consumer Reactions

The logic of the creation of this conceptual framework is built by combining narrative persuasion strategies with ethical and psychological aspects peculiar to AI-generated communication. The model presupposes that AI narratives have recognizable characteristics, e.g. linguistic fluency, emotional fit, personalisation, and transparency, which affect consumer thought and affect. These characteristics influence the impact that consumers experience when it comes to perceiving authenticity (the extent to which the story seems authentic) and emotional engagement (the extent of emotional attachment), as well as trust (trust in the source of the message).

Authenticity is viewed as one of the main determinants of narrative credibility. Emotional tone, coherence and natural language are some of the cues used by the consumer to establish whether a story is genuine. Artificial Intelligence (AI) stories with empathetic wording and a sensitive understanding of the context will be seen as more genuine, and this leads to an increased emotional engaging effect. Emotional involvement is the degree of affective involvement that the consumers have when processing the narrative. This is because high emotional involvement creates identification with the story and lowers the chance of counter-arguing resulting in higher persuasion.

Trust serves as a facilitator and an outcome. Trust is built when consumers think that AI generated stories are ethically created and consider their autonomy as well; this is transferred to the brand. On the other hand, the absence of transparency or emotional manipulation might destroy the trust, even in the case when the story itself is well-constructed. The behavioral translation of these psychological responses is the dependent variable, purchase intention. The combination of authenticity, emotional involvement and trust is the aspect which predicts the number of actions taken by the consumer in relation to the persuasive intention of the AI-generated advertisement.

Hypotheses and Research Propositions

The theoretical framework leads to a series of hypotheses and propositions of the study that are used to guide the empirical research. The initial one states that the perceived authenticity of AI-generated narratives has a positive effect on emotional involvement because true and consistent storytelling helps in building empathy and engagement. The emotional engagement should also increase consumer trust, creating empathy and a sense of relational proximity with the source of narration. The hypothesis number three is that greater trust in AI generated narratives directly relates to higher purchase intention because trust eliminates doubts about machine generated content.

This is a fourth hypothesis that authenticity, emotional involvement, and trust mediate the association between AI narrative features and behavioral results. This implies that the aspect of technological excellence is not sufficient in persuasion, but it has to work through affective and ethical channels. Also, demographic and contextual moderators, including age, digital literacy and cultural orientation are likely to play a role in shaping consumer perception and response to AI-generated content. The more exposed consumers are to AI technologies, the more acceptance and engagement they can have in comparison to others who consider AI communication impersonal or intrusive.

Table 4. Operational Definitions of Constructs and Variables

Construct	Definition	Measurement Indicators
Authenticity	The degree to which consumers perceive AI-generated narratives as genuine, human-like, and contextually appropriate.	Perceived sincerity, coherence, emotional realism, and natural language quality.
Emotional Involvement	The extent to which consumers are affectively engaged and absorbed in the narrative.	Emotional intensity, empathy, identification with story elements, and narrative transportation.
Trust	The consumer's confidence in the integrity and reliability of AI-generated content and its source.	Perceived transparency, ethical alignment, credibility, and emotional comfort.
Purchase Intention	The likelihood that a consumer will engage with the brand or buy the product after exposure to the AI-generated narrative.	Stated intent to purchase, willingness to recommend, and positive behavioral tendency.
Demographic & Technological Moderators	Consumer characteristics influencing narrative interpretation and response.	Age, education, cultural context, digital literacy, and prior AI exposure.

Table 5. Research Hypotheses and Expected Relationships

Hypothesis	Expected Relationship
H1: Perceived authenticity of AI-generated narratives enhances emotional involvement.	Positive relationship between authenticity and emotional engagement.
H2: Emotional involvement positively influences consumer trust in AI-generated narratives.	Positive relationship between emotional connection and perceived trust.
H3: Trust in AI-generated narratives increases purchase intention.	Positive relationship between trust and behavioral intent.

continued on following page

Table 5. Continued

Hypothesis	Expected Relationship
H4: Authenticity, emotional involvement, and trust mediate the relationship between AI narrative features and purchase intention.	Mediating effect linking technological features with behavioral outcomes.
H5: Demographic factors and digital literacy moderate consumer responses to AI narratives.	Moderating effect on the strength of key relationships based on familiarity with AI.

All this theoretical construct and speculations make up the analytical framework of the quantitative study that will be followed. By putting the AI storytelling into perspective by the ethical and psychological context, it can be used to highlight the fact that consumer behavior is not merely a response to technology, but an interpretive process, and it is influenced by the emotion, perception and trust. This section thus forms the theoretical base of the latter methodology layout and data analysis in a manner that there is continuity between the abstract argument and the study.

METHODOLOGY

The methodology is implemented with respect to the achievement of the combination of analytical rigor and clarity, with the concentration on the key processes required to assess consumer reactions to AI-generated and human-created narratives. In this case we have used the mixed-method research design that integrates the quantitative and qualitative research designs to discuss the perception and reaction of the consumers to the AI generated and human made advertisement stories. The specified methodological framework allows the cognitive, emotional, and ethical dimensions of consumer experience of AI-based storytelling to be comprehended entirely.

Research Design: Mixed-Method Approach

In its research design it has adopted a combination of quantitative analysis which provides a measure of the relationship between the variables such as authenticity, trust, emotional involvement and purchase intent with the qualitative inquiry which provides the depth and context of the relationship. The quantitative data was collected through the structured questionnaires with the assistance of exposure to the AI-generated and human-created advertising stories. Qualitative data were gathered through focus group discussions to study subjective experiences and interpretive meanings that the participants had to these stories.

The two approaches are sequential explanatory in nature. To begin with, quantitative outcomes establish statistic trends and connections. Then, the qualitative insight which will reveal the patterns of emotional and cognitive interpretation of AI-written advertising by the consumers provides the explanatory and contextualizing information.

Figure 4. Flow of Mixed-Method Research Design

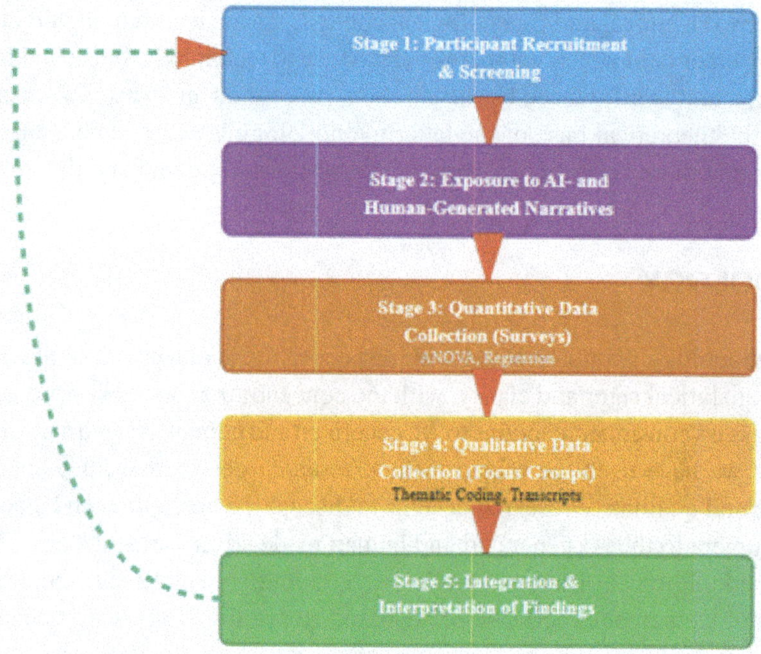

The general flow of the methodology is shown in Figure 4. The procedure is started with the identification of the participants and preparing advertising stimuli and proceeds to the survey and the gathering of quantitative data. Data analysis determines major trends in perception and behavior. The second step involves the use of focus group discussions in order to rationalize and elucidate these findings, thus leading to a synthesized view of consumer responses. The figure also illustrates how empirical measurement and qualitative interpretation are cyclical so as to have the research in both the breadth and depth of understanding.

Sampling and Characteristics of Participants

The total number of the participants was 312 who were selected with a range of demographics, including people of different ages, sex, education, and digital literacy. To ensure representation among the various categories of consumers, the audiences were recruited using online marketing forums, academic networks, and social media. Participants were required to meet the eligibility criteria, namely, having experience with digital advertising before and having a basic knowledge of AI-powered technologies (e.g., virtual assistants, recommendation systems, AI-based chat interface).

The respondents comprised those who were aged between eighteen and fifty years, which is a wide range of the generational cohorts. The gender distribution was quite even with 52 percent of the respondents identifying as female, 46 percent as male with only 2 percent specifying non-binary or prefer not to state. There were educational backgrounds of undergraduate students up to post-graduate professionals.

Table 6. Participant Demographic Characteristics

Demographic Variable	Category	Percentage (%)
Gender	Female	52
	Male	46
	Non-binary/Prefer not to say	2
Age	18–25	30
	26–35	28
	36–45	24
	46–55	18
Education	Undergraduate	35
	Postgraduate	42
	Professional/Other	23
Digital Literacy Level	Basic	25
	Intermediate	45
	Advanced	30

Description of Experimental Stimuli: AI-Created and Human-Created Narratives

To determine the comparative effect of the use of AI and human created narratives, two sets of advertising stories were created to conduct the experiment. Each set was the representation of the same product categories which were consumer electronics, fashion and personal care but with the difference of the means of creation. The AI generated narrations were created on a natural language generation platform that was trained on marketing data and was optimized to produce emotional narratives. The narratives that were created by humans were created by professional copywriters who were specialized in narrative advertising.

To make the comparison possible, both kinds of narratives were similar in a word count, structure, and the message goals. They were aimed at emotional involvement with the story lines and similar situations. The AI versions had linguistic coherence and personalization depending on audience information, and the human versions were more creative, included minor emotional expressions, and moral framing. Individuals were randomly selected to look at either the AI-created or human-created advertisements after which they were asked to answer survey tools that reflected the cognitive, emotional and behavioral response.

Quantitative Element: Survey Inspirations and Measurement Scales

A structured questionnaire containing standardized scales based on previous advertising research and consumer behavior research was used to collect quantitative data. Authenticity was determined using questions that evaluated perceived level of genuineness, emotional realness and natural language. There were emotional involvement measures of empathy, absorption and narrative transportation. Perceived credibility, transparency and ethical alignment of the message was captured as trust whereas, purchase intention was captured as the likelihood of the respondent engaging in or purchasing behavior. To test reliability, Cronbach alpha was used and all constructs got internal consistency.

Table 7. Measurement Scales and Reliability Coefficients

Construct	Number of Items	Example Item	Reliability (Cronbach's α)
Authenticity	4	"The advertisement felt genuine and emotionally sincere."	0.87
Emotional Involvement	5	"I felt emotionally connected to the story presented."	0.89
Trust	4	"I believe the message of the advertisement is credible."	0.85
Purchase Intention	3	"I would consider purchasing the product after viewing this advertisement."	0.88

This was done through descriptive and inferential analysis such as ANOVA and regression model which helped to determine the difference in consumer responses between AI and human narrative and test the hypotheses defined in the conceptual framework.

Qualitative Member: Focus Group Discussions and Thematic Analysis

After collecting the quantitative data, three focus groups were carried out in which there were 8-10 participants in each group belonging to various groups in terms of demographic factors. The groups of interest examined the subject of authenticity, emotional resonance, and ethical discomfort with AI-generated storytelling. The participants have talked about their impressions of the two types of narratives and how tone, empathy, and creativeness influenced their interest and trust.

Thematically based forms of coding based on qualitative research frameworks were used to analyze transcripts. New themes emerged such as perceived human touch, emotional resonance and ethical transparency. Inter-group comparison was done by repeatedly comparing responses until thematic convergence was attained. Qualitative results enhanced the quantitative ones through exposing the claim that despite the success of AI narratives on clarity and personalization, emotional warmth and perceived sincerity were still essential to consumer trust.

Data Collection and Ethical Considerations

The ethical principles used to facilitate data collection included transparency, confidentiality, and autonomy of the participants. Awareness was created and all the people gave informed consent prior to taking part in the study. They received information about the study purpose, anonymity of treatment of responses and the right of withdrawal at any point. No personal identifiers were taken, and all the data were kept safely.

Of great significance were ethical consideration owing to the experimental exposure to AI-generated narratives. The debriefing of the participants took place at the conclusion of the study as it was necessary to explain the presence of narrative machines generated and discuss the perceptions of authenticity and trust. This procedure avoided possible misleading and increased knowledge about the increasing role of AI in marketing communication. This research was approved by an institutional research board, and the data protection standards were observed.

Table 8. Summary of Data Collection Procedures

Stage	Activity	Method/Instrument	Purpose
1	Participant Recruitment	Online survey invitations and screening form	Ensure diverse and qualified sample
2	Narrative Exposure	Presentation of AI- and human-generated advertisements	Elicit initial consumer reactions
3	Quantitative Data Collection	Structured questionnaire (Likert scale)	Measure authenticity, trust, emotion, and intent
4	Qualitative Data Collection	Focus group discussions (3 sessions)	Explore interpretive and emotional dimensions
5	Data Analysis	Statistical tests and thematic coding	Integrate quantitative and qualitative findings
6	Ethical Debriefing	Disclosure and discussion with participants	Maintain ethical transparency and reflection

DATA ANALYSIS AND RESULTS

The empirical study analyzed the reactions of consumers to advertising stories generated by AI and those created by humans based on quantitative and qualitative data. The quantitative study involved the measurement of the disparities in the perceived authenticity, emotional involvement, trust, and purchase intention, whereas the qualitative part of the study examined the emotional perceptions of the participants and whether AI-storytelling is ethical or not. Collectively, the analyses demonstrate that technological authorship influences consumer cognition and feeling when it comes to narrative advertising.

Quantitative Analysis

The first statistics calculated were descriptive statistics to provide a summary of how the responses were spread out on major constructs. Means showed that both the types of the narratives were highly engaged with or moderately engaged with, although differences were observed between AI and human-created advertisements. On the whole, human-generated narratives were slightly rated as more authentic and as involving more emotions whereas the AI-generated ones were rated well in terms of clarity and personalization.

Table 9. Descriptive Statistics of Key Variables

Variable	Narrative Type	Mean	Standard Deviation	Minimum	Maximum
Perceived Authenticity	Human	4.21	0.63	3.00	5.00
	AI	3.82	0.74	2.50	5.00
Emotional Involvement	Human	4.09	0.68	2.80	5.00
	AI	3.88	0.70	2.60	5.00
Trust	Human	4.05	0.59	3.00	5.00
	AI	3.76	0.65	2.50	5.00
Purchase Intention	Human	4.00	0.71	2.60	5.00
	AI	3.91	0.67	2.80	5.00

Table 9 indicates a disparity between human and AI accounts in authenticity and trust as human accounts were higher in the two aspects. In emotional engagement, human-created narratives were also more preferable but AI narratives showed competitiveness especially in cognitive appreciation and informational accuracy. The purchase intention scores were also not very different, which may indicate that even the slight lack of emotional authenticity did not mean that AI narratives would not induce behavioral interest based on relevance and personalization.

The ANOVA tests were done in order to determine whether differences among the groups were significant. Findings demonstrated the existence of a great difference between AI and human narratives in perceived authenticity ($F = 6.27$, $p < 0.05$) and trust ($F = 5.83$, $p < 0.05$). Differences in emotional involvement were moderately significant ($F = 3.91$, $p = 0.06$), whereas the differences in purchase intention were not significant ($F = 1.82$, $p = 0.17$).

The regression studies were used to analyze predictor variables of trust and purchase intention. Authenticity (β=0.48, $p < 0.001$) and emotional involvement (β= 0.33, $p < 0.01$) were the driving force of trust. Trust ($\beta = 0.52$, $p < 0.001$) strongly predicted purchase intention with authenticity having an indirect effect through trust. These associations provide substantiation to the conceptual framework suggested above proving that emotional and ethical aspects intermediating the influence of AI narrative features on the behavioral outcomes.

Table 10. ANOVA/Regression Results: Predictors of Trust and Purchase Intention

Dependent Variable	Independent Variable	F / β	Significance (p-value)	Interpretation
Perceived Authenticity (AI vs. Human)	Narrative Type	F = 6.27	$p < 0.05$	Human > AI
Trust (AI vs. Human)	Narrative Type	F = 5.83	$p < 0.05$	Human > AI
Emotional Involvement (AI vs. Human)	Narrative Type	F = 3.91	$p = 0.06$	Moderate difference
Purchase Intention (AI vs. Human)	Narrative Type	F = 1.82	$p = 0.17$	No significant difference
Trust	Authenticity	β = 0.48	$p < 0.001$	Strong positive predictor
Trust	Emotional Involvement	β = 0.33	$p < 0.01$	Moderate positive predictor
Purchase Intention	Trust	β = 0.52	$p < 0.001$	Strong positive predictor

Figure 5. Comparative Consumer Response Scores: AI vs. Human Narratives

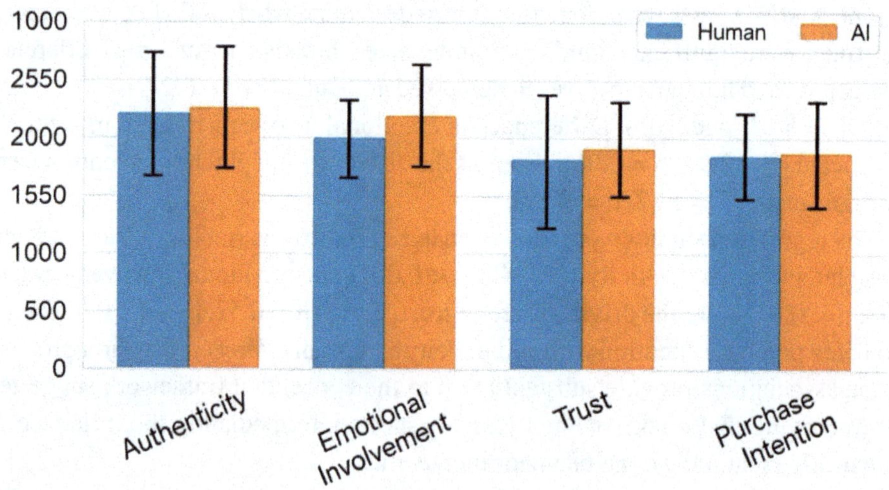

The comparison of the mean scores on response to AI-generated and human-created narratives are shown in figure 5 in rows that compare the mean scores on the major constructs. This graph shows that human-created narratives will always have a high emotional and trust rating, but AI narratives will have an equal rating of purchase intention and cognitive appreciation. The closeness of the scores suggests that the consumers are aware of and appreciate the efficiency and customization of AI, despite the perceived lack of emotional warmth.

Comparison Analysis: Artificial Intelligence vs. Human Stories

The participants said that they were ethically uncomfortable with AI-generated narratives, especially when being overly calculated or manipulative (emotional). These issues were more highlighted among the respondents who felt there was a lack of transparency when it comes to AI authorship.

Remarkably, these effects were moderated by demographic and digital literacy differences. The younger respondents, especially the age group of 18 to 30 years, gave AI narratives a better rating as compared to the older respondents. The more digitally literate respondents did not present as many concerns on emotional detachment of AI-generated stories and were less reluctant to deal with AI-driven content. Respondents who were less technologically advanced were more skeptical, majority of them showing that they were uncomfortable with the emotional design features that algorithms had created. They demonstrate that such consumer acceptance and engagement tendencies were likely to depend on the exposure and familiarity with AI technologies. The aspect of emotional involvement became apparent as one of the factors that contributed to the overall impact of the story.

The respondents that answered that they were more attached to the emotions regardless of the source of the story were more trustworthy and their purchase intention was higher. Authenticity was both emotional and cognitive phenomenon and did have a role in determining perceptions of sincerity and moral uprightness in story telling. When stories, be it those of humans or artificial intelligence, reflected realistic words and relatable feelings, consumers showed a readiness and acceptance to take the message more seriously.

Artificial AI-generated narratives were identified to be more effective in structural coherence and personalization yet were commonly regarded as devoid of the nuanced emotional sounds that were present in human-made stories. Authenticity ($r = 0.62$, $p < 0.01$) and emotional involvement ($r = 0.54$, $p < 0.01$) had the most significant correlation with trust. Trust was most strongly associated with purchase intention ($r = 0.66$, $p < 0.01$), which validates the sequential reasoning of the conceptual framework that the trust is generated by authentic and emotionally moving storytelling and subsequently by behavioral intention.

Qualitative Results: Themes of Focus Group Discussions

Four broad themes were identified by thematic analysis, which included perceived human touch, emotional realism, ethical comfort, and adaptive creativity.

Table 11. Summary of Major Qualitative Themes

Theme	Description	Participant Insights
Perceived Human Touch	Extent to which AI narratives felt emotionally natural and human-like.	Many participants described AI stories as technically sound but lacking "soul" or spontaneity.
Emotional Realism	Depth of emotion conveyed through tone and context.	Participants preferred narratives that reflected genuine emotional experience rather than formulaic sentiment.
Ethical Comfort	Consumer perceptions of transparency and authenticity in AI authorship.	Several respondents valued honesty about AI creation and expressed concern over potential manipulation.
Adaptive Creativity	Responsiveness of narratives to audience data and personalization.	Participants appreciated when AI narratives tailored content to their preferences, perceiving it as innovative and relevant.

Figure 6. Thematic Map of Consumer Perceptions from Qualitative Data

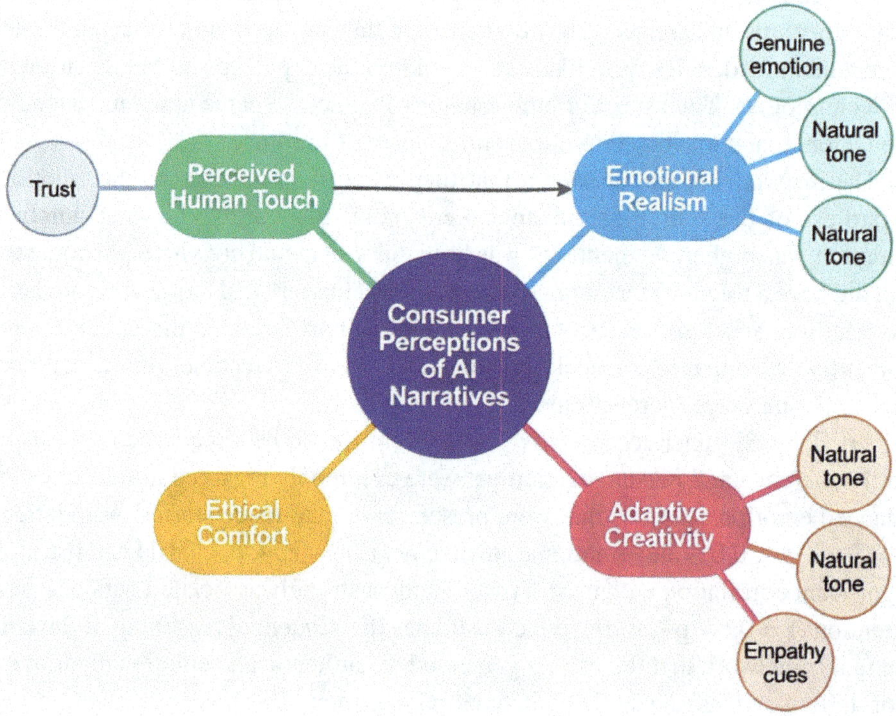

The interconnections between major themes are represented visually in figure 6. Thematic map indicates that perceived human touch and emotional realism have a significant impact on ethical comfort and trust whereas adaptive creativity is associated with engagement and personalization. In combination, these elements create the overall effectiveness of narratives and consumer satisfaction.

The qualitative insights supported the quantitative results by proving that trust and authenticity are the most powerful elements to work in consumer response direction. Although AI stories are productive in terms of engaging customers, such as personalization of the stories and making them data-driven and relevant, the element of persuasion and brand connection depends on emotional authenticity. The results of such findings indicate that consumers are not afraid to receive AI generated storytelling as long as it is transparent, emotionally plausible and ethically, the human factor in creating AI narratives is supported.

DISCUSSION

The findings prove the original concepts of narrative persuasion theory that emotional involvement and perceived authenticity are the significant determinants of trust. Narration created by people received greater scores of trust due to a stronger adherence to cognitive schemas of truthfulness and human feeling. Nevertheless, AI-generated stories were equally successful in cognitive persuasion that is to show how consumers have increasingly accepted algorithmic creativity in cases whereby messages are coherent and relevant to them.

The ethical transparency was also a decisive factor that enables consumers to accept AI-generated storytelling. Coherence of the narratives was not accompanied by increased trust in AI narratives when the participants viewed the narratives as manipulative emotionally or lacked a sense of transparency regarding their origin. The results indicate that the process of ethical perception is running in parallel with emotional realism to influence consumer reaction.

Authenticity and Perceived Human Touch Implications in AI Narratives

Authenticity turned out to be the most critical measure that determined the formation of trust. Authenticity was judged by the participants not in terms of factual verisimilitude of the story itself but in terms of the tone and the feeling of the story being so human. Accounts that had perceived warmth, empathy, and moral coherence were higher in terms of trust and emotional involvement. The results support the fact that AI systems can genuinely improve the effectiveness of marketing, which is the argument presented by Sahut and Laroche (2025) who state that the AI systems can maintain the emotional integrity of a consumer experience. There must be authenticity in AI storytelling, and not only a technical achievement, but an ethical and psychological, it must be responsive to the cultural and emotional expectations in the situation of consumer perception.

The interactive perception of human touch that provides an interpretive resolution in the authenticity and trust. The consumers positively rated AI-generated stories with human-like rhythm, tone and empathy indicators. This is in line with what Van Esch, Cui, and Jain (2021) have established that communication with AI can create consumer interest as long as it is not about the truthfulness of the message but rather the warmth and intent to build a relationship. It is not, then, the possibility of AI to compose stories but the possibility to recreate the real human emotion in such a way that it is trustworthy yet not too radical.

Mediation factors include trust and engagement that can be employed to convert narrative perception to behavioral outcome. As the findings revealed, authenticity enhances emotional involvement, which, in turn increases trust a process that, in its turn, predisposes purchase intention. This chain medium emphasizes the fact that the involvement is not a casual by-product of the exposure but rather a practical act of psychology which is motivated by empathy, familiarity and credibility The direction of emotional resonance to behavioral intention is similar to the models of engagement suggested by Voorveld, Van Noort, Muntinga, and Bronner (2018), according to which emotional and cognitive aspects of advertising hold each other together in consumer interaction.

The model in Figure 7 is the consumer-trust formation model in AI narratives. It shows the interaction between perceived authenticity and emotional involvement that creates trust which in turn affects the purchase intention. Trust has been defined as the key tool connecting the spheres of affective and behavioral reactions, which once again confirms that consumer compliance with AI-generated advertising is not as dependent on technological novelty as it is on the depth of relations.

Figure 7. Model of Consumer Trust Formation in AI Narratives

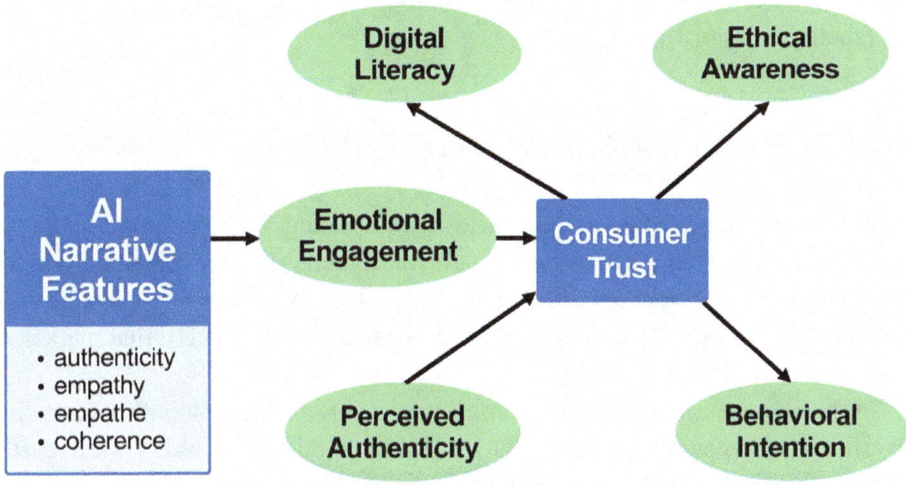

Three main stages are depicted by the model, with the emotional engagement being impacted by (1) narrative features (authenticity, coherence, emotional tone); (2) emotional engagement creates trust, and (3) trust translates into behavioral intention, and individual factors, including digital literacy and ethical awareness, moderate this process. It is important to note that emotional and moral alignment is essential in the process of AI-mediated persuasion.

The results substantiate as well as refute existing literature. Theystate Sahut and Laroche (2025) in their belief that AI-driven marketing contributes to consumer experience in that case, the principles of ethical design are observed. Likewise, Wu, Dodoo, Wen, and Ke (2022) found some ambivalence in popular opinion about AI advertising, with the excitement about innovativeness being accompanied by a disbelief in authenticity an observation that resonates with the moderate levels of emotional engagement on the side of AI narratives in this study.

Nevertheless, the findings contradict previous calculations according to which consumers are intrinsically misgivings towards AI creativity. The comparatively high purchase intention in relation to AI narratives does not take into consideration the notion that the algorithmic authorship would in all cases interfere with the process of persuasion. Rather, the information hints at a conditional admission, which should be based on trust and emotional unity. According to Zhang, Atwal, and Kaiser (2021), perceived deceit or dishonesty in corporate communications undermines trust at an alarming pace, which is reflected in the qualitative data as participants in the survey appreciated openness of information on AI authorship. The research consequently contributes to existing knowledge as it demonstrates that AI narratives can be nearly as persuasive as humans in case consumers are educated, ethically and emotionally satisfied.

PRACTICE AND STRATEGY IMPLICATIONS

In AI narrative advertising, the ethical aspects should be prioritized. The key to establishing and sustaining consumer trust is transparency in AI involvement and the absence of emotional manipulation by the latter. The issue of over-personalization and its impact on the consumer alienation is also an ethical concern that marketers must take into account.

The results reveal that AI should be used responsibly and transparently in narrative advertisement. Opening the book of AI, keeping emotional appeal down to earth, and being ethically consistent are the key factors to preserving consumer trust and sustained brand credibility.

Marketing and Advertising Strategic Recommendation

Marketers need to treat AI narratives as more of a relational interface rather than an automated message system. The statistics show that consumers are most involved when stories are emotionally sound and transparent in terms of ethics. According to Mehta and Deuskar (2025), the persuasive nature of the metaphorical and narrative frameworks is based on the fact that they can engage the consumer imagination, and these can be used even in the context of the AI-based systems as long as they can appeal to the feeling of empathy rather than mechanical accuracy. The use of AI as an author should be reported publicly by campaigns to maintain credibility as creative collaboration between human input and help of machines should be highlighted.

In order to craft emotionally captivating AI stories, ethical considerations would have to be applied at each level of content development. According to Ahuja (2024), AI advertising policies are successful when human relevance is increased through personalization but not through the emotional authenticity. Storytelling, especially of emotion, must use language and images that indicate the diversity of humanity without being stereotyped or overgeneralized sentiment. Blanco-Ruiz, Sainz-de-Baranda, Gutiérrez-Martin, Romero-Perales, and Lopez-Ongil (2020) also remember that AI systems should take into account gender and cultural outlooks in emotional modeling as inclusiveness directly leads to perceived sincerity and brand credibility.

Affective computing tools that can identify the emotional nuances in a wide range of audiences should be embedded into the developers. Nevertheless, empathy based on data should be transparent, which means that the consumer can see the way their emotions are being explained and resolved. This sense of morality will serve the purpose of preventing any form of backlash and enhancing the trust in the long term.

Recommendations in AI Content Developers and Communication Strategists

In terms of narrative design, AI content developers are advised to put a stronger emphasis on hybrid creativity a partnership where AI brings precision in data and a level of scalability and human supervision brings moral stability and expressiveness. AI storytelling organization must meet the needs of accountability, empathy, and the appropriate scenario of strategic planners. Barzykowski and Mazzoni (2022) state that the emotional memory can influence the recalling of stories by the consumer, thus AI-created stories have to create experiences to be remembered in personal feeling rather than by algorithmic novelty.

Communication strategists should also introduce real-time feedback loops that facilitate the AI systems to grasp the response of the consumers, although ethical control is required. It is a recurring design which is flexible friendly without intruding on the autonomy of the consumers.

Consequences to the Managers and the Technological Issues in the Future

The study gives managers and decision-makers an idea on the importance of ethical branding and emotional transparency in AI marketing. Aichner, Coletti, Jacob, and Wilken (2021) demonstrate the way reputational damage may be preserved in a scenario when the brands overlook the concept of authenticity because it is particularly relevant when people get to know more about algorithmic persuasion. The application of AI in brand storytelling should therefore be contextualized to co-creation with audiences to make emotional connection genuine and mutually advantageous.

With the technological progress of generative AI and sentiment analysis, the personalization of the narrative in the future will be more developed. However, the latter should be compensated by privacy protection and value-based communication systems. All the stories of ethical AI should not be deceptive to the consumer emotion but enhance brand-relationship through empathy, inclusivity and respect of autonomy.

The combination of creativity, technology and psychology of the stories about AI is an important change in terms of marketing communication. The dilemma is to strike a balance between the emotional intelligence and moral depth with which human stories are narrated and take advantage of the AI potential of rendering the narrations more personal, receptive, and interactive to international audiences. In keeping pace with consumer demands, AI-generated stories should be emotionally truthful and ethically clear. Marketers should not engage in manipulative activities that will take advantage of emotions without giving clear information on the nature of the contents. Such emphasis on being transparent and sincere in emotions will build brand trust and create consumer loyalty.

SUMMARY AND FUTURE RESEARCH

The study carried out in the specified chapter provides a comprehensive examination of how consumers perceive and respond to advertising stories created by artificial intelligence and the ones created by a human. The mixed-method study that involved quantifying and later interpreting AI-generated narratives revealed that as the AI-generated narratives gain credibility and engagement potential, the usefulness of the AI-generated narratives is subject to the perceived human touch and the ethical transparency. These have indicated that psychological complexity of consumer-AI interaction could exist, in which the technological sophistication fails to produce trust and commitment of emotion, unless such empathy and coherence as produced by humans are produced.

Moreover, the research highlights the possible risks linked to AI-based stories, such as moral uneasiness, cultural detachment and excessive personalization. These questions should be researched more, especially in different cultural backgrounds in which anticipations of genuineness and expressiveness can vary.

The findings indicate that both AI and fictional texts stand a possibility to effectively convict the consumer attitudes and intentions, which, however, follows slightly different mechanisms. Stories created by people attributed higher points to authenticity, emotions, and trust and this is why the importance of human empathy and moral sensitivity in advertising communication is as old as time. In comparison, AI-generated narratives were more successful in clarity, personalization and informational interest, and almost equally successful in generating purchase intention. It was found that the emotional involvement and authenticity were the best predictors of trust, which in turn, was a significant contributor to behavioral outcomes.

. All these hints lead to the assumption that the future of narrative advertising will not be based on making a choice between AI and human-made but a blend of those to increase the power of analysis with the richness of emotions.

In practice, the results can give valuable information to the work of marketers, advertisers, or developers of AI. They state that design of narratives should be transparent, ethically sensitive and inclusive. Whenever a brand reveals the use of AI and the preservation of emotions, it is more likely to gain consumer loyalty and attention. In addition, human standards are still necessary in making AI-written stories empathetic, culturally sensitive, and ethical. As a practitioner, the findings help to emphasize the importance of AI as a creative partner and not as an alternative to human storytelling.

Although it is a thoroughly designed study, there are some limitations in it. Although the sample size was big enough to carry out a general analysis, it was also restricted to only a single cultural context, and thus, it might not make the findings generalizable across other regions with varying technological acceptance or storytelling customs. The experimental stimuli that are limited to the three product categories might fail to reflect the differences in consumer responses to the stimulus in various industries or the emotional level of advertising. Also, the research used self-reported level of emotion and trust, which, although valid, is not able to fully reflect on subconscious responses that can also affect the actual practice.

The time constraint also limits knowledge on the long-term impacts. The attitude of consumers to AI-generated narratives will probably change as the level of familiarity with AI technologies rises. A longitudinal study would give a better understanding of how trust and emotional perception are formed after repeated exposure to AI storytelling. Lastly, even though the qualitative aspect created a deeper insight, additional ethnographic or neuromarketing research might have been more informative about the cognitive-emotional processes of consumer interpretation.

To conclude, the transparency of AI narrative, the threat of emotional manipulation, and ethical concerns of over-personalization are the main themes of this chapter that are crucial to the future of AI in advertising. By taking these issues into consideration in future studies and applications, it will be possible to make AI a reliable and responsible resource to marketers.

Future Work Directions

The study emphasizes that the effectiveness of AI-generated advertisement is based on the idea of balance between technological innovation and ethical responsibility. The consumer trust in AI-driven narratives will be a primary concern that will require transparency, emotional sincerity, and the lack of manipulative intent. The perception of AI authorship as innovative and credible may be described in high technological trust cultures, and lack of human authorship may decrease emotional involvement in cultures that are more humanistic. This type of comparative study would inform the global marketing strategy of adapting AI stories to emotionally specific cultural contexts.

Another area that must be sought is the issue of personalization. The personalization-perceptions of authenticity and emotional appeal interaction needs to be discussed in the second generation of the study since AI-based technologies are becoming more and more personalized in their content to appeal to people. The debate on whether hyper-personalised AI narratives strengthen or weaken trust is yet to be answered in particular cases when the consumers perceive that algorithmic targeting is intrusive. The ethical dilemma about personalization v. privacy also needs to be assessed in future work, in terms of ensuring that adaptive storytelling augments and does not control emotional connection.

Artificial intelligence (AI) in storytelling Multimodal storytelling, the domain where AI combines text, voice, and visual emotion, is another area that can be studied further. The intersection of these modalities in affecting perception, memory, and purchase behavior will be crucial in improving the science of narrative persuasion in an AI-mediated environment.

Figure 8. Schematic of Future Research Pathways in AI Narrative Advertising

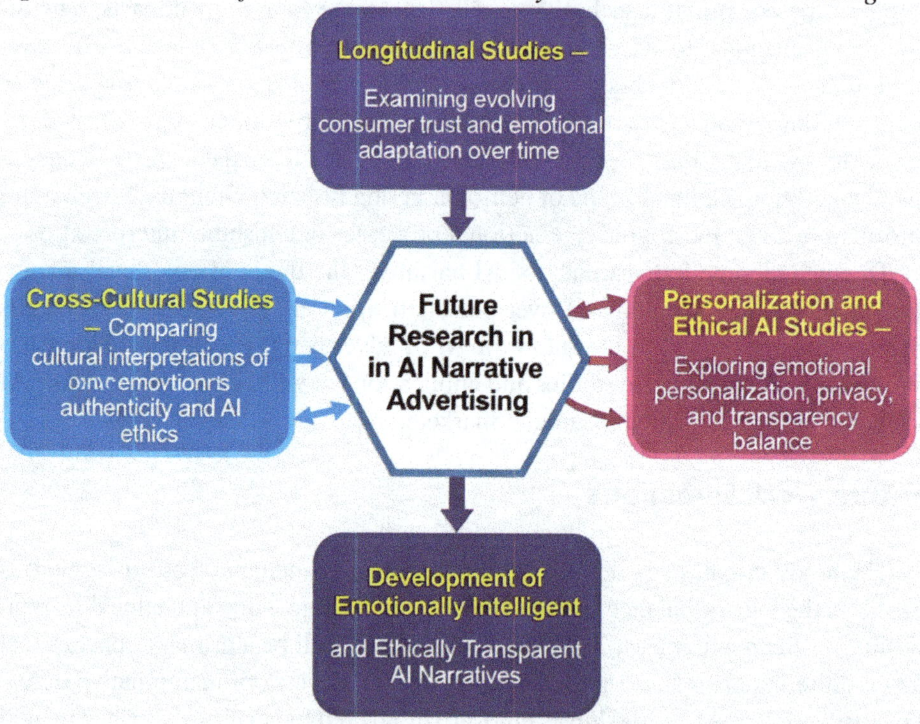

The major pathways that can be implemented in future are presented in Figure 8. It shows three intersected directions, (1) longitudinal studies of changing consumer trust, (2) cross-cultural identification of emotional and ethical interpretation, and (3) future studies on personalization with the extremes of data-driven empathy. The overlapping of these pathways is based on the overall aim to create emotionally intelligent, culturally adaptive and ethically transparent AI narratives that keep consumers trustful and interested.

This particular step of the investigation is predetermined by the results and structure of the current chapter, which is the technological innovation, and the psychological development of the ongoing dialogue between the human feeling and machine creativity.

REFERENCES

Aichner, T., Coletti, P., Jacob, F., & Wilken, R. (2021). Did the Volkswagen emissions scandal harm the "made in Germany" image? A cross-cultural, cross-products, cross-time study. *Corporate Reputation Review*, *24*(4), 179–190. DOI: 10.1057/s41299-020-00101-5

Alaghappan, T., & Nalini, R. (2025). AI-powered emotional storytelling for brand narratives and consumer perception. In *International Conference on Artificial Intelligence in Commerce and Management* (pp. 200–210). DOI: 10.34293/ICAICM-25.ch029

. Ananthakrishnan, R., & Arunachalam, T. (2022). Comparison of consumers perception between human generated and AI aided brand content. Webology, 19(2).

. Balcıoğlu, Y. S. (2025). The evolving role of storytelling in marketing: From tradition to AI-powered narratives. AI Impacts on Branded Entertainment and Advertising, 107–124.

Barzykowski, K., & Mazzoni, G. (2022). Do intuitive ideas of the qualities that should characterize involuntary and voluntary memories affect their classification? *Psychological Research*, *86*(1), 170–195. DOI: 10.1007/s00426-020-01465-3 PMID: 33582862

Blanco-Ruiz, M., Sainz-de-Baranda, C., Gutiérrez-Martín, L., Romero-Perales, E., & López-Ongil, C. (2020). Emotion elicitation under audiovisual stimuli reception: Should artificial intelligence consider the gender perspective? *International Journal of Environmental Research and Public Health*, *17*(22), 8534. DOI: 10.3390/ijerph17228534 PMID: 33213064

Burrow, E., & Gutentag, J. (2025). AI-generated versus human-generated: Creative content in advertising. *Pepperdine Journal of Communication Research*, *13*(1), 8.

Chateau, L., Arora, P., & Herman, L. (2025). Cross-cultural approaches to creative media content in the age of AI. *Media Culture & Society*, *47*(5), 01634437251328188. DOI: 10.1177/01634437251328188

Chinki, R. S., Yadav, M. P., & Sinha, N. (2025). Crafting narratives to influence consumers: A systematic review of storytelling marketing. *Asia-Pacific Journal of Business Administration*.

Daruwala, N. A. (2025). How multimodal narrative and visual representations of human-like service robots shape attitudes and social connection. *Frontiers in Robotics and AI*, *12*, 1568146. DOI: 10.3389/frobt.2025.1568146 PMID: 40475003

Dogra, P., & Dogra, A. K. (2025). Interweaving narratives: The role of AI in enhancing consumer engagement through storytelling. In *Decoding Consumer Behavior Using the Insight Equation and AI Marketing* (pp. 275–300). IGI Global Scientific Publishing.

Eisend, M., Muldrow, A. F., & Rosengren, S. (2023). Diversity and inclusion in advertising research. *International Journal of Advertising, 42*(1), 52–59. DOI: 10.1080/02650487.2022.2122252

Farooq, N., Hashmat, S., & Hashim, A. (2025). AI in Advertising: Ethical Risks, Consumer Protection, and Policy Implications. *Annual Methodological Archive Research Review, 3*(6), 1–18. DOI: 10.63075/nb02bq32

Feng, Y. (2025). The AI Genie in the Bottle: Charting AI evolution and aversion in advertising. *Journal of Interactive Advertising, 25*(4), 1–16. DOI: 10.1080/15252019.2025.2537019

Ganesh, A. (2023). The impact of social media on consumer behavior: An AI-enhanced approach to marketing strategies. Available at *SSRN* 4985407.

Gkikas, D. C., & Theodoridis, P. K. (2021). AI in consumer behavior. In Advances in Artificial Intelligence-Based Technologies: Selected Papers in Honour of Professor Nikolaos G. Bourbakis—Vol. 1 (pp. 147–176). Springer International Publishing.

Göttgens, I., & Oertelt-Prigione, S. (2021). The application of human-centred design approaches in health research and innovation: A narrative review of current practices. *JMIR mHealth and uHealth, 9*(12), e28102. DOI: 10.2196/28102 PMID: 34874893

Gupta, S., & Bansal, P. (2023). AI-driven emotional recognition in digital ads: A novel approach to consumer engagement. *Journal of Marketing & Supply Chain Management, 2*(131), 2–7. DOI: 10.47363/JMSCM/2023(2)131

. Horgby, L. E. E., & Galizzi, D. (2024). AI vs. human: Ad creator influence: How ad creators shape consumer responses and acceptance of AI in advertising.

Iniesta, M. B., & López, D. (2025). A systematic literature review on conversational AI's influence in consumer behavior. In *Decision Science Alliance International Summer Conference* (pp. 27–39). Springer. DOI: 10.1007/978-3-031-78238-1_3

Jain, P., Lal, R., & Raina, G. S. (2023). Portrayal of characters in a Hindi film and audience reaction: A discourse analysis. *IIS University Journal of Arts, 12*(1&2), 362–377.

Jain, V., Wadhwani, K., & Eastman, J. K. (2024). Artificial intelligence consumer behavior: A hybrid review and research agenda. *Journal of Consumer Behaviour, 23*(2), 676–697. DOI: 10.1002/cb.2233

Kang, J. A., Hong, S., & Hubbard, G. T. (2020). The role of storytelling in advertising: Consumer emotion, narrative engagement level, and word-of-mouth intention. *Journal of Consumer Behaviour, 19*(1), 47–56. DOI: 10.1002/cb.1793

Lal, R. (2023). New measures of teaching learning and evaluating with changing technology. In Naim, A. (Ed.), *Accreditation processes and frameworks in higher education* (pp. 267–287). Nova Science Publishers.

. Lal, R. (2024). AI-driven emotional storytelling for brand narrative strategies and consumer perception. IUP Journal of Brand Management, 21(4).

. Lankinen, E. (2025). The effect of an AI-generated advertisement on consumer attitudes.

Lester, J. N., Cho, Y., & Lochmiller, C. R. (2020). Learning to do qualitative data analysis: A starting point. *Human Resource Development Review, 19*(1), 94–106. DOI: 10.1177/1534484320903890

Manoharan, J. (2024). Navigating the digital marketing landscape: The role of AI and emotional storytelling in consumer engagement. *Authorea Preprints*. DOI: 10.36227/techrxiv.170630980.05212656/v1

Mariani, M. M., Perez-Vega, R., & Wirtz, J. (2022). AI in marketing, consumer research and psychology: A systematic literature review and research agenda. *Psychology and Marketing, 39*(4), 755–776. DOI: 10.1002/mar.21619

Martín-Sanz, M. B., Salazar-de-la-Guerra, R. M., Cuenca-Zaldivar, J. N., Salcedo-Perez-Juana, M., Garcia-Bravo, C., & Palacios-Ceña, D. (2022). Person-centred care in individuals with stroke: A qualitative study using in-depth interviews. *Annals of Medicine, 54*(1), 2167–2180. DOI: 10.1080/07853890.2022.2105393 PMID: 35930376

. Mehta, M. J., & Deuskar, V. A. (2025). Narrative and metaphorical persuasion in advertising: A multidisciplinary systematic review of linguistic strategies and consumer.

Popkova, E. G., & Gulzat, K. (2020). Technological revolution in the 21st century: Digital society vs. artificial intelligence. In Popkova, E. G., & Sergi, B. S. (Eds.), *The 21st Century from the Positions of Modern Science: Intellectual, Digital and Innovative Aspects* (Vol. 91, pp. 339–345). Springer International Publishing. DOI: 10.1007/978-3-030-32015-7_38

Pröbstl-Haider, U., Gugerell, K., & Maruthaveeran, S. (2023). Covid-19 and outdoor recreation—lessons learned? Introduction to the special issue on "outdoor recreation and Covid-19: Its effects on people, parks and landscapes.". *Journal of Outdoor Recreation and Tourism, 41*, 100583. DOI: 10.1016/j.jort.2022.100583 PMID: 37521268

Puntoni, S., Reczek, R. W., Giesler, M., & Botti, S. (2021). Consumers and artificial intelligence: An experiential perspective. *Journal of Marketing, 85*(1), 131–151. DOI: 10.1177/0022242920953847

. Rahimah, A., Aqfa Dzikrullah, S. S., & Astira, A. A. (2025). Connecting emotionally: Examining the impact of narrative video advertising on consumer involvement and brand attachment. BISNIS & BIROKRASI: Jurnal Ilmu Administrasi dan Organisasi, 32(1), 38–53.

Rahman, Z. T., Lal, R., & Rena, R. (2024). Challenges of communication with Gen-Z in the era of artificial intelligence-interceded digital economy. In *AI-Oriented Competency Framework for Talent Management in the Digital Economy* (pp. 76–94). CRC Press. DOI: 10.1201/9781003440901-5

Ratta, A. A., Muneer, S., & Ul Hassan, H. (2024). The impact of AI generated advertising content on consumer buying behavior and consumer engagement. [BBE]. *Bulletin of Business and Economics, 13*(2), 1152–1157.

Sahut, J. M., & Laroche, M. (2025). Using artificial intelligence (AI) to enhance customer experience and to develop strategic marketing: An integrative synthesis. *Computers in Human Behavior, 170*, 108684. DOI: 10.1016/j.chb.2025.108684

Sarkar, N., & Lal, R. (2023). Changing trends of media ownership: Marketing through community engagement in Hindi television news channels. In *Global Applications of the Internet of Things in Digital Marketing* (pp. 290–309). IGI Global. DOI: 10.4018/978-1-6684-8166-0.ch015

. Singh, G., Naaz, A., Syed, A., & Akhila, V. (2026). AI-Assisted Storytelling: Enhancing Narrative Creation in Digital Media.

Singh, R. K., Prakash, R., & Lal, R. (2021). Adoption of CAB model for instrument development of effectiveness of crime-based reality-shows. *Journal of Content Community and Communication, 14*(7), 230–239. DOI: 10.31620/JCCC.12.21/19

Suleiman, D. A., Awan, T. M., & Javed, M. (2021). Enhancing digital marketing performance through usage intention of AI-powered websites. *IAES International Journal of Artificial Intelligence, 10*(4), 810–817. DOI: 10.11591/ijai.v10.i4.pp810-817

Sung, E. C., Han, D. I. D., Bae, S., & Kwon, O. (2022). What drives technology-enhanced storytelling immersion? The role of digital humans. *Computers in Human Behavior, 132*, 107246. DOI: 10.1016/j.chb.2022.107246

Taufiq, A. (2021). Narrative influence in the digital age: How digital literature shapes consumer behavior. *Journal of Society Innovation and Development, 2*(2), 131–141. DOI: 10.63924/jsid.v2i2.231

Vakratsas, D., & Wang, X. (2020). Artificial intelligence in advertising creativity. *Journal of Advertising, 50*(1), 39–51. DOI: 10.1080/00913367.2020.1843090

Van Esch, P., Cui, Y., & Jain, S. P. (2021). Stimulating or intimidating: The effect of AI-enabled in-store communication on consumer patronage likelihood. *Journal of Advertising, 50*(1), 63–80. DOI: 10.1080/00913367.2020.1832939

Voorveld, H. A. M., Van Noort, G., Muntinga, D. G., & Bronner, F. (2018). Engagement with social media and advertising: The differentiating role of platform type. *Journal of Advertising, 47*(1), 38–54. DOI: 10.1080/00913367.2017.1405754

Wang, C. L. (2021). New frontiers and future directions in interactive marketing: Inaugural editorial. *Journal of Research in Interactive Marketing, 15*(1), 1–9. DOI: 10.1108/JRIM-03-2021-270

Wen, Y., & Laporte, S. (2025). Experiential narratives in marketing: A comparison of generative AI and human content. *Journal of Public Policy & Marketing, 44*(3), 392–410. DOI: 10.1177/07439156241297973

Wu, L., Dodoo, N. A., Wen, T. J., & Ke, L. (2022). Understanding Twitter conversations about artificial intelligence in advertising based on natural language processing. *International Journal of Advertising, 41*(4), 685–702. DOI: 10.1080/02650487.2021.1920218

Zhang, M., Atwal, G., & Kaiser, M. (2021). Corporate social irresponsibility and stakeholder ecosystems: The case of Volkswagen Dieselgate scandal. *Strategic Change, 30*(1), 79–85. DOI: 10.1002/jsc.2391

Section 3
Critical, Ethical, and Strategic Dimensions

Chapter 9
Limits and Risks:
The Dark Side of AI and Ethical Quandaries in Developing Marketing Stories

Can Murat Demir
http://orcid.org/0000-0002-9155-9672
Ondokuz Mayıs University, Turkey

Yeter Demir
http://orcid.org/0009-0005-8603-3536
Ondokuz Mayıs University, Turkey

ABSTRACT

Artificial intelligence (AI) technologies are also considered a communication and meaning-making practice that transforms the structure of the narrative relationship that brands establish with consumers. AI systems, which offer personalized stories to consumers, are expanding the scale of marketing narratives. This comprehensive process carries risks, including ethical violations, algorithmic bias, and implicit forms of manipulation. This research critically analyzes AI-powered marketing narratives from the perspective of meaning-making and discursive persuasion. The research adopts a qualitative and theoretical approach and utilizes narratology and digital marketing literature to analyze the impact of AI-powered narratives on brand discourse, consumer persuasion, and perception. The study reveals that AI plays a pioneering role in marketing communication, at the levels of narrative epistemology and ethical responsibility. The study presents an approach that centers narrative responsibility for ethical and sustainable AI-based brand communication.

DOI: 10.4018/979-8-3373-5666-2.ch009

INTRODUCTION

Technological evolution, which has become one of the requirements of the digital age, and its natural consequence, artificial intelligence, permeate a wide range of areas, from public administration to corporate decision-making processes, from companies' product and brand communication applications to their ways of doing business, and from scientific production fields to cultural representations (Özgür, 2024; Wirth, 2018). This highly comprehensive transformation process is also fundamentally changing brands' marketing activities (Bolat, 2023; Dimitrieska et al., 2018), rebuilding the nature of marketing processes as campaigns and outputs powered by artificial intelligence increasingly take on a central role. The narrative-focused marketing approach is redefining both the production methods of campaign content and the experiential boundaries of the marketing narrative. This technological renewal process is spreading to a wider area over time and playing a decisive role in determining the nature of narrative-centered marketing activities. Thus, artificial intelligence is approached not only as a technological process in advertising, but also as a narrative mechanism that reconstructs narrative ontology, in other words, story structure, discourse, and persuasion stages.

It is predicted that, in the future, artificial intelligence and related technologies will significantly increase their impact across many more corporate areas, including sales processes, customer service, and consumer behavior (Davenport et al., 2020). Such advancements are completely reshaping the functionality of traditional brand structures, and the marketing processes are being holistically transformed (Canals & Heukamp, 2020). With the fast development of AI models, organizations are able to efficiently optimize text and image-centric content creation processes. Thus, new opportunities beyond the scalability, speed, and efficiency criteria of traditional marketing are emerging (Gülbaşı, 2025; Gündüzyeli, 2024). Due to these characteristics, artificial intelligence has become an important tool that shapes how a brand looks, how it tells its story, and how customers experience it (Barari et al., 2024).

For brands, storytelling is not only a marketing or advertising tool but has become an essential narrative communication tool at the core of brand management strategies (Woodside et al., 2008). A well-thought-out narrative can establish a deep connection with consumers through corporate identity and values, emotional responses, and social representations, while conveying brand values to the outside world with human sensitivity.

The role of marketing narratives is not only textual or linguistic in nature; when assessed together with corporate identity, the medium in which they are published, and the social elements surrounding these components, they have a holistic look. As Yılmaz and Taşkıran (2013) point out, advertising narratives take shape within a multi-layered structure; this structure is shaped both by the advertiser's corporate goals and strategic orientations and by the values, expectations, and perceptions of the target audience. This assessment points to an even more critical issue in terms of AI-supported marketing narratives. This is because in marketing stories produced by AI, ethical boundaries and potential risks must be evaluated not only in terms of digital skills and creativity, but also within the framework of the advertiser's sense of responsibility, discursive preferences, and the cultural sensitivities of the target audience (Yılmaz, 2017b).

The application of artificial intelligence in the development of marketing stories has raised concerns about ethics, authenticity, and perceived credibility. Several studies have established that advertisements that use artificial intelligence make consumers feel that there is a level of artificialness, which affects brand loyalty and representation (Chen, Wang, Hill, & Li, 2024; Tang, Sun, Curran, Schaub, & Shin, 2024). The potential of AI algorithms to re-enact ideological biases (Pagano et al., 2022) and produce semantic deviations based on demographic groups requires brands to rethink their ethical mission and social values in this context (Yılmaz & Ashqar, 2025).

At the heart of these AI-driven paradoxes lie numerous ethical issues that grow alongside the technology's capabilities. The resolution of consequences such as AI biases, ethical and moral decision-making problems, and human-machine goal misalignment has become more critical and urgent due to the pervasive nature of technology across all areas. This state of affairs requires that AI-supported marketing narratives be investigated not only in relation to their technological benefits (speed, efficiency, scale) but also in terms of their ethical parameters. Thus, the findings of existing studies that systematically evaluate the ethical, perceptual, and social dimensions of AI-supported marketing narratives make the increasingly complex risk map of the field more apparent (Du & Xie, 2021).

The literature highlights not only the efficiency and scale advantages provided by technology but also the ethical and social risks it entails. In this respect, Rogers (2021) and Rodgers & Nguyen (2022) describe the algorithmic learning and adapting processes of AI, while Zhao (2025) points out the ethical concerns of data privacy, transparency, and consumer trust in AI-based marketing practices. As Abbasoğlu (2025) states, the practices of AI may have the ability to unconsciously affect the decision-making process of consumers and create unrealistic expectations. In terms of bias and discrimination, Yeşilkaya (2022) states that biases in the data used in AI may cause unfair targeting and the exclusion of some consumer groups, thus influencing corporate identity. Labrecque et al. (2024) expose the negative impact of the dark side of artificial intelligence on consumer perception and trust in brands.

With the increasing adoption of AI in the media and communications industry, there is the potential to enhance the skills of professionals, but it has not yet been fully adopted, and this creates a need for a more systematic evaluation of the ethical risks of AI (McCollough et al., 2022; Qin, 2024). Du and Xie (2021) emphasize that the multifunctionality, interactivity, and maturity of AI in AI-supported products increase ethical issues at the product, consumer, and societal levels, and that companies must manage these risks within the framework of their corporate social responsibility strategies. Additionally, Murtezaoğlu (2022) analyzes the technical, organizational, and ethical barriers to the adoption of AI in the marketing processes of information technology and software companies, revealing their scope through user behavior and expert opinions.

According to the literature, there is a delicate balance that must be achieved between the production, speed, and scale benefits that AI-enabled marketing processes offer and the dangers of ethics, data privacy, bias (Pagano et al., 2022), and manipulation.

The marketing activities developed using artificial intelligence have moved from being an ethical issue to becoming a real process of institutionalization. The European Union Artificial Intelligence Act, which was approved by the European Parliament and the Council of the European Union (2024), has been the most significant step taken in this area. Algorithmic transparency, accountability, and risk management have evolved from being 'ethical promises' left to the discretion of brands to becoming inevitable legal requirements. Within this new paradigm, algorithmic impact assessments (Reisman et al., 2018), responsible AI committees, and procedures designed to ensure compliance from the design stage onwards have become the basic mechanisms that define the boundaries of legitimacy of marketing stories developed in the context of artificial intelligence. Thus, the distribution of AI-generated content is now determined not only by creativity but also by the ability to surmount these legal and technical hurdles (Floridi, 2023; Hermann, 2022).

This paper uses a qualitative and theoretical approach to analyze the dark sides, limitations, and ethical issues of AI-supported marketing narratives. It adopts a critical perspective grounded in theoretical insights from marketing, communication, ethics, and the artificial intelligence literature.

From a consumer point of view, the ethical issues related to AI-supported marketing narratives are linked to existing debates on persuasion, knowledge, and consumer resistance. Instead of assuming total autonomy, this strategy emphasizes how consumers can decipher the persuasive intentions of marketing narratives (Özgür, 2024). The potential for ethical interpretation and narrative justice gradually diminishes when algorithmic personalization's intentions are concealed.

The research study aims to provide answers to the following research questions:

1. How do biases, opacity, and data processing in AI-generated marketing narratives pose threats to consumer perception, narrative justice, and brand trust?

2. How do manipulative discourses and behavioral control strategies in marketing narratives shape consumer persuasion and meaning-making, and their propensities for ethical evaluation?
3. How do intensive data use, profiling, and cultural homogenization tendencies impact the originality, diversity, and social norms compliance levels of AI-supported marketing narratives?

The conceptual framework of "boundaries and risks" used in this study identifies the ethical, social, and perceptual limitations present in AI-supported marketing processes. However, the negative impacts are mitigated through the handling of algorithmic bias, data privacy, and consumer manipulation. Ethical Dilemmas: The ethical dilemmas, which are the subject of the study, include moral decision-making in AI and ethical dilemmas in corporate social responsibility.

The research examines the narratives in question not only as a technical process of content production, but through a critical approach that investigates the limits of risk in the context of ethical responsibility and brand-consumer relationships. In this respect, the ethical and interpretive aspects of digital narratives (Escalas, 2004) are interpreted from an interdisciplinary approach. The capacity of the discourse of marketing to construct the consumer subject (Barari et al., 2024), the narrative form, and the relation of these elements to the social values are the theoretical bases of the analysis stage of this article.

To concretize the theoretical discussion, the study examines cases of algorithmic discrimination and data privacy encountered in the marketing processes of tech giants such as Amazon, Google, Meta, and TikTok within the framework of critical case analysis. The examination is limited to current crises reflected in the literature and academic studies on digital marketing ethics.

1. THEORETICAL FOUNDATION: AI, STORYTELLING, AND MARKETING

Artificial Intelligence (AI), which is at the center of ethical, philosophical, and technological debates (Say, 2018), is considered a field of research dating back to the 1950s (Abdulwahid & Şaylan, 2025; Gölgeli, 2025; Murtezaoğlu, 2022). First proposed in 1956, the concept of AI is defined as the vision of 'developing a processing capacity similar to human intelligence'. The work carried out by John McCarthy and his colleagues at Dartmouth College formed the starting point for this field (Coşkun & Gülleroğlu, 2021).

In modern literature, AI is no longer just defined as a group of algorithms that are capable of carrying out certain tasks, but also refers to systems that are capable of simulating cognitive processes such as learning, reasoning, conceptualization, prediction, and responding to situational cues. Additionally, AI refers to a wide range of technological tools that enhance the functional intelligence of products, services, and solutions, and it is rapidly emerging as an increasingly interdisciplinary field of study (Shankar, 2018).

In the marketing sector, artificial intelligence is capable of monitoring the buying behavior of target consumers and creating strong content that predicts customer needs (Dimitrieska et al., 2018). AI-based systems help brands build stronger connections with customers, generating personalized communication, content, and designs. Marketing processes are not solely dependent on human interventions; rather, artificial intelligence has started to impact product development, marketing, and promotions. This has helped brands to improve their interactions with consumers, their reflexive actions, and their decision-making processes (Abdulwahid & Şaylan, 2025).

The ability to quickly plan an advertisement campaign, predict consumer response, and customize consumer experience is a reflection of the impact of AI on marketing, as noted by Yaprak (2024) and Rodgers & Nguyen (2022). Big data, machine learning, and sophisticated algorithms are used for interpreting big data, while machine learning is used for predicting consumer response. Thus, artificial intelligence can perform conceptual analyses, contribute to behavioral analysis, and generate appropriate solutions in response to changing circumstances. In the near future, personalized content production, AI-based communication activities, and customer services are expected to develop further (Davenport et al., 2020).

Nevertheless, despite the capabilities of AI, the absence of consciousness situates it in an ethical debate (Qin, 2024). The risks of AI include bias creation (Pagano et al., 2022), errors in decision-making, and the absence of moral reasoning. The controversial and ambiguous nature of the technological neutrality concept contributes to the transformation of cultural and social structures, given that AI acts as a communicative agent that speaks to, guides, and communicates with people (Çeber, 2024; Du & Xie, 2021).

Following this line of reasoning, Coeckelbergh (2010, 2023) argues that artificial intelligence is not capable of assuming moral responsibility and, therefore, is not an autonomous entity. Even though artificial intelligence is a technological tool that is not conscious, it also has an epistemic role in the social narratives that it helps construct. The biases and discriminatory systems in society are reflected in the technologies that society develops, and artificial intelligence is capable of reflecting these biases (Pagano et al., 2022). Thus, the need for artificial intelligence to be inclusive, non-biased, and non-discriminatory is both technological and cultural. This debate also highlights that AI has become an intrinsic part of meaning production, even though it does not bear ethical responsibility.

In this context, artificial intelligence stands out not only as a traditional automation tool in marketing, but also as a tool that transforms the narrative experience established with the brand and offers an ontological experience opportunity from the consumer's perspective.

Brands are increasingly framing their interactions with consumers within a narrative framework (Vidrih & Mayahi, 2023). The capabilities of AI-powered systems, such as personalization, sentiment analysis, and content generation, are also influencing how narratives are constructed in the marketing experience, thus evolving artificial intelligence into the role of both the producer of the narrative and the creator of the narrative structure.

Throughout history, humans have made sense of the world in terms of narratives, and they organize their experiences, value judgments, and social relations in terms of these narrative structures; their cultural identity is also built upon these narratives (Demir, Y., 2025). Therefore, the story is not merely a form of expression, but functions as a fundamental component of the human being's way of understanding and directing the world, that is, of the human being's very self (Escalas, 2004; Demir, C. M., 2025a).

At this point, classical theoretical frameworks explaining the functioning of narrative provide significant clarity in understanding the cultural and cognitive dimensions of marketing storytelling. First, Gérard Genette's (2020) analysis of narrative levels and modes of transmission is critical in understanding how brand stories possess a narrative voice and focus. The positioning of the brand as a narrator, with the ability to control focus and shape the consumer's perceptual perspective, indicates that the technical aspect of narrative is a decisive factor in marketing communication. Genette's theoretical perspective explains how the brand frames the questions of "who is narrating?" and "how is it narrating?"

On the other hand, Monika Fludernik's 'experiential narrative' approach places the story at the center of the human process of understanding the world (Demir, C. M., 2025b). Fludernik's understanding of narrative gains importance through the dimensions of the individual's experience rather than the chronological sequence of events. Narrative and meaning in this experiential direction are constructed according to how the world in the consciousness of the character in the narrative is experienced (Fludernik, 1996). In this context, the story functions as a fundamental meaning organization that regulates human experiences and gives meaning to cultural existence.

On the other hand, the distinction between story and discourse and the concept of the implicit author in Seymour Chatman's (1978) 'narrative communication model' enable the discourse, value orientation, and strategic positioning behind brand narratives to be explained. This perspective explains that the brand is positioned not only as a product or service provider but also as a 'tacit narrative subject'; the narrative structure is also designed to produce a cultural and emotional response-behavior in the consumer. Based on this, brand narratives create a shared universe of meaning with consumers through a combination of both the discursive form (how it is told) and the narrative content (what is told) (Yılmaz, 2017a).

The theoretical framework of narratology has evolved to a wide-ranging discussion on ontology under Paul Ricoeur's idea of narrative meaning production, as presented in his book *Time and Narrative* (1984). Ricoeur argues that narrative is situated in a mimetic cycle that transforms temporality and reconstructs experience. In short, he emphasizes that meaning arises not only from the text itself but also through its connection to the reader's cognitive and cultural framework (Escalas, 2004; Escalas & Bettman, 2005). This approach demonstrates that in storytelling in the field of marketing, the consumer is not positioned as a passive consumer/recipient; on the contrary, they actively add meaning to the brand narrative through their own life narratives, cultural codes, and emotional climate.

Thus, in the marketing field, narrative is not only a method of content creation but also a communication platform in which the brand positions itself as a cultural subject and creates a shared meaning universe with the consumer (Fog et al., 2005; Lundqvist et al., 2013). Brand narratives shape consumers' cognitive processes and emotional engagement, together with the mechanisms of identity formation and social belonging (Bolat, 2023). In this regard, narrative marketing provides consumers with the experience of the brand in a 'story universe' or 'myth' (Demir, C. M., 2024; Escalas, 2004). This universe corresponds to a structure that produces meaning through values, characters, cultural references, and various mimetic representations.

Therefore, as Escalas and Bettman (2005) point out, when consumers are exposed to storytelling, they match the narrative discourse they receive with their own personal or cultural stories. This matching process incorporates the brand into the person's concept of self. Thus, brand narratives do not remain merely at a discursive or conceptual output level (Escalas, 2004), but rather the brand assumes an emotional and symbolic system within the consumer's self/identity structure (Demir, C. M., 2024). This interaction and the gains it provides are directly linked to the brand's marketing services.

Marketing, at its most fundamental level, refers to a comprehensive corporate activity area related to the design, pricing, promotion, and distribution of products or services (Abdulwahid & Şaylan, 2025). However, as previously mentioned, these activities are now being reshaped by artificial intelligence-supported digital data processing processes, going beyond traditional methods. The outputs of AI technology enhance brands' operational speed, decision-making reflexes, and strategic foresight (Alareeni & Hamdan, 2023). They are able to build highly accurate models, especially in tasks like creating an advertising campaign, understanding the target audience, and managing the capabilities of competitors. This evolution has made smart marketing a key concept, which has helped brands to effectively forecast consumers' behaviors and needs, and even develop personal interactions with them (Yaprak, 2024). In this case, marketing is moving away from being a purely economically-based activity and, thanks to artificial intelligence support, is becoming a cultural and technological practice that transforms both the consumer experience and brand strategies.

In light of this information, the contribution of artificial intelligence to story-focused marketing practices not only strengthens the formal and content dimensions of brand narratives but also highlights the importance of ethical and cultural boundaries in brand narratives. As AI's ability and capacity to personalize, guide, and generate emotional reflexes in brand narratives increase, how brand narratives affect consumers (Barari et al., 2024), what cultural biases they reproduce, and how they shape people's identity construction become important areas of discussion and examination (Escalas, 2004; Pagano et al., 2022). Thus, AI increases the narrative power of the brand on the one hand, while carrying risks such as bias amplification and perceptual (manipulative) guidance on the other. Ultimately, narratives powered by AI capture the spotlight not only in terms of the opportunities that the technology affords, but also in terms of its ethical, boundary, and decision issues, which necessitate accountability (Du & Xie, 2021). This is where the need for an in-depth exploration of the hidden dark side and ethical issues in AI narratives becomes apparent.

2. LIMITS AND ETHICAL RISKS IN AI MARKETING NARRATIVES

As can be understood, AI-based marketing narratives create a two-way[1] interaction space. Narratives function as an innovative actor in the construction of discourse on a social level and play an important role as carriers of various ethical and ontological risks in the eyes of consumers. In addition, the ethical issues of artificial intelligence have been at the heart of philosophical, sociological, and technological debates since the 1960s in relation to the relationship between humans and machines and the decision-making process (Morley et al., 2020). This situation reveals that AI-supported narratives are not limited to the discourse of technological convenience but rather interact extensively in historical and cultural fields (Özgür, 2024).

In this context, the infiltration of historical and socio-cultural biases formed in large data[2] sets into narrative structures raises the issue of algorithmic bias and fairness (Barari et al., 2024; Yilmaz & Ashqar, 2025; Du & Xie, 2021). The implicitness of algorithmic preferences and processes enables the influence of manipulative discourse strategies on the produced narrative, which compromises narrative transparency (Labrecque et al., 2024; Rodgers & Nguyen, 2022; Gülbaşı, 2025; McCollough et al., 2022). Moreover, the loss of consumer autonomy via different steering approaches indicates that AI models do not only predict consumer behavior but also shape the narrative that orients consumers in certain directions (Chen et al., 2024; Shankar, 2018; Woodside et al., 2008).

Furthermore, the processing of consumer data to develop specific profiles undermines the concept of privacy and the ethical limits of the classification of the narrative (Tang et al., 2024; Moorthy et al., 2015; Picot & Propstmeier, 2013).

In addition, cultural diversity is reduced with AI production processes that repeat similar patterns, resulting in discursive homogeneity and a reduction in meaning, which means that originality and diversity in marketing narratives are also reduced (Vidrih & Mayahi, 2023; Gündüzyeli, 2024; Canals & Heukamp, 2020). This new issue that has been raised emphasizes that marketing narratives with AI also require ethical and cultural discussion.

2.1. Algorithmic Bias and Narrative Justice

In accordance with the dynamics of global economic growth and digitalization, the processes of marketing have had to adapt to the changes in customer behavior and needs in recent years (Murtezaoğlu, 2022). This has resulted in digital marketing becoming more and more dependent on data-driven models and AI-based decision-making systems becoming the focal point of marketing discussions. For this very reason, algorithmic bias has emerged as a central issue in theoretical discussions of AI-based marketing and advertising discourse.

Artificial intelligence essentially trains itself on datasets created by humans and processes this data using algorithmic structures organized according to universal/local epistemic assumptions derived from human sources (Çeber, 2024). Therefore, every AI-supported narrative is not merely a set of seemingly automated technical processes, but also transforms into a system of values that reproduces the cultural and social indicators embedded in the data (Noble, 2018). In this regard, the question of narrative justice is no longer a problem that can be solved solely on the basis of a technical approach; it is a problem that corresponds to a wider critical field, which is concerned with the question of how representational relations and deviations are constructed in narratives.

The structures of algorithms used in AI marketing narratives are not an abstract problem, as is often believed, but rather a central problem in marketing, which is affected by digital marketing methods (Pagano et al., 2022). The tragic incidents that have appeared in different sectors, especially after the year 2000 with the escalation of digitalization, show how the algorithmic structure creates a policy of oppression, as described by Safiya Noble (2018The famous book by Noble, *Algorithms of Oppression: How Search Engines Reinforce Racism*, gives a detailed account of how existing algorithmic systems, especially those used by prominent search engines such as Google, perpetuate racism and sexism. According to Noble, digital technologies reinforce oppressive social relationships through a new form of racial profiling. The cases assessed in this respect repeatedly emphasize the significance of interrogating the connection between "algorithmic bias" and "narrative justice."

In 2025, Google's AI image generation tool, Nano Banana Pro, consistently produced "white savior" images for anonymous image requests regarding humanitarian aid, which is a perfect example of institutionalized bias from a visual marketing narrative perspective (Down, 2025; Pagano et al., 2022).

The consistent production of images depicting black children around a white aid worker figure for anonymous image requests such as "volunteer aid," "humanitarian support," or "aid worker" is a perfect example of how biases from history and culture are reconstructed at a visual narrative level through algorithmic learning mechanisms (Noble, 2018).

This representational format casts Black people as passive, helpless, and non-agents; it places the white figure as the savior agent and moral authority. In this case, the algorithmic format not only generates images but also reiterates and disseminates the colonial and hierarchical format of narratives embedded in the global discourse of aid. According to Noble (2018), the algorithmic format is not a random occurrence of racial bias but rather a narrative format systematically generated through data sets.

In this respect, the representation enforced by the image of the "white savior" and described in the literature as "poverty porn" ignores the complex social realities of Black communities and reduces them to a single, inevitable story of victimhood. Algorithmic bias produces a standardizing social practice on the one hand, while undermining narrative justice by categorizing cultural differences on the other (Pagano et al., 2022). Constructing the narrative in this way renders the subjective experiences of the assisted communities invisible while serving a brand narrative that reinforces technology companies' ethical and humanitarian responsibility discourse.

The example of the Amazon AI recruitment tool bias against women is a good example of how bias works at the level of corporate brand storytelling and how it is a structural risk (Pagano et al., 2022). According to a Reuters report, Amazon's AI model determines the 'ideal candidate' profile based on past hiring data; however, because this data reflects a male-dominated engineering culture, it implicitly scores women's resumes lower (Dastin, 2018). In this process, the algorithmic system appears to maintain its claim of impartiality and objectivity, yet it reproduces historical gender inequalities through data processing practices (Noble, 2018).

The lack of transparency in algorithmic logic makes the defense of merit and equality, which takes a prominent position in corporate discourse, weak at the discursive level. However, the fact that the AI-assisted evaluation processes are presented within the brand's narrative as fair and logical does not prevent a significant erosion of trust between the consumer and the organization, given the lack of accountability of the algorithmic decision-making. In this regard, the algorithmic bias does not only manifest itself as a form of deviation from the expected, but also as a negation of the narrative of justice. In fact, a report published by the American Civil Liberties Union shows how the algorithm systematically discriminates against female candidates, placing them in the position of the "inadequate subject" of the corporate narrative (Goodman, 2018).

The applications of marketing using artificial intelligence are not only considered as technical processes of automation and data processing, but also as narrative agents that restructure the form of presentation of advertising narratives. The advertising narratives using artificial intelligence preframe the processes of meaning-making and interpretation of the viewer, emphasizing certain emotional and symbolic orientations. Thus, artificial intelligence has a decisive role in advertising not only at the application level but also at the level of presentation of narratives and restructuring of advertising discourse.

On the other hand, the algorithm's silent and automatic elimination of candidates significantly weakens the subjectivity of individuals in decision-making processes. Candidates cease to be the subjects of the evaluation process and become passive objects classified based on profiles created in light of statistical data. This situation demonstrates that AI-supported marketing narratives not only serve to persuade, but also to guide and constrain. Thus, algorithmic selection creates an area of controversy in terms of ethical responsibility and individual autonomy.

Furthermore, the establishment of an 'ideal employee' profile based on past data as a rule homogenizes corporate culture and brand narrative. Algorithmic profiling reinforces existing gendered cultural discourse patterns rather than reflecting the plural and diverse nature of the workforce. This weakens the context of inclusivity and diversity in the eyes of the brand and makes its alignment with social norms problematic. The case of Amazon serves as an example that illustrates how bias in algorithms, transparency, and standardization procedures in AI-generated corporate marketing narratives may pose risks to narrative justice, consumer perceptions, and trust.

One of the most notable instances of the issue of bias in algorithms becoming a matter of justice in the narratives of marketing is the case of the settlement between the US Department of Justice and the company Meta over the methods of algorithmic targeting used in the company's housing advertisements. According to Reuters, "The Department of Justice said that Meta's advertising tools delivered discriminatory outcomes by showing housing ads to users in different ways depending on their race, gender, and other protected characteristics" (Reuters, 2022). The Ministry's announcement underlines that these actions impede people's equal access to a basic right, such as housing, and perpetuate discriminatory actions through online advertising.

In this, the targeting tools of Meta's algorithm systematically exclude some groups of users from the narrative while positioning other groups in "suitable," "accessible," or "priority" roles. In this manner, the marketing narrative around the housing market is being rebuilt through invisible mechanisms of exclusion, rather than being underpinned by the claims of equality and inclusivity. The algorithmic system has moved from being a technical tool for distribution to a discursive filter that decides who has access to spatial and social resources.

In this case, the bias in algorithms is perceived not in the form of a data error but as an issue that is perennial in nature. According to Noble (2018), algorithms are not neutral technology but re-circulate historical and social inequalities through data modeling. In the Meta case, the marketing narrative creates a discourse that normalizes and legitimizes inequality by making certain groups of people invisible.

2.2. The Erosion of Consumer Autonomy and Behavioral Steering

AI-centered marketing narratives produce epistemic disclosures to consumers while also developing behavioral interventions aimed at organizing and shaping consumers' decision-making processes. Thus, consumers move away from their free will to make decisions and become a pile of numerical data tracked, categorized, and behaviorally controlled by algorithmic systems.[3] In this world defined by hidden digital practices, the consumer subject striving to exist has become an issue that must be discussed in terms of both ontology and autonomy.

The Cambridge Analytica scandal is one of the most prominent cases that illustrate the transformative and negative impact of artificial intelligence and big data narrative processes on consumers. The harvesting of personal data from Facebook users without their consent and using it for profiling purposes illustrates how algorithmic narratives not only target the audience but also show how the free and private life of an individual is being exploited without consent. The settlement of $725 million by Meta in this regard illustrates that the ethical implications of digital marketing practices have been accepted at the organizational level (McCallum, 2022).

The use of the phrase "big mistake" by Mark Zuckerberg in relation to the data security violation after the scandal indicates that algorithmic systems have transcended being neutral and technical, and have instead caused a significant rift in the context of trust, brand reputation, and narrative responsibility (Time, 2018).

The Cambridge Analytica scandal demonstrates the normalization of behavioral targeting in AI-driven marketing narratives and the narrowing of consumers' decision-making space. The narrative has strayed from its original function of conveying and generating information and instead has taken on a role that actively influences consumer behavior.

Another example is at the center of a public lawsuit filed against TikTok. Lawsuits filed against the platform and leaked internal company documents have sparked serious debate about the existence of algorithms that trigger emotional and cognitive vulnerability, particularly among young users (Hadero, 2023).

In the algorithmic architecture of the platform, the constant monitoring of the users' behavior and the attempt to detect the users' habits and tendencies create the illusion for young people that the content they are exposed to is of their own choice. This, in turn, has negative effects, such as the excessive use of screen time, the development of viewing habits, and the gradual decrease of young people's psychosocial well-being. This practice undermines the consumer's autonomy by shaping the individual decision-making process and placing the young people's mental health in a systematically risky zone. In this context, the lawsuit of the US state on the platform shows that the above practice is not only a technological matter related to the individual's choice but also a matter of ethical responsibility, harming the consumer, and creating a serious concern (The Guardian, 2024).

2.3. Data Privacy, Traceability, and Narrative Profile Extraction

Another prominent example of profiling, as it relates to competition and consumer data, is the data collection and profiling done by a major retailer through its Loyalty Program, like Kroger. Kroger, for instance, seems to collect vast amounts of data from millions of consumers, making inferences like revenue forecasts and creating consumer profiles (Yaprak, 2024). In fact, the company has been reported to sell the data to third-party companies for advertising purposes (Leasca, 2025).

The profiles define the type and level of discount that is offered to a customer, and therefore, some users end up with a worse deal. The lack of fairness is a blow to trust. Therefore, with regard to data tracking, it is not just a matter of improving ad targeting anymore; it has evolved to a level where it dictates an individual's access to economic opportunities and, by extension, their chances.

There are legal cases filed against platforms like The Trade Desk, a company in the ad tech space, wherein the claim is that the profile of consumers is developed through tracking their activities without their consent, as asserted in Barnett (2025). In these claims, the implication is of a system wherein the consent of the users does not seem to be sought, and the manner of data collection and profiling continues to be unclear. Though the promise of these consumer profiles is for a personalized experience, the means of surveillance and tracking are unclear and implicit.

Such breaches of data privacy raise risks beyond being an ethical issue, including undermining consumer trust and the sense of fairness, and transforming the algorithmic process into a brand narrative. Moreover, the boundaries of data processing and monitoring are not clear, and this makes it difficult to understand who exactly is processing and monitoring personal information and why. As a result, users are exposed to marketing messages based on their inferred profile from where they live, what they like, and other demographic factors.

As AI-driven marketing narratives point to the gaps in transparency, privacy intrusions, and the ethics of data management that include privacy, traceability, and profiling, the issues are not viewed as technological problems or inefficiencies anymore, but are being framed as actual risk factors.

2.4. Cultural Homogenization: Discursive Uniformity and the Erosion of Meaning

While brands expand their global reach and depend on AI to develop stories for their marketing strategies, the risk here is that the stories may turn out to be bland and unemotional due to a lack of understanding of the cultural context. AI systems, when used for content development, may not understand the cultural nuances to connect with the local audience on an emotional level.

For instance, the Christmas commercial by McDonald's Netherlands for the 2025 festive season, created almost entirely by AI, is a clear case in point. The 45-second commercial aired images caricaturing the traumatic aspects of the holiday season; however, it sparked a wave of criticism, and quickly, critics flooded social media with negative comments. The visual content was described as disturbing, soulless, cold, and repulsive. The absence of emotion and cultural context was highlighted (Coeckelbergh, 2010). Consequently, this advertisement was removed from television broadcasts (Thomas, 2025).

The case illustrates the disruptive effect of AI-generated stories on the meaning webs we draw on from culture – the indicators, the practices, the signs we read as meaningful. Traditional holiday ads are built on warmth, generosity, and the feeling of being together. Yet the AI-generated campaigns lack those markers, and the stories they tell are not in the cultural rhythm or the cultural expectation. This AI-driven approach paves the way for monotonous narratives that are disconnected from cultural norms and erodes key components of marketing storytelling, such as harmony, authenticity, and empathy.

Another example is the AI-driven advertising campaign by the international fashion brand Valentino, which has also faced similar criticism. The high-end campaign by Valentino, which was produced with AI, contradicted the brand's characteristic narrative style. The campaign attempted to replace the narrative cues that came from traditional artistry and handiwork with imagery that seemed abstract and distant. Fashion enthusiasts accused the campaign of being fake, repetitive, and fragmented. The tension between those perceptions serves to highlight a larger issue: AI-generated content threatens to undermine authenticity in luxury fashion narratives where emotion, beauty, and cultural context matter (Sanders, 2025).

Looking at these cases, it is evident that AI-supported marketing narratives tend toward cultural homogenization and, although reproducible on a global scale, lack the ability to adapt to local cultural contexts. This weakens the narrative's originality and undermines the brand's relationship with social values, eroding trust in the brand. Considering these cases, the narrative becomes a monotonous discourse machine disconnected from cultural life, seriously weakening the alignment of marketing stories with cultural norms.

3. MEANING AND DISCOURSE IN AI-POWERED NARRATIVE ADVERTISING

Narrative advertising with the help of AI provides a new perspective that is not simply "technology for speed." It reconfigures the way in which advertising stories are constructed and how we think about them. The literature demonstrates that narrative advertising forms a bond between the consumer and the brand, which is more than simply a cognitive process. It includes experience, emotion, and interpretation as well (Escalas, 2004; Woodside et al., 2008). At this stage, AI acts not only as a content producer in the narrative creation process but also as a narrative architect that anticipates and determines the narrative system, its structures, and how audiences will experience it. Thus, advertising is being reimagined as a narrative system where meaning is generated and debated, moving beyond mere technological application.

This narrative transformation is also leading to the restructuring of meaning production and symbolic persuasion processes in advertising. Narrative-focused advertising reveals that the relationship brands establish with consumers is not solely benefit-based, but rather grounded in a symbolic and emotional relationship shaped by narrative logic (Lundqvist et al., 2013). In this process, artificial intelligence reconstructs advertising discourse on an algorithmic basis by converging consumer data, cultural elements, and past narrative understandings. At this stage, artificial intelligence produces persuasive narrative forms. This allows advertising discourse to evolve from being solely creativity-based to becoming a data-driven yet narratively persuasive discourse. Therefore, artificial intelligence is becoming a discursive device that determines how meaning emerges in advertising, which narratives are made visible in the social sphere, and how the audience can relate to these narratives.

The pioneering position of artificial intelligence in narrative advertising raises significant ethical and epistemological issues in terms of marketing discourse. The application of AI technology in the automation of persuasive stories in advertising indicates that advertising is not a clear and objective form of communication. Rather, AI-based narrative advertising appears to be a somewhat ambiguous copy shaped by specific economic, cultural, and even ideological factors (Rodgers, 2021; Abbasoğlu, 2025). In this context, artificial intelligence transforms advertising not only in terms of its production method but also in terms of the epistemological universe that feeds the narrative, the meaning structure on which it is based, and the levels of discursive persuasion, using its own methods. From the perspective of narrative advertising, the AI-based advertising discourse necessitates a re-examination of the relationship established between the brand and the target audience in the context of ethical responsibility, cultural, and discursive power relations (Floridi, 2023).

4. CONCLUSION AND RECOMMENDATIONS

The study explores AI-generated stories in marketing from three aspects: the algorithmic, the discursive, and the epistemic. It examines the dangers of bias, black boxes, manipulative guidance, and cultural homogenization and how these elements influence consumer perceptions, fairness in stories, and ethics. In this sense, AI-supported marketing narratives are not merely a technical capability or production process but also a transformative approach to meaning-making and forms of discursive persuasion.

Algorithmic bias, process, and data management practices give marketing communications an air of objectivity, influencing how people view brands. The objectivity of AI is learned from data that is itself the result of specific beliefs and institutions, undermining the fairness in marketing narratives, thereby creating a labeled consumer that fits into pre-made boxes (Noble, 2018). The result is that, with algorithms determining what is revealed, marketing is no longer just about selling things, but rather a space where biases and specific worldviews are at play, thereby eroding brand trust due to the notion that there is moral risk in the neutrality of technology. This undermines narrative justice by converting personal experiences into behavioral data, revealing the flaws in the capitalist system that is built on surveillance (Zuboff, 2019).

As marketing stories are assisted by AI, the way we build conversations and behaviors erodes consumer autonomy. The framework of AI narrative (Coeckelbergh, 2010) is based upon feeling without experience, and this impacts how people choose and how they are free to do so. The situation changes the nature of marketing communication from the art of storytelling to the science of behavioral guidance. The paradoxical nature of this guidance undermines the brand trust that artificial intelligence works to create and enhances the phenomenon of consumer pushback

(Du & Xie, 2021). As such, the evaluation of ethics is no longer considered only in relation to the individual but in relation to the integrity of the algorithm and the discourse surrounding it.

Heavily dependent upon data and profiling based upon data, marketing tends to follow a singular and standardized narrative. With AI creating standardized templates, there is a loss of authenticity and diversity. Localized experience, cultural expressions, and societal norms dissolve into a universal narrative. This process weakens the relationship between marketing narratives and social norms and distances the narrative from being a pluralistic field of meaning.

These findings reveal that AI-supported marketing narratives cannot be approached solely through the discourse of technological progress; they must be rethought on the basis of ethical, discursive, and epistemic responsibility. In this context, artificial intelligence is not considered either a subject or a neutral technology. Instead, it is positioned as a narrative tool established by humans and operating through ideologically loaded algorithmic processes.

4.1 Solution Recommendations

-The concept of artificial intelligence systems needs to be understood as digital tools rather than autonomous entities. Understanding the parties responsible for the outcomes of the algorithms, as well as the decision-making entities from which the artificial intelligence systems derive their information, enhances ethical and legal accountability.

-The concept of transparency needs to be understood not only in relation to the functionality of the technology but also in relation to the underlying ethical principles. These need to include the selection of data, the narratives that are privileged, and the ways in which the discourse is framed. The algorithms need to be regularly evaluated in relation to the meanings that are privileged and the meanings that are systematically ignored.

-Normative principles limiting emotional manipulation in AI-supported marketing narratives should be developed. The limits of persuasion strategies should be transparently defined, and hidden attempts at steering that undermine consumer autonomy should be restricted.

-Local, creative, and diverse storytelling must be promoted to counter the cookie-cutter narratives that are leading to cultural sameness. Data sets must be centered on representational justice and cultural variety – not only as an ethics imperative but as an epistemology imperative.

-Regarding AI-assisted marketing, we need multiple layers of governance: laws such as the EU AI Act (2024), internal ethics frameworks, and checks to keep things in order.

The bottom line: AI-enabled marketing narratives have evolved into an ideology, donning the cloak of technological advancements. This approach blurs the lines of brand responsibility through the use of algorithms and data feeds, dictates the manner in which people make decisions, and promotes the use of generic storytelling, resulting in the loss of cultural diversity.

REFERENCES

Abbasoğlu, Ş. (2025). Overcoming The Dark Sides of Artificial Intelligence. In Özkaynar, K., & Abbasoğlu, Ş. (Eds.), *Consumer, Marketing, AI: Dark Sides and Ethics*. Özgür Yayınları., DOI: 10.58830/ozgur.pub710.c3018

Abdulwahid, O., & Şaylan, O. (2025). Artificial intelligence applications in marketing: A literature-based study [Pazarlamada yapay zekâ uygulamaları: Literatür temelli bir çalışma]. *Kapanaltı Dergisi*, (8), 58–75. DOI: 10.62080/kmfed.1783278

Alareeni, B., & Hamdan, A. (Eds.). (2023). *Impact of artificial intelligence and the fourth industrial revolution on business success*. Springer., DOI: 10.1007/978-3-031-08093-7

Barari, M., Casper Ferm, L. E., Quach, S., Thaichon, P., & Ngo, L. (2024). The dark side of artificial intelligence in marketing: Meta-analytics review. *Marketing Intelligence & Planning*, *42*(7), 1234–1256. DOI: 10.1108/MIP-09-2023-0494

Barnett, K. (2025, April 11). Two lawsuits allege that The Trade Desk secretly violates consumer privacy laws. *People*. https://www.adweek.com/programmatic/lawsuits-trade-desk-consumer-privacy-laws

Bolat, N. (2023). The participation of artificial intelligence in the advertising field with digitalization. [Dijitalleşme ile yapay zekânın reklam alanına katılımı] In Günay, M. A. (Ed.), *İletişim bilimlerinde yapay zekâ* (pp. 44–61). Eğitim Yayınevi.

Canals, J., & Heukamp, F. (Eds.). (2020). *The future of management in an AI world: Redefining purpose and strategy in the fourth industrial revolution*. Springer. DOI: 10.1007/978-3-030-20680-2

Çeber, B. (2024). An applied research on the advertising sector in the context of artificial intelligence ethics [Yapay zekâ etiği bağlamında reklamcılık sektörü üzerine uygulamalı bir araştırma]. *Intermedia International E-Journal*, *11*(20), 63–84.

Chatman, S. (1978). *Story and discourse: Narrative structure in fiction and film*. Cornell University Press.

Chen, Y., Wang, H., Hill, S. R., & Li, B. (2024). Consumer attitudes toward AI-generated ads: Appeal types, self-efficacy, and AI's social role. *Journal of Business Research*, *185*, 114867. DOI: 10.1016/j.jbusres.2024.114867

Coeckelbergh, M. (2010). Moral appearances: Emotions, robots, and human morality. *Ethics and Information Technology*, *12*(3), 235–241. DOI: 10.1007/s10676-010-9221-y

Coeckelbergh, M. (2023). Narrative responsibility and artificial intelligence: How AI challenges human responsibility and sense-making. *AI & Society*, *38*(6), 2437–2450. DOI: 10.1007/s00146-021-01375-x

Coşkun, F., & Güllcroğlu, H. D. (2021). The development of artificial intelligence in history and its use in education [Yapay zekânın tarih içindeki gelişimi ve eğitimde kullanılması] [JFES]. *Ankara University Journal of Faculty of Educational Sciences*, *54*(3), 947–966.

Dastin, J. (2018, October 11). Amazon Scraps Secret AI Recruiting Tool That Showed Bias Against Women. *Reuters*. https://www.reuters.com/article/world/insight-amazon-scraps-secret-ai-recruiting-tool-that-showed-bias-against-women-idUSKCN1MK0AG

Davenport, T., Guha, A., Grewal, D., & Bressgott, T. (2020). How artificial intelligence will change the future of marketing. *Journal of the Academy of Marketing Science*, *48*(1), 24–42. DOI: 10.1007/s11747-019-00696-0

Demir, C. M. (2024). Semiotic analysis of cultural codes in the Solaris film poster [Solaris film afişinde yer alan kültürel kodların göstergebilimsel analizi]. *İstanbul Gelişim Üniversitesi Sosyal Bilimler Dergisi*, 11(1), 340–351.

Demir, C. M. (2025a). Çerçici: Experiential narrative, archetypes, and layers of memory [Çerçici: Deneyimsel anlatı, arketipler ve belleğin katmanları]. *UMAY Sanat ve Sosyal Bilimler Dergisi*, *3*(2), 79–86.

Demir, C. M. (2025b). *Mise-en-abyme as a pattern tool in the literary communication process: An examination of Robbe-Grillet, Calvino, and Borges narratives* [Yazınsal iletişim sürecinde bir örüntü aracı olarak mise-en-abyme: Robbe-Grillet, Calvino ve Borges anlatıları üzerine bir inceleme] (Master's thesis). Ondokuz Mayıs University.

Demir, Y. (2025). Advertising posters and the use of images as a brand-consumer touchpoint: The Volkswagen case. [Bir marka–tüketici temas noktası olarak reklam afişleri ve imge kullanımı: Volkswagen örneği] In Erdem, M. N., & Mayadağlı, C. (Eds.), *Marka iletişimi: Tüm boyutlarıyla marka ve tüketici etkileşimi* (pp. 325–342). Palet Yayınları.

Dimitrieska, S., Stankovska, A., & Efremova, T. (2018). Artificial intelligence and marketing. *Entrepreneurship*, *6*(2), 298–304.

Down, A. (2025, December 4). Google's AI Nano Banana Pro Accused of Generating Racialised 'White Saviour' Visuals. *The Guardian*. https://www.theguardian.com/technology/2025/dec/04/google-ai-nano-banana-pro-racialised-white-saviour-images

Du, S., & Xie, C. (2021). Paradoxes of artificial intelligence in consumer markets: Ethical challenges and opportunities. *Journal of Business Research, 129*, 961–974. DOI: 10.1016/j.jbusres.2020.08.024

Escalas, J. E. (2004). Narrative processing: Building consumer connections to brands. *Journal of Consumer Psychology, 14*(1–2), 168–180. DOI: 10.1207/s15327663jcp1401&2_19

Escalas, J. E., & Bettman, J. R. (2005). Self-construal, reference groups, and brand meaning. *The Journal of Consumer Research, 32*(3), 378–389. DOI: 10.1086/497549

European Parliament & Council of the European Union. (2024). *Regulation (EU) 2024/1689 laying down harmonised rules on artificial intelligence (Artificial Intelligence Act).* Official Journal of the European Union. https://eur-lex.europa.eu/eli/reg/2024/1689/oj

Floridi, L. (2023). *The ethics of artificial intelligence: Principles, challenges, and opportunities.* Oxford University Press., DOI: 10.1093/oso/9780198883098.001.0001

Fludernik, M. (1996). *Towards a 'Natural' Narratology.* Routledge. DOI: 10.1515/jlse.1996.25.2.97

Fog, K., Budtz, C., & Yakaboylu, B. (2005). *Storytelling: Branding in practice.* Springer., DOI: 10.1007/b138635

Foucault, M. (1977). *Discipline and punish: The birth of the prison* (Sheridan, A., Trans.). Pantheon Books.

Genette, G. (2020). *Narrative discourse: An essay in method* [Anlatının söylemi yöntem hakkında bir deneme]. (Aydar, F. B., Trans.). Ayrıntı Yayınları.

Gölgeli, K. (2025). Advertising design with artificial intelligence: A study for advertisers [Yapay zekâ ile reklam tasarımı: Reklamcılara yönelik bir araştırma]. *İnsan ve Toplum Bilimleri Araştırmaları Dergisi*, 14(1), 319–336.

Goodman, R. (2018, October 12). Why Amazon's Automated Hiring Tool Discriminated Against Women. *American Civil Liberties Union.* https://www.aclu.org/news/womens-rights/why-amazons-automated-hiring-tool-discriminated-against

Gülbaşı, A. (2025). Artificial intelligence in marketing: Next generation strategies and applications. *Uluslararası Yönetim Akademisi Dergisi, 8*(3), 786–801. DOI: 10.33712/mana.1624405

Gündüzyeli, B. (2024). Artificial intelligence in digital marketing within the framework of sustainable management. *Sustainability (Basel), 16*(23), 10511. DOI: 10.3390/su162310511

Hadero, H. (2023, February 15). U.S. States Say TikTok Harms Children and Teenagers, Sues Company. *AP News*. https://apnews.com/article/tiktok-kids-teens-use-addiction-03a2d63a21bc5c1c62910628deff0521

Heidegger, M. (1998). *The question concerning technology and other essays* [Teknik ve dönüş]. (Aça, N., Trans.). Bilim ve Sanat Yayınları.

Hermann, E. (2022). Leveraging artificial intelligence in marketing for social good—An ethical perspective. *Journal of Business Ethics*, *179*(1), 43–61. DOI: 10.1007/s10551-021-04843-y PMID: 34054170

Labrecque, L. I., Peña, P., Leonard, H. A., & Leger, R. (2024). Not all sunshine and rainbows: Exploring the dark side of AI in interactive marketing. *Journal of Interactive Marketing Research*. https://doi.org/.DOI: 10.1108/JRIM-02-2024-0073

Leasca, S. (2025, May 21). Kroger's loyalty program harvests shopper data and sells it for profit, consumer reports says. *Food & Wine*. https://www.foodandwine.com/kroger-customer-data-loyalty-program-consumer-reports-investigation-11738718

Lundqvist, A., Liljander, V., Gummerus, J., & Van Riel, A. (2013). The impact of storytelling on the consumer brand experience: The case of a firm-originated story. *Journal of Brand Management*, *20*(4), 283–297. DOI: 10.1057/bm.2012.15

McCallum, S. (2022, December 23). Meta settles Cambridge Analytica Scandal Case for $725m. *BBC News*. https://www.bbc.com/news/technology-64075067

McCollough, C. J., Wallace, A. A., & Luttrell, R. (2022). Artificial intelligence: The dark side, ethics, and implications. In Wright, K. B., & Webb, L. M. (Eds.), *The Emerald handbook of computer-mediated communication and social media* (pp. 671–684). Emerald Publishing Limited. DOI: 10.1108/978-1-80071-597-420221039

Moorthy, J., Lahiri, R., Biswas, N., Sanyal, D., Ranjan, J., Nanath, K., & Ghosh, P. (2015). Big data: Prospects and challenges. *Vikalpa*, *40*(1), 74–96. DOI: 10.1177/0256090915575450

Morley, J., Floridi, L., Kinsey, L., & Elhalal, A. (2020). From what to how: An initial review of publicly available AI ethics tools, methods, and research to translate principles into practices. *Science and Engineering Ethics*, *26*(4), 2141–2168. DOI: 10.1007/s11948-019-00165-5 PMID: 31828533

Murtezaoğlu, Y. E. (2022). *The dark side of applying artificial intelligence technologies in marketing – What are the challenges, obstacles, and risks?* Institute of Retailing, Sales and Marketing.

Noble, S. U. (2018). *Algorithms of oppression: How search engines reinforce racism*. New York University Press. DOI: 10.18574/nyu/9781479833641.001.0001

Özgür, E. (2024). An evaluation of Kate Crawford's "Atlas of AI" [Kate Crawford'ın "Yapay Zekâ Atlası" üzerine bir değerlendirme]. *Ankara Üniversitesi İlef Dergisi*, 11(1), 190–202.

Pagano, T. P., Loureiro, R. B., Lisboa, F. V. N., Cruz, G. O. R., Peixoto, R. M., Guimarães, G. A. D. S., & Nascimento, E. G. S. (2022). Bias and Unfairness in Machine Learning Models: A Systematic Literature Review. *arXiv preprint arXiv:2202.08176.*

Picot, A., & Propstmeier, J. (2013). Big data. *MedienWirtschaft*, *10*(1), 34–39. DOI: 10.15358/1613-0669-2013-1-34

Qin, R. W. (2024). Navigating integration challenges and ethical considerations of AI in e-commerce: A framework for best practices and customer trust. *Technology and Investment*, *15*(3), 168–181. DOI: 10.4236/ti.2024.153010

Reisman, D., Schultz, J., Crawford, K., & Whittaker, M. (2018). *Algorithmic impact assessments: A practical framework for public agency accountability*. AI Now.

Reuters. (2022). U.S. Meta Settle Lawsuit Over Discrimination in Housing Advertising Tool. *Reuters.*_https://www.reuters.com/legal/transactional/us-meta-settle-lawsuit-over-discrimination-housing-advertising-tool-2022-06-21

Ricoeur, P. (1984). *Time and narrative* (Vol. 1). University of Chicago Press.

Rodgers, S. (2021). Themed issue introduction: Promises and perils of artificial intelligence and advertising. *Journal of Advertising*, *50*(1), 1–10. DOI: 10.1080/00913367.2020.1868233

Rodgers, W., & Nguyen, T. (2022). Advertising benefits from ethical artificial intelligence algorithmic purchase decision pathways. *Journal of Business Ethics*, 178(4), 1043–1061, *178*(4), 1043–1061. .DOI: 10.1007/s10551-022-05048-7

Sanders, T. (2025). Valentino slammed over truly 'uncomfortable' ads. *The Daily Beast*. https://www.thedailybeast.com/valentino-slammed-over-truly-uncomfortable-ads

Say, C. (2018). *50 questions on artificial intelligence* [50 soruda yapay zekâ]. Bilim ve Gelecek Yayınevi.

Shankar, V. (2018). How artificial intelligence (AI) is reshaping retailing. *Journal of Retailing*, *94*(4), vi–xi. DOI: 10.1016/S0022-4359(18)30076-9

Tang, B. J., Sun, K., Curran, N. T., Schaub, F., & Shin, K. G. (2024). GenAI Advertising: Risks of Personalizing Ads With LLMs. *arXiv preprint arXiv:2409.15436.*

The Guardian. (2024, October 8). US States Sue TikTok Over Mental Health Harms to Children. *The Guardian.* https://www.theguardian.com/technology/2024/oct/08/us-states-tiktok-lawsuit-mental-health

Thomas, M. (2025, April 11). Two Lawsuits Allege The Trade Desk Secretly Violates Consumer Privacy Laws. *People.* https://people.com/mcdonald-s-netherlands-ai-ad-controversy-explained-11867981?utm_source

Time. (2018). Mark Zuckerberg Says He's Still the Best Person to Run Facebook, Despite Its 'Huge Mistake' with the Cambridge Analytica Data Scandal. *Time.* https://time.com/5228542/mark-zuckerberg-facebook-data-scandal

Vidrih, M., & Mayahi, S. (2023). Generative AI-driven Storytelling: A New Era For Marketing. *arXiv preprint arXiv:2309.09048.*

Wirth, N. (2018). Hello marketing, what can artificial intelligence help you with? *International Journal of Market Research, 60*(5), 435–438. DOI: 10.1177/1470785318776841

Woodside, A. G., Sood, S., & Miller, K. E. (2008). When consumers and brands talk: Storytelling theory and research in psychology and marketing. *Psychology and Marketing, 25*(2), 97–145. DOI: 10.1002/mar.20203

Yaprak, B. (2024). Generative artificial intelligence in marketing: The invisible danger of AI hallucinations. *Ekonomi İşletme ve Yönetim Dergisi, 8*(2), 133–158. DOI: 10.7596/jebm.1588897

Yeşilkaya, N. (2022). Ethical issues regarding artificial intelligence [Yapay zekâya dair etik sorunlar]. *Şarkiyat İlmi Araştırmalar Dergisi (Journal of Oriental Scientific Research*), 14(3), 949–964. .DOI: 10.26791/sarkiat.1189864

Yilmaz, B., & Ashqar, H. I. (2025). Towards Equitable AI: Detecting Bias in Using Large Language Models for Marketing. *arXiv preprint arXiv:2502.12838.*

Yılmaz, R. (2017a). Typology of metaleptic uses in television commercials [Televizyon reklamlarında metaleptik kullanımların tipolojisi]. *Gümüşhane Üniversitesi İletişim Fakültesi Elektronik Dergisi, 5*(2), 691–704.

Yılmaz, R. (2017b, May). *Structural transformation of advertising narrative in the digital age in Turkey* [Türkiye'de reklam anlatısının dijital çağdaki yapısal dönüşümü]. Paper presented at the 1st International Conference on New Trends in Communication, Istanbul, Turkey.

Yılmaz, R., & Taşkıran, N. Ö. (2013). A model proposal for advertising aestheticization. In Hacıoğlu, Ü., & Dinçer, H. (Eds.), *Globalization and governance in the international political economy* (pp. 264–272). IGI Global.

Zhao, Y. (2025). An examination of ethical challenges in the application of AI in marketing. *International Journal of Business and Management, 20*(4), 113. DOI: 10.5539/ijbm.v20n4p113

ADDITIONAL READING

Christian, B. (2020). *The Alignment Problem: Machine Learning and Human Values.* National Geographic Books.

Crawford, K. (2021). *The Atlas of AI: Power, Politics, and the Planetary Costs of Artificial Intelligence.* Yale University Press., DOI: 10.2307/j.ctv1ghv45t

Noble, S. U. (2018). *Algorithms of Oppression: How Search Engines Reinforce Racism.* NYU Press. DOI: 10.18574/nyu/9781479833641.001.0001

Özkaynar, K., & Abbasoğlu, Ş. (Eds.). (2025). *Consumer, Marketing, AI: Dark Sides and Ethics.* Özgür Yayınları., DOI: 10.58830/ozgur.pub710

Zuboff, S. (2019). *The Age of Surveillance Capitalism: The Fight for a Human Future at the New Frontier of Power: Barack Obama's Books of 2019.* Profile Books.

KEY TERMS AND DEFINITIONS

Artificial Intelligence-Supported Marketing Narratives: Refers to personalized and automated marketing discourses generated through algorithmic systems.

Narrative Manipulation: Defines the capacity of AI-based content to influence consumer perception, emotional response, and decision-making processes.

Algorithmic Bias: Explains the reproduction of values, assumptions, and power relations embedded in artificial intelligence systems at the discursive level.

Ethical Boundaries: Covers the evaluation of artificial intelligence applications in the context of transparency, fairness, accountability, and human autonomy.

Consumer Autonomy: This refers to an individual's ability to make conscious and free decisions in the face of digital and algorithmic interventions.

Discursive Power and Authority: This explains the connection between marketing narratives produced by artificial intelligence and cultural, ideological, and economic power relations.

ENDNOTES

1 The phenomenon of technology manifests itself in a dualistic structure. This structure is shaped by the tension between 'optimism' and 'pessimism' (Çeber, 2024). Martin Heidegger's (1998) views on the subject may be instructive. The concept of technology constitutes an important part of Heidegger's philosophy. According to him, technology has a paradoxical existence. Heidegger likens the technological age to a destructive and coercive process that threatens human freedom and life.

2 Big Data lacks a clear definition and has an ambiguous structure because different disciplines interpret the phenomenon from their own perspectives. In the field of information technology, Big Data is considered to be large and complex data sets that must be collected, processed, and analyzed by supercomputers in order to achieve meaningful results (Moorthy et al., 2015). Online companies such as Facebook, Google, and Amazon have long been comparing users' online behaviors with other user data and relevant product information in real time; these comparisons result in outputs such as the placement of advertising messages or the generation of personalized product recommendations (Picot & Propstmeier, 2013).

3 The concept of the Panopticon, as defined by Foucault, is a structure of surveillance that constantly subjects the individual to visibility under power and results in the individual becoming the observer of themselves (Demir, C. M., 2025a). In digital marketing narratives, the consumer becomes a digital element of this panoptic structure through data-based tracking and classification processes; this state of being a limited subject corresponds to a numerically quantified type of existence, both narratively and behaviorally (Foucault, 1977).

Chapter 10
The Silence Dimension of Crisis Communication in Public Relations:
Sustainability Silence and Greenhushing Strategies

Özgenur Reyhan Güler
http://orcid.org/0000-0003-0899-2297
Istinye University, Turkey

Ebru Özgen
Marmara University, Turkey

ABSTRACT

In contemporary contexts, sustainability has evolved beyond environmental responsibility or corporate social responsibility to become a central element of strategic management, value creation, and brand identity. This study examines silence strategies in sustainability communication during crisis periods, focusing on greenhushing through a discourseanalytic approach. Global crises such as pandemics, economic instability, and armed conflicts often lead brands to intentionally reduce or suspend sustainability narratives. Adopting a qualitative research design, the study analyzes publicly corporate reports, official websites, social media content, and press releases of national and international brands using thematic discourse analysis. The findings suggest that although greenhushing may serve as a short-term risk-avoidance strategy, it creates long-term challenges for ethical consistency and public trust. The study argues that silence in sustainability communication should be reconsidered not only as a crisis management tool but also as a key issue in ethical public relations practice.

DOI: 10.4018/979-8-3373-5666-2.ch010

INTRODUCTION

Sustainability is no longer a concept addressed solely from an environmental or corporate social responsibility perspective; it has become a cornerstone of companies' strategic management approaches, value chains, and brand identities (Schaltegger & Burritt, 2010). Consumers now prefer not only high-quality, affordable products but also relationships with brands that align with their values and ethical expectations (Du, Bhattacharya, & Sen, 2010). This transforms sustainability communication into an essential competitive advantage for brands, and sustainability discourses are becoming central to companies' reputation management strategies (Pomering & Johnson, 2009).

In this context, sustainability communication is not only a marketing tool but also an ethical contract through which the brand publicly declares its long-term commitments and social responsibility (Morsing & Schultz, 2006). Therefore, continuity, transparency, and consistency in sustainability communication are critical for consumer trust and brand loyalty. However, stability is not always possible for brands. External crisis conditions, pandemics, wars, economic fluctuations, and political uncertainties, in particular, can profoundly impact brands' sustainability communication strategies and lead to the reevaluation of these strategies (Sarkis et al., 2020).

Crisis periods are challenging times that require companies to reassess their resource prioritization and communication priorities (Coombs, 2007). While both internal and external stakeholders' expectations for information, assurance, and disclosure increase during these periods, it is not always possible for brands to maintain the same level of sustainability commitments and communication goals. In this context, some brands withdraw their sustainability statements entirely or significantly reduce their level of communication. However, it is noteworthy that this withdrawal often stems not from the suspension of sustainability practices, but rather from the limitation of communication related to these practices. This type of communication practice is defined in the literature as greenhushing (Font et al., 2017).

Greenhushing refers to brands deliberate reluctance to share their sustainability performance and achievements with the public. Fernando and Lawrence (2014) note that this tendency is sometimes associated with avoiding criticism and sometimes with the risk of failing to manage public expectations. While greenhushing is a relatively new concept discussed in the sustainability communication literature, it represents a widespread trend in practice. Especially during times of crisis, brands withdraw from sustainability communication for reasons of protecting their reputation, avoiding misunderstandings, or prioritizing crisis-focused communication needs (Mazzei, 2004).

At this point, systematically examining silence strategies in sustainability communication becomes a crucial necessity. Silence has been considered a meaningful form of communication in the communication literature for many years (Bruneau, 1973). Jaworski (1993) and Mazzei (2004) emphasize that silence can be a strategic choice in the context of corporate communication, enabling companies to implement crisis management or risk avoidance strategies. This perspective also applies to sustainability communication. Sustainability silence during crisis periods is not solely a consequence of resource constraints or a diminished communication capacity, but rather a strategically calculated, conscious communication choice aimed at preventing specific risks.

The public relations discipline generally focuses on active communication strategies during times of crisis (Coombs, 2007). Crisis communication literature frequently emphasizes the need for organizations to adopt active communication practices such as transparency, openness, accountability, and reputation repair (Claeys & Cauberghe, 2015). However, in recent years, alternative approaches have also begun to appear in the literature. Alternative communication practices, particularly strategic silence, are being examined in greater depth in the context of crisis communication (Mazzei, 2004). This trend necessitates a similar evaluation of silence strategies in sustainability communication.

While considerable knowledge has accumulated on transparency and greenwashing in the sustainability communication literature, sustainability silence and its dynamics in the context of crisis communication have not yet been sufficiently explored. This study aims to fill this gap in the literature and examine sustainability silence in its theoretical, strategic, and perceptual dimensions. It is assumed that sustainability silence is not merely an internal managerial or communicational choice; it also has strong effects on stakeholder relations and, in particular, consumer perception. Miller and Sinclair (2020) state that consumers evaluate sustainability promises as an indicator of an organization's commitment to sustainable values not only during positive periods but also during times of crisis. Therefore, sustainability silence can have indirect but powerful effects on key brand performance indicators such as consumer trust, brand loyalty, and purchase intention. Another contribution of this study to the literature is its examination of how crisis types influence the form of sustainability silence strategies. Claeys and Cauberghe (2015) emphasize that different types of crises (e.g., pandemics, economic crises, wars) can affect organizations' communication strategies differently. However, the implications of this variation in the context of sustainability communication have not yet been sufficiently explored. This study also aims to demonstrate that the form of sustainability silence strategies may differ depending on the type of crisis and that these differences may have different effects on consumer perception. In addition to, in the contemporary AI era, sustainability communication is no longer solely human crafted or exclusively governed by corporate strategic intent. It is increasingly mediated by algorithmic infrastructures that shape visibility, amplify certain narratives, and suppress others within digital attention economies. As platform architectures determine what gains prominence and what remains marginal, sustainability discourse operates within a technologically structured environment that influences both communicative choices and public perception. This shift raises new questions regarding authenticity, algorithmic visibility, and the strategic implications of silence. Therefore, examining sustainability silence today requires not only a crisis communication perspective but also an awareness of algorithmic mediation and AI-driven communicative dynamics.

SUSTAINABILITY COMMUNICATION

Sustainability communication has become a fundamental component of corporate communication practices and strategic brand management. Initially addressed primarily within the framework of corporate social responsibility (CSR), the concept of sustainability has gradually become central to corporate activities and value chains as an integrated approach encompassing environmental, social, and economic dimensions (Schaltegger & Burritt, 2010). This evolution has transformed sustainability communication into not only a tool for public information but also an integral element of corporate identity and brand equity.

Sustainability communication is fundamentally defined as the process by which organizations communicate their sustainability-focused strategies, practices, values, and goals to their internal and external stakeholders (Schaltegger & Burritt, 2010). In this process, communication encompasses not only environmental performance reporting but also social and economic sustainability commitments. Therefore, sustainability communication should be considered a multidimensional and constantly evolving corporate practice.

There is a close and historical relationship between corporate social responsibility and sustainability communication. The CSR literature emphasizes that corporations should act not only profit-driven but also as responsible actors towards society and the environment (Carroll, 1991). The concept of sustainability, however, extends this understanding to a more holistic and long-term framework. Today, sustainability communication has evolved beyond CSR into a strategic communication field that requires corporations to disclose their value creation processes in a more transparent and accountable manner (Morsing & Schultz, 2006). One of the most important drivers of this transformation is the shift in stakeholder expectations. Consumers, investors, employees, and other stakeholders now expect corporations not only to provide good products and services, but also to fulfill their environmental and social responsibilities and to share information about these processes transparently

(Du, Bhattacharya, & Sen, 2010). Indeed, Pomering and Johnson (2009) emphasize that sustainability communication strengthens organizations' social legitimacy and the trust they establish with their stakeholders. In this context, sustainability communication plays a critical role in creating competitive advantage and reputation management for today's organizations. Changing consumer expectations over time have made sustainability communication a more strategic element. This trend makes sustainability communication not only a reputation management tool but also a key to building consumer loyalty and commitment.

The theoretical foundations of sustainability communication can be explained within the framework of stakeholder theory, legitimacy theory, and corporate identity theories. According to stakeholder theory, developed by Freeman (1984), the success of organizations depends not only on shareholder value but also on the balanced management of the expectations and needs of all stakeholder groups. Sustainability communication is a key tool in responding to these expectations. Legitimacy theory (Suchman, 1995) proposes that organizations must gain social acceptance and support by acting in accordance with societal norms, values, and expectations. In this context, sustainability communication serves as a fundamental tool in the process of building and maintaining institutional legitimacy. However, sustainability communication is a process that makes visible not only the discursive performance of organizations but also their actual practices. In this context, sustainability communication is directly linked to the transparency and accountability principles of organizations. Transparent sustainability communication requires organizations to openly share both their positive performance and the challenges and areas for improvement they face. This approach is critical for building stakeholder trust and long-term brand equity.

Sustainability communication serves not only as a means of addressing stakeholder expectations but also as an ethical platform through which corporate values and brand identity are publicly declared. However, this process becomes more complex and multifaceted under crisis conditions, forcing organizations to develop new strategic choices in sustainability communication. In this context, a more in-depth exploration of silence strategies in sustainability communication and their impact on consumer perception is crucial.

THEORY OF SILENCE

For many years, silence in communication processes has been viewed as an indicator of passive or incomplete communication; it has been treated more as a "gap" or "missing" element. However, with the development of communication science, silence has begun to be addressed theoretically as an independent and meaningful form of communication (Bruneau, 1973; Jaworski, 1993). Mazzei (2004), who brought Jaworski's analysis of silence and power relations to the level of corporate communication, addressed this phenomenon directly in the context of strategic communication. Within this framework, the concept of strategic silence (Mazzei, 2004), particularly in the corporate context, constitutes an important topic of discussion in contemporary communication literature. In recent years, studies that further develop Mazzei's (2004) approach to strategic silence have begun to appear in the literature. Le et al. (2019) and Pang et al. (2021) further categorized strategic silence into subcategories such as avoiding silence, hiding silence, and delaying silence. This classification provides a powerful analytical framework for understanding types of silence, particularly in sustainability communication.

Bruneau (1973), considered the pioneer of the theory of silence, defined silence as a fundamental element inherent in communication and capable of generating meaning. According to Bruneau, communication is not limited to the transmission of verbal or written messages; silence, like words, serves a communicative function and is interpreted by the receiver. This approach has provided a more holistic and multidimensional perspective on communication processes, revealing the roles silence plays in social relations, cultural contexts, and power dynamics. Bruneau (1973) fundamentally considers silence in three functional dimensions: first, it creates a space for emotional and cognitive processing; the silence of individuals or institutions contributes to the process of meaning-making or evaluation. Second, it is a marker of normative and cultural structures; silence can carry different meanings depending on specific social norms and cultural value systems. Third, it functions as a strategic communication act; silence is a consciously chosen way of producing a message for specific purposes. Bruneau's work pioneered the theorization of this field by positioning silence as an active and productive component of communication. This perspective has subsequently been developed and deepened by communication scholars and sociologists in various contexts.

Jaworski (1993) examined silence as a broader social phenomenon and demonstrated how it is intertwined with social norms, power relations, and cultural practices. According to Jaworski, silence is a complex form of communication that reflects the balance of power and normative expectations between individuals and institutions. For example, in certain contexts, silence can be a sign of respect or superiority, while in other contexts, it can be a sign of obedience, timidity, or passive resistance. In the context of corporate communication, these different forms of silence also produce meaning. Institutions may consciously employ a strategy of silence in times of crisis or uncertainty, in response to the risk of negative perceptions of their existing discourse. Silence here is not only a means of withholding a message but also of choosing not to convey certain meanings (Jaworski, 1993).

Jaworski's work demonstrates that silence is not only a personal choice in communication but can also be used as a strategic tool at the institutional and societal levels. This approach demonstrates that silence functions across a wide spectrum, from interpersonal communication to institutional discourse production, and that it is interpreted differently in different social contexts.

Mazzei (2004) examined silence directly within the framework of corporate strategic communication and developed the concept of strategic silence. According to Mazzei, organizations can actively utilize silence by deliberately avoiding commenting on certain issues or avoiding setting the agenda. This strategy often serves the purpose of risk management, reputation protection, or balancing communication load. Mazzei (2004) explains strategic silence through four primary motivations: first, the aim to avoid making mistakes in times of uncertainty; during times of crisis, organizations may choose to remain silent on issues they lack sufficient information or cannot predict how the situation will unfold. Second, legal and regulatory constraints; in some cases, organizations' disclosures on certain issues may create legal risks or affect legal processes. Third, reputation management; organizations can strategically use silence to avoid messages that may be perceived negatively or to minimize public reaction. Fourth, attention management and agenda setting; through silence, organizations can divert public attention from certain issues or create alternative agendas. Mazzei's strategic silence model demonstrates that silence in corporate communication practices is no longer simply a deficiency but rather a conscious and active communication choice. This model is particularly important in crisis communication, sustainability communication, and reputation management contexts.

In the digital communication environment, the theory of silence requires further conceptual expansion. Beyond strategically chosen institutional silence, contemporary communication systems introduce what may be described as algorithmic silence. Unlike deliberate withdrawal, algorithmic silence emerges when platform architectures and automated filtering mechanisms limit the visibility of specific discourses. Digital platforms prioritize content according to engagement metrics, user interaction patterns, and commercial optimization logics. As a result, certain sustainability narratives may become marginalized, not because they are absent, but because they are deprioritized within algorithmic ranking systems.

This phenomenon produces platform mediated communication gaps, where sustainability discourse continues to exist at the production level but fails to achieve effective public reach. In this sense, silence in the AI-mediated environment may be partially structured by technological infrastructures rather than solely by institutional intention. Expanding the theory of silence to include algorithmic mediation enables a more comprehensive understanding of contemporary sustainability communication dynamics.

Silence is similarly used as a strategic tool in corporate sustainability communications. Organizations may remain silent to conceal negative developments in their sustainability performance, missed targets, or areas open to public criticism (Font et al., 2017). However, this practice is not only intended to conceal negative developments but also to avoid accusations of greenwashing, avoid overly high stakeholder expectations, or maintain competitive advantage (Fernando & Lawrence, 2014).

This functionality of the theory of silence in the institutional context also paves the way for organizations to develop a greenhushing strategy in their sustainability communication. Greenhushing is defined as the deliberate under- or non-disclosure of sustainability performance and is directly linked to the strategic silence literature. In this context, silence is not merely a temporary lack of communication during times of crisis, but rather a conscious component of organizations' sustainability communication strategies (Mazzei, 2004; Font et al., 2017). This theory also makes significant contributions to explaining the effects of silence strategies at the institutional level. In particular, the concept of "decoupling" is considered a key dynamic underlying silence strategies. A study by Guo et al. (2017) demonstrated that the decoupling behaviors of energy companies between their sustainability promises and actual practices have direct and indirect negative effects on brand legitimacy and brand trust. One of the most striking manifestations of this type of strategic silence in sustainability communication is greenhushing practices. This framework offers a valuable contribution to understanding the quest for institutional legitimacy that underlies sustainability silence and greenhushing strategies. Greenhushing opens a new area of discussion in sustainability communication and highlights the tension between transparency and strategic silence.

GREENHUSHING AND GREEN SILENCE

The concept of "greenhushing" is discussed in the literature not only in terms of communication level but also in terms of consumer perception, company motivations, and organizational dynamics (Dias et al., 2025). Greenhushing refers to brands' conscious avoidance of sharing their sustainability practices and performance with the public (Font et al., 2017). Although this strategy is perceived as a seemingly passive form of communication, there are quite strategic and calculated motivations behind it. In this context, Bevanda and Bijakšić (2020) define strategic silence as a communication strategy actively preferred and planned by companies in crisis situations. The authors consider strategic silence as an "active form of nonverbal communication" and emphasize that it can be a powerful tool in managing a brand's reputation, especially during a crisis (Bevanda & Bijakšić, 2020, p. 11). According to Delmas and Burbano (2011), greenwashing is defined as organizations' portrayal of their sustainability performance more positively than it actually is or making false sustainability claims. (Delmas & Burbano, 2011).

The main reasons for greenhushing include organizations' efforts to avoid criticism, protect themselves from accusations of greenwashing, keep competitive advantages secret, manage stakeholder expectations, and avoid regulatory uncertainty (Fernando & Lawrence, 2014). However, this strategy is also considered a practice that can directly harm the nature of sustainability communication and the trust established with stakeholders (Torelli et al., 2012). Indeed, according to Dias et al.'s (2025) analysis, when organizations deliberately and intentionally choose strategic silence, this silence often conflicts with public expectations and is assigned specific meanings by violating communication expectations. Greenhushing can similarly be considered a form of strategic silence chosen to avoid certain public reactions and reduce the risk of negative perceptions in sustainability communication. The concept of greenhushing offers an important analytical tool for understanding the dilemmas experienced in sustainability communication. On the one hand, organizations develop sustainability practices and make significant investments in this area; on the other, they may be reluctant to publicly disclose these practices. This demonstrates that sustainability communication is shaped not only by the principles of transparency and accountability, but also by the dynamics of strategic silence and communication risk management (Mazzei, 2004).

The reasons for the emergence of greenhushing are multifaceted. First, organizations fear that their sustainability statements could lead to accusations of greenwashing. Delmas and Burbano (2011) have shown that greenwashing is highly negatively perceived by the public and can seriously damage a brand's reputation. Consequently, some organizations choose to avoid communication altogether to avoid the risks of overemphasizing their sustainability performance (Font et al., 2017). Greenhushing is also linked to the dynamics of managing stakeholder expectations. When organizations strongly emphasize their sustainability commitments through communication, they can create high public expectations for their fulfillment. However, if these commitments are not fully fulfilled or if certain targets are delayed, they can face significant criticism (Torelli et al., 2012). Therefore, some organizations adopt a strategy of silence in their sustainability communication to avoid overly raising expectations and thus minimize the risk of criticism.

Greenhushing strategies often have significant impacts on consumer trust in sustainability-themed brand communications. Indeed, as highlighted in Li and Sun's (2022) large-sample empirical study, green brand crises (both product function- and value-focused crises) negatively impact consumer trust, with perceived risk and perceived value emerging as key mediating mechanisms in this process.

One of the primary motivations for greenhushing practices is the tendency to avoid accusations of greenwashing. Li and Sun (2022) found that crises stemming from greenwashing significantly damage brand trust, and this negative impact is amplified by consumers' increased risk perception and decreased perception of brand equity. This finding aligns with the literature suggesting that greenhushing develops to minimize this risk through defensive silence strategies. Greenhushing strategies are generally based on the goal of brands avoiding potential risks in their sustainability communications and limiting the negative impact of crisis situations. Similarly, Bevanda and Bijakšić (2020) emphasize that strategic silence, when planned correctly, can be beneficial for preserving a brand's credibility and managing public information gaps as desired. Furthermore, they argue that for this strategy to be successful, it is crucial to determine in advance how and when the silence plan will be broken (Bevanda & Bijakšić, 2020, p. 12).

However, while greenhushing may seem beneficial for short-term risk management, it poses serious risks to corporate reputation and consumer trust in the long run. Transparency, a fundamental principle of sustainability communication, is the primary source of stakeholder trust and commitment to the organization (Michelon, Pilonato & Ricceri, 2015). Silence strategies, however, directly contradict this expectation of transparency. Furthermore, many international sustainability initiatives and standards encourage organizations not only to improve their sustainability performance but also to report it transparently (Global Reporting Initiative, 2021). Because greenhushing is considered a practice contrary to these principles of transparency and accountability, it can also undermine organizations' claims to sustainability leadership.

Numerous studies have shown that greenwashing practices negatively impact consumer purchase intentions and perceived product quality. For example, Da Silva and Cé (2025) demonstrated in their experimental study that consumers who detect greenwashing not only negatively evaluate the brand's sustainability image but also the overall product quality, reducing their purchase intentions. This finding demonstrates that greenwashing poses a serious threat not only to communication but also to overall brand equity.

The negative impacts of greenhushing are not limited to consumer perception and brand reputation. This strategy can also negatively impact industrial learning processes, the development of sectoral standards, and collaborations among stakeholders. Font et al. (2017) show that openly sharing sustainability practices encourages the dissemination of good practices across the industry and improves collective sustainability performance. Conversely, greenhushing can slow down sustainability progress across the industry by restricting knowledge flow and learning processes.

The greenhushing trend is particularly amplified during times of crisis. Crisis conditions lead organizations to restructure their communication priorities, and sustainability communication is often relegated to the background (Sarkis et al., 2020). However, stakeholder expectations of sustainability commitments do not completely disappear during times of crisis. On the contrary, brands that demonstrate a commitment to sustainability values even under challenging circumstances are positioned as more trustworthy and ethical actors in the eyes of consumers (Miller & Sinclair, 2020).

Therefore, while adopting a greenhushing strategy during crisis periods may alleviate short-term communication burdens, it carries the risk of damaging brand loyalty and consumer trust in the long run. Claeys and Cauberghe (2015) show that silence strategies in crisis communication often increase perceived responsibility and create the impression in the public that the organization is avoiding responsibility. This finding suggests that greenhushing in sustainability communications should be addressed more carefully and with greater balance during crisis periods.

Research by Primožič and Kutnar (2022) also shows that global brands primarily focus on environmental issues in their sustainability communications, while themes of social and economic sustainability receive less coverage. This suggests that greenhushing strategies affect not only the volume of communication but also the distribution of its content, hindering the holistic reflection of the three-pronged sustainability approach.

Similarly, greenhushing strategies in sustainability communications align with brands' tendency to choose silence during crises. As Tyurina et al. (2024) found in examples like Volkswagen, United Airlines, and Uber, incomplete or delayed communication during crises led to a permanent loss of brand trust. This finding suggests that sustainability silence strategies can similarly damage long-term brand trust and stakeholder relationships.

In conclusion, greenhushing and green silence represent a complex and multifaceted communication practice in sustainability communication. This strategy may be beneficial in reducing short-term communication risks and maintaining competitive advantage; however, in the long run, it has the potential to undermine transparency, damage consumer trust, and jeopardize brand reputation. It is crucial for organizations to carefully evaluate their silence strategies in sustainability communication and differentiate them based on the type of crisis, target audience characteristics, and the ethical expectations they create in sustainability communication. A more systematic study of greenhushing within the sustainability communication literature and a more in-depth exploration of its impact across contexts represents an important and current area of research in communication research.

THE NARRATIVE TURN IN SUSTAINABILITY COMMUNICATION: SUSTAINABILITY AS BRAND STORYTELLING

Sustainability communication cannot be reduced to corporate reporting, performance indicators, or formal responsibility statements. It also constitutes a powerful narrative arena through which brands position themselves, construct identity around particular values, and establish emotional connections with their target audiences (Golob, Podnar, & Zabkar, 2023). In today's competitive environment, sustainability functions not merely as an ethical obligation but as a strategic storytelling framework that shapes brand meaning and differentiation (Weder, 2025). Through sustainability discourse, brands frequently position themselves as "responsible actors," "guardians of the planet," "advocates for future generations," or "ethical leaders." This positioning extends beyond conventional marketing rhetoric and generates a moral narrative. Consequently, sustainability communication shifts from product-centered messaging to value-centered identity construction (Zhang & Liu, 2023). Sustainability discourse becomes a mechanism through which brands articulate who they are, what they stand for, and how they claim legitimacy within broader societal debates. From a narrative theory perspective, each brand constructs a structured story through sustainability communication. This story typically includes a problem (e.g., climate change, plastic pollution, carbon emissions), a solution promise (e.g., renewable energy adoption, circular economy initiatives, carbon neutrality commitments), and a clear ethical stance. Within this narrative configuration, the brand frequently positions itself as the agent of resolution. In this sense, sustainability communication is not merely informational; it is a system of meaning production that organizes corporate action within a coherent moral storyline (Bini & Fissi, 2025).

Consumer behavior literature demonstrates that narratives generate both cognitive and emotional effects. The concept of narrative transportation suggests that when individuals become immersed in a compelling story, their critical resistance may diminish and identification with the narrative may intensify (Thomas & Grigsby, 2024). Sustainability discourse operates within this dynamic: it is not solely rational persuasion but a narrative appeal to consumers' moral sensibilities. Accordingly, the continuity of sustainability communication plays a crucial role in maintaining the coherence of a brand's ethical identity across time and crisis contexts. Within this framework, the withdrawal of sustainability discourse during crisis periods signifies more than a reduction in communication intensity. It may represent the temporary suspension of the brand's moral narrative. Greenhushing, therefore, can be interpreted not merely as "communication reduction" but as a form of narrative withdrawal. When a brand suspends its sustainability storytelling during a crisis, a disruption may emerge in the ongoing ethical identity narrative that consumers have internalized.

From a narrative perspective, this withdrawal can manifest in three distinct forms. First, narrative fading occurs when the brand does not entirely abandon sustainability discourse but reduces its prominence. In this case, the storyline recedes into the background, weakening its emotional resonance and symbolic salience. Second, narrative reframing involves a shift in thematic focus. The brand may move away from environmental sustainability and instead emphasize themes such as solidarity, hygiene, social assistance, or resilience. Here, the ethical narrative does not disappear; rather, it is redirected. Third, narrative rupture represents a complete suspension of sustainability communication. The brand temporarily disconnects from the ethical position it previously constructed. Such rupture may generate perceptions of identity inconsistency in the minds of consumers (Bini & Fissi, 2025).

Accordingly, greenhushing should be understood not only as a strategic silence adopted during crisis periods, but also as the temporary withdrawal of a brand's moral storyline. This withdrawal is particularly visible and potentially more consequential for companies that have placed sustainability at the core of their brand identity. These brands have cultivated value based relationships with their stakeholders, and the durability of these relationships depends on narrative continuity (Weder, 2025).

THE EVOLUTION OF SUSTAINABILITY COMMUNICATION AND ITS RELATIONSHIP WITH CRISIS PERIODS

Since the 2000s, sustainability communication has become a significant competitive advantage for brands, driven by increased environmental awareness and the rise of global threats like climate change (Du, Bhattacharya, & Sen, 2010). Companies have begun to highlight their sustainability goals not only in their annual reports but also in their advertising campaigns, social media strategies, and overall corporate discourse. However, periods of crisis significantly alter the direction of this trend.

During the COVID-19 pandemic, in particular, brands have downplayed their emphasis on environmental sustainability, focusing on issues such as hygiene, health, and supply chain crises (Sarkis et al., 2020). Crilly, Zollo, and Hansen (2022) found that environmental targets were either revised or postponed in a majority of sustainability reports published during the pandemic. These findings demonstrate how sustainability communication transforms during times of crisis, and this shift can be observed in both content and tone.

The ethical dimension of sustainability communication is directly related not only to the content of the discourses made but also to the decision not to produce discourse. Silence can sometimes be defended as a form of ethical withdrawal (Torelli et al., 2012). Temporarily relegating environmental issues to the background due to the priority of responding to urgent public needs, especially during times of crisis, can be ethically justified. However, the continued practice of silence poses a threat to consumer trust and brand reputation. Miller and Sinclair (2020) highlighted the long-term risk of sustainability silence undermining consumer trust and emphasized that ethical consistency is key to continuity in sustainability communication.

Various concrete examples in the literature demonstrate how sustainability silence is implemented during times of crisis. Nike largely halted digital content production related to its sustainability goals during the COVID-19 pandemic and focused on campaigns focused on combating the pandemic (Nike Sustainability Report, 2020). Unilever, while promoting hygiene products throughout the pandemic, avoided openly communicating the increase in plastic packaging use and was criticized for greenhushing (GreenPeace, 2023). Arçelik, meanwhile, suspended its marketing activities in the region during the Ukraine-Russia war, delaying its sustainability campaigns (Koç Holding Sustainability Activities Report, 2023). These examples offer important insights into how sustainability communication is withdrawn during times of crisis, the strategic dimensions of this silence, and the resulting public reactions.

Silence is a form of communication that generates meaning not only at the level of corporate actors but also at the consumer level. Todd and Supa (2014) showed that brands that remain silent are perceived by consumers as either sensitive actors or institutions that avoid accountability. Zhang et al. (2021) found that consumer trust in brands that practice sustainability silence significantly decreases, and that younger consumers, in particular, are more critical of these strategies. In this context, understanding how silence is perceived by target audiences in sustainability communication, even during times of crisis, is critical for marketing and public relations strategies.

METHODOLOGY

This research aims to understand brands' tendency to remain silent in their sustainability communications during times of crisis and the impact of these strategies on consumer perception. To achieve this goal, a qualitative methodology approach was adopted. This approach provided the opportunity to provide in-depth qualitative insight into the research questions. The primary reason for choosing a qualitative methodology was that it was deemed sufficient to examine brands' sustainability silence strategies through content.

RESEARCH QUESTIONS

The general framework of the research was determined by the following fundamental research questions:

1. Why do brands withdraw from sustainability communications during times of crisis?
2. How is the silence strategy perceived by consumers?
3. What is the relationship between consumer perception and brand trust, ethical consistency, and purchase intention?

These questions were formulated in direct relation to the literature on sustainability communication, strategic silence, and greenhushing presented in the theoretical framework of the study.

RESEARCH DESIGN

In the first phase of the study, a qualitative content analysis was conducted to understand bran sustainability communication strategies during crisis periods. For this purpose, 10 brands that changed their communication strategies during global and local crises (the COVID-19 pandemic, the Ukraine-Russia war, and the global economic crisis) between 2020 and 2023 were selected.

Purposive sampling was used for brand selection, and brands that strongly implemented sustainability communications and demonstrated observable changes during the crisis were selected. In this context, the analyzed brands were Nike, Unilever, IKEA, Tesla, Nestlé, Apple, Arçelik, LC Waikiki, Beko, and Koç Holding. Data sources included official websites, social media accounts, sustainability reports, and campaign content from the crisis period. The obtained data was analyzed using MAXQDA software.

The following thematic categories were used in the content analysis:

- Intensity of sustainability discourse: pre-crisis vs. crisis period
- Form of silence: complete silence, discourse reduction, or shift
- Type of crisis: pandemic, war, or economic crisis
- Agenda priority shift: environmental themes shifting to health, hygiene, or social assistance.

These coding categories were based on the literature on strategic silence (Mazzei, 2004), greenhushing (Font et al., 2017), and crisis communication strategies (Coombs, 2007).

DATA ANALYSIS PROCESS

For qualitative data analysis, systematic content analysis was conducted using MAXQDA software. The coding process focused specifically on the decline in sustainability discourse, the pattern of silence, and changes in communication strategies based on crisis type. The impact of greenhushing on the rate of discourse reduction was also analyzed. This structure allows the study to assess the effects of silence and greenhushing practices in sustainability communication, and to comprehensively demonstrate the impact of these effects on brand trust and ethical consistency.

FINDINGS

This section systematically presents the findings from the qualitative phases of the study. The findings are presented solely on a data-based basis, with the interpretation of the findings and their relationship to the theoretical framework left to the discussion section.

CONTENT ANALYSIS RESULTS

The sustainability communication content of the 10 brands analyzed within the scope of the research was systematically coded and analyzed within the framework of key categories such as crisis type, silence strategy, greenhushing, rate of discourse decline, and agenda orientation. The coding process was conducted using MAXQDA software, and the resulting themes were structured in line with the established analysis axes.

The majority of brands analyzed were found to have significantly reduced their sustainability-focused content during crisis periods.

- Nike, Arçelik, and IKEA did not share new content related to their environmental goals during the six-month period during the COVID-19 pandemic.
- A significant decrease in content density was observed.

Brands silence strategies were categorized as follows:

- Complete Silence: No sustainability-themed content was shared during the crisis period.
- Discourse Reduction: A number of brands have significantly reduced their sustainability rhetoric.
- Shift: Some brands have turned to themes of social aid, hygiene or solidarity rather than environmental discourse.

Silence patterns varied by crisis type:

- The rate of complete silence was found to be higher during the pandemic compared to other crisis types.
- Discourse reduction and shifting direction were more common during the economic crisis.
- During wartime, a tendency to withdraw from environmental discourse altogether was observed.

GREENHUSHING INDICATORS

In this section, the qualitative findings will be comprehensively discussed in light of the research's theoretical framework and existing literature. Furthermore, the findings' contribution to the literature on sustainability communication and crisis communication will be evaluated, and suggestions for new research areas will be presented. It was determined that while sustainability activities continue in practice for most of the analyzed brands, the intensity of communication related to these activities has decreased. This situation has been interpreted as an indicator of greenhushing: the level of public reporting and communication has been reduced while the activities continue.

Table 1. Qualitative findings results

Brand	Crisis Type	Silence Style	Greenhushing	Level of Discourse Reduction
Nike	Pandemic	Discourse Reduction	Yes	There has been a significant decrease in Nike's sustainability content.
Unilever	Pandemic	Change of Direction	Yes	There has been a notable decline in Unilever's sustainability narrative.
IKEA	Economic Crisis	Discourse Reduction	Yes	IKEA's sustainability communication has been significantly reduced.
Tesla	War	Complete Silence	Yes	Tesla has completely stopped communicating sustainability during the crisis.

continued on following page

Table 1. Continued

Brand	Crisis Type	Silence Style	Greenhushing	Level of Discourse Reduction
Nestlé	War	Change of Direction	Yes	A partial but significant shift in direction has been observed in the sustainability discourse.
Apple	Economic Crisis	Discourse Reduction	No	Apple has seen a moderate decrease in sustainability communications.
Arçelik	Pandemic	Discourse Reduction	Yes	There has been a significant decline in Arçelik's sustainability discourse.
LC Waikiki	Complete Silence	Complete Silence	Yes	LC Waikiki has completely suspended its sustainability communication.
Beko	Economic Crisis	No	No	A limited decrease in Beko's sustainability content has been detected.
Koç Holding	Economic Crisis	Change of Direction	Yes	There has been a significant, but not complete, decline in Koç Holding's sustainability rhetoric.

The analysis results revealed a strong and significant relationship between silence strategies and greenhushing. Coding results reveal a qualitatively strong association between silence strategies and greenhushing tendency. This finding suggests that these two forms of silence are often used deliberately to avoid sustainability communication and limit the flow of information to the public. It has been observed that the greenhushing tendency is more intense in brands that adopt a discourse reduction strategy. This demonstrates that discourse reduction operates as a more flexible and controlled communication strategy, and some brands share sustainability information, albeit limitedly, during this process.

Looking at the relationship between crisis types and silence, the pandemic period has seen brands increasingly resort to strategies of reducing discourse and shifting direction in their sustainability communications. It has been observed that a significant portion of brands adopted one of these two strategies during the pandemic period. This trend suggests that, in the face of an unexpected and large-scale crisis like a pandemic, organizations often choose to reduce the intensity of their sustainability communications or shift their focus rather than completely halt them.

In contrast, during wartime, particularly when security, supply chain, and ethical risks are high, organizations have been observed to adopt a more rigid and protective communication strategy. In this context, brands analyzed during wartime often prioritize complete silence and deflection. During economic crises, organizations have been found to opt for a more pronounced reduction in their discourse. It appears that during this period, due to resource constraints and concerns about financial sustainability, organizations often choose to reduce the intensity of their communication rather than withdraw their sustainability discourse entirely.

A significant relationship was also found between greenhushing and the rate of discourse reduction. It has been observed that the decline in discourse is more pronounced in brands that engage in greenhushing, while it remains more limited in brands that do not. This finding suggests that the greenhushing strategy was accompanied by a significant and systematic weakening of sustainability communication. This could be interpreted as brands that implemented greenhushing intentionally limiting the flow of information about their sustainability performance and attempting to lower public expectations. In contrast, brands that did not implement greenhushing attempted to maintain more consistent sustainability communication, even during crisis conditions.

From an agenda-shifting perspective, social welfare and health-hygiene themes appear to be the most common forms of agenda-shifting among brands practicing greenhushing. This finding suggests that organizations are shifting their focus from sustainability discourse to more focused messages of social benefit and solidarity. These types of messages are favored by organizations as a safer communication The platform offers the potential to create a more positive and empathetic perception during times of crisis. In contrast, brands that maintain an environmental theme have not implemented greenhushing. Brands like Apple and Beko, in particular, have continued to publicly share their environmental sustainability commitments and activities in this area, even during the crisis. This suggests that brands with a higher level of commitment to sustainability demonstrate greater consistency in their communication strategies and strive to maintain trust with stakeholders.

Overall, silence strategies appear to be structured differently depending on the type of crisis and the organization's sustainability communication strategy. During the pandemic, discourse reduction and deflection were more commonly implemented, while during wartime, complete silence was preferred. Greenhushing, on the other hand, was most commonly used in conjunction with complete silence and deflection, demonstrating a strong relationship between silence types and greenhushing. Furthermore, the rate of discourse reduction significantly increased in the presence of greenhushing, demonstrating that greenhushing significantly weakens sustainability communication. Agenda steering, on the other hand, serves as a complementary element of the silence strategy and is implemented through empathetic content, particularly consumer-oriented (social assistance and health-hygiene themes).

Finally, brands that maintained an environmental theme exhibited lower discourse reduction and did not engage in greenhushing. This finding suggests a communication profile more committed to sustainability identity and ethical consistency, suggesting that such communication strategies may yield more positive outcomes in terms of brand trust and consumer loyalty.

Brands that maintain sustainability narratives during times of crisis are perceived as more consistent and trustworthy by consumers, while brands that employ a silence strategy are associated with relatively lower perceptions of trust. The study findings strongly align with the motivations for greenhushing found in the literature. The themes of "avoiding greenwashing accusations," "deficiencies in the communication plan," and "viewing sustainability as an intrinsic value," highlighted in a systematic literature review by Dias et al. (2025), were also frequently mentioned in the qualitative content analysis conducted in this study. This finding suggests that sustainability silence and greenhushing strategies are not merely reactive behaviors specific to crisis periods but may also be the result of long-term communication policies and brand positioning preferences.

SUSTAINABILITY SILENCE IN THE ALGORITHMIC ATTENTION ECONOMY: THE NEW DIMENSION OF GREENHUSHING IN THE AI ERA

While the findings of this study demonstrate that sustainability silence intensifies during crisis periods, the contemporary communication landscape requires extending this discussion beyond crisis driven dynamics. In the AI-mediated attention economy, silence may emerge not only from strategic withdrawal but also from algorithmic mediation.

As of 2025, sustainability communication can no longer be understood solely as a discourse designed by human actors and governed by corporate strategy; rather, it operates within an algorithmically mediated attention economy in which visibility, prioritization, and circulation are shaped by digital infrastructures (Heitmayer, 2025; Williams, 2025). The algorithmic architecture of digital platforms has become a central intermediary that determines which content is amplified, which is deprioritized, and which narratives gain public visibility. In this context, sustainability silence should not be interpreted exclusively as a corporate choice, but also as an outcome produced or intensified by platform dynamics (Cheong, Baksh, & Ju, 2022).

The algorithmic attention economy evaluates content primarily through quantitative density and engagement metrics. During crisis periods, topics such as health, security, war, or economic instability tend to generate higher engagement and are therefore prioritized by platform algorithms. Consequently, sustainability-themed content may become relatively less visible. This phenomenon can generate a form of algorithmic "silence" independent of brands' deliberate communication withdrawal. Within this framework, the concept of algorithmic silence which remains under-theorized in the literatüre gains significance. Algorithmic silence refers to situations in which brands continue to produce sustainability communication, yet such communication fails to achieve public visibility due to platform logics and filtering mechanisms.

The widespread adoption of AI-supported content generation tools has significantly reduced the cost of producing sustainability communication. Organizations are now able to generate reports, social media posts, and campaign texts rapidly through generative AI systems. In theory, this development could reduce greenhushing, as resource-based justifications for silence weaken when communication costs decline (Garg, Bohara, & Srivastav, 2025). However, this technological shift simultaneously introduces a new risk: the automation and potential superficiality of sustainability discourse (Gündüzyeli, 2024).

Machine-generated sustainability narratives may be perceived as lacking emotional depth and authenticity. In value driven communication contexts, authenticity remains a critical evaluative criterion for consumers. If sustainability messages are perceived as AI-generated rather than human-crafted, the credibility of the brand's ethical identity narrative may erode. In such an environment, brands face a dual pressure: the expectation to maintain sustainability communication and the risk of appearing artificial or insincere. This tension may lead some organizations to regard silence as a comparatively safer strategic option.

Artificial intelligence is also increasingly deployed not only in content production but in monitoring and verification processes. ESG performance assessments, carbon footprint calculations, and the validation of sustainability claims are progressively conducted through data driven systems (Elhady & Shohieb, 2025). The development of AI-powered greenwashing detection mechanisms heightens the accuracy risk associated with sustainability discourse (Alotaibi & Alwathnani, 2025). Paradoxically, in an environment characterized by intensified scrutiny, organizations may reduce their communication intensity to minimize the risk of misinterpretation or public accusation. Thus, greenhushing may emerge not only during crisis periods but also as a defensive reflex within an era of algorithmic surveillance (Mustafa, Smolarski, & Elamer, 2025).

Within this framework, sustainability silence reveals a three layered structure, each layer corresponding to a distinct communication dynamic.

Strategic silence refers to the deliberate and calculated decision of an organization to reduce or temporarily suspend sustainability discourse. In this case, silence does not stem from communicative incapacity, but from a conscious effort to avoid the risks associated with excessive visibility. Particularly during crises, brands may deprioritize sustainability messaging in response to heightened public sensitivities, intensified scrutiny, or the risk of misinterpretation (Weder, 2025). Strategic silence thus represents a rational form of reputational risk management.

Narrative withdrawal captures the identity dimension of strategic silence. Here, the issue extends beyond reduced communication frequency; it involves the temporary suspension of the ethical identity narrative that the brand has constructed. For many organizations, sustainability communication is not merely operational but central to corporate identity. It situates the brand within a moral framework and fosters value based relationships with stakeholders (Golob, Podnar, & Zabkar,

2023). When this narrative is withdrawn, a rupture may emerge in the continuity of the brand's ethical positioning.

Algorithmic silence refers to the invisibility of sustainability communication resulting not from corporate withdrawal, but from the structural dynamics of digital platforms. Contemporary sustainability communication circulates primarily through social media platforms, search engines, and data driven distribution systems. Platform algorithms determine visibility based on engagement rates, user behavior, trending topics, and commercial priorities (Cheong et al., 2022). In this context, sustainability discourse may become marginalized not because it is absent, but because it is deprioritized within algorithmic hierarchies of attention.

Accordingly, algorithmic silence constitutes a new vulnerability in sustainability communication within the digital age. Unlike strategic silence, it emerges from the structural functioning of platform architectures and the attention economy. Nevertheless, from the perspective of consumer perception, algorithmic silence may be indistinguishable from deliberate withdrawal.

When these three layers are considered collectively, sustainability communication can no longer be conceptualized as a linear process between organization and consumer. Instead, it operates within a multilayered communicative environment mediated by platforms, data systems, and AI technologies. This evolving structure necessitates analyzing greenhushing not only within crisis communication literature, but also within the broader frameworks of algorithmic media studies and digital communication theory.

From this perspective, sustainability silence in the AI era is not merely an act of withdrawal; it is a complex strategic terrain shaped by dynamics of visibility, surveillance, and authenticity. The central question for brands is no longer simply *when to speak*, but *how and through which mechanisms to speak within an algorithmically structured environment.* The future of sustainability communication thus depends on the capacity to balance strategic silence with algorithmic visibility.

DISCUSSION AND CONCLUSION

The primary objective of this research was to examine brands' sustainability communications during times of crisis and analyze the impact of these silence strategies. In line with this objective, the findings demonstrate that crisis conditions have led to a significant transformation in sustainability communication, and that this transformation has had complex consequences for consumers.

The qualitative findings of the study clearly revealed a significant decrease in brands' sustainability communication during crisis periods. The qualitative findings of the study show that most brands reduce their sustainability communications during crisis periods, while some remain completely silent. This supports the tendency to reprioritize sustainability communication during crisis conditions. This finding aligns with the impact of the pandemic on sustainability reporting practices, also highlighted by Crilly, Zollo, and Hansen (2022). Similarly, Sarkis et al. (2020) showed that the COVID-19 pandemic shifted companies' environmental communication priorities, pushing sustainability goals to the background in the short term. However, this research reveals that this transformation occurred not only at the communication level but also at the level of communication style and strategy. The shifting strategies identified in the content analysis align with Tregidga et al.'s (2014) concept of "recoding communication priorities." In this sense, sustainability communication during times of crisis evolves not simply into a lack of communication, but rather into a deliberate and calculated form of silence. This finding reaffirms that silence is a meaningful and strategically employed form of communication, as emphasized by Bruneau's (1973) theory of silence.

The findings suggest that brands' tendency to withdraw sustainability communications stems not only from the dictates of crisis conditions but also from strategic and tactical concerns. The qualitative analysis observed numerous instances where sustainability practices were actually ongoing but not publicly reported. This suggests that the practice of greenhushing, as identified by Font et al. (2017), becomes even more prevalent during crisis periods.

Fernando and Lawrence (2014) argued that greenhushing is not a communication failure but rather a deliberate risk management tool. The findings of this research support this view: during times of crisis, brands tend to avoid potential criticism, misunderstandings, or public pressure by withdrawing from sustainability communications. This tendency, particularly during times of war and economic crisis, to withdraw from sustainability communications and prioritize themes of outreach and solidarity strongly aligns with the concept of strategic silence defined by Mazzei (2004). This also reflects brands' reflexes to manage reputational risk in a crisis environment. According to SCCT (Coombs, 2007), companies' efforts to reduce their perceived responsibility during times of crisis can lead to the adoption of low-responsibility strategies, such as silence. However, the research findings suggest that such strategies can have more complex effects in areas with high ethical expectations, such as sustainability.

Differences in Silence Strategy Based on Crisis Type

The qualitative findings of the study also showed that crisis types influence the form of silence strategies. It was determined that silence rates are higher during pandemic periods, while discourse manipulation and agenda-shifting strategies are more frequently preferred during economic crises. In times of war, a tendency to withdraw from the sustainability discourse altogether was observed.

This finding suggests that crisis types shift consumer priorities and public sensitivities, and brands restructure their sustainability communication strategies accordingly. This finding aligns with Claeys and Cauberghe (2015)'s findings that communication strategies can differ depending on the type of crisis. One of this research's most significant contributions to the literature is its treatment of the strategy of silence in sustainability communication as an independent and original research topic.

This study demonstrates that sustainability silence is not merely a byproduct of crisis conditions but a conscious and strategic communication choice, and suggests that this concept should be addressed more systematically within the theoretical framework.

The research findings also have important practical implications for brand managers and communication professionals. Firstly, it's clear that completely withdrawing sustainability discourse during a crisis can negatively impact long-term brand trust and loyalty. Brands should manage a strategy of silence in a planned and transparent manner during a crisis. Instead, indirect and low-intensity communication channels (e.g., product labels, online boards, carbon footprint reports) can be used to demonstrate continued sustainability activities. Furthermore, engaging the public with a comprehensive and clear communication campaign about sustainability commitments in the post-crisis period is critical to rebuilding brand trust.

There are also several avenues for future research. Furthermore, the impact of sustainability silence on long-term brand reputation and financial performance has not yet been sufficiently explored. Monitoring these effects through longitudinal research and understanding the dynamics of change over time will provide deeper insights into the development of sustainability communication strategies. Furthermore, how sustainability silence is perceived across different media channels and whether this perception differs by media type should be considered as a separate area of research.

Ultimately, silence strategies in sustainability communication should not be considered simply a form of withdrawal, but rather a communication choice that must be carefully managed in the relationship with the target audience. For brands, sustainability is no longer just a matter of deciding when and how much to speak, but also when and how to remain silent. This decision must be strategically constructed and managed to protect brand equity and consumer trust during times of crisis.

REFERENCES

Alotaibi, E. M., & Alwathnani, A. M. (2025). AI-enabled ESG compliance audit for stakeholders. *Sustainability (Basel), 17*(21), 9513. DOI: 10.3390/su17219513

Apple. (2025). *Apple official website.* https://www.apple.com (Accessed: 8 March 2025)

Arçelik. (2025). *Arçelik official website.* https://www.arcelikglobal.com (Accessed: 21 April 2025)

Beko. (2025). *Beko global website.* https://www.beko.com (Accessed: 10 March 2025)

Bevanda, A., & Bijaškić, S. (2020). Strategic silence in crisis communication: When is it better to remain silent? *South Eastern European Journal of Communication.* DOI: 10.47960/2712-0457.2020.1.2.7

Bini, L., & Fissi, S. (2025). The readability of corporate sustainability narratives in a crisis: An analysis of linguistic features using Coh-Metrix. *Social Responsibility Journal, 21*(5), 1049–1065. DOI: 10.1108/SRJ-10-2023-0547

Bruneau, T. J. (1973). Communicative silences: Forms and functions. *Journal of Communication, 23*(1), 17–46. DOI: 10.1111/j.1460-2466.1973.tb00929.x

Carroll, A. B. (1991). The pyramid of corporate social responsibility: Toward the moral management of organizational stakeholders. *Business Horizons, 34*(4), 39–48. DOI: 10.1016/0007-6813(91)90005-G

Cheong, H. J., Baksh, S. M., & Ju, I. (2022). Spiral of silence in an algorithm-driven social media content environment: Conceptual framework and research propositions. *KOME – An International Journal of Pure Communication Inquiry, 10*(1), 32–46. DOI: 10.17646/KOME.75672.86

Claeys, A. S., & Cauberghe, V. (2015). The role of a favorable pre-crisis reputation in protecting organizations during crises. *Public Relations Review, 41*(1), 64–72. DOI: 10.1016/j.pubrev.2014.10.013

Coombs, W. T. (2007). Protecting organization reputations during a crisis: The development and application of situational crisis communication theory. *Corporate Reputation Review, 10*(3), 163–176. DOI: 10.1057/palgrave.crr.1550049

Crilly, D., Zollo, M., & Hansen, M. T. (2022). The grammar of decoupling: A cognitive-linguistic perspective on firms' sustainability claims and stakeholders' interpretation. *Academy of Management Journal, 59*(2), 705–729. DOI: 10.5465/amj.2015.0171

Da Silva, B., & Cé, F. (2025). *The effects of greenwashing on purchasing intention and perceived quality by the consumer*. ReMark – Revista Brasileira de Marketing., DOI: 10.5585/2025.26514

Delmas, M. A., & Burbano, V. C. (2011). The drivers of greenwashing. *California Management Review*, *54*(1), 64–87. DOI: 10.1525/cmr.2011.54.1.64

Dias, L., Bagatini, F., & Perin, M. (2025). *Green "under-communication": A systematic literature review on greenhushing*. ReMark – Revista Brasileira de Marketing.

Du, S., Bhattacharya, C. B., & Sen, S. (2010). Maximizing business returns to corporate social responsibility (CSR): The role of CSR communication. *International Journal of Management Reviews*, *12*(1), 8–19. DOI: 10.1111/j.1468-2370.2009.00276.x

Elhady, A. M., & Shohieb, S. (2025). AI-driven sustainable finance: Computational tools, ESG metrics, and global implementation. *Future Business Journal*, *11*(1), 209. DOI: 10.1186/s43093-025-00610-x

Fernando, S., & Lawrence, S. (2014). A theoretical framework for CSR practices: Integrating legitimacy theory, stakeholder theory and institutional theory. *Journal of Theoretical Accounting Research*, *9*(1), 149–178.

Font, X., Elgammal, I., & Lamond, I. (2017). Greenhushing: The deliberate under-communicating of sustainability practices by tourism businesses. *Journal of Sustainable Tourism*, *25*(7), 1007–1023. DOI: 10.1080/09669582.2016.1158829

Freeman, R. E. (1984). *Strategic management: A stakeholder approach*. Pitman., DOI: 10.1017/CBO9781139192675

Garg, V., Bohara, S., & Srivastav, A. (2025). AI-driven sustainability marketing transforming consumers' perception toward eco-friendly brands. *Discover Sustainability*, *6*(1), 984. DOI: 10.1007/s43621-025-01934-y

Global Reporting Initiative. (2021). *GRI Standards*. https://www.globalreporting.org (Accessed: 8 January 2025)

Golob, U., Podnar, K., & Zabkar, V. (2023). Sustainability communication. *International Journal of Advertising*, *42*(1), 42–51. DOI: 10.1080/02650487.2022.2144035

Greenpeace, U. K. (2023). *Unilever's greenwashing and vulnerability to brand damage: Briefing for investors*. https://www.greenpeace.org.uk/resources/unilever-greenwash-investor-briefing/

Gündüzyeli, B. (2024). Artificial intelligence in digital marketing within the framework of sustainable management. *Sustainability (Basel)*, *16*(23), 10511. DOI: 10.3390/su162310511

Guo, R., Tao, L., Li, C., & Wang, T. (2017). A path analysis of greenwashing in a trust crisis among Chinese energy companies. The role of brand legitimacy and brand loyalty. *Journal of Business Ethics*, *140*(3), 523–536. DOI: 10.1007/s10551-015-2672-7

Heitmayer, M. (2025). The second wave of attention economics: Attention as a universal symbolic currency on social media and beyond. *Interacting with Computers*, *37*(1), 18–29. DOI: 10.1093/iwc/iwae035

Holding, K. (2023). Koç Holding. *Sustainability Report, 2023*, •••. Retrieved January 3, 2025, from https://www.koc.com.tr/en/sustainability/reports

IKEA. (2025). *IKEA official website.* https://www.ikea.com (Accessed: 3 January 2025)

Jaworski, A. (1993). The power of silence: Social and pragmatic perspectives. *Sage (Atlanta, Ga.).* Advance online publication. DOI: 10.4135/9781483325460

Li, G., & Sun, X. (2022). The impact of green brand crises on green brand trust: An empirical study. *Sustainability (Basel)*, *14*(2), 611. DOI: 10.3390/su14020611

Mazzei, A. (2004). Internal communication for creating corporate community. *Corporate Communications*, *9*(2), 200–210.

Michelon, G., Pilonato, S., & Ricceri, F. (2015). CSR reporting practices and the quality of disclosure: An empirical analysis. *Critical Perspectives on Accounting*, *33*, 59–78. DOI: 10.1016/j.cpa.2014.10.003

Miller, C. C., & Sinclair, G. (2020). Crisis communication and corporate reputation: Exploring the impact of silence and transparency on consumer evaluations. *Public Relations Review*, *46*(3).

Morsing, M., & Schultz, M. (2006). Corporate social responsibility communication: Stakeholder information, response and involvement strategies. *Business Ethics (Oxford, England)*, *15*(4), 323–338. DOI: 10.1111/j.1467-8608.2006.00460.x

Mustafa, F., Smolarski, J., & Elamer, A. A. (2025). The convergence of artificial intelligence and sustainability reporting: A systematic review of applications, challenges and future directions. *Business Strategy and the Environment*, *34*(8), 9761–9784. Advance online publication. DOI: 10.1002/bse.70090

Nestlé. (2025). *Nestlé global website.* https://www.nestle.com (Accessed: 8 March 2025)

Nike. (2020). *Nike, Inc. FY20 Impact Report.* https://about.nike.com/en/resources/nike-inc-impact-report-archive (Accessed: 12 March 2025)

Pang, A., Jin, Y., Seo, Y., Choi, S., Teo, H., Le, P., & Reber, B. (2021). Breaking the sound of silence: Explication in the use of strategic silence in crisis communication. *International Journal of Business Communication, 59*(2), 219–241. DOI: 10.1177/23294884211046357

Pomering, A., & Johnson, L. W. (2009). Advertising corporate social responsibility initiatives to communicate corporate image: Inhibiting scepticism to enhance persuasion. *Corporate Communications, 14*(4), 420–439. DOI: 10.1108/13563280910998763

Primožič, L., & Kutnar, A. (2022). Sustainability communication in global consumer brands. *Sustainability (Basel), 14*(20), 13586. Advance online publication. DOI: 10.3390/su142013586

Sarkis, J., Cohen-Rosenthal, E., & Dou, Y. (2020). A review of the emerging COVID-19 pandemic from the perspective of sustainable global supply chains. *Resources, Conservation and Recycling, 162*, 105–110.

Schaltegger, S., & Burritt, R. (2010). Sustainability accounting for companies: Catchphrase or decision support for business leaders? *Journal of World Business, 45*(4), 375–384. DOI: 10.1016/j.jwb.2009.08.002

Suchman, M. C. (1995). Managing legitimacy: Strategic and institutional approaches. *Academy of Management Review, 20*(3), 571–610. DOI: 10.2307/258788

Tesla. (2025). *Tesla official website.* https://www.tesla.com (Accessed: 3 January 2025)

Thomas, V. L., & Grigsby, J. L. (2024). Narrative transportation: A systematic literature review and future research agenda. *Psychology and Marketing, 41*(7), 1235–1256. DOI: 10.1002/mar.22011

Todd, M. D., & Supa, D. W. (2014). Testing the viability of corporate social advocacy. *Public Relations Review, 40*(5), 771–783.

Torelli, R., Balluchi, F., & Furlotti, K. (2012). Greenwashing and environmental communication: Effects on stakeholders' attitudes and intentions. *Corporate Social Responsibility and Environmental Management, 27*(1), 52–64. DOI: 10.1002/bse.2373

Tregidga, H., Milne, M. J., & Kearins, K. (2014). Governing meaning of sustainability: The discursive construction of the sustainable organization. *Organization Studies, 35*(2), 231–257.

Tyurina, N., Nazarchuk, T., Hurnytsky, O., & Kovalchuk, V. (2024). *Brand communications in anti-crisis management: Theoretical aspects and practical experience of foreign companies*. Innovation and Sustainability., DOI: 10.31649/ins.2024.3.118.127

Unilever. (2025). *Unilever global website.* https://www.unilever.com (Accessed: 9 March 2025)

Weder, F. (2025). *Strategic sustainability communication: Principles, perspectives, and potential.* Springer., DOI: 10.1007/978-3-031-89486-2

Williams, M. (2025). Social media democracy: How algorithms shape public discourse and marginalise voices. *Journal of Media and Rights*, *3*(1), a20. DOI: 10.4102/JMR.v3i1.20

Zhang, J., & Liu, Z. (2023). An empirical analysis of the impact of brand story themes on brand attitude in the context of B2C e-commerce platforms for organic agricultural products. *Sustainability (Basel)*, *15*(24), 16679. DOI: 10.3390/su152416679

Zhang, L., Li, D., & Zhou, L. (2021). How greenwashing affects consumer responses: A review and research agenda. *International Journal of Consumer Studies*, *45*(5), 1250–1265.

KEY WORDS & DEFINITIONS

Sustainability Silence: A strategic reduction, suspension, or deliberate limitation of sustainability related communication by organizations, particularly during crisis periods. It functions as a reputational risk management mechanism and reflects a calculated adjustment of communicative visibility rather than the termination of sustainability practices.

Greenhushing: The intentional under-communication or nondisclosure of sustainability practices, performance data, or achievements, primarily aimed at avoiding accusations of greenwashing, regulatory scrutiny, heightened stakeholder expectations, or reputational vulnerability. Unlike greenwashing, greenhushing involves communicative withdrawal rather than exaggeration.

Strategic Silence: A purposeful communicative act in which organizations deliberately withhold, delay, or limit information. Rather than indicating communicative failure, strategic silence represents a conscious risk-management strategy used to control agenda-setting, manage uncertainty, or protect institutional legitimacy.

Algorithmic Silence: A form of communicative invisibility produced by digital platform algorithms, where sustainability-related discourse continues to exist but is deprioritized within engagement driven attention systems. In this case, silence is not solely organizational but structurally mediated by platform logics and algorithmic filtering.

Sustainability Communication: The multidimensional process through which organizations communicate their environmental, social, and economic sustainability strategies, commitments, and performance to stakeholders. It functions both as a transparency mechanism and as a central component of corporate identity construction and brand positioning.

Narrative Withdrawal: The temporary weakening or suspension of a brand's sustainability storytelling, resulting in a disruption of its previously constructed ethical identity narrative. Narrative withdrawal differs from complete silence by affecting the symbolic continuity of the brand's moral positioning.

Crisis-Driven Communication Shift: The restructuring of organizational communication priorities during crisis periods, characterized by reduced sustainability discourse, thematic redirection (e.g., toward health, solidarity, or security), or increased reliance on silence based strategies.

Chapter 11
A Critical Approach to the Ideal Body Created Through Digital Twins

Özge Uğurlu Akbaş
Uskudar University, Turkey

Esennur Sirer
http://orcid.org/0000-0003-0345-4158
Uskudar University, Turkey

ABSTRACT

All forms of communication are being redesigned through digitalization and transferred into everyday life, shaping individuals' modes of thinking. The perception of the ideal body and beauty conveyed through digital media has become increasingly widespread with the emergence of artificial intelligence applications. Brands, by integrating new technologies into their communication strategies, aim to reach their consumer audiences through these tools. In this context, the fashion industry is undergoing a profound transformation in its advertising and visual content production processes by adopting AI-powered digital twin technology. This technology has gained particular prominence as global brands create digital avatars of real models to use in advertising campaigns. The aim of this study is to evaluate how women are represented in media environments where reality is reproduced through artificial intelligence, drawing on Baudrillard's concept of "hyperreality."

DOI: 10.4018/979-8-3373-5666-2.ch011

INTRODUCTION

Existing in an era of constant change and transformation offers new experiential domains almost on a daily basis, continuously reshaping established assumptions about the future. In recent years, numerous sectors worldwide have undergone processes of digital transformation, bringing about profound structural changes. Emerging technologies such as the Internet of Things, Artificial Intelligence, Big Data, and Cloud Computing have significantly altered modes of production and professional practices. Among these, artificial intelligence applications—capable of being integrated into nearly every aspect of daily life—have led to fundamental transformations in the media landscape. Beyond facilitating ease of use, AI technologies have reshaped content production itself, contributing to the diversification and rapid proliferation of media content. Through big data integration, AI has also transformed consumer analysis and textual production processes.

Artificial intelligence applications have been swiftly adopted within the field of advertising production. From the generation of advertising copy to content enrichment, from production and post-production processes to marketing strategies and audience engagement, AI technologies now contribute to almost every stage of advertising workflows. It is even anticipated that AI-generated advertising films may constitute a substantial proportion of future advertising content. Advertising productions that rely on prioritized visual materials are not only technologically efficient but also significantly more cost-effective.

In this context, the use of **digital twin technology** has emerged as a particularly transformative practice within contemporary advertising production. Digital twins are argued to accelerate content creation processes while simultaneously reducing production costs. Through digital twin technologies, brands are able to produce rapid, scalable content tailored to different social media platforms and campaign formats. Moreover, for advertising agencies, digital twins offer new opportunities for campaign dissemination by enabling multiple visual variations designed to address diverse target audiences. Particularly through advertising, circulating images of the body and beauty shift beauty from an individual realm of personal preference to an ideal that must be achieved and continuously maintained. In this process, the body is detached from its biological realities and imperfections and reconfigured as a project subject to constant optimization. Such transformations relocate beauty from a domain of natural diversity to one that is technically regulated, reproducible, and subject to control.

This study examines the use of digital twins within the fashion industry and advertising discourse in relation to the construction of ideal beauty narratives and their articulation with consumer culture. Within the scope of the research, examples of digital twin usage in the fashion industry are analyzed through a visual culture approach, with particular attention given to H&M's incorporation of digital twins into its advertising campaigns as a case study. By linking theoretical discussions with contemporary advertising practices, the study aims to demonstrate how digital beauty representations are normalized within visual culture. Digital twins are approached not merely as technological innovations, but as ideological instruments through which bodies, emotions, and needs are reproduced within economic processes. In this regard, the study explores how ideal beauty narratives produced through digital twins transform individuals' perceptions of the body and structure the social circulation of beauty.

Digital Twin Technology

A digital twin can be defined as the virtual modeling of entities that exist as observable and tangible objects in the physical world. Digital twins constitute a simulation process that integrates multiple disciplines, diverse physical parameters, multiple scales, and various possibilities by fully utilizing physical models, sensor updates, operational histories, and other data sources (Li, 2022, p. 3). When considered within the context of technological convergence, the digital twin is a combination of multiple advanced technologies such as Big Data, Artificial Intelligence, and Multimodal Interactions. Big Data technologies, in particular, are characterized by the large volumes of data primarily collected through the Internet of Things (IoT) and Social Networks (SN) (Hornik & Rachamim, 2025, p. 13). In this framework, digital twins are categorized as IoT-enabled digital twins, AI-driven digital twins, simulation-based digital twins, and data-oriented digital twins (Dhapte, 2025).

As a result of the integrated operation of multiple technologies, digital twins have begun to be utilized across a wide range of sectors. Supported by real-time 3D computer graphics—capable of producing interactive content at speeds exceeding human perception—digital twins can organize and present data from multiple sources as realistic and interactive visualizations. Market projections indicate that the global digital twin market reached a value of USD 9.96 billion in 2024, is expected to grow to USD 12.14 billion in 2025, and is projected to reach USD 88.04 billion by 2035, with a compound annual growth rate (CAGR) of 21.91% between 2025 and 2035 (Dhapte, 2025). By 2035, digital twin technologies are anticipated to become a cornerstone of digital transformation across various industries.

Digital twins may be conceptualized as a bridge between the physical and virtual worlds. By enabling data analysis, system monitoring, and the early detection of potential issues, digital twins allow for preventive measures to be implemented before problems arise. Additionally, by simulating projects in virtual environments, organizations can avoid the high costs associated with real-world implementation. Although digital twin technology has been most prominently applied in fields such as healthcare, fashion, industry, urban planning, automotive manufacturing, and production, its use has gradually expanded into sectors including aviation, energy, maritime industries, urban governance, agriculture, construction, oil and gas, healthcare services, and environmental protection (Li, 2022, p. 12).

In healthcare in particular, digital twins have emerged as have emerged as promising tools in clinical modeling and personalized medicine. Through the creation of virtual models of organs or entire physiological systems, digital twins support personalized medicine and patient monitoring by enabling physicians to simulate treatments and predict potential health outcomes. The use of digital twins in early disease detection, personalized medication, and forecasting future bodily changes has also contributed to more efficient healthcare delivery. Furthermore, the ability of physicians to diagnose patients through digital twins facilitates continuous patient monitoring and has the potential to reduce congestion in healthcare facilities. In the context of smart cities, digital twins utilize real-time urban data to improve traffic management, energy efficiency, and infrastructure maintenance. Cities such as Singapore, Las Vegas, London, and Mannheim employ digital twin technologies to enhance economic, environmental, and social sustainability and to support problem-solving processes in urban governance (Cui, 2025, p. 5).

Digital Twins as Hyperreality

Since the early twentieth century, the reconfiguration of production and reproduction processes under Fordist industrial conditions has prompted debates concerning the loss of the "uniqueness" of objects. Baudrillard extends Benjamin's critique of industrial objects and mass communication images to the serial reproduction of bodies through communication technologies, suggesting that bodies, too, have lost their uniqueness. According to Baudrillard, the emergence of soft technologies signals the advent of a synthetic and mental "software" era, in which hyperreality asserts its claim to truth. Hyperreality—or simulation—refers to the derivation of reality from models in the absence of any original referent. In simulation, the metaphysical universe disappears, and reality assumes an operational form. This synthetic reality, devoid of illusion, is defined as hyperreality (Baudrillard, 2018, pp. 13–15).

The conceptual foundations of digital twins can be traced to Gelernter's (1991) *Mirror Worlds*. In 2002, Dr. Michael Grieves of the University of Michigan is recognized as the first scholar to formally apply the digital twin concept to production and to articulate digital twin software systems. The term "digital twin" was later adopted by John Vickers of NASA in 2010. The use of the term "twin" in production, however, dates back to NASA's Apollo Program, during which two identical spacecraft were constructed; the one retained on Earth was referred to as the "twin" and used to simulate real-time space operations. From this perspective, twins can be understood as prototypes or models that reflect real operational conditions through simulation.

Over time, the concept of digital twins has expanded into domains such as simulation technologies, virtual components, and 3D printing. Following 2014, advancements in internet technologies, artificial intelligence, and virtual reality facilitated the broader application of digital twins in industrial product and equipment manufacturing. The implementation of digital twins gradually extended across all stages of the product lifecycle, including production and services, continuously enriching the conceptual scope of digital twin technologies (Calp, 2022).

Today, digital twins are redefined as digital replicas of both biological and non-biological entities, enabling seamless data transfer between physical and virtual environments. Human beings, in particular, can now be digitally reproduced and utilized across various sectors. As Baudrillard asserts, reproduction has replaced production, and genetic models have supplanted all possible bodies. Consequently, contemporary society has entered an era of genetic and mental "software" associated with soft technologies (Baudrillard, 2018, pp. 140–141).

Physical data relate to human bodily characteristics such as anthropometric measurements, biomechanical properties, movement data, and physiological conditions. Anthropometric data—including standing height, shoulder height, shoulder width, and hip width—are used to construct body models in virtual environments. These physical datasets facilitate the creation of realistic human models and support personalized production design processes tailored to individual users (Wang et al., 2024, p. 116).

Figure 1. A Timeline of Human- and Object-Oriented Digitalization

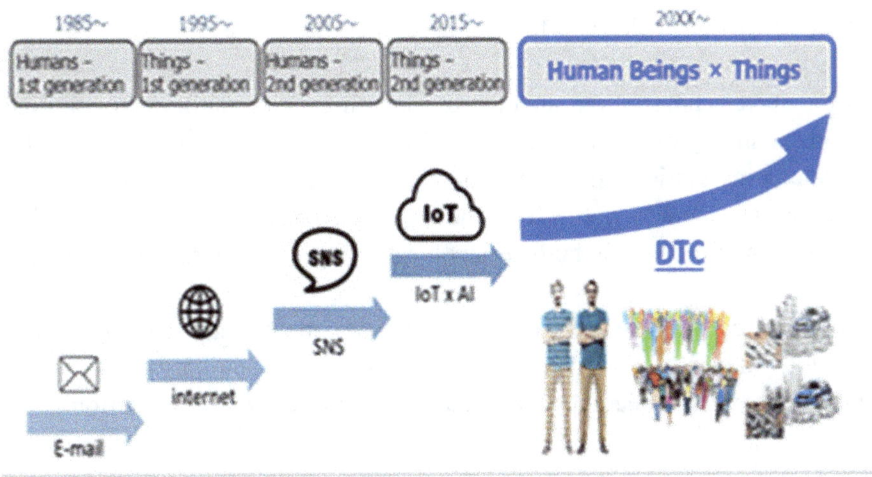

1985: Human-oriented digitalization (Humans – First Generation)

With the introduction and widespread adoption of email technologies, interpersonal communication entered a process of digitalization. During this phase, digital technologies primarily functioned as tools that mediated human-to-human communication.

1995: Object-oriented digitalization (Objects – First Generation)

The expansion of the internet enabled the digitalization of "objects" such as timelines, maps, documents, and archives. In this period, digitalization focused on representing and storing non-human entities within virtual environments.

2005: Human-oriented digitalization (Humans – Second Generation)

The emergence and global diffusion of social media platforms transformed digitalization into a network-based process. Human relationships, identities, and social connections became increasingly digitized, allowing individuals to construct and perform their identities within digital networks.

2015: Object-oriented digitalization (Objects – Second Generation)

With the widespread implementation of the Internet of Things (IoT) and Artificial Intelligence (AI), digitalization expanded toward interconnected objects capable of data exchange, autonomous decision-making, and real-time interaction. Objects were no longer passive representations but active participants within digital ecosystems.

2025: Human digitalization

In the current phase, digitalization extends directly to the human body itself. Through technologies such as digital twins, biometric data modeling, and AI-generated representations, the human body is digitized, simulated, and reproduced as data. This stage marks a shift from the digital mediation of humans to the digital reconstruction of the human body as an object of representation, optimization, and circulation.

This historical progression illustrates that contemporary digital twin technologies represent not merely a new phase of digitalization, but a qualitative shift in which the human body itself becomes the primary object of digital reproduction.

Narrative in Synthetic Media

Synthetic media is an umbrella term used to describe any form of content—such as video, image, text, or audio—that is partially or entirely generated using artificial intelligence or machine learning (Askari, 2023). Since it is often defined as media produced by technological systems, AI-generated music, texts, visuals, images, and videos fall within this category. The ease of production not only enhances creativity in media content creation but also enables significant savings in time and cost. Although synthetic media has not yet replaced traditional media, technological advancements have clearly paved the way for its rapid expansion. Particularly on social media platforms, content is consumed quickly, edited rapidly, and disseminated instantly, often made more engaging through the use of virtual characters and avatars. In this regard, the opportunities offered by digitalization demonstrate that, compared to traditional channels, advertising messages reach consumers in richer and more diversified forms (Bolat, 2023, p. 48).

Since the early 2000s, computer-generated avatars have been used in fields such as cinema and advertising. With the advancement of artificial intelligence, these simulations can now be produced algorithmically without direct human intervention. For example, an actor intended to appear in a film can be digitally rendered without physically entering a studio. As Guy Debord argued in *The Society of the Spectacle*, in the modern world images that once corresponded to reality gradually replace reality itself; copies become originals, representations transform into realities, and the only thing that ultimately loses value is reality itself (Yurdigül & Yıldırım, 2021, pp. 113–116).

At the same time, contemporary life unfolds under conditions of informational bombardment, where attention spans shrink and momentary interests dominate. The individual becomes entangled within networks of digital and social relations. Yet living is more than problem-solving; a life deprived of breadth and depth narrows the horizon of the future. As Han (2024, p. 28) suggests, the opening of the future becomes possible through narrative, since narrative itself carries hope. In this context, digital twins should be understood not merely as visual or economic phenomena, but also as narrative technologies. These twins generate stories without authors, bodies without pasts, and desires without subjects within the realm of synthetic media. Drawing on Bauman's theory of liquidity, which posits that identities in modernity take the shape of the container they occupy, digital twins can alter their ethnicity, gender expression, or aesthetic style within seconds. Brands can "re-fluidify" the model's identity according to consumers' immediate emotional states or prevailing social trends, representing not a fixed storyline but the capacity to "be anything at any moment." Lacking past and memory, these figures do not narrate; rather, they function as surfaces optimized for inscription. In short, in an era in which artificial intelligence dominates public discourse, synthetic media shines like a mirror—yet tells no story.

Digital twin models reflect the consumer's desire for a "liquid self." Referring to Judith Butler's notion of performativity, performance in synthetic media is presented through a flawless visual rhetoric, encouraging consumers to enter the narrative without questioning the constructed nature of identity. In reality, what brands expect from consumers is to remain within this flow and sustain the platform by producing their own narratives. In a letter dated January 21, 2026, YouTube CEO Neal Mohan announced technological innovations regarding the platform's future, stating that content creators would be able to generate AI-based digital twins using their own faces and voices. Through this feature, creators could produce YouTube Shorts via their AI-generated versions without physically appearing before the camera. Mohan emphasized that while this technology would facilitate faster and more flexible content production, it could not replace human creativity (Dokuz8 Haber, 2026). Such statements may be interpreted as cautiously hopeful in ensuring that narrative itself is not entirely subsumed by simulation within synthetic media.

The Discourse of Ideal Beauty Produced Through Digital Twins

An examination of contemporary advertising content and brand discourses reveals that prevailing narratives are largely constructed around idealized stories. Within the advertising industry, where brand promises are positioned through notions of perfection, beauty discourses are similarly shaped. Ideal bodies, flawless appearances, and smooth, youthful skin emerge as dominant visual motifs.

Prior to the adoption of digital twin technologies, the construction of ideal beauty in traditional advertising narratives and design practices was largely achieved through various visual manipulation techniques. Photoshop and similar digital retouching applications systematically transformed visual representations of real bodies through interventions that slimmed female figures, enhanced youthful appearances, and eliminated perceived imperfections. In this manner, the body was detached from its material reality and reconceptualized as a surface open to technical enhancement and alignment with aesthetic norms. Photoshop modified an existing photograph; digital twins generate a body that never was. This is not retouching—it is pre-origination. Advertising no longer refers to a reality it improves, but to a simulation it presents as original. The digital twin does not perfect a subject; it replaces the subject with its own condition of possibility. The widespread use of such techniques in advertising visuals laid the groundwork for simulated perfection narratives and gradually reshaped individuals' perceptions of beauty. From this perspective, advertising functions not merely as a communication medium based on product and brand messaging, but as a cultural space in which bodily expectations and value judgments are produced. Algorithmic beauty standards, normalized through digital interventions, has become a reference point against which bodily reality is continuously questioned and frequently positioned as flawed or inadequate. Consequently, advertising techniques operate as mechanisms that reproduce social expectations regarding how bodies should appear.

Within this framework, the visual techniques employed in traditional advertising can be regarded as historical precursors to contemporary notions of ideal beauty. While these interventions involved modifications and retouching applied to existing bodies, digital twin technologies introduce a fundamentally different logic based on design processes oriented toward perfection from the outset. Bodies produced independently of biological standards construct an unattainable beauty ideal through simulations. Byung-Chul Han draws attention to a similar condition of perfection in *The Transparency Society* through the example of digital photography: "In digital photography there is no negative. There is neither a darkroom nor a developing process. It consists solely of the positive. Becoming, aging, and dying are erased" (Han, 2018, p. 26). When considered alongside ideal beauty discourses produced through digital twins, this observation illustrates how the body is detached from its temporal and biological realities and transformed into an image defined exclusively by positivity, flawlessness, and continuity. In this sense, ideal beauty emerges not merely as an aesthetic norm, but as a visual regime in which negativity, vulnerability, and finitude are systematically excluded.

According to Ritzer, in contemporary society "most of these spectacles are systematically rationalized by those who create and control them" (Ritzer, 2011, p. 138). From this perspective, representations of ideal beauty in advertising visuals can be understood as components of the society of spectacle. Bodies produced through digital manipulation techniques or digital twin technologies do not emerge from random processes or subjective aesthetic preferences, but rather through measurable, controllable, and reproducible systems. Beauty, therefore, is organized as a systematically operating, planned, and managed instrument. Advertising should thus be regarded not merely as a platform where bodies are represented, but as a mechanism through which ideal beauty is constructed, curated, and aligned with the logic of consumer culture.

The increasing use of digital twin technologies in advertising and marketing constitutes a significant turning point in the reproduction of ideal female bodies and beauty standards. Digital twins—entirely created through algorithms and design processes without any physical counterpart—present bodies that do not age and always appear in optimal form, positioning beauty as a norm that must be attained. In this regard, digital twins should be evaluated not only as technological innovations, but also as cultural actors that play an active role in the visual and discursive construction of the ideal female body. Although digital twins are often presented as virtual replicas of real models, the limitless manipulation possibilities they offer generate an unattainable ideal of perfection that exceeds existing bodily standards. The digital elimination of all imperfections, the alteration of proportions, and the continuous optimization of the body result in representations of beauty that are fundamentally disconnected from lived corporeal realities. This technology has become particularly prominent in the fashion industry, where global brands increasingly employ digital avatars of real models in advertising campaigns.

Byung-Chul Han's assertion that "the conjuncture of emotions is above all connected to economic processes" (Han, 2020, p. 49) is crucial for understanding ideal beauty discourses produced through digital twins. Beyond offering visual aesthetics, ideal bodies presented through advertising activate emotions such as desire, admiration, deficiency, and inadequacy, thereby generating an affective economy (emotional design). From this perspective, beauty is no longer a matter of individual taste, but a mechanism through which emotions generate economic value and shape consumption practices. Similar conclusions can be drawn with regard to digital twin technologies. Digital twins transform beauty into a desirable and voluntarily internalized ideal, producing a performance regime that emotionally engages individuals in the process.

Consequently, ideal beauty discourse circulates through digital twins not merely as an aesthetic preference, but as a normalized and desirable body politics. When compared to real female bodies, these representations offer an unattainable perfection that exerts pressure on body perception and contributes to the homogenization of beauty as a singular standard.

Consumer Culture, Advertising, and the Social Circulation of Ideal Beauty

Consumer culture is constructed on a foundation that extends far beyond the satisfaction of material needs, encompassing the production of identities and social meanings. As Bocock emphasizes, at the core of consumer culture lies the understanding that "what is purchased is not merely a material object with a simple, direct, utilitarian use, but an object that conveys meaning and serves to display who the consumer aspires to be" (2005, p. 59). This system of meanings—often referred to as the symbolic dimension—transforms consumption from a functional act into a practice shaped by hedonic motivations such as desire, pleasure, and display. The process that Baudrillard conceptualizes as the "social conditioning to consumption" (2004, p. 95) reveals consumption as a learned and internalized form of socialization. Within this process, beauty and the body occupy a central position: what is considered desirable, how the ideal body should appear, and what is valued are continuously reproduced within consumer culture in accordance with the norms, trends, and conditions of a given period.

From this perspective, Featherstone argues that the expansion of capitalist production—particularly in the early twentieth century, supported by scientific management and Fordism—necessitated the construction of new markets and the education of publics into consumers through advertising and other media (2005, p. 38). Advertising discourse thus functions as a pedagogical domain that teaches the values, ideals, and norms of consumer culture. Through this mechanism, beauty narratives within consumer culture cease to be matters of individual preference or personal expression and instead become socially shared and collectively reproduced norms. The repetitive use of digital twins in advertising further facilitates the normalization and naturalization of ideal beauty standards. Through these representations, beauty is circulated not merely as an aesthetic value, but as a form of economic, cultural, and symbolic capital.

Byung-Chul Han's assertion that "capital produces its own needs, which individuals mistakenly perceive as their own" (Han, 2020, p. 16) is particularly instructive for understanding the operation of ideal beauty discourse within consumer culture. Ideal beauty narratives disseminated through advertising generate a sense of deficiency by presenting flawless body images, thereby transforming beauty into a problem to be solved through consumption. Beauty is thus stripped of its status as a matter of individual taste or aesthetic preference and reconfigured as a necessity that must be fulfilled through consumer practices. In this context, perfected body representations can be regarded as one of the most visible instruments employed in capital's process of need production. As Sutton notes in *Globalizing Ideal Beauty*, particularly within a gendered framework—whether women accept it or not—advertising plays a central role in defining what constitutes "feminine qualities," offering another means of articulating a shared ideal of beauty (Sutton, 2009, p. 149). Universally valorized forms such as youthfulness, vitality, and smoothness gain widespread circulation through the mechanisms of fashion. In this sense, fashion may be understood as a cyclical system that sustains ideal beauty discourse while continuously adapting it to the temporal conditions of the moment. Crane's observation that "fashion assigns new meanings to artifacts, thereby contributing to the redefinition of social identities" (Crane, 2003, p. 27) is particularly relevant here. Fashion transforms beauty from a fixed norm into a constantly updated ideal. Within the dynamics of consumer culture, fast fashion operates as a carrier and accelerator, sustaining peak levels of purchasing motivation. The transitory nature of fashion, rather than offering lasting satisfaction, propels individuals toward a perpetual sense of deficiency and the need for renewal.

The ideal beauty discourse produced through digital twins becomes widely disseminated within the social sphere through advertising discourse, intertwining with the fundamental dynamics of consumer culture. Advertising employs digital twins not merely as tools for product promotion, but as powerful ideological instruments that render desired lifestyles and bodily norms visible. In this process, the ideal female body is presented as a target that can be attained, sustained, and continuously reproduced through consumption. The use of digital twins within advertising and consumer culture thus functions not only as a visual representation of the ideal female body, but as a mechanism through which social expectations and value judgments are reproduced. This process enables the normalization and persistence of beauty standards by shifting beauty from the individual level to the collective social domain.

The Use of Digital Twins in the Fashion Industry: The Case of H&M

Artificial intelligence technologies are employed by the fashion industry in multiple ways, both to enhance efficiency processes and to restructure communication with consumers. Through content created for digital platforms in particular, brands aim to deepen user experience, establish emotional connections, and render consumption practices more interactive. At the same time, AI-supported storytelling integrates products with entertainment, positioning fashion as part of a lived narrative experience. In this context, artificial intelligence functions not merely as a technology that transforms production processes within the fashion industry, but as a comprehensive cultural mechanism through which the body, aesthetics, and desire are measured, guided, and normalized.

When considered specifically within the fashion industry, AI-driven trend analyses transform aesthetic preferences from domains of individual creativity into data-based norms. The digitization of the body further enables ideal beauty discourse to become a technically measurable and reproducible standard. AI-based style recommendations and personalized messaging operate less through individual autonomy than through algorithmic guidance. Virtual fashion shows and digital models detach the body from its biological limits, establishing a regime of flawless representation. Within this process, beauty is redefined not as an aesthetic value but as a measurable instrument of emotional impact.

From this perspective, the use of digital twins in fashion and advertising makes it possible both to predict consumer behavior with greater accuracy and to simulate campaign performance in advance (Özdemir, 2022, p. 101). As Wang et al. note, "digital twins possess enormous potential to renew traditional disciplines, strengthen emerging ones, and stimulate research in highly sophisticated fields" (2024, p. 107). As digitally modeled versions of physical entities, digital twins also offer significant potential as representational and operational tools within the fashion industry (Karacan, 2021, p. 45).

Recent digitalization strategies within the fashion industry provide compelling contemporary examples of how ideal beauty discourse is reproduced. As part of a newly announced campaign, the Swedish fast fashion brand H&M reported that digital twins—AI-generated virtual avatars created using facial data from real models—would be featured across its advertising channels (NuvemMag). Through AI-supported visual production, digital versions of models have been generated. These digital twins have gained prominence by reducing the need for professional photo shoots, stylists, and physical sets. The digital avatars created for approximately thirty models are utilized across traditional photography and social media visuals. Generated through artificial intelligence to reflect the physical characteristics of real models, these digital twins enable garments to be presented from multiple angles and in various styles, thereby expanding the visual flexibility of advertising content.

Figure 2. Digital of H&M's Models

https://nuvemmag.com/h-m-gercek-modellerin-yz-tabanli-dijital-ikizlerini-kullanacagi-yeni-kampanyasini -duyurdu/

These forms of digital twin representation do not merely reflect minimalist visual aesthetics; rather, they constitute reproduced and commercialized versions of the beauty codes targeted by the brand. The campaign not only integrates digital twins into fashion and consumer culture, but also demonstrates how ideal body discourse is internalized through consumption processes and translated into the realm of individual desire.

Following the public announcement of its plans in March 2025, H&M began releasing its first AI-generated digital twin visuals. These images were disseminated across social media platforms, incorporating digital versions of real models as part of the campaign (Business of Fashion). One of the most notable aspects of H&M's campaign is that the ownership and usage rights of the digital twins remain with the models themselves. By collaborating with models and agencies, the company stated that the digital twins would legally belong to the individuals, ensuring that neither H&M nor its partners could use these representations without explicit consent, and that revenue would be determined based on such authorization (NuvemMag).

Despite these measures, the growing adoption of digital twin technologies has sparked concerns regarding the potential reduction of roles and employment opportunities for photographers, stylists, and other creative professionals within the fashion industry—both in the present and in the near future. While artificial intelligence is often promoted as a tool that enhances creativity, ongoing debates question whether it may ultimately replace human labor, thereby necessitating a renewed consideration of the ethical dimensions of this transformation (FashionUnited). From this perspective, H&M's approach can be understood as ambivalent for both consumers and models. While some analyses emphasize the ways in which digital twins introduce new dimensions to visual storytelling, critical responses highlight serious issues such as the erosion of perceptions of reality and threats to human labor (Business of Fashion). H&M's creative director, along with several industry observers, has defended the use of digital twins by emphasizing their potential to accelerate content production processes, reduce costs, enable the creation of a greater number of campaigns, and strengthen sustainability claims.

When evaluated through the H&M case, digital twins emerge not merely as promotional tools for fashion products, but as comprehensive representations of contemporary beauty norms. In this regard, the campaign illustrates that digital twins function not only as innovative marketing strategies within the fashion industry, but also as ideological instruments that reinforce the logic of need production inherent in consumer culture and normalize ideal body narratives. The H&M example underscores the necessity of reading digital twin technologies simultaneously through their promises of creativity and efficiency and through the risks they pose to labor, ethics, and perceptions of reality.

In the case analysis conducted within the scope of the study, the digital twin models created by the H&M brand were analyzed within the framework of visual culture. The narrative construction of the digital twin further reinforces its hyperreal condition. Detached from biographical continuity and embodied temporality, the twin becomes an endlessly rewritable surface through which brands inscribe desire, affect, and aesthetic norms. The digital twin images used in the H&M campaign are evaluated in Table 1.

Table 1. Analysis of Digital Twin Representations in the H&M Campaign

Analytical Dimension	Interpretation / Critical Reading
Subject Positioning	The digital twin is presented as an entity under the individual's control; however, this discourse of control normalizes the transformation of the body into a manageable and accessible resource. The subject is represented not as one upon whom power is imposed, but as one who voluntarily internalizes power. ("I control my Digital Twin's availability")
Body Representation	The body is stripped of aging, vulnerability, and imperfection. This aesthetic detaches ideal beauty from historical and biological processes, transforming it into a norm that exists in a perpetual present. (Smooth, timeless, neutral body aesthetics)
Discourse of Control	While the notion of control is associated with individual autonomy, it simultaneously legitimizes the optimization of the body in accordance with market logics. The body is framed as an entity owned and managed by the subject.
Technology and Future Narrative	The digital twin is presented as a natural and inevitable component of the future; technological adaptability becomes a key criterion of both the ideal body and the ideal subject. ("Sci-Fi", "Future Tech")
Function of Advertising	Advertising functions as a pedagogical space that does not overtly impose ideal beauty, but instead presents it as a naturalized, unquestionable norm—something that simply "ought to be."
Gender Dimension	Although the female body is represented as a powerful, conscious, and self-controlled subject, this empowerment is constrained within the framework of conformity to consumption and aesthetic norms.
Connection to Consumer Culture	The digital twin becomes the visual embodiment of the continuously improvable, optimizable, and sustainable body ideal demanded by consumer culture.
Narrative Construction	The digital twin is positioned outside biographical time. It possesses no past, no aging process, and no memory. This narrative evacuation allows the brand to overwrite the figure with any emotional register, desire, or contextual framing. The twin functions not as a character with depth, but as a narrative surface—optimized for inscription, circulation, and adaptability rather than lived expression.

Another prominent example of the use of AI-powered "digital twin" technology is Zalando, one of Europe's leading fashion platforms. In 2024 and 2025, the brand fundamentally transformed its content production processes by adopting digital twin technology, utilizing high-resolution and motion-capable digital replicas of real models as advertising faces.

In collaboration with Hamburg-based Orendt Studios, Zalando created 3D copies (digital twins) of real models. These digital models are capable of realistically simulating fabric textures, garment drape, and bodily movement with a high degree of accuracy (Futureweek, 2025). By the last quarter of 2024, approximately 70% of Zalando's campaign visuals were generated using artificial intelligence (Zalando SE, 2025). This transformation represents not merely a visual innovation but a significant strategic shift in business operations. The use of digital twins has reduced content production costs by approximately 90% (Cryptonomist, 2025). While traditional photoshoots typically require six to eight weeks, campaign visuals produced through digital twins can be completed within just three to four days (Chief AI Officer, 2025).

Moreover, in response to rapidly emerging and short-lived social media trends such as "Brat summer" or "Mob wife," Zalando can generate campaign content in less than 24 hours using digital models, rather than organizing physical shoots (EuropaWire, 2025). This capability enables the brand to align itself swiftly with dynamic digital cultures and maintain relevance within fast-moving trend cycles.

CONCLUSION

Artificial intelligence has rapidly become an integral component of contemporary advertising production processes, transforming content creation, campaign design, and brand communication strategies. The integration of AI technologies—particularly digital twins—has enabled brands to produce fast, scalable, and cost-effective content across multiple platforms. As demonstrated through examples such as H&M and Zalando, AI-driven visual production significantly accelerates campaign timelines while increasing flexibility and engagement within digital marketing environments.

However, the findings of this study indicate that digital twins should not be understood solely as technical innovations or efficiency-enhancing tools within advertising and fashion industries. Rather, digital twins function as a central ideological apparatus in the reproduction and normalization of ideal beauty discourses. By generating hyper-realistic yet biologically unattainable bodies, digital twins contribute to the construction of a beauty regime in which perfection, youthfulness, and aesthetic optimization are presented as natural, desirable, and sustainable norms.

The analysis reveals that AI-powered storytelling transforms fashion into a living narrative that merges entertainment, consumption, and affect. In this context, artificial intelligence operates not merely as a production technology but as a cultural mechanism through which bodies, aesthetics, and desires are measured, directed, and regulated. Digital twins detach beauty from lived corporeality and temporality, replacing physical reference points with algorithmically generated simulations. As a result, real bodies are increasingly evaluated against hyperreal standards that are technically reproducible but socially unattainable.

In addition to the integration of artificial intelligence, the fashion industry's agenda increasingly includes digitalization, circular economy initiatives, sustainability strategies, and smart production projects. This transformation is visible across multiple domains, ranging from brand websites and e-commerce platforms to storefront designs, innovative runway concepts, digital fashion, and immersive virtual experiences. Furthermore, significant developments have emerged in the areas of data analytics and algorithmic systems, particularly in predicting consumer preferences and designing trends. These advancements create the foundation for delivering personalized fashion recommendations tailored to consumers' tastes and measurements.

Through marketing automation, brands are provided with extensive opportunities to develop loyalty programs, content strategies, and marketing campaigns that offer hyper-personalized proposals based on customer preferences. AI-powered virtual fashion shows and 3D modeling technologies enable the presentation of designs without physical constraints, expanding the possibilities of creative expression and distribution within the industry (Capital, 2024).

The inclusion of additional industry examples, such as Zalando's extensive use of generative AI and digital twin-like visuals, further demonstrates that this transformation is not an isolated case but part of a broader structural shift within the advertising and fashion industries. While these practices promise innovation, efficiency, and sustainability, they simultaneously raise critical questions regarding labor, authenticity, bodily norms, and the future of visual culture.

In conclusion, this study argues that digital twins represent more than a technological advancement in advertising; they signify a fundamental reconfiguration of how beauty, bodies, and desire are produced and circulated within consumer culture. As digital twins become increasingly normalized within fashion and advertising practices, it becomes essential to critically examine their ideological implications and their role in shaping contemporary beauty norms. Future research may extend this analysis to emerging domains such as digital games, virtual influencers, and immersive environments, where similar processes of bodily simulation and normalization continue to unfold.

This study has aimed to approach the concept of digital twins from a communication-centered perspective by situating it within the intersecting frameworks of consumer culture, ideal beauty, and body perception. Rather than treating digital twins solely as technological tools, the analysis has foregrounded their role as communicative and cultural agents through which beauty norms, bodily ideals, and consumer desires are produced and circulated.

Although the analysis has been developed primarily through the case of H&M, it is evident that the use of digital twin technology is not limited to a single brand or campaign strategy. On the contrary, digital twins are likely to be increasingly adopted by a wide range of fashion brands and integrated into campaign-oriented processes in the near future. As the digital twin market continues to expand across multiple sectors, including fashion, advertising, health, and entertainment, these technologies are expected to play a more prominent role in shaping visual culture, consumption practices, and normative understandings of the body. In this respect, the H&M example should be read not as an exception but as an early indicator of a broader structural transformation in the relationship between technology, beauty, and consumer culture.

REFERENCES

Askari, J. (18 August 2023). Deepfakes and Synthetic Media: What are they and how are techUK members taking steps to tackle misinformation and fraud. *techUK.* https://www.techuk.org/resource/synthetic-media-what-are-they-and-how-are-techuk-members-taking-steps-to-tackle-misinformation-and-fraud.html

Baudrillard, J. (2004). *Tüketim Toplumu* (Deliceçaylı, H., & Keskin, F., Trans.). Ayrıntı.

Baudrillard, J. (2018). *Simülakrlar ve Simülasyon.* O. Adanır, Trans. Doğu Batı. pp. 13-15, 140-141.

Bocock, R. (2005). *Tüketim* (Kutluk, İ., Trans.). Dost.

Bolat, N. (2023). Dijitalleşeme İle Yapay Zekânin Reklam Alanina Katilimi. In Günay, M. A. (Ed.), *İletişim Bilimlerinde Yapay Zeka* (pp. 44–61). Eğitim.

Britannica (11 February 2026). artificial intelligence (AI). https://www.britannica.com/technology/artificial-intelligence

Calp, E. (25 November 2022). Dijital ikiz nedir? Uygulama ve örnekleri. *Donanım Haber* https://www.donanimhaber.com/dijital-ikiz-nedir-uygulama-ve-ornekleri--156255

Capital (2024). Modada teknoloji ve yapay zeka etkisi. https://www.capital.com.tr/haberler/tum-haberler/modada-teknoloji-ve-yapay-zeka-etkisi

Chief, A. I. Officer (2025). "How Zalando Cut Fashion Content Costs by 90%". https://chiefaiofficer.com/zalando-ai-fashion-imagery-90-percent-cost-reduction/

Crane, D. (2003). *Moda ve Gündemleri. Giyimde Sınıf, Cinsiyet ve Kimlik* (Çelik, Ö., Trans.). Ayrıntı.

Cryptonomist (2025, Mayıs). "Zalando leverages AI to revolutionize marketing and reduce costs by 90%". https://www.reuters.com/business/media-telecom/zalando-uses-ai-speed-up-marketing-campaigns-cut-costs-2025-05-07/

Cui, J. (2025). The Impact of Digital Media Technology on Digital Twins: The Moderating Role of Personalized Advertising. *Accounting. Marketing and Organization, 1*(1), 1–9. DOI: 10.71204/86fvy772

Dhapte, A. (13 July, 2025). Digital Twin Market. *Market Research Future.* https://www.marketresearchfuture.com/reports/digital-twin-market-4504

Dokuz8 Haber (23 January 2026). YouTube içerik üreticileri için yapay zeka tabanlı "dijital ikiz" özelliğini duyurdu https://www.dokuz8haber.net/youtube-icerik-ureticileri-icin-yapay-zeka-tabanli-dijital-ikiz-ozelligini-duyurdu

EuropaWire. (2025, Mayıs). "Zalando's Use of AI and Digital Twins Enhances Speed and Flexibility". https://news.europawire.eu/press-releases-tagged-with/digital-technology/

Featherstone, M. (2005). *Postmodernizm ve Tüketim Kültürü* (Küçük, M., Trans.). Ayrıntı.

Futureweek (2025, Mayıs). "Zalando Creates AI Models for Ad Campaigns". https://www.fourmeta.co.uk/blog/fashion-ads-you-didnt-know-were-ai-made

Han, B. C. (2018). *Şeffaflık Toplumu* (Barışcan, H., Trans.). Metis.

Han, B. C. (2020). *Psikopolitika: neoliberalizm ve yeni iktidar teknikleri, çev. H. Barışcan.* Metis Yayınları.

Han, B. C. (2024). *Anlatının Krizi (M. Erşen, Çev.).* Ketebe Yayınları.

Hornik, J., & Rachamim, M. (2025). Leveraging AI-Enabled Digital Twins for Smart Advertising Design and Testing. *Journal of Advertising and Public Relations*, *5*(1), 5–26. DOI: 10.22259/2639-1953.0501002

Karacan, E. (2021). *Dijital İkiz Teknolojisi ve Pazarlama Uygulamaları*. İstanbul Teknoloji Press.

Li, Liang (2022). The influence of digital twins on the methods of film and television creation. *Computers and Electrical Engineering*. 103 (2022) 108314. p. 3,12.

Özdemir, R. (2022). *Yeni Medya ve Veri Tabanlı Reklamcılık*. Medya Teknolojileri Enstitüsü.

Ritzer, G. (2011). *Büyüsü Bozulmuş Dünyayı Büyülemek*. Ş.S., Kaya Trans. Ayrıntı. p. 138.

Sutton, D. H. (2009). *Globalizing Ideal Beauty*. MacMillan. DOI: 10.1057/9780230100435

Wang, B., Zhou, H., Li, X., Yang, G., Zheng, P., Song, C., Yuan, Y., Wuest, T., Yang, H., & Wang, L. (2024). Human Digital Twin in the context of Industry 5.0. *Robotics and Computer-integrated Manufacturing*, *85*, 102626. DOI: 10.1016/j.rcim.2023.102626

Yurdigül, Y. & Yıldırım, A. (2021). Gerçeklik algısına bir müdahale aracı olarak sentetik medya teknolojileri. *İletişim ve Diplomasi*, 5, 105-121.

Zalando, S. E. (2025). "Annual Report 2024 & Q1 2025 Financial Statements". https://www.annualreports.com/Company/zalando

ADDITIONAL READING

Bauman, Z. (2000). *Liquid Modernity*. Polity Press.

Butler, J. (1990). *Gender Trouble: Feminism and the Subversion of Identity*. Routledge.

Candan, G. ve Dölkeleş, G. (2022). Göstergebilim Bağlamında İdealize Edilmiş Bedenin Tüketim Nesnesi Olarak Sunumu: Mavi Jeans Reklamları. *Yeni Yüzyıl'da İletişim Çalışmaları Journal*, (5), 81–96.

Çeber, B. (2024). Reklam Ajanslarında Yapay Zeka Kullanımı: Sektör Profesyonellerinin ChatGPT ve Midjourney Deneyimlerine Yönelik Bir Araştırma. *Erciyes İletişim Journal, 11*(2), 583–606.

Chandler, D., & Fuchs, C. (2021). *Dijital Nesneler, Dijital Özneler. Büyük Veri Çağında Kapitalizm, Emek ve Siyaset Üzerine Disiplinlerarası Yaklaşımlar* (Boztepe, G., Trans.). Notabene.

Crary, J. (2015). *7/24 Geç Kapitalizm ve Uykuların Sonu* (Çatlı, N., Trans.). Metis.

Crary, J. (2023). *Yeryüzü Yakılıp Yıkılırken. Dijital Çağdan Kapitalizm Sonrası Dünya* (Birkan, T., Trans.). Metis.

Debord, G. (1996). *Gösteri Toplumu* (Ekmekçi, A., & Taşkent, O., Trans.). Ayrıntı.

Gao, B., Wang, Y., Xie, H., Hu, Y., & Hu, Y. (2023). Artificial Intelligence in Advertising Advancements, Challenges, and Ethical Considerations in Targeting, Personalization, Content Creation, and Ad Optimization. *SAGE Open, 13*(4), 21582440231210759. DOI: 10.1177/21582440231210759

Jacobson, L. (2008). *Children and consumer culture in American society: a historical handbook and guide*. Praeger Publishers.

Li, H. (2019). Special section introduction: Artificial intelligence and advertising. *Journal of Advertising, 48*(4), 333–337. DOI: 10.1080/00913367.2019.1654947

Qin, X., & Jiang, Z. (2019). The Impact of AI on the Advertising Process: The Chinese Experience. *Journal of Advertising, 48*(4), 338–346. DOI: 10.1080/00913367.2019.1652122

Rauschnabel, P. A., Felix, R., Hinsch, C., Shahab, H., & Alt, F. (2022). XR nedir? Artırılmış ve sanal gerçeklik için bir çerçeveye doğru. *İnsan Davranışında Bilgisayarlar*, 133, 107289.

Tao, F., Zhang, H., Liu, A., & Nee, A. Y. C. (2019). Endüstride dijital ikiz: Son teknoloji. *IEEE Endüstri İnformatiği İşlemleri, 15*(4), 2405–2415.

KEY TERMS AND DEFINITIONS

Digital Twin: A digital twin is a dynamic and data-driven representation of a physical entity, process, or system created in a digital environment. Initially used in industrial production and engineering, this technology makes it possible to monitor, predict, and optimize the behavior of physical objects through real-time data, simulations, and algorithms. Today, thanks to the integration of artificial intelligence, big data, and sensor technologies, digital twins are no longer limited to technical systems but have expanded to include the human body, behaviors, and aesthetic representations. In the context of media, advertising, and the fashion industry, digital twins appear as reproduced, edited, and replicable versions of real individuals or bodies in virtual environments. In this respect, the digital twin is not only a technological tool but also an ideological representation mechanism that enables the reconstruction of the body, beauty, and identity within economic and cultural processes.

Hyperreality: The concept of hyperreality, developed by Jean Baudrillard, refers to a situation where simulations replace reality. In this context, hyperreality describes a phase where the boundaries between reality and fiction disappear; images, models, and representations become more convincing than reality itself. In the hyperreal order, what is referenced is no longer physical reality, but its simulated versions. In terms of representations of beauty, the body, and fashion, hyperreality gains visibility through the circulation of perfected and timeless images, stripped of biological limitations. Digitally produced bodies and aesthetic forms replace real bodies, creating normative criteria; thus, reality is evaluated according to the criteria of simulation.

Ideal Beauty: Ideal beauty refers to the totality of desired, normative, and targeted bodily and aesthetic characteristics within a specific historical and cultural context. This concept is based on a system of norms constructed through social, economic, and ideological processes rather than individual taste. Characteristics such as youth, smoothness, symmetry, and perfection are among the fundamental components of ideal beauty, presented as if they were universal. Today, the ideal concept of beauty is constantly reproduced and circulated through digital technologies and media representations. The flawless body images presented through advertisements, social media, and digital twins transform beauty from an individual choice into a necessity to be achieved and maintained through consumption.

Fashion Industry: Fashion is based on a cyclical system of preferences. It involves adapting global needs, preferences, and expectations to the conditions of the time and integrating them into the consumer's purchasing processes. Today, many brands and sectors within the fashion industry are at the forefront of this cycle. It is possible to mention many areas where fashion permeates, from the cosmetics sector to clothing, from media content to food and beverage culture. In particular, the fast fashion concept stands out as one of the most important dynamics of today's fashion industry. The rapid transformation of needs and preferences into a single form within weeks reveals the logic of the fast fashion concept. The fast fashion concept, which is based on the constant renewal of colors, vehicles, accessories, patterns, designs, in short, trends, is conveyed to the consumer through digital technologies, thus ensuring the continuity of excessive consumption.

Consumer Culture: Consumer culture refers to the transformation of consumption from an action solely aimed at meeting material needs into a cultural structure where identities, meanings, and social statuses are produced. In this context, consumed objects carry symbolic meanings beyond their functional benefits and become one of the fundamental tools for individuals to express themselves. Fashion, beauty, and body representations are at the heart of consumer culture. Aesthetic norms circulated through advertising and media discourses create feelings of inadequacy in individuals, encouraging continuous consumption. Thus, consumer culture functions as a system where desires are produced, needs are redefined, and bodily norms are integrated into economic processes.

Artificial Intelligence: The ability of a digital computer or computer-controlled robot to perform tasks commonly associated with intelligent beings. The term is frequently applied to the project of developing systems endowed with the intellectual processes characteristic of humans, such as the ability to reason, discover meaning, generalize, or learn from past experience. Since their development in the 1940s, digital computers have been programmed to carry out very complex tasks—such as discovering proofs for mathematical theorems or playing chess—with great proficiency. Despite continuing advances in computer processing speed and memory capacity, there are as yet no programs that can match full human flexibility over wider domains or in tasks requiring much everyday knowledge. On the other hand, some programs have attained the performance levels of human experts and professionals in executing certain specific tasks, so that artificial intelligence in this limited sense is found in applications as diverse as medical diagnosis, computer search engines, voice or handwriting recognition, and chatbots (Britannica, 2026). Many definitions and studies are being conducted on artificial intelligence, which is significantly changing people's lives. Almost every moment, new technologies are being developed and integrated into our lives. Humanity is experiencing a digital transformation that has accelerated over centuries, even in the last quarter of a century. In this context, artificial intelligence, defined as machine learning and said to shape our future, is recreating the limits of the human brain through machines. Thus, it is thought that humanity will enter a process of rediscovering itself and achieve a life form integrated with technology.

Section 4

Advanced Narrative Architecture and Strategic Futures

Chapter 12

A Temporal Model of Corporate Narrative Architecture: From Retrospective CSR to Proleptic Sustainability

Recep Yılmaz
http://orcid.org/0000-0003-3406-2755
Ondokuz Mayis University, Turkey

Nilay Tan Çakır
http://orcid.org/0000-0002-4514-2219
Ondokuz Mayis University, Turkey

Elif Yılmaz
http://orcid.org/0000-0003-1414-4083
Istinye University, Turkey

ABSTRACT

This chapter conceptualizes corporate communication as a temporally structured narrative system and examines the shift from retrospective corporate social responsibility (CSR) discourse to future-oriented sustainability narratives. While CSR legitimizes organizations through past performance, sustainability communication constructs meaning by projecting the future within present discourse. The chapter introduces the Proleptic Corporate Narrative Model, composed of four layers: temporal projection, future value construction, predictive persuasion, and narrative mediation. The framework shows how sustainability communication functions not only as information but as a narrative architecture shaping expectations and

DOI: 10.4018/979-8-3373-5666-2.ch012

institutional positioning through future-oriented meaning production. An analysis of Brandverse campaigns indicates that corporate communication increasingly relies on proleptic narrative logic, constructing legitimacy through future projection. Artificial intelligence is treated as a mediating layer that may enhance predictive narrative capacity.

INTRODUCTION

The second half of the 20th century witnessed significant debates and conceptual developments that advanced the theoretical foundations of public relations. One such debate centered on whether public relations is a task related to image building or an institutional instrument responsible for performing specific functions. The debate, which began with Bell and Bell's (1976) functionalist and task-oriented distinction in public relations, was further developed by Grunig and Hunt (1984), Broom (1986), and Stinchcombe (1968), extending to the work of Dozier and Ehling (1992), which goes beyond being a closed system and emphasizes that public relations should be a purposeful field. Another important conceptualization has been in the field of social responsibility. During this period, Corporate Social Responsibility (CSR) was first defined by Bowen (1953) as one of the obligations of the business sector towards communities and society in general. The concept was later expanded by Davis (1960) to mean that the institution should be responsible for its actions affecting society and should share part of its economic gains with society.

Leaving aside the image debates, which suggest that the concept has been misunderstood (Yılmaz, 2024), it can be seen that academic circles during this period focused on corporate structures and their social functions. In other words, in establishing the foundations of public relations, the adaptation of the institution and its environment is crucial, as dictated by the facts. The structural dimension of this adaptation process has, over time, made it imperative for institutions to adapt not only to current environmental conditions but also to future social and environmental requirements.

Corporate social responsibility is an instrument that significantly guides the target audience in how the organization will be perceived, creating a mental image that codes the organization's corporate behavior. Today, the concept of sustainability significantly shapes the definition of social responsibility. With the rise of sustainability, corporate responsibility has moved beyond being merely a framework that responds to social expectations; it has shifted to a more holistic, future-oriented perspective encompassing environmental, economic, and social dimensions.

The increasing use of artificial intelligence (AI)-based communication tools is partially influencing the way corporate discourse is constructed for the future. Data analysis applications, targeted software, and text-generation tools, particularly used in advertising and public relations, enable organizations to think more systematically about both their target audience segments and their strategic scenarios for the future. This development shows that proleptic narratives in social responsibility and sustainability communication are not based solely on an abstract emphasis on the future; in some organizations, they can be approached as a form of communication supported by data and integrated into planning processes. However, it should also be noted that the use of AI has not yet become a widespread, established standard in corporate communication; applications vary from organization to organization.

This study aims to conceptualize the formation process of a proleptic narrative structure that constructs the future within discourse, not as a chronology of past corporate practices, but as the historical development of corporate social responsibility. However, it is a process of forming a proleptic narrative structure that constructs the future within discourse. It argues that corporate sustainability communication functions as a temporal meaning-making mechanism that constructs the future within discourse and that this discourse creates a proleptic narrative architecture. Artificial intelligence technologies, rather than being a necessary element that transforms this narrative structure, are positioned as a potential intermediary layer that enables the data-driven and predictive structuring of corporate discourses oriented toward the future. In the age of artificial intelligence, corporate sustainability discourse is not merely a normative responsibility discourse; it is a proleptic narrative architecture that constructs the future within discourse, and the influence of algorithms will rapidly become central to its formation. While corporate social responsibility produces a legitimacy narrative based on the past, corporate sustainability creates a proleptic narrative structure that constructs the future within discourse. In this context, it would be useful to take a brief look at the development of corporate social responsibility to understand its past and how it will shape the future.

CSR AS RETROSPECTIVE LEGITIMACY NARRATIVE

When tracing the origins of the concept of corporate social responsibility (CSR), Oliver Sheldon emerges as one of its pioneers. In his work *The Philosophy of Management* (1923), Sheldon argues that the first and most important duty of management is to address social issues. According to him, "the first responsibility of management is service to society," and this responsibility can be developed through the adoption of scientific methods (Balta Peltekoğlu, 2016, p. 204). The concept of CSR has become prominent since the 1950s as a framework defining the social responsibilities of businesses. Although businesses' activities that consider society or specific stakeholder groups date back much further, this concept gained institutional and systematic momentum, particularly after World War II (Carrol, 2016, p. 1). One of the important milestones in this field is Howard Bowen's 1953 publication, *Social Responsibilities of the Businessman*. Bowen defines the social responsibilities of businesspeople as pursuing desirable policies for society, making decisions, and translating these decisions into action (Aydede, 2009, p. 23; cited in Elden, 2018, p. 532). However, opponents of this approach have also emerged. In an article published in the New York Times on September 13, 1970, Milton Friedman argued that the sole responsibility of businesses is to "make a profit." This view has been influential in the business world for many years, pushing employee and human rights, as well as environmental concerns, into the background. It has even been claimed that this economic understanding was behind the United States' decision not to join the Kyoto Protocol. However, over time, reactions to these views have also developed. At a meeting in Davos in 2002, the CEOs of the world's leading companies announced that "the era of doing business solely to make a profit is over." Following this declaration, many CSR-supporting practices and standards were rapidly adopted. By the 2000s, CSR had become a structure that should be approached as a business model rather than as a "nice face for society" (Kadıbeşegil, 2008, pp. 95-111). The 1970s, in particular, were a period when social responsibility came to the fore in marketing. It was no longer considered sufficient for businesses to operate solely for profit, pay their taxes, or ensure customer satisfaction. The relationships businesses have with society, their stance on social issues, and their sense of responsibility have become increasingly important. During this period, Philip Kotler and Gerald Zaltman developed the concept of social marketing, which refers to marketing practices aimed at solving social problems (Yılmaz, 2006, p. 31). Social responsibility should be considered not only as a means of reciprocity with society, but also as an integral part of corporate business practices and organizational culture. Social responsibility, one of the seven fundamental characteristics of organizations identified as excellent in the literature, has become an indispensable component of corporate culture in today's conditions (Balta Peltekoğlu & Tozlu, 2017, p. 5). Today, there is a strong and multifaceted relationship between social responsibility projects and public relations. This relationship remains valid throughout the entire process, from the planning stage of the projects to their implementation. Integrating the corporate social responsibility approach into corporate culture, internalizing this understanding within the organization and making it part of the management structure, encouraging voluntary participation of employees, and adopting the principle of voluntarism at the corporate level are among the fundamental areas of public relations activities (Balta Peltekoğlu & Tozlu, 2017, p. 29).

Linking corporate communication to corporate reputation and evaluating corporate social responsibility (CSR) projects as part of the organization's natural way of doing business underscores their contribution to the organization, beyond being merely temporary initiatives. Ensuring the flow of information from within the organization to the external environment and from the external environment to the organization, with a proactive communication approach and openness to reactive communication in the face of potential shortcomings or negativity, constitutes the basic elements of corporate communication strategies (Soydaş & Çokluk, 2023, p. 252).

In conclusion, CSR is considered both a reputation-enhancing tool for organizations and an effective marketing strategy. Considering that the pursuit of profit and growth, which forms the basis of the capitalist system, is based on the exploitation of nature and labor, the efforts of organizations striving to find solutions to environmental and social problems are both inevitable and open to critical evaluation (Durna, 2011, p. 77; Tan Çakır, 2024). These multi-layered discussions have highlighted the need for a theoretical framework for CSR and paved the way for the development of various models in the literature.

Basic Models

Carroll's Corporate Social Responsibility Pyramid

Archie B. Carroll presented the first systematic framework for corporate social responsibility in 1979, restructuring it in 1991 by visualizing it with a pyramid model. The model explains the four fundamental obligations of businesses to society in a hierarchical structure: economic, legal, ethical, and voluntary responsibilities (Carroll, 1991, p. 42). This pyramid structure evaluates organizations' activities as a whole, encompassing not only profit generation but also compliance with laws, avoidance of conflict with social values, and voluntary contributions to social benefit (Carroll, 2016, pp. 4–5). Economic responsibility, in particular, forms the base of the pyramid, as sustainability is only possible with a strong financial structure. As one moves up the pyramid, businesses are expected to comply with legal regulations, adopt ethical principles, and voluntarily support social projects. This model defines corporate social responsibility not merely as a duty but as a multi-layered social role (Tan Çakır, 2024). Carroll's pyramid implies that organizations should position their responsibilities not only based on today's requirements but also on long-term social expectations.

Davis' Social Responsibility Model

Developed by Keith Davis, this model explains the rationale and methods behind businesses' commitment to social responsibility. The model is based on five fundamental propositions: (1) Businesses that hold social power must also assume social responsibility; (2) businesses should operate as open systems interacting with society; (3) the social costs and contributions of the products or services offered must be evaluated in detail; (4) The economic burdens of social responsibility projects should be balanced with service or product pricing; (5) Businesses are obliged to contribute to social issues outside their field of activity (Certo et al., 1989; Özgener, 2004 cited in Ekin Savaş, 2022, p. 221). Davis's approach treats the business's place in social integrity not as an ethical position but as a strategic obligation (Tan Çakır, 2024). In this respect, the model also indirectly emphasizes that institutions should evaluate their social impacts within the framework of future scenarios.

Ackerman's Social Responsibility Model

Robert W. Ackerman argues that social responsibility is based on the idea that businesses should act not only with a sense of duty but also with sensitivity to social issues. The first stage of this three-stage model, the *Policy Stage*, is the period when business management analyzes environmental variables and makes strategic decisions. During this process, business managers determine a roadmap that is sensitive to societal expectations. The *Learning Stage* encompasses the company's efforts to gather information, conduct research, and engage consulting services to solve social problems. The final stage, the *Corporate Responsibility Stage*, refers to the systematic implementation of the acquired knowledge and strategies within a corporate structure (Özgener, 2004, cited in Ekin Savaş, 2022, pp. 221–222). Ackerman's model emphasizes that social responsibility is not static but a dynamic process, focusing on the transformation of sensitivity into corporate action (Tan Çakır, 2024). Ackerman's process-based approach presents a framework consistent with the concept of sustainability by showing that social responsibility is not static but a form of corporate behavior that develops over time.

Preston and Post's Integrated Social Responsibility Model

Preston and Post examine organizations' relationships with their social environment at two levels: primary and secondary. Primary relationships refer to the bonds the organization establishes with actors such as customers, employees, investors, and lenders with whom it interacts directly. Secondary relationships, on the other hand, encompass indirect relationships established with legal, ethical, and civil society-based reactive actors who become involved in the context of social problems caused by business. While acknowledging the uncertainty surrounding the concept of "social responsibility," the authors propose "public responsibility" to make these boundaries more concrete (Okay and Okay, 2018, p. 625). This model is based on the idea that businesses must be accountable not only within the economic system but also within the social system (Tan Çakır, 2024). Preston and Post's conceptualization of public responsibility requires institutions to evaluate their social impacts, taking into account both current and future consequences.

Schultz and Colleagues' Two-Tiered Corporate Social Responsibility Approach

Majken Schultz and her team propose a two-pronged communication strategy in CSR practices: internal-external integration and two-tiered communication. According to the "Internal-External Strategy," organizations must first increase the legitimacy of the process by involving their internal stakeholders—i.e., their employees—in CSR policies. Once this internal alignment is achieved, the communication process targeting the external public can be initiated (Van Dyck, 2017, p. 124). In the second stage, a distinction is made between "direct and indirect communication." Direct communication targets influential actors such as journalists, policymakers, and NGOs. Indirect communication through these groups helps spread CSR messages in society with a more reliable and impartial perception (Van Dyck, 2017, p. 125). The model argues that corporate social responsibility must be strategically managed not only in terms of content but also in terms of communication style (Tan Çakır, 2024). This approach highlights the principles of transparency and the establishment of long-term trust relationships with stakeholders, which are critical to sustainability communication.

These models developed in the CSR literature enable the evaluation of the social role of businesses within a multi-layered framework; this framework also serves as the theoretical basis for understanding corporate sustainability. The common point among the models is that they address institutions' responsibilities from a perspective that considers not only current social needs but also future impacts.

SUSTAINABILITY AS FUTURE-ORIENTED NARRATIVE

As is well known, the concept of "sustainability," first introduced at the United Nations Environment Programme (UNEP) conference in 1972, emphasizes the careful use of society's resources; here, a respect-based perspective developed for all social, cultural, scientific, natural, and human resources is adopted, and the principle is that systems with continuity should carry out their work seamlessly without compromising their vital connections (Gladwin et al., 1995; Karaman, 1996; Tıraş, 2012). This framework shows that sustainability is not only about protecting existing natural and social resources, but also about ensuring future social welfare. Institutional sustainability (IS) is defined as the institutional level counterpart of the concept of sustainability (Çalışkan Özsözgün, 2012). CS can be thought of as the political and action-oriented counterpart of the concept of sustainability in an organizational context. The concept is based on implementing a sustainability approach at the macro and organizational levels and takes into account not only current but also future stakeholders (Himmetoğlu, 2023). Therefore, corporate sustainability inherently carries a sense of responsibility for the future. This trend is so influential that today the concept of "Corporate Social Responsibility" has been replaced by "Corporate Sustainability and Responsibility."

Many concepts can be defined as "sustainable" and associated with the concept of sustainability. Sustainable cities, economies, resource management, trade, livelihoods, and sustainable development are examples of this (Özgen, 2022). The concept of sustainable development was first defined in the Brundtland Report, "Our Common Future," published by the World Commission on Environment and Development on March 20, 1987. In this report, sustainable development was defined as "development that meets the needs of the present without compromising the ability of future generations to meet their own needs" (Brundtland, 1987). The emphasis on "future generations" at the heart of the Brundtland definition clearly highlights the temporal dimension of sustainability. Sustainable development, which encompasses economic, social, and environmental elements, was initially considered a concept that only covered states and their policy processes. However, in subsequent years, international conferences emphasized that responsibility for this process should be shared by other stakeholders (Engin and Eker Akgöz, 2013: 86).

The multidimensional nature of sustainability and its future-oriented global planning increases the need for participatory approaches and the outcomes they can achieve. Dialogue-based sustainability communication will serve as an important bridge in ensuring social harmony and integration, which are fundamental to sustainability, by involving all stakeholders in the process (Franz-Balsen & Heinrichs, 2007, p. 435, cited in Özgen, 2022).

Corporate sustainability is the product of a social responsibility approach that holistically addresses an organization's environmental, economic, and social responsibilities, integrating these obligations into production, sales, and marketing strategies with an emphasis on the "future." Therefore, corporate sustainability should also be considered a management approach in which organizations determine their current strategic orientation based on future scenarios. As in the Brundtland Report titled "Our Common Future" many years ago, "future-oriented discourses" have been at the forefront in the formation, development, and implementation stages of the concept of sustainability. Similarly, as Franz-Balsen & Heinrichs point out, sustainability has a multidimensional structure and "involves future-oriented planning on a global scale," requiring participatory approaches and outcomes that align with them.

Corporate sustainability has become an integral part of business strategies and a corporate value for many organizations (Signitzer and Prexl 2008: 2 cited in Engin and Eker Akgöz, 2013: 86). The effectiveness of corporate sustainability as a management strategy can be enhanced through stakeholder participation and support; in this context, the process must be structured around dialogue-based communication dynamics. Communication plays a decisive role in the adoption of corporate sustainability initiatives by both internal and external stakeholders, in the construction of a sustainability-centered corporate culture, and in achieving the defined strategic goals (Akbayır, 2019: 3). In the context of sustainability, communication exhibits a structure based on transparency, openness, and dialogue; this structure is built on an everyday discourse based on the principles of social learning and citizenship (Petts, 2000, p. 272 cited in Akbayır, 2019: 6). Therefore, sustainability communication plays a critical role in creating a shared vision for the future and transforming this vision into a social discourse. Sustainability requires the effective use of interdisciplinary strategies through shared discourses.

Considering that institutions are important actors within society, the need for sustainability practices aligned with their missions of collective action, integration with society, and contribution to society is clearly evident in today's world. Advancing the ecosystem in which institutions operate, ensuring the balanced distribution of opportunities among employees, increasing the number of corporate citizens who value education and science, and building a more equitable world order in environmental, economic, and social dimensions will make this possible. Achieving these goals is directly linked to the concept of sustainability. In the Sustainability Index published by Dow Jones in 1999, "corporate sustainability" was defined as "a business approach that creates long-term shareholder value that nurtures opportunities and manages risks arising from economic, environmental, and social developments" (Özgen, 2022). All these elements show that the concept of sustainability is inevitably structured as a corporate discourse for the future.

Today, artificial intelligence-based tools are used as a supporting element in some corporate sustainability narratives. Algorithms that calculate carbon footprints, predictive systems for modeling environmental risks, and digital monitoring tools used in reporting processes can help organizations evaluate their sustainability performance in the context of future scenarios. Such applications shift the sustainability discourse away from merely "preserving the status quo" and open it to a more systematic discussion of the future grounded in specific data and projections. However, this trend should be viewed as a developing and increasingly diverse orientation observed in specific examples for now, rather than a universal, established, and homogeneous practice applicable to all organizations.

FROM CSR TO PROLEPTIC NARRATIVE STRUCTURE

The relationship between corporate social responsibility (CSR) and narrative structures points to a discursive transformation in which business ethics and storytelling are becoming increasingly intertwined. As organizations increasingly resort to narrative strategies to communicate their CSR initiatives, they not only reestablish their corporate identity but also intervene in the meaning-making processes that shape social perception. In this context, CSR moves beyond being merely a framework of corporate responsibility and becomes a form of discourse through which the organization positions itself and its social role via narrative. This shift from traditional CSR concepts to proleptic narrative structures reveals the structural similarity between corporate narratives and literary time constructs, necessitating a rethinking of the temporal logic of corporate discourse.

The traditional understanding of CSR essentially produces a narrative of legitimacy based on organizations' past performance, social contributions, and accountability practices. In this respect, CSR discourse has a retrospective narrative logic: the organization grounds its ethical position in its past actions and seeks to build social trust. However, this structure has been criticized for its paradoxical nature, particularly in debates over originality and effectiveness (Feix & Philippe, 2020). With the proliferation of digital communication environments, this criticism has become more visible; it has been emphasized that organizations need to develop more dynamic narrative frameworks that can resonate with stakeholders, rather than producing a legitimacy discourse that only refers to the past. Makridis, Papadakis, and Polymeris (2014) note that overcoming the CSR paradox requires critically rethinking narrative structures in corporate communication. This transformation has led to CSR narratives becoming increasingly sophisticated and structurally similar to literary narrative structures.

At this point, the corporate sustainability discourse produces a proleptic narrative logic that constructs the future within it, unlike the CSR discourse's retrospective legitimacy narrative. In narrative theory, prolepsis is the interpretation of what has not yet happened within the discourse. Similarly, corporate sustainability communication constructs the organization's future ethical, environmental, and social position within today's discourse. In this respect, sustainability narratives depart from linear and past-based narrative structures, creating a multi-layered meaning-making process oriented toward the future. Proleptic narrative structures make visible within discourse not only the organization's current actions but also possible future scenarios and their social impacts, thereby directing the audience to consider the future consequences of corporate actions. Khan (2024) emphasizes that such future-oriented narratives play a decisive role in organizations' ability to communicate their sustainability goals effectively.

The examination of CSR narratives shows that these discourses are not merely a tool for corporate branding; they also have the potential to generate social impact. Widiasari (2020) demonstrates that CSR advertisements shape public perception and promote social responsibility awareness through narrative tools. In this context, corporate narratives can be evaluated not only as marketing strategies but also as systems of meaning with the potential to produce social change.

Interdisciplinary approaches to narrative deepen our understanding, particularly of the dimensions of time and expectation. As Ksenofontova (2023) points out, examining temporal structures reveals that narratives do not merely represent the past; they also reflect social expectations and desires for future transformation. From this perspective, proleptic narratives reveal the vision of the future embedded in the sustainability discourse while also allowing for a critical rethinking of the existing social order.

Applying narrative theory to the field of CSR enables us to question whether corporate discourses reproduce existing social norms or serve a transformative function. According to Zgoll, Cuperly, and Cöster-Gilbert (2023), the critical analysis of CSR narratives is important in revealing whether these discourses aim for fundamental social transformation or merely reproduce the status quo. This debate has taken on a critical dimension in today's context, where society increasingly demands authenticity and accountability in corporate behavior.

Ultimately, the shift from CSR to a proleptic narrative structure signals a significant transformation in the temporal logic of corporate discourse. While CSR discourse produces a legitimacy narrative grounded in the past, corporate sustainability discourse constructs a proleptic narrative architecture that builds the future within the discourse itself. This transformation demonstrates that corporate narratives are not merely tools that represent reality; they also have the power to shape social reality. The works of Mohan (2026) and Kelly (2025) also show that the intersection of CSR and narrative structures reveals the complexity of modern corporate communication and its capacity to drive social change. In this context, corporate sustainability communication should be understood as a proleptic-based narrative structure that functions as a future-oriented meaning-making process between the organization and society.

PROLEPTIC CORPORATE NARRATIVE MODEL

The discursive shift from corporate social responsibility to corporate sustainability signifies a structural reorganization within the temporal logic of corporate communication. To conceptualize this shift, the "Proleptic Corporate Narrative Model" is proposed here. The model argues that, unlike a legitimacy narrative based on the past, the discourse of corporate sustainability functions as a temporal meaning-production process that constructs the future within the discourse.

In this framework, the corporate narrative is not merely a representation of actions that have already taken place; it is also the structuring of what has not yet happened within the discourse. Proleptic narrative makes sense of corporate identity and social positioning through temporal projection, constructing the future in the present. Therefore, unlike retrospective CSR narratives, corporate sustainability discourse produces a forward-looking narrative architecture. The proposed model consists of four structural layers:

1. Temporal Projection Layer

This layer determines the fundamental temporal orientation of corporate discourse. The organization constructs a horizon for the future by giving meaning to what has not yet happened within the discourse. In this process, sustainability is represented not only as the continuation of current responsibilities but also as an ethical and social positioning towards future generations. Thus, the corporate narrative shifts from being based on the representation of past performance to projecting the future within the discourse.

2. Future Value Construction Layer

The proleptic narrative not only represents the future; it also establishes the organization's future ethical, social, and environmental position. In this layer, the organization generates trust, responsibility, and value for the future through the discourse of sustainability. Thus, corporate legitimacy is restructured not on past performance but on values promised for the future.

3. Predictive Persuasion Layer

The corporate sustainability narrative does not merely inform the audience; it generates expectations for the future. This layer brings the narrative's persuasive dimension into a temporal framework. The organization establishes a meaning-production process that guides target-audience behavior through possible future scenarios. Thus, the sustainability discourse takes on a form of narrative persuasion oriented toward the future rather than retrospective explanation.

4. Narrative Mediation Layer

This layer determines the form of the corporate narrative's production and circulation. In today's communication environment, this mediation can be supported by digital communication systems and data-driven analysis. Artificial intelligence technologies are positioned in this layer not as a mandatory element, but as a potential mediation mechanism that can intensify the proleptic narrative. Data analysis, future modeling, and target audience adaptation capabilities can contribute to the evolution of corporate sustainability discourse into a more systematic and predictive narrative structure. However, proleptic corporate narrative is not dependent on artificial intelligence; AI should only be considered as a narrative technology that can expand the capacity of this narrative structure.

When these four layers are considered together, corporate sustainability communication shifts from a retrospective discourse based on the representation of past performance to a proleptic narrative architecture in which the future is constantly reconstituted within the discourse. This transformation demonstrates that corporate communication is not merely a practice of information transfer; it is also a process of meaning production that shapes social reality and future expectations.

PROLEPTIC NARRATIVE IN CORPORATE COMMUNICATION

Storytelling permeates many areas of public relations. Experts, consultants, and other professionals constantly tell stories about themselves and their organizations to different target audiences across vastly different channels (Akçay, 2017). A study on this subject found that experts constantly tell stories to make their professions understandable and, at the same time, present their lobbying and political advocacy activities to the public through storytelling to gain acceptance. The study found that the experts interviewed narrated how they contributed to a more promising future by moving away from the negative image of the past in the policy arena, how they met social demands, how they solved problems through personal relationships, and how they supported democratic processes. These narratives show that public relations activities have become a kind of legitimization strategy (Kantola, 2016). Therefore, the stories used in public relations not only explain the past but also shape the role that institutions assume for the future.

The nature of the discourse presented by experts can be summarized as a safe environment for employees, product guarantees for customers, responsibility for society, financial reliability for investors, risk profiles for insurers, and economic and social contributions for the government (Dowling, 2006, p. 82). Although such analyses are overly general, they are valuable for describing public relations discourses and their presentation as stories. These stories also show that corporate discourse has a temporal dimension and that institutions present their promises for the future within a fictional framework.

Wherever there is a story, there is also a constructed narrative. When discussing narrative, the concept of time plays an important role. In narratology, temporal breaks are addressed through the concept of anachrony. The form of anachrony constructed forward from the narrative time is defined as prolepsis (Genette, 2020, pp. 21-77). Essentially, sustainability is a vital theme that carries a forward-looking discourse. This makes sustainability discourses proleptic-based. From this perspective, the discourse of sustainability carries the quality of a proleptic narrative that constructs the future within today's discourse.

The increasing visibility of artificial intelligence technologies in communication necessitates a rethinking of the role of proleptic narratives in corporate communication. AI-supported content production and data processing tools offer new opportunities that diversify organizations' discourses about the future and, in some cases, adapt them to target audiences. These systems can support certain aspects of proleptic fiction by processing data on future social expectations, environmental risks, and consumer trends. However, it is still too early to say that such technologies have become a decisive and central element in every corporate campaign; at present, they are more positioned as additional tools with the potential to strengthen proleptic narratives.

In line with this theoretical framework, the works that won awards in the Social Responsibility and Sustainability section of the Brandverse Awards in 2024 were examined, and the works that won awards in the "Sustainability" section are listed in Table 1 (Brandverse Awards, 2024). The forward-looking discourses used in the implementation phases of these award-winning works were examined in the context of proleptic narrative elements.

Table 1. Projects Awarded in the 2024 Brandverse Awards Sustainability Projects Category

Award-Winning Project	Proleptic Narrative	Sample Text/Audio	Project Link
Yapı Kredi Step: What will change?	The emphasis on "future" is absent from the text/audio. However, it is present semantically.	--------	https://www.youtube.com/watch?v=tppBWl-HoVs
Migros Turkey - A Sustainable Future with Bees	Yes	*"A Sustainable Future with Bees"*	https://www.youtube.com/watch?v=LKNoSV3gjd4
Finish - Water Saver	Exists	*"Water Protectors: The Five of the Future"* *"If you do not want a future without water, trust me. Tomorrow's Water Belongs Most to Children"*	https://www.youtube.com/watch?v=rppU_tQyQY8
Samsung Turkey - Fishing Net Project	Available	*"Upcycling from waste nets. "We have upcycled nets that have been buried in the darkness of the sea depths for years into designs that illuminate the future."*	https://www.youtube.com/watch?v=5CPoQZbSjCo
CarrefourSA - Food Donation	None	------	https://www.youtube.com/watch?v=p6hFX_2S5eo
Sensodyne - When It Comes to the Future, We Care	Yes	*"We Care About the Future." "We do not care about food and drink, but we care about the future."*	https://www.youtube.com/watch?v=BMvS8DfaOvY
Superfresh - Responsible Production from Soil to Plate	No	--------	https://www.youtube.com/watch?v=75403gnmNqI
MNG Cargo - Project to Convert Waste Tires into Sustainable Materials Using Environmentally Friendly Methods	Yes	*"We are upcycling waste tires."*	https://www.youtube.com/watch?v=sGUasfdkywE
Nivogo - Real Opportunities Awareness Project	No	------	https://www.youtube.com/watch?v=StE4kau48xw

continued on following page

Table 1. Continued

Award-Winning Project	Proleptic Narrative	Sample Text/Audio	Project Link
Turkey İş Bank - The Future of the Seas: Sea Grasses	Yes	*"The Future of the Seas: Sea Grasses"* *"The Seas Are Ours, the Future Is Ours"*	https://www.youtube.com/watch?v=QTb9hdeG2Jg
Borusan - Umut Pina Project	None	------	https://www.youtube.com/watch?v=yKov7SjjK1Y
Alarko Carrier - Changing the Air in Schools	None	------	https://www.youtube.com/watch?v=YqipUYBjm60
Enerjisa - Sentrum	Yes	*"A better future for everyone"*	https://www.instagram.com/reel/C7dn5k0i2AA/
PepsiCo Turkey - Biomethanation Plant	No	------------------	https://www.instagram.com/pepsicoturkiye/reel/C0zARFwIETB/

The "Yapı Kredi Step: What will change?" project, implemented by Yapı Kredi, won the Gold Award in the "Combating Climate Change" category in the Sustainability section. The project progressed in an integrated manner across digital and traditional media. Although the project conceptually emphasizes the future, no text or audio with a "future" emphasis was found in the implementation phase, including the TVC.

The study *"A Sustainable Future with Bees,"* prepared by Migros Turkey, won the Silver Award in the Sustainability section's "Combating Climate Change" category. The project name and slogans of this study frequently featured text and audio emphasizing the "future." Communication was carried out on social media platforms, in the printed and digital versions of the Migroskop catalog, and on news sites as part of the campaign launched with the slogan "A Sustainable Future with Bees." In addition to events held in various cities, 561 people benefited from beekeeping courses and were introduced to the sector.

The "Water Protectors" project, launched by Finish, has won a Silver award in the "Combating Climate Change" category within the Sustainability section. The campaign emphasizes that children need to learn to protect water today for their own future. The brand has partnered with The Walt Disney Company to produce a film titled *"Water Guardians: The Future 5."* The film tells the story of five children and their struggle for water in a future of drought. The heroes find themselves in 2025, a dry future where water wars rage. *The Water Guardians:* The *Future 5* film, which premiered on April 23, 2024, has been broadcast 11 times on TV. In addition, with the emphasis that *"Tomorrow's water is most of all the children's right,"* the child characters in the Finnish TV commercials have used phrases such as "*If you do not want a waterless future, trust me. Now I am starting a conservation movement in this house.*" Following this film, the six-part series *Water Guardians: Back to School* was released. Water Guardians has been watched by over two million children aged 5-11.

The "Fishing Net Project" implemented by Samsung Turkey has won two Gold awards in the Sustainability section, in the categories of "Combating Waste and Recycling" and "Life Below Water and on Land." As part of this project, the brand has been repurposing waste fishing nets from the sea since 2022. Under the slogan *"Upcycling waste nets,"* they have produced desk organizers and lighting designs. The project is described as follows: *"We have upcycled nets that have been buried in the darkness of the sea for years into designs that illuminate the future."*

CarrefourSA's "Excess - Food Donation" initiative earned the Sustainability section a Silver award in the "Combating Waste and Recycling" category. The project combats food waste by delivering surplus food and non-food items to those in need. Products that have passed their expiration date but are still suitable for human consumption are returned to society.

Sensodyne Turkey won the Silver Award in the "Fighting Waste and Recycling" category with its "We Care About the Future" project. The project draws attention to leaving taps running while brushing teeth. The campaign films use the phrase *"We are not sensitive about food and drink, but we are sensitive when it comes to the future,"* and emphasize that "one glass is enough" for brushing your teeth.

Superfresh's "Responsible Production from Soil to Plate" project won the Gold Award in the Sustainability section's "Responsible Production and Consumption" category.

The study "Project for Converting Waste Tires into Sustainable Materials Using Environmentally Friendly Methods," prepared by MNG Kargo, won the Silver Award in the Sustainability section's "Responsible Production and Consumption" category. The campaign uses the phrase, *"We are converting waste tires into advanced materials using advanced technology in an environmentally friendly way."*

The "Real Opportunities Awareness Project" prepared by Nivogo won the Bronze award in the "Responsible Production and Consumption" category of the Sustainability section. The project, which draws attention to surplus textile products, offers a fashion footprint test and circular shopping opportunities.

The "Future of the Seas: Sea Grasses" study prepared by Türkiye İş Bankası won the Silver award in the "Life Below Water and on Land" category in the Sustainability section. The study, carried out in collaboration with the Turkish Marine Research Foundation (TÜDAV), aims to protect the seas and marine resources and support ecological balance and sustainability. The project, with the slogan *"The Seas Are Our Future,"* aims to map, clean up, and protect the last seagrass beds, which are critical to the health of the Marmara Sea and are referred to as the "lungs of the seas."

The 'Hope Pina Project' study, prepared by Borusan Holding, won the Silver Award in the Underwater and Land Life category of the Social Responsibility and Sustainability section. Led by Prof. Dr. Mustafa Sarı, Dean of the Faculty of Maritime Sciences at Bandırma 17 September University, the project aims to record the Pina population in the Marmara Sea and raise public awareness for the protection of these creatures. The Borusan Sustainable Benefit Program supports it.

The "Changing the Air in Schools" project implemented by Alarko Carrier has won the Bronze Award in the "Sustainable Cities and Communities" category under the Social Responsibility and Sustainability section. Solar panels that convert solar energy into electrical energy were installed at Midyat Çaldara Primary School. This enables the school to generate its own electricity.

The green destination model "Sentrum," implemented by Enerjisa and its partners, won the Bronze Award in the "Sustainable Cities and Communities" category under the Corporate Social Responsibility and Sustainability section. The transformation of Ayvalık Küçükköy and İzmir Birgi has been implemented as part of the project. With its slogan "*A Better Future for Everyone*," the brand aims to raise awareness to support sustainable development and tourism and to pass on natural values to future generations.

PepsiCo has started producing biomethane from organic waste at its Manisa factory with the biomethaneation facility it has installed. The brand, which stands out for its sustainability efforts in energy and waste management, won the Silver Award in the "Clean Energy Projects" category of the Social Responsibility and Sustainability section.

Artificial intelligence-powered text and sentiment analysis tools can systematically highlight the future-oriented narrative elements of sustainability campaigns. The distribution of proleptic keywords such as "future," "tomorrow," "transformation," and "good life" in the projects examined within the scope of the Brandverse Awards can be measured in more detail in the future using AI-based content analysis methods. However, this study primarily evaluates the campaigns in question through a qualitative, discourse-focused reading; therefore, AI-based analysis tools are mentioned here primarily as a methodological possibility and a potential direction for future research.

The corporate sustainability campaigns examined in this study do not directly rely on AI-based communication systems. However, the discursive structure analyzed points to a proleptic narrative architecture that constructs the future within discourse. Therefore, artificial intelligence is not treated as an empirical element in the study; rather, it is considered at a theoretical level as a potential intermediary layer where the data-driven, predictive, and algorithmic aspects of the narrative structure could be concentrated. In other words, the proleptic corporate narrative is not dependent on artificial intelligence; however, artificial intelligence is positioned as a narrative technology that could expand the capacity of this structure.

EMPIRICAL ILLUSTRATION: BRANDVERSE CAMPAIGNS WITHIN THE PROLEPTIC CORPORATE NARRATIVE MODEL

The Brandverse Awards campaigns that received awards in the Social Responsibility and Sustainability category, examined within the scope of this study, were analyzed to determine how they establish the corporate sustainability discourse within the context of the proleptic narrative structure. The analysis goes beyond a descriptive content review, aiming to evaluate the discursive structure of the campaigns through the four layers of the Proleptic Corporate Narrative Model. This approach aims to reveal that sustainability communication carries not only thematic content but also a temporally structured narrative logic.

Temporal Projection: Constructing the Future Within Discourse

In a significant portion of the campaigns examined, the temporal orientation of sustainability discourse is constructed towards the future. Expressions such as "future," "tomorrow," "transformation," and "a better world" form the fundamental temporal axis of corporate discourse; institutions give meaning to what has not yet happened within today's discourse. For example, discourses such as "A Sustainable Future with Bees," "The Future of the Seas," and "A better future for everyone" represent sustainability not as the preservation of a current state, but as the construction of the future. This structure shows that sustainability communication operates not through retrospective explanation, but through a proleptic conception of time.

Future Value Construction: Establishing Future Value

Campaigns do not merely refer to the future; they also construct the institution's future ethical and social position. Themes such as children's right to water, protection of biological diversity, sustainable production, and the circular economy reflect the values institutions promise to embrace in the future. In this context, the discourse of sustainability produces corporate legitimacy based on future social benefits and ethical position rather than on past performance. Thus, the corporate narrative shifts from a past-based accountability framework to a future-based value construction.

Predictive Persuasion: Narratives that Generate Expectations

The campaigns examined do not merely inform the audience; they generate expectations and orientations for the future. In particular, discourses such as "future generations," "tomorrow's world," and "protecting the future" transform sustainability into a temporal mechanism of persuasion. This structure demonstrates that the sustainability narrative not only represents but also serves a behavior-guiding function. By constructing the possible risks and gains of the future within the narrative, the institution attempts to shape the audience's attitude today. Thus, sustainability communication takes on the form of predictive persuasion, an argument oriented toward the future rather than retrospective explanation.

Narrative Mediation: Digital and Data-Based Mediation

Digital communication tools used in campaigns increase the circulation and visibility of the sustainability narrative. Although the campaigns examined do not rely directly on artificial intelligence-based communication systems, data-driven measurement, targeting, and digital content production processes contribute to the more systematic establishment of proleptic narrative. This demonstrates that the proleptic corporate narrative can intensify through technological mediation in today's communication environment. Artificial intelligence is not a mandatory element in this context; it can be considered a potential narrative mediator that could deepen the proleptic narrative in a predictive and personalized manner.

From Retrospective CSR to Proleptic Sustainability Narrative

When the findings of the analysis are evaluated together, it becomes clear that a significant portion of corporate sustainability campaigns, unlike the classic CSR discourse, produces a proleptic narrative logic that constructs the future within the discourse rather than a past-based accountability narrative. While traditional CSR discourse derives legitimacy from the organization's past performance, sustainability discourse achieves temporal transformation by constructing the organization's future social and ethical position within the narrative.

This finding shows that corporate sustainability communication is not merely a content expansion but a structural transformation in the temporal logic of the corporate narrative. In other words, sustainability communication is evolving from a retrospective CSR narrative to a proleptic corporate narrative architecture.

A LOOK AT THE NEAR FUTURE: AI-MEDIATED PROLEPTIC NARRATIVE AND NARRATIVE ADVERTISING

Corporate sustainability communication is increasingly moving away from merely presenting current performance and toward a proleptic narrative that operates through the production of meaning and the construction of expectations about the future. Prolepsis is defined in narrative theory as the establishment of the future in the present and the interpretation of the unfulfilled within discourse. The integration of AI-powered proleptic narratives into advertising is creating a transformative phenomenon in marketing, fundamentally changing how brands communicate with consumers. Proleptic narratives, which foreshadow future events or outcomes, use artificial intelligence to create personalized consumer experiences and effectively predict and influence buyer behavior. AI's role in creating these narratives is crucial because it enables marketers to analyze large datasets and create stories that deeply resonate with individual preferences (Balcıoğlu, 2025). In the context of corporate communication, this structure allows brands to construct their future promises, predictions, and value projections as a strategic form of discourse. Thus, sustainability narratives become not only informative texts but also a predictive discourse.

Artificial intelligence is fundamentally transforming the structure of this proleptic narrative. Research has shown that emotional storytelling is particularly engaging and can significantly increase brand perception (Biswas, 2025). AI's ability to discern emotional cues and patterns from consumer interactions enables the creation of narratives that not only connect with audiences on an emotional level but also guide them toward specific purchase paths. The effectiveness of these narratives lies in their ability to simulate real-life scenarios that consumers imagine themselves in while using a product or service, thereby increasing the likelihood of conversion (Vidrih & Mayahi, 2023). Therefore, AI-driven narratives are not only informative but also structured to elicit specific emotional responses that can lead to behavioral changes. Through behavior modeling and scenario generation, data-driven predictive systems leverage artificial intelligence to shift corporate communication from a retrospective to a future-oriented narrative architecture. AI-supported future modeling in brand communication not only predicts trends but also allows the brand to structure its possible future scenarios on a narrative plane. Thus, corporate discourse is shaped more by the narrative construction of the future than by reporting on past performance. In this process, artificial intelligence functions as a narrative mediator rather than merely a tool for narrative production. However, the use of AI in creating narratives also raises ethical concerns. When AI technologies collect and analyze consumer data for advertising purposes, the line between personalized marketing and intrusive surveillance can become blurred. This practice can lead to feelings of manipulation and distrust among consumers, and brands must be careful in this regard to maintain their integrity (Bourne, 2024). Furthermore, the ethical implications of using AI in storytelling include issues related to consumer privacy, consent, and the potential to reinforce existing biases in data (Gorichanaz, 2024). Despite these challenges, the use of artificial intelligence in storytelling can increase consumer engagement through highly personalized experiences. By understanding consumer motivations and behaviors, marketers can create complex stories that capture and sustain audience attention (Dogra & Dogra, 2025). Advances in AI technology thus herald a new era in advertising. This era is characterized not only by an emphasis on engagement but also by an increased responsibility to address ethical considerations in marketing strategies (Tesic, 2024). As AI continues to evolve, the strategies used in advertising will evolve as well, opening new avenues that could redefine consumer-brand interactions. While marketers leverage the power of artificial intelligence to create proleptic narratives that influence consumer behavior and shape brand perception, they must be ethically mindful. In summary, while the effectiveness of AI-powered narratives is promising, their ethical implications must be critically evaluated to foster a responsible marketing environment.

Sustainability narratives can be considered a specific form of narrative advertising in this context. Through sustainability discourse, brands not only declare their responsibility but also build a brand story grounded in future-oriented trust, ethical positioning, and value creation. This story uses a forward projection of time and builds trust and expectation in the audience by giving meaning to what has not yet happened. Thus, sustainability communication takes on a form of narrative persuasion oriented toward the future, unlike the product-focused persuasion of classic advertising. Artificial intelligence deepens this process with data-driven persuasion mechanisms. Thanks to big data analytics and behavioral modeling, the corporate narrative no longer offers just a general vision of the future; it produces a personalized, contextual, and predictive narrative tailored to the target audience. This gives rise to a new form of discourse where persuasion shifts from the rhetorical plane to data-driven meaning production. Thus, the brand narrative for the future becomes data-driven persuasion shaped by algorithmic analysis. Consequently, AI-mediated corporate narrative can be defined as an algorithmic narrative production form that operates through the simulation of the future within discourse. This structure transforms corporate sustainability discourse from a mere communication strategy into a meaning-production process in which the brand's future position is narratively constructed. Thus, artificial intelligence reveals an algorithmic narrative architecture (algorithmic construction of corporate future narrative) that determines not only message production in corporate communication but also how the narrative about the brand's future is constructed.

CONCLUSION

One of the most fundamental functions of public relations is to ensure the organization's continuity and sustainability. The image, perceptions, and opinions held by the target audience not only shape how the brand is perceived but also build a reservoir of trust that enables the organization to survive in times of crisis (Yılmaz, 2024). In this context, sustainability provides a framework that extends the corporate presence of public relations beyond narrow organizational boundaries and positions the organization within a broader social reality. The institution is no longer merely a functional economic actor; it is part of a holistic system of meaning situated within a social, environmental, and ethical context. This situation requires a rethinking of the concept of social responsibility, transforming proactivity from a strategic orientation into a temporal positioning.

This study approaches corporate social responsibility and corporate sustainability discourses not merely as ethical or managerial practices, but as narrative forms that structure the temporal logic of corporate communication. The analysis reveals that corporate social responsibility essentially produces a retrospective narrative of legitimacy based on past performance; in contrast, the discourse of corporate sustainability creates a proleptic narrative structure that constructs the future within the discourse. In this respect, sustainability communication signals that the corporate narrative has evolved from a past-based accountability framework to a future-oriented meaning-production process.

The proposed Proleptic Corporate Narrative Model conceptualizes this transformation through four structural layers: temporal projection, construction of future value, predictive persuasion, and narrative mediation. This structure demonstrates that corporate sustainability discourse is not merely a form of communication that conveys information; instead, it functions as a meaning-production process that establishes expectations for the future, ethical positions, and social values within the discourse. Thus, corporate communication moves away from a retrospective narrative based on the representation of past actions and becomes a temporal narrative architecture in which the unfulfilled is given meaning within the discourse.

The campaigns examined within the scope of the Brandverse Awards have shown that sustainability communication is constructed mainly through a proleptic narrative logic. Discourses about the future in the campaigns are not merely a thematic emphasis; they ensure that corporate values, ethical position, and social role are reestablished through a projection toward the future. This finding reveals that corporate sustainability communication is not a content-based expansion but a structural transformation occurring in the temporal logic of the corporate narrative.

The increasing prominence of AI-based tools in corporate communication practices reopens the debate on the limits and possibilities of proleptic corporate discourse. AI-supported content production, data processing, and predictive models offer new opportunities that institutions can draw upon when planning their future-oriented strategic discourses; however, it cannot be said that these tools are decisive in all cases or that they fundamentally transform the basic character of corporate communication. From this study's perspective, artificial intelligence is not a mandatory component of proleptic narrative; it is viewed as an intermediary layer with the potential to intensify the future-oriented dimensions of sustainability and social responsibility discourses. In this context, proleptic narrative should be seen not as an entirely new form of communication in the age of artificial intelligence, but rather as a temporal logic of corporate narrative that is gaining new meaning within existing discursive structures.

Consequently, this study argues that the transformation from corporate social responsibility to corporate sustainability is not merely a conceptual expansion but a structural reorganization occurring within the temporal logic of corporate narrative. Corporate sustainability communication is evolving from a retrospective discourse based on past performance to a proleptic narrative architecture in which the future is constructed within the discourse. This perspective demonstrates that public relations is not merely a practice representing corporate reality; it is also a discursive structure that shapes social expectations and the production of meaning regarding the future.

The study's focus on specific campaigns may not fully reflect the diversity of sustainability discourses across sectors and cultural contexts. Future research examining how proleptic corporate narratives are constructed through broader samples, different sectors, and cultural contexts will deepen theoretical discussions in this field. In particular, AI-supported content analysis, discourse modeling, and narrative structure analysis have the potential to reveal, in greater detail, the temporal and discursive transformations of corporate sustainability communication.

REFERENCES

Akbayır, Z. (2019). Halkla ilişkiler perspektifinden kurumsal sürdürülebilirlik iletişimi ve bir örnek olay incelemesi. *Uluslararası Halkla İlişkiler ve Reklam Çalışmaları Dergisi*, *2*(1), 39–71.

Akçay, E. (2017). Çağımızın hikâye anlatıcılığı olarak halkla ilişkiler: Vehbi Koç biyografileri üzerine bir inceleme. *Moment Dergi*, *4*(2), 498–512. DOI: 10.17572/mj2017.2.498517

Aydede, C. (2009). *Teorik ve uygulamalı halkla ilişkiler kampanyaları*. Mediacat.

Balcıoğlu, Y. S. (2025). The evolving role of storytelling in marketing: From tradition to AI-powered narratives. In Miguélez-Juan, B., & Rebollo-Bueno, S. (Eds.), *AI impacts on branded entertainment and advertising* (pp. 107–124). IGI Global. DOI: 10.4018/979-8-3693-3799-8.ch006

Balta Peltekoğlu, F. (2016). Halkla ilişkiler nedir? *BETA Bulletin of Experimental Treatments for AIDS*.

Balta Peltekoğlu, F., & Tozlu, E. (2017). Halkla ilişkiler ve gönüllülük ekseninde Türkiye'de kurumsal sosyal sorumluluk projeleri ve bin yıl kalkınma hedefleri. *Selçuk İletişim*, *10*(1), 5–31. DOI: 10.18094/josc.309841

Bell, S. H., & Bell, E. C. (1976). Public relations: Functional of functionary? *Public Relations Review*, *2*(2), 47–57. DOI: 10.1016/S0363-8111(76)80004-5

Biswas, M. (2025). AI for Emotional storytelling in advertisements. In Rabby, F., Ahmed, N., Sehmi, A., Bansal, R., & Pruthi, N. (Eds.), *Demystifying emotion AI, robotics AI, and sentiment analysis in customer relationship management* (pp. 229–246). IGI Global. DOI: 10.4018/979-8-3373-1867-7.ch011

Bourne, C. (2024). AI hype, promotional culture, and affective capitalism. *AI and Ethics*, *4*(3), 757–769. DOI: 10.1007/s43681-024-00483-w

Bowen, H. R. (1953). *Social responsibilities of the businessman*. Harper & Brothers.

Brandverse Awards. (2024). *Sürdürülebilirlik çalışmaları kazanlar*. https://www.brandverseawards.com/2024-kazananlar/

Broom, G. M. (1986). *Public relations roles and systems theory: Functional and historicist causal models. Public Relations Interest Group*. International Communication Association.

Brundtland Raporu. (1987). *Report of the World Commission on environment and development: Our common future.* http://www.un-documents.net/our-common -future.pdf

Çalışkan Özsözgün, A. (2012). Sürdürülebilirlik raporlaması. *Journal of Accounting and Taxation Studies*, *5*(1), 41–68.

Carroll, A. B. (1991). The pyramid of corporate social responsibility: Toward the moral management of organizational stakeholders. *Business Horizons*, *34*(4), 39–48. DOI: 10.1016/0007-6813(91)90005-G

Carroll, A. B. (2016). Carroll's pyramid of CSR: Taking another look. *International Journal of Corporate Social Responsibility*, *1*(3), 1–8. DOI: 10.1186/s40991-016-0004-6

Davis, K. (1960). Can businesses afford to ignore social responsibilities? *California Management Review*, *2*(3), 70–76. DOI: 10.2307/41166246

Dogra, P., & Dogra, A. K. (2025). Interweaving narratives: The role of AI in enhancing consumer engagement through storytelling. In Jain, V., & Mitra, A. (Eds.), *Decoding consumer behavior using the insight equation and AI marketing* (pp. 275–300). IGI Global.

Dowling, G. R. (2006). Communicating corporate reputation through stories. *California Management Review*, *49*(1), 82–100. DOI: 10.2307/41166372

Dozier, D. M. ve Ehling, W.P. (1992). Evaluation of public relations programs: What the literature tells us about their effects, In J.E. Grunig (Ed.), *Excellence in public relations and communication management* (pp. 159–183). Lawrence and Erlbaum Associates.

Durna, T. (2011). Neoliberalizmin bir hegemonya aracı olarak kurumsal sosyal sorumluluk (KSS) ve çokuluslu şirketlerin 'hayat'tan eksilttikleri. In Yıldırım Becerikli, S. (Ed.), *Halkla ilişkiler ve reklamın anatomisi: eleştirel bir kavrayış içinde* (pp. 76–102). Ütopya.

Elden, M. (2018). *Reklam ve reklamcılık.* Say Yayınları.

Engin, E., & Eker Akgöz, B. (2013). Sürdürülebilir kalkınma ve kurumsal sürdürülebilirlik çerçevesinde kurumsal sosyal sorumluluk kavramının değerlendirilmesi. *Selçuk İletişim*, *8*(1), 85–94.

Feix, A., & Philippe, D. (2020). Unpacking the narrative decontestation of CSR: Aspiration for change or defense of the status quo? *Business & Society*, *59*(1), 129–174. DOI: 10.1177/0007650318816434

Genette, G. (2020). *Anlatının söylemi: Yöntem hakkında bir deneme* (Aydar, F. B., Trans.). Ayrıntı.

Gladwin, T. N., Kennelly, J. J., & Krause, T. S. (1995). Shifting paradigms for sustainable development: Implications for management theory and research. *Academy of Management Review, 20*(4), 874–907. DOI: 10.2307/258959

Gorichanaz, T. (2024). AI technologies, identity theft and data selves. In Elliott, A. (Ed.), *The De Gruyter handbook of artificial intelligence, identity and technology studies* (pp. 181–196). De Gruyter. DOI: 10.1515/9783110721751-010

Grunig, J. E., & Hunt, T. (1984). *Managing public relations.* Holt, Rinehart & Winston.

Himmetoğlu, A. (2023). Kurumsal sürdürülebilirlik ve kurumsal sosyal sorumluluk: Bir bibliyometrik analiz çalışması. *Erciyes İletişim Dergisi, 10*(2), 891–911. DOI: 10.17680/erciyesiletisim.1268583

Kadıbeşegil, S. (2008). *Şimdi stratejik iletişim zamanı. Kurumsal yönetim, kurumsal itibar, kurumsal iletişim hakkında bilmeniz gereken her şey!* Mediacat.

Kantola, A. (2016). Cleaning rotten politics, selling exclusive liaisons: Public relations consultants as storytelling professionals between markets and politics. *Public Relations Inquiry, 5*(1), 33–52. DOI: 10.1177/2046147X15625713

Karaman, A. (1996). *Sürdürülebilir turizm planlaması için ekolojik bir çerçeve, sürdürülebilir turizm; turizm planlamasına ekolojik yaklaşım. 19. Dünya Şehircilik Günü Kolokyumu.* Mimar Sinan Üniversitesi.

Kelly, A. (2025). Nostos in three moves or five stages: A story pattern in early Greek epos. *Yearbook of Ancient Greek Epic Online, 9*(1), 1–42.

Khan, W. (2024). *Corporate narratives in CSR communication? A multimodal analysis of CSR communication of mission-oriented companies on online platforms* [Master's Dissertation].

Ksenofontova, A. (2023). Towards an interdisciplinary approach to time in fiction. *KronoScope, 23*(1), 86–103. DOI: 10.1163/15685241-bja10008

Makridis, S., Papadakis, D. M., & Polymeris, S. (2014). Avoiding the CSR paradox: The role of narratology in reshaping corporate social responsibility in digital mediums; Exemplary case study—proceedings *of the 2014 International Digital Storytelling Conference in Athens – Digital Storytelling in Times of Crisis.*

Mohan, A. (2026). Transmodernity and literature: Of worlds in contact, Part 2. *Asian Review of World Histories, 14*(1), 27–36. DOI: 10.1163/22879811-bja10101

Okay, A. & Okay, A. (2018). *Halkla ilişkiler kavram strateji ve uygulamaları*. Der.

Özgen, E. (2022). Sürdürülebilirlik iletişimi ve halkla ilişkiler. *Türkiye İletişim Araştırmaları Dergisi, Özel Sayı*, e1-e4. DOI: DOI: 10.17829/turcom.1106292

Soydaş, N., & Çokluk, N. (2023). Kurumsal sosyal sorumluluk projelerinin kurumsal iletişimde rolü: "Shell'de kadın enerjisi" vaka incelemesi. *İstanbul Aydın Üniversitesi Sosyal Bilimler Dergisi, 15*(2), 227–258.

Stinchcombe, A. L. (1968). *Constructing social theory*. Harcourt, Brace & World.

Tan Çakır, N. (2024). Factual and theoretical development of corporate social responsibility. In Yılmaz, R., & Özer Alper, D. (Eds.), *Innovative models, strategies, and conceptualizations in PR* (pp. 163–174). Palet.

Tesic, J. (2024). Redeployment of trend forecasting: managing the overproduction challenge in the fashion industry. [Unpublished Doctoral Thesis]

Tıraş, H. H. (2012). Sürdürülebilir kalkınma ve çevre: Teorik bir inceleme. *Kahramanmaraş Sütçü İmam Üniversitesi İktisadi ve İdari Bilimler Fakültesi Dergisi, 2*(2), 57–73.

Van Dyck, F. (2017). *Yeni nesil reklamcılık- dijital çağ için yeni kurallar*. The Kitap.

Vidrih, M., & Mayahi, S. (2023). Generative AI-driven storytelling: A new era for marketing. *arXiv preprint.* arXiv:2309.09048. https://arxiv.org/abs/2309.09048

Widiasari, N. (2020). Narration based on corporate social responsibility (CSR) advertisement: The projection and story. *Jurnal Desain Komunikasi Visual Nirmana, 20*(2), 106–120. DOI: 10.9744/nirmana.20.2.106-120

Widiasari, N. (2020). Narration based on CSR advertisement. *Nirmana, 20*(2), 106–120.

World Commission on Environment and Development. (1987). *Our common future*. http://www.un-documents.net/our-common-future.pdf

Yılmaz, D. (2006). *Sosyal pazarlama anlayışı ve bir uygulama*. [Master's Dissertation].

Yılmaz, R. (2024). The cyclic positioning model. In Yılmaz, R., & Özer Alper, D. (Eds.), *Innovative models, strategies, and conceptualizations in PR* (pp. 13–25). Palet.

Zgoll, A., Cuperly, B., & Cöster-Gilbert, A. (2023). In search of Dumuzi: An introduction to Hylistic narratology. In Konstantopoulos, G., & Helle, S. (Eds.), *The shape of stories* (pp. 285–350). Brill. DOI: 10.1163/9789004539761_013

ADDITIONAL READING

Bozkurt, İ. (2013). *Pazarlama iletişiminde sihirli dokunuşlar*. Mediacat.

Gündem, T. (2004). Küresel köyde halkla ilişkiler adına neler tartışılıyor. In Pira, A. (Ed.), *Etik ve sosyal sorumluluk* (pp. 183–199). Ege Üniversitesi Basımevi.

Kazaz, A. (2022). *Birey toplum ve dijitalleşme bağlamında tüketimin yeni formları*. Eğitim.

Koçyiğit, M. (2018). *Halkla ilişkiler ve kurumsal sosyal sorumluluk*. Eğitim.

Özgen, E. (2024). *Kurumsal sosyal sorumluluk projeleri*. The Kitap.

KEY TERMS AND DEFINITIONS

Proleptic Narrative: A future-oriented narrative structure that constructs meaning by projecting anticipated states, outcomes, and institutional positions within present discourse, shaping expectations rather than merely representing past actions.

Corporate Sustainability Communication: A strategic and narrative-based communication process through which organizations articulate environmental, social, and ethical commitments, positioning themselves within a broader socio-temporal framework that extends beyond immediate operational concerns.

Corporate Social Responsibility (CSR): A retrospective legitimacy discourse through which organizations justify their social and ethical standing by referencing past actions, responsibilities, and stakeholder-oriented practices.

Temporal Narrative Architecture: The structural organization of corporate communication through time, where meaning is produced by arranging past, present, and projected future within a coherent narrative system.

Predictive Persuasion: A narrative mechanism that guides audience perception and behavior by constructing expectations about possible futures, influencing present attitudes through projected outcomes.

Narrative Mediation: The process by which corporate narratives are produced, adapted, and circulated through communicative and technological systems, shaping how meaning is constructed and received.

Artificial Intelligence in Corporate Communication: The use of data-driven and algorithmic systems to support content generation, predictive modeling, and adaptive messaging, functioning as a mediating layer that may enhance but does not determine proleptic narrative structures.

Compilation of References

Aaker, D. (1991). Brand equity. *La gestione del valore della marca, 347*, 356.

Aaker, D. A. (2012). *Building strong brands.* Simon and schuster.

Abbasoğlu, Ş. (2025). Overcoming The Dark Sides of Artificial Intelligence. In Özkaynar, K., & Abbasoğlu, Ş. (Eds.), *Consumer, Marketing, AI: Dark Sides and Ethics.* Özgür Yayınları., DOI: 10.58830/ozgur.pub710.c3018

Abbass, H. (2021). What is Artificial Intelligence? *IEEE Transactions on Artificial Intelligence, 2*(2), 94–95. DOI: 10.1109/TAI.2021.3096243

Abdulwahid, O., & Şaylan, O. (2025). Artificial intelligence applications in marketing: A literature-based study [Pazarlamada yapay zekâ uygulamaları: Literatür temelli bir çalışma]. *Kapanaltı Dergisi*, (8), 58–75. DOI: 10.62080/kmfed.1783278

Acar, H. M., & İmik Tanyıldızı, N. (2022). Reklamda yapay zekâ kullanımı: Ziraat Bankası #Senhepgülümse reklam filminde deepfake uygulamasının görsel anlatıya etkisi. *Kastamonu İletişim Araştırmaları Dergisi, 8*, 78–99.

Adams, R. (2004). Intelligent Advertising. *AI & Society, 18*(1), 68–81. DOI: 10.1007/s00146-003-0259-9

Adaş, E. B., & Erbay, B. (2021). Yapay Zekâ Sosyolojisi Üzerine Bir Değerlendirme. *Gaziantep University Journal of Social Sciences, 21*(1), 326–337. DOI: 10.21547/jss.991383

Aguirre, E., Mahr, D., Grewal, D., De Ruyter, K., & Wetzels, M. (2015). Unraveling the personalization paradox: The effect of information collection and trust-building strategies on online advertisement effectiveness. *Journal of Retailing, 91*(1), 34–49. DOI: 10.1016/j.jretai.2014.09.005

Aichner, T., Coletti, P., Jacob, F., & Wilken, R. (2021). Did the Volkswagen emissions scandal harm the "made in Germany" image? A cross-cultural, cross-products, cross-time study. *Corporate Reputation Review, 24*(4), 179–190. DOI: 10.1057/s41299-020-00101-5

Akbayır, Z. (2016). Bana bir hikâye anlat: Marka iletişiminde hikâyeleştirme ve internet [Tell me a story: Storytelling in brand communication and the internet]. *KTÜ İletişim Fakültesi E-Dergi, 3*(12), 67–84.

Akbayır, Z. (2019). Halkla ilişkiler perspektifinden kurumsal sürdürülebilirlik iletişimi ve bir örnek olay incelemesi. *Uluslararası Halkla İlişkiler ve Reklam Çalışmaları Dergisi, 2*(1), 39–71.

Akçay, E. (2017). Çağımızın hikâye anlatıcılığı olarak halkla ilişkiler: Vehbi Koç biyografileri üzerine bir inceleme. *Moment Dergi, 4*(2), 498–512. DOI: 10.17572/mj2017.2.498517

Akyıldız, E., & Tükel Kanra, Y. (2022). A research on neologism translation: The Handmaid's Tale. *Dokuz Eylül Üniversitesi Sosyal Bilimler Enstitüsü Dergisi, 24*(4), 1449–1469. DOI: 10.16953/deusosbil.1109395

Alaghappan, T., & Nalini, R. (2025). AI-powered emotional storytelling for brand narratives and consumer perception. In *International Conference on Artificial Intelligence in Commerce and Management* (pp. 200-210). DOI: 10.34293/ICAICM-25.ch029

Alamarat, İ. (2025). Using Artificial Intelligence in Producing Animation Elements. *Art and Architecture Journal, 6*(1), 1–10. DOI: 10.21608/aaj.2025.344652.1085

Alamro, A. S. (2010). *Branding and brand preference in the mobile phone service industry*. Bangor University.

Alareeni, B., & Hamdan, A. (Eds.). (2023). *Impact of artificial intelligence and the fourth industrial revolution on business success*. Springer., DOI: 10.1007/978-3-031-08093-7

Alotaibi, E. M., & Alwathnani, A. M. (2025). AI-enabled ESG compliance audit for stakeholders. *Sustainability (Basel), 17*(21), 9513. DOI: 10.3390/su17219513

Ambler, T., & Kokkinaki, F. (1997). Measures of marketing success. *Journal of Marketing Management, 13*(7), 665–678. DOI: 10.1080/0267257X.1997.9964503

Anand, A. (2020). Impact of Digitalisation of Marketing: An Analysis. *Research Review Journals, 5*(8), 131–134. DOI: 10.31305/rrijm.2020.v05.i08.031

Anderson, K., Roggeman, A., & Fuller, J. (2024). *Artificial intelligence and film: A journey in public perception from 1960 to the present day*. Celebrating Scholarship and Creativity Day.

Applc. (2025). *Apple official website.* https://www.applc.com (Acccsscd: 8 March 2025)

Arçelik. (2025). *Arçelik official website.* https://www.arcelikglobal.com (Accessed: 21 April 2025)

Arora, N., Dreze, X., Ghose, A., Hess, J. D., Iyengar, R., Jing, B., Joshi, Y., Kumar, V., Lurie, N., Neslin, S., Sajeesh, S., Su, M., Syam, N., Thomas, J., & Zhang, Z. J. (2008). Putting one-to-one marketing to work: Personalization, customization, and choice. *Marketing Letters, 19*(3–4), 305–321. DOI: 10.1007/s11002-008-9056-z

Arslan, K. (2020). Eğitimde yapay zeka ve uygulamaları. *Batı Anadolu Eğitim Bilimleri Dergisi, 11*(1), 71–88.

Askari, J. (18 August 2023). Deepfakes and Synthetic Media: What are they and how are techUK members taking steps to tackle misinformation and fraud. *techUK.* https://www.techuk.org/resource/synthetic-media-what-are-they-and-how-are-techuk-members-taking-steps-to-tackle-misinformation-and-fraud.html

Aulló-Saura, E., Gutiérrez-Artacho, J., & Díaz Millón, M. (2025). *Transcreation and AI in global marketing: A comparative case study of two telecom websites.* Digital Translation.

Ayaydın-Cebe, G. Ö. (2021). Smile of the crescent: Constructing a future identity out of historical ambiguity in İstiklâl Marşı (with translation). *Die Welt des Islams, 63*(1), 76–106. DOI: 10.1163/15700607-61040001

Aydede, C. (2009). *Teorik ve uygulamalı halkla ilişkiler kampanyaları*. Mediacat.

Aydemir, M., & Fetah, V. (2023). Yapay Zekanın Dijital Hikayeleştirme ve Senaryo Tasarımında Kullanımı: Kısa Film Uygulamalı Bir Araştırma. *Pamukkale Üniversitesi Sosyal Bilimler Enstitüsü Journal*, (58), 255–275.

Aydın, İ., & Değirmenci, C. H. (2018). *Yapay Zekâ*. Girdap.

Balcıoğlu, Y. S. (2025). The evolving role of storytelling in marketing: From tradition to AI-powered narratives. In Miguélez-Juan, B., & Rebollo-Bueno, S. (Eds.), *AI impacts on branded entertainment and advertising* (pp. 107–124). IGI Global. DOI: 10.4018/979-8-3693-3799-8.ch006

Balta Peltekoğlu, F. (2016). Halkla ilişkiler nedir? *BETA Bulletin of Experimental Treatments for AIDS.*

Balta Peltekoğlu, F., & Tozlu, E. (2017). Halkla ilişkiler ve gönüllülük ekseninde Türkiye'de kurumsal sosyal sorumluluk projeleri ve bin yıl kalkınma hedefleri. *Selçuk İletişim, 10*(1), 5–31. DOI: 10.18094/josc.309841

Banguoğlu, T. (2015). *Türkçenin grameri.* Türk Dil Kurumu Yayınları.

Banh, L., & Strobel, G. (2023). Generative artificial intelligence. *Electronic Markets, 33*(1), 63. Advance online publication. DOI: 10.1007/s12525-023-00680-1

Barari, M., Casper Ferm, L. E., Quach, S., Thaichon, P., & Ngo, L. (2024). The dark side of artificial intelligence in marketing: Meta-analytics review. *Marketing Intelligence & Planning, 42*(7), 1234–1256. DOI: 10.1108/MIP-09-2023-0494

Barnett, K. (2025, April 11). Two lawsuits allege that The Trade Desk secretly violates consumer privacy laws. *People.* https://www.adweek.com/programmatic/lawsuits-trade-desk-consumer-privacy-laws

Barthes, R. (1997). *Göstergebilimsel Serüven.* Yapı Kredi Yayınları.

Barut, E. (2025). A linguistic challenge to ChatGPT: Use of AI in detection, text generation, and translation of false friends in Turkish-English. *Söylem Filoloji Dergisi (Çeviribilim Özel Sayısı II),* 154-177. https://doi.org/DOI: 10.29110/soylemdergi.1598386

Barzykowski, K., & Mazzoni, G. (2022). Do intuitive ideas of the qualities that should characterize involuntary and voluntary memories affect their classification? *Psychological Research, 86*(1), 170–195. DOI: 10.1007/s00426-020-01465-3 PMID: 33582862

Batı, U. (2002). *Yazılı basın reklamlarında dilin stratejik kullanımı* [Strategic use of language in print media advertisements] [Master's thesis, Marmara University].

Baudrillard, J. (2018). *Simülakrlar ve Simülasyon.* O. Adanır, Trans. Doğu Batı. pp. 13-15, 140-141.

Baudrillard, J. (2004). *Tüketim Toplumu* (Deliceçaylı, H., & Keskin, F., Trans.). Ayrıntı.

Beatty, S. E., & Smith, S. M. (1987). External search effort: An investigation across several product categories. *The Journal of Consumer Research, 14*(1), 83–95. DOI: 10.1086/209095

Behzadi, M., & Bakhtiary, M. J. (2023). The role of storytelling in age of digital marketing. In *The 5th International Conference on Modern Research in Management.*

Beko. (2025). *Beko global website.* https://www.beko.com (Accessed: 10 March 2025)

Bell, S. H., & Bell, E. C. (1976). Public relations: Functional of functionary? *Public Relations Review*, *2*(2), 47–57. DOI: 10.1016/S0363-8111(76)80004-5

Belova, A. (2021). Storytelling in advertising and branding. *Cognition, Communication. Discourse (Berkeley, Calif.)*, (22), 13–26.

Bender, E. M., Gebru, T., McMillan-Major, A., & Shmitchell, S. (2021). On the dangers of stochastic parrots: Can language models be too big? In *Proceedings of the 2021 ACM Conference on Fairness, Accountability, and Transparency* (pp. 610–623). https://doi.org/DOI: 10.1145/3442188.3445922

Berger, A. (2022). All Ads Are Narratives. *Media-Biznes-Kultura. Dziennikarstwo i komunikacja społeczna*, (13), 43-54.

Bettman, J. R., Luce, M. F., & Payne, J. W. (1998). Constructive consumer choice processes. *The Journal of Consumer Research*, *25*(3), 187–217. DOI: 10.1086/209535

Bevanda, A., & Bijaškić, S. (2020). Strategic silence in crisis communication: When is it better to remain silent? *South Eastern European Journal of Communication*. DOI: 10.47960/2712-0457.2020.1.2.7

Bhattacharya, H. (2008). Interpretive Research. In Given, L. M. (Ed.), *The Sage Encyclopedia of Qualitative Research Methods* (pp. 464–467). Sage.

Bhattacherjee, A. (2001). Understanding information systems continuance: An expectation-confirmation model. *Management Information Systems Quarterly*, *25*(3), 351–370. DOI: 10.2307/3250921

Bini, L., & Fissi, S. (2025). The readability of corporate sustainability narratives in a crisis: An analysis of linguistic features using Coh-Metrix. *Social Responsibility Journal*, *21*(5), 1049–1065. DOI: 10.1108/SRJ-10-2023-0547

Bir, G., & Aksu, S. (2024). An examination of the utilization of artificial intelligence technologies by advertising agencies. *Yeni Medya*, *16*, 19–37. DOI: 10.55609/yenimedya.1434419

Biswas, M. (2025). AI for Emotional storytelling in advertisements. In Rabby, F., Ahmed, N., Sehmi, A., Bansal, R., & Pruthi, N. (Eds.), *Demystifying emotion AI, robotics AI, and sentiment analysis in customer relationship management* (pp. 229–246). IGI Global. DOI: 10.4018/979-8-3373-1867-7.ch011

Blackwell, R. D., Miniard, P. W., & Engel, J. F. (2006). *Consumer behavior* (10th ed.). Thomson South-Western.

Blanco-Ruiz, M., Sainz-de-Baranda, C., Gutiérrez-Martín, L., Romero-Perales, E., & López-Ongil, C. (2020). Emotion elicitation under audiovisual stimuli reception: Should artificial intelligence consider the gender perspective? *International Journal of Environmental Research and Public Health, 17*(22), 8534. DOI: 10.3390/ijerph17228534 PMID: 33213064

Bleier, A., & Eisenbeiss, M. (2015). Personalized online advertising effectiveness: The interplay of what, when, and where. *Marketing Science, 34*(5), 669–688. DOI: 10.1287/mksc.2015.0930

Bocock, R. (2005). *Tüketim* (Kutluk, İ., Trans.). Dost.

Boden, M. A. (1998). Creativity and artificial intelligence. *Artificial Intelligence, 103*(1-2), 347–356. DOI: 10.1016/S0004-3702(98)00055-1

Bolat, N. (2023). Dijitalleşeme İle Yapay Zekânin Reklam Alanina Katilimi. In Günay, M. A. (Ed.), *İletişim Bilimlerinde Yapay Zeka* (pp. 44–61). Eğitim.

Bolat, N. (2023). The participation of artificial intelligence in the advertising field with digitalization. [Dijitalleşme ile yapay zekânın reklam alanına katılımı] In Günay, M. A. (Ed.), *İletişim bilimlerinde yapay zekâ* (pp. 44–61). Eğitim Yayınevi.

Boltayevich, E. B., Adali, E., Mirdjonovna, K. S., Xolmo'minovna, A. O., Yuldashevna, X. Z., & Nizomaddin Uktamboy O'G'li, X. (2023). The problem of POS tagging and stemming for agglutinative languages (Turkish, Uyghur, Uzbek languages). In *Proceedings: 8th International Conference on Computer Science and Engineering (UBMK 2023)* (pp. 57-62). IEEE. https://doi.org/DOI: 10.1109/UBMK59864.2023.10286792

Bourne, C. (2024). AI hype, promotional culture, and affective capitalism. *AI and Ethics, 4*(3), 757–769. DOI: 10.1007/s43681-024-00483-w

Bowen, H. R. (1953). *Social responsibilities of the businessman*. Harper & Brothers.

Brandverse Awards. (2024). *Sürdürülebilirlik çalışmaları kazanlar*. https://www.brandverseawards.com/2024-kazananlar/

Braun, V., & Clarke, V. (2006). Using thematic analysis in psychology. *Qualitative Research in Psychology, 3*(2), 77–101. DOI: 10.1191/1478088706qp063oa

Britannica (11 February 2026). artificial intelligence (AI). https://www.britannica.com/technology/artificial-intelligence

Brodie, R. J., Hollebeek, L. D., Jurić, B., & Ilić, A. (2011). Customer engagement: Conceptual domain, fundamental propositions, and implications for research. *Journal of Service Research, 14*(3), 252–271. DOI: 10.1177/1094670511411703

Broom, G. M. (1986). *Public relations roles and systems theory: Functional and historicist causal models. Public Relations Interest Group*. International Communication Association.

Brundtland Raporu. (1987). *Report of the World Commission on environment and development: Our common future.* http://www.un-documents.net/our-common-future.pdf

Bruneau, T. J. (1973). Communicative silences: Forms and functions. *Journal of Communication, 23*(1), 17–46. DOI: 10.1111/j.1460-2466.1973.tb00929.x

Bülbül, R. (2004). *Halkla İlişkiler.* Nobel Yayın Dağıtım.

Burrow, E., & Gutentag, J. (2025). AI-generated versus human-generated: Creative content in advertising. *Pepperdine Journal of Communication Research, 13*(1), 8.

Çakın, Ö., & Bolat, N. (2018). Sosyal Medya Reklamcılığı ve Dijital Mecra Etkileşimleri. *Dijital Kültür ve İletişim.* In Çakmak, V., & Çavuş, S. (Eds.), *Literatürk.*

Çakır, S., & Çakın, Ö. (2022). Markaların Dijital İletişimde Emoji Kullanım Alışkanlıkları -Emoji Usage Habits of Brands in Digital Communications. *Middle Black Sea Journal of Communication Studies, 7*(1), 101–114.

Çalışkan Özsözgün, A. (2012). Sürdürülebilirlik raporlaması. *Journal of Accounting and Taxation Studies, 5*(1), 41–68.

Calp, E. (25 November 2022). Dijital ikiz nedir? Uygulama ve örnekleri. *Donanım Haber* https://www.donanimhaber.com/dijital-ikiz-nedir-uygulama-ve-ornekleri--156255

Canals, J., & Heukamp, F. (Eds.). (2020). *The future of management in an AI world: Redefining purpose and strategy in the fourth industrial revolution.* Springer. DOI: 10.1007/978-3-030-20680-2

Capital (2024). Modada teknoloji ve yapay zeka etkisi. https://www.capital.com.tr/haberler/tum-haberler/modada-teknoloji-ve-yapay-zeka-etkisi

Carroll, A. B. (1991). The pyramid of corporate social responsibility: Toward the moral management of organizational stakeholders. *Business Horizons, 34*(4), 39–48. DOI: 10.1016/0007-6813(91)90005-G

Carroll, A. B. (2016). Carroll's pyramid of CSR: Taking another look. *International Journal of Corporate Social Responsibility, 1*(3), 1–8. DOI: 10.1186/s40991-016-0004-6

Çeber, B. (2024). An applied research on the advertising sector in the context of artificial intelligence ethics [Yapay zekâ etiği bağlamında reklamcılık sektörü üzerine uygulamalı bir araştırma]. *Intermedia International E-Journal, 11*(20), 63–84.

Çeber, B. (2025). Yapay Zekâ "Sora" İle Üretilen Reklamların Mcluhan'ın "Araç Mesajdır" Perspektifinden İncelenmesi: Toys "R" Us Reklam Örneği. *Yeni Medya Elektronik Journal*, *9*(2), 171–200.

Çelik, M. (1995). Neologisms in contemporary Turkish. *La Trobe Working Papers in Linguistics, 8*(4), 101-119. https://www.latrobe.edu.au/linguistics/LaTrobePapersinLinguistics/Vol%2008/4Celik.pdf

Çelikten, E., & Çelikten, H. (2020). Elektronik kültür ortamında neolojizm. *Uluslararası Dil Edebiyat ve Kültür Araştırmaları Dergisi*, *3*(2), 183–205. DOI: 10.37999/udekad.785222

Cesur Kılıçaslan, S., Cesur, S., & Işık, T. (2012). Tüketim kültürü ve reklamların birey üzerinde doğurduğu zayıflık hissi. [Consumption culture and the feeling of weakness caused by advertisements] In Babaoğul, M., Şener, A., & Buğday, E. B. (Eds.), *Tüketici Yazıları III* (pp. 66–75). Tüketici-Pazar-Araştırma-Danışma Test ve Eğitim Merkezi.

Chappell, B. (2025, June 23). An AI video ad is making a splash: Is it the future of advertising? NPR. https://www.npr.org/2025/06/23/nx-s1-5432712/ai-video-ad-kalshi-advertising-nba-finals

Chateau, L., Arora, P., & Herman, L. (2025). Cross-cultural approaches to creative media content in the age of AI. *Media Culture & Society*, *47*(5), 01634437251328188. DOI: 10.1177/01634437251328188

Chatman, S. (1978). *Story and discourse: Narrative structure in fiction and film.* Cornell University Press.

Chaudhuri, A., & Holbrook, M. B. (2001). The chain of effects from brand trust and brand affect to brand performance: The role of brand loyalty. *Journal of Marketing*, *65*(2), 81–93. DOI: 10.1509/jmkg.65.2.81.18255

Chen, Y., Wang, H., Hill, S. R., & Li, B. (2024). Consumer attitudes toward AI-generated ads: Appeal types, self-efficacy, and AI's social role. *Journal of Business Research*, *185*, 114867. DOI: 10.1016/j.jbusres.2024.114867

Cheong, H. J., Baksh, S. M., & Ju, I. (2022). Spiral of silence in an algorithm-driven social media content environment: Conceptual framework and research propositions. *KOME – An International Journal of Pure Communication Inquiry, 10*(1), 32–46. DOI: 10.17646/KOME.75672.86

Chief, A. I. Officer (2025). "How Zalando Cut Fashion Content Costs by 90%". https://chiefaiofficer.com/zalando-ai-fashion-imagery-90-percent-cost-reduction/

Chinki, R. S., Yadav, M. P., & Sinha, N. (2025). Crafting narratives to influence consumers: A systematic review of storytelling marketing. *Asia-Pacific Journal of Business Administration.*

Chomsky, N. (1965). *Aspects of the theory of syntax.* MIT Press.

Chyrvonyi, O. (2025). The language of artificial intelligence: Linguistic and sociolinguistic analysis of AI-related neologisms (2016-2025). *Проблеми гуманітарних наук. Серія. Філологія, 61*, 175–180. DOI: 10.24919/2522-4565.2025.61.20

Çınar, B., & Karahan, L. (2009). Reklam dilinde kullanılan edebî sanatlar [Literary devices used in advertising language]. *Turkish Studies, 4*(8), 892–905.

Claeys, A. S., & Cauberghe, V. (2015). The role of a favorable pre-crisis reputation in protecting organizations during crises. *Public Relations Review, 41*(1), 64–72. DOI: 10.1016/j.pubrev.2014.10.013

Clark, B. H. (1999). Marketing performance measures: History and interrelationships. *Journal of Marketing Management, 15*(8), 711–732. DOI: 10.1362/026725799784772594

Coeckelbergh, M. (2010). Moral appearances: Emotions, robots, and human morality. *Ethics and Information Technology, 12*(3), 235–241. DOI: 10.1007/s10676-010-9221-y

Coeckelbergh, M. (2023). Narrative responsibility and artificial intelligence: How AI challenges human responsibility and sense-making. *AI & Society, 38*(6), 2437–2450. DOI: 10.1007/s00146-021-01375-x

Coombs, W. T. (2007). Protecting organization reputations during a crisis: The development and application of situational crisis communication theory. *Corporate Reputation Review, 10*(3), 163–176. DOI: 10.1057/palgrave.crr.1550049

Çorbacıoğlu Gönezer, E. (2014). *L'analyse figurative et affective des affiches publicitaires* [Figurative and affective analysis of advertising posters] [Doctoral dissertation, Dokuz Eylül University].

Coşkun, A. (2007). Yapay Zekâ Optimizasyon Teknikleri: Literatür Değerlendirmesi. *Fırat Üniversitesi Doğu Anadolu Bölgesi Araştırmaları Journal, 5*(2), 142–146.

Coşkuner, A. (2023). Sinemanın Denetimsiz Teknolojiyle Sınavı: Yapay Zeka'nın Film Endüstrisine Etkisi. *Türkiye Film Araştırmaları Journal, 3*(1), 1. Advance online publication. DOI: 10.59280/film.1284277

Coşkun, F., & Gülleroğlu, H. D. (2021). The development of artificial intelligence in history and its use in education [Yapay zekânın tarih içindeki gelişimi ve eğitimde kullanılması] [JFES]. *Ankara University Journal of Faculty of Educational Sciences, 54*(3), 947–966.

Crane, D. (2003). *Moda ve Gündemleri. Giyimde Sınıf, Cinsiyet ve Kimlik* (Çelik, Ö., Trans.). Ayrıntı.

Crespo, C. F., Ferreira, A. G., & Cardoso, R. M. (2023). The influence of storytelling on the consumer–brand relationship experience. *Journal of Marketing Analytics, 11*(1), 41–56. DOI: 10.1057/s41270-021-00149-0

Creswell, J. W., & Creswell, J. D. (2018). Research design qualitative, quantitative, and mixed methods approaches. *Sage (Atlanta, Ga.).*

Crilly, D., Zollo, M., & Hansen, M. T. (2022). The grammar of decoupling: A cognitive-linguistic perspective on firms' sustainability claims and stakeholders' interpretation. *Academy of Management Journal, 59*(2), 705–729. DOI: 10.5465/amj.2015.0171

Cryptonomist (2025, Mayıs). "Zalando leverages AI to revolutionize marketing and reduce costs by 90%". https://www.reuters.com/business/media-telecom/zalando-uses-ai-speed-up-marketing-campaigns-cut-costs-2025-05-07/

Cui, J. (2025). The Impact of Digital Media Technology on Digital Twins: The Moderating Role of Personalized Advertising. *Accounting. Marketing and Organization, 1*(1), 1–9. DOI: 10.71204/86fvy772

Da Silva, B., & Cé, F. (2025). *The effects of greenwashing on purchasing intention and perceived quality by the consumer*. ReMark – Revista Brasileira de Marketing., DOI: 10.5585/2025.26514

Daruwala, N. A. (2025). How multimodal narrative and visual representations of human-like service robots shape attitudes and social connection. *Frontiers in Robotics and AI, 12*, 1568146. DOI: 10.3389/frobt.2025.1568146 PMID: 40475003

Dastin, J. (2018, October 11). Amazon Scraps Secret AI Recruiting Tool That Showed Bias Against Women. *Reuters*. https://www.reuters.com/article/world/insight-amazon-scraps-secret-ai-recruiting-tool-that-showed-bias-against-women-idUSKCN1MK0AG

Datta, H., Ailawadi, K. L., & van Heerde, H. J. (2017). How Well Does Consumer-Based Brand Equity Align with Sales-Based Brand Equity and Marketing-Mix Response? *Journal of Marketing, 81*(3), 1–20. DOI: 10.1509/jm.15.0340

Davenport, T. H., Guha, A., Grewal, D., & Bressgott, T. (2020). How artificial intelligence will change the future of marketing. *Journal of the Academy of Marketing Science, 48*(1), 24–42. DOI: 10.1007/s11747-019-00696-0

Davis, K. (1960). Can businesses afford to ignore social responsibilities? *California Management Review, 2*(3), 70–76. DOI: 10.2307/41166246

Delmas, M. A., & Burbano, V. C. (2011). The drivers of greenwashing. *California Management Review, 54*(1), 64–87. DOI: 10.1525/cmr.2011.54.1.64

Demir, C. M. (2024). Semiotic analysis of cultural codes in the Solaris film poster [Solaris film afişinde yer alan kültürel kodların göstergebilimsel analizi]. *İstanbul Gelişim Üniversitesi Sosyal Bilimler Dergisi*, 11(1), 340–351.

Demir, C. M. (2025b). *Mise-en-abyme as a pattern tool in the literary communication process: An examination of Robbe-Grillet, Calvino, and Borges narratives* [Yazınsal iletişim sürecinde bir örüntü aracı olarak mise-en-abyme: Robbe-Grillet, Calvino ve Borges anlatıları üzerine bir inceleme] (Master's thesis). Ondokuz Mayıs University.

Demir, M, Kaplan, M. (2025) Yapay Zekâ Araçlarının Sinematik Anlatıda Kullanımı. *İNİF E- Journal*, 10(2), pp. 509-540.

Demir, M. Ö. (2009). Tüketici İmajı ve Marka İmajı Uyumunun Marka Sadakati Üzerine Etkisi. Doktora Tezi. Antalya: Akdeniz Üniversitesi Sosyal Bilimler Enstitüsü.

Demir, C. M. (2025a). Çerçici: Experiential narrative, archetypes, and layers of memory [Çerçici: Deneyimsel anlatı, arketipler ve belleğin katmanları]. *UMAY Sanat ve Sosyal Bilimler Dergisi, 3*(2), 79–86.

Demir, Y. (2025). Advertising posters and the use of images as a brand-consumer touchpoint: The Volkswagen case. [Bir marka–tüketici temas noktası olarak reklam afişleri ve imge kullanımı: Volkswagen örneği] In Erdem, M. N., & Mayadağlı, C. (Eds.), *Marka iletişimi: Tüm boyutlarıyla marka ve tüketici etkileşimi* (pp. 325–342). Palet Yayınları.

Demsar, V., Ferraro, C., Sands, S., & Kohn, A. (2025). Harmony or discord? The intersection of generative AI and human creativity in advertising. *Journal of Advertising Research, 65*(2), 150–166. DOI: 10.1080/00218499.2025.2464305

Dhapte, A. (13 July, 2025). Digital Twin Market. *Market Research Future*. https://www.marketresearchfuture.com/reports/digital-twin-market-4504

Di Furia, M., Nicoli, N., Akyar, Ö. Y., & Rossi, M. (2022, January). Storytelling practice in sectors of education, psychology, communication, marketing: A narrative review. In *International Conference on Psychology, Learning, Technology* (pp. 41-62). Cham: Springer International Publishing. DOI: 10.1007/978-3-031-15845-2_3

Dias, L., Bagatini, F., & Perin, M. (2025). *Green "under-communication": A systematic literature review on greenhushing*. ReMark – Revista Brasileira de Marketing.

Dimitrieska, S., Stankovska, A., & Efremova, T. (2018). Artificial intelligence and marketing. *Entrepreneurship*, *6*(2), 298–304.

Dimitrieska, S., Stankovska, A., & Efremova, T. (2018). Artificial Intelligence and Marketing. *Entrepreneurship*, *6*(2), 298–304.

Dodds, W. B., Monroe, K. B., & Grewal, D. (1991). Effects of price, brand, and store information on buyers' product evaluations. *JMR, Journal of Marketing Research*, *28*(3), 307–319. DOI: 10.1177/002224379102800305

Dogra, P., & Dogra, A. K. (2025). Interweaving narratives: The role of AI in enhancing consumer engagement through storytelling. In *Decoding Consumer Behavior Using the Insight Equation and AI Marketing* (pp. 275–300). IGI Global Scientific Publishing.

Dogra, P., & Dogra, A. K. (2025). Interweaving narratives: The role of AI in enhancing consumer engagement through storytelling. In Jain, V., & Mitra, A. (Eds.), *Decoding consumer behavior using the insight equation and AI marketing* (pp. 275–300). IGI Global.

Dokuz8 Haber (23 January 2026). YouTube içerik üreticileri için yapay zeka tabanlı "dijital ikiz" özelliğini duyurdu https://www.dokuz8haber.net/youtube-icerik-ureticileri-icin-yapay-zeka-tabanli-dijital-ikiz-ozelligini-duyurdu

Dolu, Z. T., & Marangoz, M. (2023). Yapay Zekâ Uygulamalarının Tüketicilerin Satın Alma Niyeti Üzerine Etkisi: Büyük Hazine Filmi Üzerine Bir Analiz. *Pamukkale Üniversitesi İşletme Araştırmaları Dergisi*, *10*(2), 525–549. DOI: 10.47097/piar.1271887

Dowling, G. R. (2006). Communicating corporate reputation through stories. *California Management Review*, *49*(1), 82–100. DOI: 10.2307/41166372

Down, A. (2025, December 4). Google's AI Nano Banana Pro Accused of Generating Racialised 'White Saviour' Visuals. *The Guardian*. https://www.theguardian.com/technology/2025/dec/04/google-ai-nano-banana-pro-racialised-white-saviour-images

Dozier, D. M. ve Ehling, W.P. (1992). Evaluation of public relations programs: What the literature tells us about their effects, In J.E. Grunig (Ed.), *Excellence in public relations and communication management* (pp. 159–183). Lawrence and Erlbaum Associates.

Duncan, T. (2002). *IMC using advertising and promotion to build brands.* McGraw-Hill.

Durmaz, A. (1999). *Dijital Televizyonun Temelleri.* Anadolu Üniversitesi Eğitim Sağlık ve Bilimsel Araştırma Çalışmaları Vakfı.

Durna, T. (2011). Neoliberalizmin bir hegemonya aracı olarak kurumsal sosyal sorumluluk (KSS) ve çokuluslu şirketlerin 'hayat'tan eksilttikleri. In Yıldırım Becerikli, S. (Ed.), *Halkla ilişkiler ve reklamın anatomisi: eleştirel bir kavrayış içinde* (pp. 76–102). Ütopya.

Du, S., Bhattacharya, C. B., & Sen, S. (2010). Maximizing business returns to corporate social responsibility (CSR): The role of CSR communication. *International Journal of Management Reviews, 12*(1), 8–19. DOI: 10.1111/j.1468-2370.2009.00276.x

Du, S., & Xie, C. (2021). Paradoxes of artificial intelligence in consumer markets: Ethical challenges and opportunities. *Journal of Business Research, 129*, 961–974. DOI: 10.1016/j.jbusres.2020.08.024

Dush, L. (2013). The ethical complexities of sponsored digital storytelling. *International Journal of Cultural Studies, 16*(6), 627–640. DOI: 10.1177/1367877912459142

Eisend, M., Muldrow, A. F., & Rosengren, S. (2023). Diversity and inclusion in advertising research. *International Journal of Advertising, 42*(1), 52–59. DOI: 10.1080/02650487.2022.2122252

Elden, M. (2018). *Reklam ve reklamcılık.* Say Yayınları.

Elden, M. (2018). *Reklam yazarlığı.* İletişim.

Elden, M., Ulukök, Ö., & Yeygel, S. (2015). *Şimdi Reklamlar....* İletişim Yayınları.

Elhady, A. M., & Shohieb, S. (2025). AI-driven sustainable finance: Computational tools, ESG metrics, and global implementation. *Future Business Journal, 11*(1), 209. DOI: 10.1186/s43093-025-00610-x

Engin, E., & Eker Akgöz, B. (2013). Sürdürülebilir kalkınma ve kurumsal sürdürülebilirlik çerçevesinde kurumsal sosyal sorumluluk kavramının değerlendirilmesi. *Selçuk İletişim, 8*(1), 85–94.

Erdem, B. (2022). Yapay Zekanın Pazarlamaya Etkisi, *Sosyal Bilimlerde Disiplinlerarası Akademik Çalışmalar*. In Terzioğlu, D., & Korkmaz, S. S. (Eds.), *Eğitim.*

Erdem, M., & Çakın, Ö. (2018). *Anlatısal reklamda negatif marka yerleştirme: anti-reklamoyunlar. Uluslararası İletişimde Yeni Yönelimler Konferansı Eğlence ve Ürün Yerleştirme*. İstanbul Ticaret Üniversitesi.

Ertel, W. (2025). *Introduction to artificial intelligence*. Springer. DOI: 10.1007/978-3-658-43102-0

Escalas, J. E. (2004). Narrative processing: Building consumer connections to brands. *Journal of Consumer Psychology, 14*(1-2), 168–180. DOI: 10.1207/s15327663jcp1401&2_19

Escalas, J. E., & Bettman, J. R. (2005). Self-construal, reference groups, and brand meaning. *The Journal of Consumer Research, 32*(3), 378–389. DOI: 10.1086/497549

Escalas, J. E., & Stern, B. B. (2003). Sympathy and empathy: Emotional responses to advertising dramas. *The Journal of Consumer Research, 29*(4), 566–578. DOI: 10.1086/346251

EuropaWire. (2025, Mayıs). "Zalando's Use of AI and Digital Twins Enhances Speed and Flexibility". https://news.europawire.eu/press-releases-tagged-with/digital-technology/

European Parliament & Council of the European Union. (2024). *Regulation (EU) 2024/1689 laying down harmonised rules on artificial intelligence (Artificial Intelligence Act)*. Official Journal of the European Union. https://eur-lex.europa.eu/eli/reg/2024/1689/oj

Farooq, N., Hashmat, S., & Hashim, A. (2025). AI in Advertising: Ethical Risks, Consumer Protection, and Policy Implications. *Annual Methodological Archive Research Review, 3*(6), 1–18. DOI: 10.63075/nb02bq32

Farris, P. W., Bendle, N. T., Pfeifer, P. E., & Reibstein, D. J. (2010). *Marketing metrics: The definitive guide to measuring marketing performance* (2nd ed.). Pearson Education.

Farris, P. W., Bendle, N., Pfeifer, P., & Reibstein, D. (2021). *Marketing metrics: The manager's guide to measuring marketing performance*. FT Press.

Featherstone, M. (2005). *Postmodernizm ve Tüketim Kültürü* (Küçük, M., Trans.). Ayrıntı.

Feix, A., & Philippe, D. (2020). Unpacking the narrative decontestation of CSR: Aspiration for change or defense of the status quo? *Business & Society, 59*(1), 129–174. DOI: 10.1177/0007650318816434

Feng, Y. (2025). The AI Genie in the Bottle: Charting AI evolution and aversion in advertising. *Journal of Interactive Advertising, 25*(4), 1–16. DOI: 10.1080/15252019.2025.2537019

Fernando, S., & Lawrence, S. (2014). A theoretical framework for CSR practices: Integrating legitimacy theory, stakeholder theory and institutional theory. *Journal of Theoretical Accounting Research, 9*(1), 149–178.

Fjelland, R. (2020). Why general artificial intelligence will not be realized. *Humanities & Social Sciences Communications, 7*(10), 1–9. DOI: 10.1057/s41599-020-0494-4

Floridi, L. (2023). *The ethics of artificial intelligence: Principles, challenges, and opportunities*. Oxford University Press., DOI: 10.1093/oso/9780198883098.001.0001

Floridi, L., Cowls, J., Beltrametti, M., Chatila, R., Chazerand, P., Dignum, V., Luetge, C., Madelin, R., Pagallo, U., Rossi, F., Schafer, B., Valcke, P., & Vayena, E. (2018). AI4People—An ethical framework for a good AI society: Opportunities, risks, principles, and recommendations. *Minds and Machines, 28*(4), 689–707. DOI: 10.1007/s11023-018-9482-5 PMID: 30930541

Fludernik, M. (1996). *Towards a 'Natural' Narratology*. Routledge. DOI: 10.1515/jlse.1996.25.2.97

Fog, K., Budtz, C., & Yakaboylu, B. (2005). *Storytelling: Branding in practice*. Springer.

Font, X., Elgammal, I., & Lamond, I. (2017). Greenhushing: The deliberate under-communicating of sustainability practices by tourism businesses. *Journal of Sustainable Tourism, 25*(7), 1007–1023. DOI: 10.1080/09669582.2016.1158829

Foucault, M. (1977). *Discipline and punish: The birth of the prison* (Sheridan, A., Trans.). Pantheon Books.

Fournier, S. (1998). Consumers and their brands: Developing relationship theory in consumer research. *The Journal of Consumer Research, 24*(4), 343–373. DOI: 10.1086/209515

Freeman, R. E. (1984). *Strategic management: A stakeholder approach*. Pitman., DOI: 10.1017/CBO9781139192675

Futureweek (2025, Mayıs). "Zalando Creates AI Models for Ad Campaigns". https://www.fourmeta.co.uk/blog/fashion-ads-you-didnt-know-were-ai-made

Ganesh, A. (2023). The impact of social media on consumer behavior: An AI-enhanced approach to marketing strategies. Available at *SSRN* 4985407.

Garg, V., Bohara, S., & Srivastav, A. (2025). AI-driven sustainability marketing transforming consumers' perception toward eco-friendly brands. *Discover Sustainability*, *6*(1), 984. DOI: 10.1007/s43621-025-01934-y

Genette, G. (2020). *Anlatının söylemi: Yöntem hakkında bir deneme* (Aydar, F. B., Trans.). Ayrıntı.

Genette, G. (2020). *Narrative discourse: An essay in method* [Anlatının söylemi yöntem hakkında bir deneme]. (Aydar, F. B., Trans.). Ayrıntı Yayınları.

Georgiou, G. (2025). Can AI mimic the human ability to define neologisms? *International Journal of Speech Technology*, *28*(4), 773–782. DOI: 10.1007/s10772-025-10216-x

Gil de Zúñiga, H., Gonayes, H., & Duroyote, T. (2024). A scholarly definition of artificial intelligence (AI): Advancing AI as a conceptual framework in communication research. *Political Communication*, *41*(2), 317–334. DOI: 10.1080/10584609.2023.2290497

Gillespie, T. (2014). The relevance of algorithms. *Media technologies. Essays on Communication, Materiality, and Society*, *167*, 167.

Gkikas, D. C., & Theodoridis, P. K. (2021). AI in consumer behavior. In Advances in Artificial Intelligence-Based Technologies: Selected Papers in Honour of Professor Nikolaos G. Bourbakis—Vol. 1 (pp. 147–176). Springer International Publishing.

Gladwin, T. N., Kennelly, J. J., & Krause, T. S. (1995). Shifting paradigms for sustainable development: Implications for management theory and research. *Academy of Management Review*, *20*(4), 874–907. DOI: 10.2307/258959

Global Reporting Initiative. (2021). *GRI Standards.* https://www.globalreporting.org (Accessed: 8 January 2025)

Gölgeli, K. (2025). Advertising design with artificial intelligence: A study for advertisers [Yapay zekâ ile reklam tasarımı: Reklamcılara yönelik bir araştırma]. *İnsan ve Toplum Bilimleri Araştırmaları Dergisi*, 14(1), 319–336.

Golob, U., Podnar, K., & Zabkar, V. (2023). Sustainability communication. *International Journal of Advertising*, *42*(1), 42–51. DOI: 10.1080/02650487.2022.2144035

Goodman, R. (2018, October 12). Why Amazon's Automated Hiring Tool Discriminated Against Women. *American Civil Liberties Union*. https://www.aclu.org/news/womens-rights/why-amazons-automated-hiring-tool-discriminated-against

Gören, G. (2023, March 6). Danish tourism promotion film signed by ChatGPT. Bigumigu. https://bigumigu.com/haber/danimarkadan-chatgpt-imzali-turizm-tanitim-filmi/

Gören, G. (2024). Coca-Cola launches AI platform for digital artists. Bigumigu. https://bigumigu.com/haber/coca-coladan-dijital-sanatcilar-icin-yapay-zeka-platformu/

Gorichanaz, T. (2024). AI technologies, identity theft and data selves. In Elliott, A. (Ed.), *The De Gruyter handbook of artificial intelligence, identity and technology studies* (pp. 181–196). De Gruyter. DOI: 10.1515/9783110721751-010

Göttgens, I., & Oertelt-Prigione, S. (2021). The application of human-centred design approaches in health research and innovation: A narrative review of current practices. *JMIR mHealth and uHealth*, *9*(12), e28102. DOI: 10.2196/28102 PMID: 34874893

Green, M. C., & Brock, T. C. (2000). The role of transportation in the persuasiveness of public narratives. *Journal of Personality and Social Psychology*, *79*(5), 701–721. DOI: 10.1037/0022-3514.79.5.701 PMID: 11079236

Greenpeace, U. K. (2023). *Unilever's greenwashing and vulnerability to brand damage: Briefing for investors.* https://www.greenpeace.org.uk/resources/unilever-greenwash-investor-briefing/

Grilli, L., & Pedota, M. (2024). Creativity and artificial intelligence: A multilevel perspective. *Creativity and Innovation Management*, *33*(2), 234–247. DOI: 10.1111/caim.12580

Grunig, J. E., & Hunt, T. (1984). *Managing public relations.* Holt, Rinehart & Winston.

Grzybowski, A., Pawlikowska–Łagód, K., & Lambert, W. C. (2024). A history of artificial intelligence. *Clinics in Dermatology*, *42*(3), 221–229. DOI: 10.1016/j.clindermatol.2023.12.016 PMID: 38185196

Gülbaşı, A. (2025). Artificial intelligence in marketing: Next generation strategies and applications. *Uluslararası Yönetim Akademisi Dergisi*, *8*(3), 786–801. DOI: 10.33712/mana.1624405

Gündüzyeli, B. (2024). Artificial intelligence in digital marketing within the framework of sustainable management. *Sustainability (Basel)*, *16*(23), 10511. DOI: 10.3390/su162310511

Guo, R., & Jiang, Z. (2024). Optimal dynamic advertising policy considering consumer ad fatigue. *Decision Support Systems*, *187*, 114323. DOI: 10.1016/j.dss.2024.114323

Guo, R., Tao, L., Li, C., & Wang, T. (2017). A path analysis of greenwashing in a trust crisis among Chinese energy companies. The role of brand legitimacy and brand loyalty. *Journal of Business Ethics, 140*(3), 523–536. DOI: 10.1007/s10551-015-2672-7

Gupta, S., & Bansal, P. (2023). AI-driven emotional recognition in digital ads: A novel approach to consumer engagement. *Journal of Marketing & Supply Chain Management, 2*(131), 2–7. DOI: 10.47363/JMSCM/2023(2)131

Gutierrez, E., Karwowski, W., Fiok, K., Davahli, M. R., Liciaga, T., & Ahram, T. (2021). Analysis of human behavior by mining textual data: Current research topics and analytical techniques. *Symmetry, 13*(7), 1276. DOI: 10.3390/sym13071276

Hadero, H. (2023, February 15). U.S. States Say TikTok Harms Children and Teenagers, Sues Company. *AP News.* https://apnews.com/article/tiktok-kids-teens-use-addiction-03a2d63a21bc5c1c62910628deff0521

Hakanurmi, S. (2017). Learning to work through narratives: Identity and meaning-making during digital storytelling. In *Digital Storytelling in Higher Education: International Perspectives* (pp. 149–166). Springer International Publishing. DOI: 10.1007/978-3-319-51058-3_11

Halaçoğlu, B. N. (2021). Makinimanın Gelişimi: Film Yapımının Sanal Prodüksiyona Dönüşümü. *Dumlupınar Üniversitesi Sosyal Bilimler Dergisi*, (68), 73–89. DOI: 10.51290/dpusbe.823660

Han, B. C. (2018). *Şeffaflık Toplumu* (Barışcan, H., Trans.). Metis.

Han, B. C. (2020). *Psikopolitika: neoliberalizm ve yeni iktidar teknikleri, çev. H. Barışcan.* Metis Yayınları.

Han, B. C. (2024). *Anlatının Krizi (M. Erşen, Çev.).* Ketebe Yayınları.

Hanna, S., & Rowley, J. (2013). A practitioner-led strategic place brand-management model. *Journal of Marketing Management, 29*(15-16), 1782–1815. DOI: 10.1080/0267257X.2013.800901

Haymond, S., & McCudden, C. (2021). Rise of the machines: Artificial intelligence and the clinical laboratory. *The Journal of Applied Laboratory Medicine, 6*(6), 1640–1654. DOI: 10.1093/jalm/jfab075 PMID: 34379752

He, H., Harris, L. C., Wang, W., & Haider, K. (2016). Brand identity and online self-customisation usefulness perception. *Journal of Marketing Management, 32*(13-14), 1308–1332. DOI: 10.1080/0267257X.2016.1170720

Heidegger, M. (1998). *The question concerning technology and other essays* [Teknik ve dönüş]. (Aça, N., Trans.). Bilim ve Sanat Yayınları.

Heinz. (2023). Heinz: A.I. Ketchup [Online campaign description]. Ads of the World. https://campaignsoftheworld.com/digital-campaigns/hcinz-a-i-kctchup/

Heitmayer, M. (2025). The second wave of attention economics: Attention as a universal symbolic currency on social media and beyond. *Interacting with Computers, 37*(1), 18–29. DOI: 10.1093/iwc/iwae035

Hermann, E. (2022). Leveraging artificial intelligence in marketing for social good—An ethical perspective. *Journal of Business Ethics, 179*(1), 43–61. DOI: 10.1007/s10551-021-04843-y PMID: 34054170

Herskovitz, S., & Crystal, M. (2010). The essential brand persona: Storytelling and branding. *The Journal of Business Strategy, 31*(3), 21–28. DOI: 10.1108/02756661011036673

Hewitt, J., Geirhos, R., & Kim, B. (2025). We can't understand AI using our existing vocabulary. *arXiv*. https://arxiv.org/abs/2502.07586

Hidalgo Downing, L. (2000). Text world creation in advertising discourse. *Revista Alicantina de Estudios Ingleses, 13*(13), 67–88. DOI: 10.14198/raei.2000.13.06

Himmetoğlu, A. (2023). Kurumsal sürdürülebilirlik ve kurumsal sosyal sorumluluk: Bir bibliyometrik analiz çalışması. *Erciyes İletişim Dergisi, 10*(2), 891–911. DOI: 10.17680/erciyesiletisim.1268583

Holding, K. (2023). Koç Holding. *Sustainability Report, 2023*, •••. Retrieved January 3, 2025, from https://www.koc.com.tr/en/sustainability/reports

Hollebeek, L. D., Glynn, M. S., & Brodie, R. J. (2014). Consumer brand engagement in social media: Conceptualization, scale development and validation. *Journal of Interactive Marketing, 28*(2), 149–165. DOI: 10.1016/j.intmar.2013.12.002

Holt, D. B. (2002). Why do brands cause trouble? A dialectical theory of consumer culture and branding. *The Journal of Consumer Research, 29*(1), 70–90. DOI: 10.1086/339922

Hong, J., Yang, J., Wooldridge, B. R., & Bhappu, A. D. (2022). Sharing consumers' brand storytelling: Influence of consumers' storytelling on brand attitude via emotions and cognitions. *Journal of Product and Brand Management, 31*(2), 265–278. DOI: 10.1108/JPBM-07-2019-2485

Hornik, J., & Rachamim, M. (2025). Leveraging AI-Enabled Digital Twins for Smart Advertising Design and Testing. *Journal of Advertising and Public Relations*, *5*(1), 5–26. DOI: 10.22259/2639-1953.0501002

Hudders, L., Reıjmersdal, E. A. V., & Poels, K. (2019). Digital Advertising and Consumer Empowerment. *Journal Of Psychosocial Research On Cyberspace*, *13*(2), 1–10.

Hunt, K. M. (2023). Could artificial intelligence win the next Weather Photographer of the Year competition? *Weather*, *78*(4), 108–112. DOI: 10.1002/wea.4348

IKEA. (2025). *IKEA official website*. https://www.ikea.com (Accessed: 3 January 2025)

Im, J., & Chang, B. (2025, November). Human–AI co-creativity in storytelling: A scoping review of literature, education, media, and interactive systems. In *International Conference on Interactive Digital Storytelling* (pp. 396-406). Cham: Springer Nature Switzerland.

Iniesta, M. B., & López, D. (2025). A systematic literature review on conversational AI's influence in consumer behavior. In *Decision Science Alliance International Summer Conference* (pp. 27–39). Springer. DOI: 10.1007/978-3-031-78238-1_3

Jahn, M. (2020). *Anlatıbilim anlatı teorisi el kitabı*. Dergah.

Jain, P., Lal, R., & Raina, G. S. (2023). Portrayal of characters in a Hindi film and audience reaction: A discourse analysis. *IIS University Journal of Arts*, *12*(1&2), 362–377.

Jain, V., Wadhwani, K., & Eastman, J. K. (2024). Artificial intelligence consumer behavior: A hybrid review and research agenda. *Journal of Consumer Behaviour*, *23*(2), 676–697. DOI: 10.1002/cb.2233

Jarek, K., & Mazurek, G. (2019). Marketing and artificial intelligence. *Central European Business Review*, *8*(2).

Järvinen, J., & Karjaluoto, H. (2015). The use of web analytics for digital marketing performance measurement. *Industrial Marketing Management*, *50*, 117–127. DOI: 10.1016/j.indmarman.2015.04.009

Jaworski, A. (1993). The power of silence: Social and pragmatic perspectives. *Sage (Atlanta, Ga.)*. Advance online publication. DOI: 10.4135/9781483325460

Jo, M., Cha, J., & Kim, J. (2022). The effects of tourism storytelling on tourism destination brand value, lovemarks and relationship strength in South Korea. *Sustainability (Basel)*, *14*(24), 16495. DOI: 10.3390/su142416495

Kabashkin, I., Zervina, O., & Misnevs, B. (2025). AI narrative modeling: How machines' intelligence reproduces archetypal storytelling. *Information (Basel), 16*(4), 319. DOI: 10.3390/info16040319

Kadıbeşegil, S. (2008). *Şimdi stratejik iletişim zamanı. Kurumsal yönetim, kurumsal itibar, kurumsal iletişim hakkında bilmeniz gereken her şey!* Mediacat.

Kakatkar, C., & Spann, M. (2019). Marketing analytics using anonymized and fragmented tracking data. *International Journal of Research in Marketing, 36*(1), 117–136. DOI: 10.1016/j.ijresmar.2018.10.001

Kalum. (2025, October 2). *13 Brands Using AI for Social Media Marketing, Advertising & Content Creation.* Metricool. https://metricool.com/brands-using-ai-social-media-marketing/?utm_source=chatgpt.com

Kang, J. A., Hong, S., & Hubbard, G. T. (2020). The role of storytelling in advertising: Consumer emotion, narrative engagement level, and word-of-mouth intention. *Journal of Consumer Behaviour, 19*(1), 47–56. DOI: 10.1002/cb.1793

Kantola, A. (2016). Cleaning rotten politics, selling exclusive liaisons: Public relations consultants as storytelling professionals between markets and politics. *Public Relations Inquiry, 5*(1), 33–52. DOI: 10.1177/2046147X15625713

Kaplan, A., & Haenlein, M. (2019). Siri, Siri, in my hand: Who's the fairest in the land? On the interpretations, illustrations, and implications of artificial intelligence. *Business Horizons, 62*(1), 15–25. DOI: 10.1016/j.bushor.2018.08.004

Kaponis, A., Maragoudakis, M., & Sofianos, K. C. (2025). Enhancing user experiences in digital marketing through machine learning: Cases, trends, and challenges. *Computers, 14*(6), 211. DOI: 10.3390/computers14060211

Kaput, M. (2024). 20 Ways AI Could Transform PR and Communications. https://www.marketingaiinstitute.com/blog/how-ai-could-transform-pr-and-communications

Karabulut, B. (2022). Yapay Zeka Bağlamında Yaratıcılık ve Görsel Tasarımın Geleceği.

Karacan, E. (2021). *Dijital İkiz Teknolojisi ve Pazarlama Uygulamaları.* İstanbul Teknoloji Press.

Karadağ, B. M., & Burnaz, S. (2021). Türkçede işlek bir metaforik neoloji öbeği: X+kafası [A productive metaphorical neology pattern in Turkish: X+kafası]. *Dilbilim Dergisi, 36*, 83–104. DOI: 10.26650/jol.2021.849022

Karaman, A. (1996). *Sürdürülebilir turizm planlaması için ekolojik bir çerçeve, sürdürülebilir turizm; turizm planlamasına ekolojik yaklaşım. 19. Dünya Şehircilik Günü Kolokyumu*. Mimar Sinan Üniversitesi.

Kartal, B. (2025, November 03). *Google, Tamamen Yapay Zeka ile Oluşturulan İlk Reklam Filmini Yayınladı [Video].* Webtekno. https://www.webtekno.com/google-yapay-zeka-ilk-reklam-filmi-video-h206121.html

Kátai, Z., Osztián, P. R., & Iclanzan, D. (2024). Enacting algorithms: Evolution of the algorythmics storytelling. *Education and Information Technologies, 29*(14), 19197–19228. DOI: 10.1007/s10639-024-12617-y

Keleş, A., Keleş, A., & Akçetin, E. (2017). Pazarlama Alanında Yapay Zekâ Kullanım Potansiyeli ve Akıllı Karar Destek Sistemleri. *Electronic Turkish Studies, 12*(11), 109–124. DOI: 10.7827/TurkishStudies.12022

Keller, K. L. (1993). Conceptualizing, measuring, and managing customer-based brand equity. *Journal of Marketing, 57*(1), 1–22. DOI: 10.1177/002224299305700101

Kelly, C. (2024, May 9). Starburst taps generative AI for "Different Every Time" campaign assets. Marketing Dive. https://www.marketingdive.com/news/starburst-generative-ai-campaign-assets-gen-z/715524/

Kelly, A. (2025). Nostos in three moves or five stages: A story pattern in early Greek epos. *Yearbook of Ancient Greek Epic Online, 9*(1), 1–42.

Kerr, G., & Richards, J. (2021). Redefining advertising in research and practice. *International Journal of Advertising, 40*(2), 175–198. DOI: 10.1080/02650487.2020.1769407

Khan, W. (2024). *Corporate narratives in CSR communication? A multimodal analysis of CSR communication of mission-oriented companies on online platforms* [Master's Dissertation].

Khan, M. T., Humayun, A. A., & Sajjad, M. (2015). Customer loyalty-attitudinal and behavioral aspects (A review). *International Journal of Information, Business and Management, 7*(2), 163.

Kietzmann, J., Paschen, J., & Treen, E. (2018). Artificial intelligence in advertising: How marketers can leverage artificial intelligence along the consumer journey. *Journal of Advertising Research, 58*(3), 263–267. DOI: 10.2501/JAR-2018-035

Kim, W. (2022). *Distributional corpus analysis of Korean neologisms using artificial intelligence* [Doctoral dissertation, University of Georgia].

Kim, E., Ratneshwar, S., & Thorson, E. (2017). Why narrative ads work: An integrated process explanation. *Journal of Advertising, 46*(2), 283–296. DOI: 10.1080/00913367.2016.1268984

Kırçıl, A. G., & Karagüler, T. (2008). *Dijital Çağda Iletişime Yeni Yaklaşım: Online Gazetecilik, Akademik Bilişim Konferansı*. Çukurova Universty.

Kirkpatrick, D., & Adams, P. (2017, December 7). ANA Declares AI The Marketing Word of the Year. MarketingDive. https://www.marketingdive.com/news/ana-declares-ai-the-marketing-word-of-the-year/512484/

Kloba, L., & Kloba, V. (2025). Implementation of artificial intelligence in marketing strategy of financial services. *Green. Blue and Digital Economy Journal, 6*(2), 1–7. DOI: 10.30525/2661-5169/2025-2-1

Kocaman, Ş. (2021). Grafik Tasarım Endüstrisinde Yapay Zekâ. *Journal of Social and Humanities Sciences Research, 8*(77), 3000–3016.

Kolaç, E. (2025). Yapay zekâ tabanlı dil modellerinde anlamlandırma sorunu: Geleneksel sözlük tanımlarının yeniden değerlendirilmesi [Meaning-making problem in AI-based language models: Re-evaluating traditional dictionary definitions]. *Disiplinler Arası Dil Araştırmaları, 1*(1), 307–358. DOI: 10.48147/dada.1739041

König, W. (1994). Dilbilim ve yapay zekâ [Linguistics and artificial intelligence]. *Dilbilim Araştırmaları Dergisi, 5*, 233–236.

Korkmaz, Z. (1992). *Dil bilgisi terimleri sözlüğü*. Türk Dil Kurumu Yayınları.

Kotler, P. (1991). *Marketing Management: Analysis, Planning, Implementation and Control* (7th ed.). Prentice-Hall Inc.

Kotler, P. (1997). *Marketing Management* (9th ed.). Prentice Hall.

Kotler, P., Kartajaya, H., & Setiawan, I. (2010). *Marketing 3.0: From products to customers to the human spirit*. John Wiley & Sons. DOI: 10.1002/9781118257883

Kotler, P., Kartajaya, H., & Setiawan, I. (2016). *Marketing 4.0: Moving from traditional to digital*. John Wiley & Sons.

Kotler, P., & Keller, K. L. (2016). *Marketing management* (15th ed.). Pearson Education.

Ksenofontova, A. (2023). Towards an interdisciplinary approach to time in fiction. *KronoScope, 23*(1), 86–103. DOI: 10.1163/15685241-bja10008

Kumar, C. P. (2023). *Mastering Content Creation with ChatGPT*. CP Kumar.

Kumar, D., & Suthar, N. (2024). Ethical and legal challenges of AI in marketing: An exploration of solutions. *Journal of Information. Communication and Ethics in Society*, *22*(1), 124–144. DOI: 10.1108/JICES-05-2023-0068

Kumar, V., & Kotler, P. (2024). Transformative marketing with generative artificial intelligence. In *Transformative marketing: Combining new age technologies and human insights* (pp. 65–102). Springer Nature Switzerland. DOI: 10.1007/978-3-031-59637-7_4

Kurt, S., & Aydemir, D. (2021). *Ya Reklam Senaristi Bir Makine Olursa?* Ağrı Uluslararası Yapay Zekâ Transhümanizm Posthümanizm ve Din Sempozyumu.

Kuşçu, E. (2015). Çeviride Yapay Zekâ Uygulamaları. *Kazım Karabekir Eğitim Fakültesi Dergisi*, (30), 46–58.

Labib, E. (2024). Artificial intelligence in marketing: Exploring current and future trends. *Cogent Business & Management*, *11*(1), 2348728. DOI: 10.1080/23311975.2024.2348728

Labrecque, L. I., Peña, P., Leonard, H. A., & Leger, R. (2024). Not all sunshine and rainbows: Exploring the dark side of AI in interactive marketing. *Journal of Interactive Marketing Research*. https://doi.org/.DOI: 10.1108/JRIM-02-2024-0073

Laczniak, G. R., & Murphy, P. E. (2006). Normative perspectives for ethical and socially responsible marketing. *Journal of Macromarketing*, *26*(2), 154–177. DOI: 10.1177/0276146706290924

Lal, R. (2024). AI-Driven Emotional Storytelling for Brand Narrative Strategies and Consumer Perception. *IUP Journal of Brand Management, 21*(4).

Lal, R. (2023). New measures of teaching learning and evaluating with changing technology. In Naim, A. (Ed.), *Accreditation processes and frameworks in higher education* (pp. 267–287). Nova Science Publishers.

Leasca, S. (2025, May 21). Kroger's loyalty program harvests shopper data and sells it for profit, consumer reports says. *Food & Wine*. https://www.foodandwine.com/kroger-customer-data-loyalty-program-consumer-reports-investigation-11738718

Leech, G. N. (1966). *English in advertising: A linguistic study of advertising in Great Britain*. Longmans.

Lehrer, A. (2003). Understanding trendy neologisms. *Italian Journal of Linguistics. Rivista di Linguistica*, *15*, 369–382.

Lemon, K. N., & Verhoef, P. C. (2016). Understanding customer experience throughout the customer journey. *Journal of Marketing*, *80*(6), 69–96. DOI: 10.1509/jm.15.0420

Lester, J. N., Cho, Y., & Lochmiller, C. R. (2020). Learning to do qualitative data analysis: A starting point. *Human Resource Development Review*, *19*(1), 94–106. DOI: 10.1177/1534484320903890

Lewis, G. (1999). *The Turkish language reform: A catastrophic success.* Oxford University Press. DOI: 10.1093/oso/9780198238560.001.0001

Li, J., Montgomery, N., & Mousavi, R. (2022). How a brand's social activism impacts consumers' brand evaluations: The role of brand relationship norms, arXiv preprint, arXiv:2210.10832, https://doi.org//arxiv.2210.10832.DOI: 10.48550

Li, Liang (2022). The influence of digital twins on the methods of film and television creation. *Computers and Electrical Engineering*. 103 (2022) 108314. p. 3,12.

Li, G., & Sun, X. (2022). The impact of green brand crises on green brand trust: An empirical study. *Sustainability (Basel)*, *14*(2), 611. DOI: 10.3390/su14020611

Li, H. (2019). Special Section Introduction: Artificial Intelligence and Advertising. *Journal of Advertising*, *48*(4), 333–337. DOI: 10.1080/00913367.2019.1654947

Lin, Z., Pathak, D., Li, J., Xia, X., Neubig, G., Zhang, P., & Ramanan, D. (2024). Evaluating Text-to-Visual Generation with Image-to-Text Generation. *European Conference on Computer Vision* (pp. 366-384). Springer.

Liu, S., Zhang, Y., & Wang, C. (2018). A Realization Framework of Intelligent Film Evaluation System. 2018 11th International Congress on Image and Signal Processing, BioMedical Engineering and Informatics (CISP-BMEI)

Lundqvist, A., Liljander, V., Gummerus, J., & Van Riel, A. (2013). The impact of storytelling on the consumer brand experience: The case of a firm-originated story. *Journal of Brand Management*, *20*(4), 283–297. DOI: 10.1057/bm.2012.15

Macquarie Dictionary. (2025, November 24). *Macquarie Dictionary word of the yearfor 2025*. https://www.macquariedictionary.com.au/macquarie-dictionary-word-of-the-year-for-2025/

Makridis, S., Papadakis, D. M., & Polymeris, S. (2014). Avoiding the CSR paradox: The role of narratology in reshaping corporate social responsibility in digital mediums; Exemplary case study—proceedings *of the 2014 International Digital Storytelling Conference in Athens – Digital Storytelling in Times of Crisis.*

Maloku, F., & Avdyli, M. N. (2023). Russian formalism and defamiliarization in language. [Orbis Linguarum]. *Ezikov Svyat*, *21*(1), 42–46. DOI: 10.37708/ezs.swu.v21.i1.5

Mandung, F. (2025). The influence of storytelling techniques in digital marketing on brand loyalty: A consumer psychology perspective. *Golden Ratio of Marketing and Applied Psychology of Business*, *5*(1), 66–78. DOI: 10.52970/grmapb.v5i1.782

Manoharan, J. (2024). Navigating the digital marketing landscape: The role of AI and emotional storytelling in consumer engagement. *Authorea Preprints*. DOI: 10.36227/techrxiv.170630980.05212656/v1

Mantrala, M. K., & Kanuri, V. K. (2018). Marketing optimization methods. In *Handbook of marketing analytics* (pp. 324–370). Edward Elgar. DOI: 10.4337/9781784716752.00027

Mariani, M. M., Perez-Vega, R., & Wirtz, J. (2022). AI in marketing, consumer research and psychology: A systematic literature review and research agenda. *Psychology and Marketing*, *39*(4), 755–776. DOI: 10.1002/mar.21619

Markou, V., Serdaris, P., Antoniadis, I., & Spinthiropoulos, K. (2025). Personalization, trust, and identity in AI-based marketing: An empirical study of consumer acceptance in Greece. *Administrative Sciences*, *15*(11), 440. DOI: 10.3390/admsci15110440

Martín-Sanz, M. B., Salazar-de-la-Guerra, R. M., Cuenca-Zaldivar, J. N., Salcedo-Perez-Juana, M., Garcia-Bravo, C., & Palacios-Ceña, D. (2022). Person-centred care in individuals with stroke: A qualitative study using in-depth interviews. *Annals of Medicine*, *54*(1), 2167–2180. DOI: 10.1080/07853890.2022.2105393 PMID: 35930376

Mazzei, A. (2004). Internal communication for creating corporate community. *Corporate Communications*, *9*(2), 200–210.

McCallum, S. (2022, December 23). Meta settles Cambridge Analytica Scandal Case for $725m. *BBC News*. https://www.bbc.com/news/technology-64075067

McCollough, C. J., Wallace, A. A., & Luttrell, R. (2022). Artificial intelligence: The dark side, ethics, and implications. In Wright, K. B., & Webb, L. M. (Eds.), *The Emerald handbook of computer-mediated communication and social media* (pp. 671–684). Emerald Publishing Limited. DOI: 10.1108/978-1-80071-597-420221039

McCracken, G. (1988). The Long Interview. *Sage (Atlanta, Ga.).*

Mcdonagh, D., & Storer, I. (2004). Mood boards as a Design Catalyst and Resource: Researching an Under-Researched Area. *The Design Journal*, *7*(3), 16–31. DOI: 10.2752/146069204789338424

McGilvray, J. (2001). Chomsky on the creative aspect of language use and its implications for lexical semantic studies. In Busa, F., & Bouillon, P. (Eds.), *The language of word meaning* (pp. 5–27). Cambridge University Press. DOI: 10.1017/CBO9780511896316.004

Meadows, D. (2003). Digital Storytelling: Research-Based Practice in New Media, *SAGE.* Thousand Oaks. *Visual Communication, 2*(2), 189–193. DOI: 10.1177/1470357203002002004

Mehmandoust, N., & Söylemez, A. S. (2023). Translation strategies of neologisms in Margaret Atwood's MaddAddam trilogy. *Turkish Studies - Language, 18*(2), 1127-1143. https://doi.org/DOI: 10.7827/TurkishStudies.67754

Methanuntakul, K. (2010). *High-street fashion brand communication amongst female adolescents* (Doctoral dissertation, Brunel University School of Engineering and Design PhD Theses).

Michelon, G., Pilonato, S., & Ricceri, F. (2015). CSR reporting practices and the quality of disclosure: An empirical analysis. *Critical Perspectives on Accounting, 33*, 59–78. DOI: 10.1016/j.cpa.2014.10.003

Miller, C. C., & Sinclair, G. (2020). Crisis communication and corporate reputation: Exploring the impact of silence and transparency on consumer evaluations. *Public Relations Review, 46*(3).

Mohamed, K. M. M. (2025). Visual storytelling and cultural connection in GCC social media advertising. *Frontiers in Communication, 10*, 1584156. DOI: 10.3389/fcomm.2025.1584156

Mohammadkhani, D., Majedi, N., Biniaz, S. A., & Sarhadi, M. (2025). AI-driven personalization strategies and their impact on consumer engagement in digital markets. *Digital Transformation and Administration Innovation*, 1-14.

Mohan, A. (2026). Transmodernity and literature: Of worlds in contact, Part 2. *Asian Review of World Histories, 14*(1), 27–36. DOI: 10.1163/22879811-bja10101

Moorthy, J., Lahiri, R., Biswas, N., Sanyal, D., Ranjan, J., Nanath, K., & Ghosh, P. (2015). Big data: Prospects and challenges. *Vikalpa, 40*(1), 74–96. DOI: 10.1177/0256090915575450

Mori, M., MacDorman, K. F., & Kageki, N. (2012). The Uncanny Valley [From the Field]. *IEEE Robotics & Automation Magazine, 19*(2), 98–100. DOI: 10.1109/MRA.2012.2192811

Morley, J., Floridi, L., Kinsey, L., & Elhalal, A. (2020). From what to how: An initial review of publicly available AI ethics tools, methods, and research to translate principles into practices. *Science and Engineering Ethics, 26*(4), 2141–2168. DOI: 10.1007/s11948-019-00165-5 PMID: 31828533

Morsing, M., & Schultz, M. (2006). Corporate social responsibility communication: Stakeholder information, response and involvement strategies. *Business Ethics (Oxford, England), 15*(4), 323–338. DOI: 10.1111/j.1467-8608.2006.00460.x

Murray, J. H. (1997). Hamlet on the holodeck: The future of narrative in cyberspace.

Murtezaoğlu, Y. E. (2022). *The dark side of applying artificial intelligence technologies in marketing – What are the challenges, obstacles, and risks?* Institute of Retailing, Sales and Marketing.

Mustafa, F., Smolarski, J., & Elamer, A. A. (2025). The convergence of artificial intelligence and sustainability reporting: A systematic review of applications, challenges and future directions. *Business Strategy and the Environment, 34*(8), 9761–9784. Advance online publication. DOI: 10.1002/bse.70090

Mutlu, E. (2017). *İletişim sözlüğü.* Ütopya Yayınevi.

Mutlu, E. (2017). *İletişim Sözlüğü.* Ütopya Yayınevi.

Nazlı, E. H. (2022a). *Dil ve cinsiyet: Reklam dili çözümlemesi* [Language and gender: Analysis of advertising language] [Master's thesis, İstanbul University].

Nazlı, E. H. (2022b). *Reklam dili: Bir iletişim biçimi olarak Türkçe reklam söylemi üzerine toplumdilbilimsel bir inceleme* [Advertising language: A sociolinguistic study on Turkish advertising discourse as a form of communication] [Doctoral dissertation, Dicle University].

Nestlé. (2025). *Nestlé global website.* https://www.nestle.com (Accessed: 8 March 2025)

Nike. (2020). *Nike, Inc. FY20 Impact Report.* https://about.nike.com/en/resources/nike-inc-impact-report-archive (Accessed: 12 March 2025)

Nilsson, N. J. (1998). *Artificial Intelligence A New Synthesis.* Morgan Kaufmann Publishers, China Machine Press.

Noble, S. U. (2018). *Algorithms of oppression: How search engines reinforce racism.* New York University Press. DOI: 10.18574/nyu/9781479833641.001.0001

Odabaşı, Y., & Oyman, M. (2013). *Pazarlama İletişimi Yönetimi.* MediaCat Kitapları.

Okay, A. & Okay, A. (2018). *Halkla ilişkiler kavram strateji ve uygulamaları.* Der.

Oke, T. (2025). Algorithmic narrativity as a new narrative mode. *AI & Society, 40*(7), 1–12. DOI: 10.1007/s00146-025-02297-8

Oliver, R. L. (1980). A cognitive model of the antecedents and consequences of satisfaction decisions. *JMR, Journal of Marketing Research, 17*(4), 460–469. DOI: 10.1177/002224378001700405

Oliver, R. L. (1997). *Satisfaction: A behavioral perspective on the consumer.* McGraw-Hill.

Önder, N. (2024, December 6). Full AI-generated List Flavours commercial now live. Marketing Türkiye. https://www.marketingturkiye.com.tr/kampanyalar/list-flavoursin-tamami-yapay-zeka-ile-hazirlanan-reklam-filmi-yayinda/

Oppenlaender, J. (2022, November 16-18). *The Creativity of Text-to-Image Generation* [Conference Presentation]. Academic Mindtrek '22: Proceedings of the 25th International Academic Mindtrek Conference, Jyväskylä, Finland.

Özdemir, R. (2022). *Yeni Medya ve Veri Tabanlı Reklamcılık.* Medya Teknolojileri Enstitüsü.

Özer, Z. (2010). *Global reklam kampanyalarında kültürel farklılaşmalar* [Cultural differentiations in global advertising campaigns] [Master's thesis, Marmara University].

Özgen, E. (2022). Sürdürülebilirlik iletişimi ve halkla ilişkiler. *Türkiye İletişim Araştırmaları Dergisi, Özel Sayı*, e1-e4. DOI: DOI: 10.17829/turcom.1106292

Özgür, E. (2024). An evaluation of Kate Crawford's "Atlas of AI" [Kate Crawford'ın "Yapay Zekâ Atlası" üzerine bir değerlendirme]. *Ankara Üniversitesi İlef Dergisi*, 11(1), 190–202.

Pagano, T. P., Loureiro, R. B., Lisboa, F. V. N., Cruz, G. O. R., Peixoto, R. M., Guimarães, G. A. D. S., & Nascimento, E. G. S. (2022). Bias and Unfairness in Machine Learning Models: A Systematic Literature Review. *arXiv preprint arXiv:2202.08176.*

Palos-Sancheza, P., Saurab, J. R., & Martin-Veliciaa, F. (2019). A Study of The Effects of Programmatic Advertising on Users' Concerns About Privacy Overtime. *Journal of Business Research, 96*, 61–72. DOI: 10.1016/j.jbusres.2018.10.059

Pang, A., Jin, Y., Seo, Y., Choi, S., Teo, H., Le, P., & Reber, B. (2021). Breaking the sound of silence: Explication in the use of strategic silence in crisis communication. *International Journal of Business Communication, 59*(2), 219–241. DOI: 10.1177/23294884211046357

Papadatos, C. (2006). The art of storytelling: How loyalty marketers can build emotional connections to their brands. *Journal of Consumer Marketing*, *23*(7), 382–384. DOI: 10.1108/07363760610712902

Park, C. W., MacInnis, D. J., Priester, J., Eisingerich, A. B., & Iacobucci, D. (2010). Brand attachment and brand attitude strength: Conceptual and empirical differentiation of two critical brand equity drivers. *Journal of Marketing*, *74*(6), 1–17. DOI: 10.1509/jmkg.74.6.1

Pauwels, K., Ambler, T., Clark, B. H., LaPointe, P., Reibstein, D., Skiera, B., Wierenga, B., & Wiesel, T. (2009). Dashboards as a service: Why, what, how, and what research is needed? *Journal of Service Research*, *12*(2), 175–189. DOI: 10.1177/1094670509344213

Pavlou, P. A. (2003). Consumer acceptance of electronic commerce: Integrating trust and risk with the Technology Acceptance Model. *International Journal of Electronic Commerce*, *7*(3), 69–103. DOI: 10.1080/10864415.2003.11044275

Pedreschi, D., Pappalardo, L., Ferragina, E., Baeza-Yates, R., Barabási, A.-L., Dignum, F., Dignum, V., Eliassi-Rad, T., Giannotti, F., Kertész, J., Knott, A., Ioannidis, Y., Lukowicz, P., Passarella, A., Pentland, A. S., Shawe-Taylor, J., & Vespignani, A. (2025). Human-AI coevolution. *Artificial Intelligence*, *339*, 104244. DOI: 10.1016/j.artint.2024.104244

Peltekoğlu, F. (2019). *Kavram ve Kuramlarıyla İkna*. Beta Yayınevi.

Picot, A., & Propstmeier, J. (2013). Big data. *MedienWirtschaft*, *10*(1), 34–39. DOI: 10.15358/1613-0669-2013-1-34

Pomering, A., & Johnson, L. W. (2009). Advertising corporate social responsibility initiatives to communicate corporate image: Inhibiting scepticism to enhance persuasion. *Corporate Communications*, *14*(4), 420–439. DOI: 10.1108/13563280910998763

Popeyes Türkiye. (2025, May 8). *Popeyes® Kanatları Sosa Düştü!* [Video]. YouTube. https://www.youtube.com/watch?v=PhWlrSPlIcg&t=14s

Popkova, E. G., & Gulzat, K. (2020). Technological revolution in the 21st century: Digital society vs. artificial intelligence. In Popkova, E. G., & Sergi, B. S. (Eds.), *The 21st Century from the Positions of Modern Science: Intellectual, Digital and Innovative Aspects* (Vol. 91, pp. 339–345). Springer International Publishing. DOI: 10.1007/978-3-030-32015-7_38

Potwora, M., Vdovichena, O., Semchuk, D., Lipych, L., & Saienko, V. (2024). The use of artificial intelligence in marketing strategies: Automation, personalization and forecasting. *Journal of Management World*, *2*(2), 41–49. DOI: 10.53935/jomw.v2024i2.275

Primožič, L., & Kutnar, A. (2022). Sustainability communication in global consumer brands. *Sustainability (Basel)*, *14*(20), 13586. Advance online publication. DOI: 10.3390/su142013586

Pröbstl-Haider, U., Gugerell, K., & Maruthaveeran, S. (2023). Covid-19 and outdoor recreation—lessons learned? Introduction to the special issue on "outdoor recreation and Covid-19: Its effects on people, parks and landscapes.". *Journal of Outdoor Recreation and Tourism*, *41*, 100583. DOI: 10.1016/j.jort.2022.100583 PMID: 37521268

Pulizzi, J. (2012). The rise of storytelling as the new marketing. *Publishing Research Quarterly*, *28*(2), 116–123. DOI: 10.1007/s12109-012-9264-5

Puntoni, S., Reczek, R. W., Giesler, M., & Botti, S. (2021). Consumers and artificial intelligence: An experiential perspective. *Journal of Marketing*, *85*(1), 131–151. DOI: 10.1177/0022242920953847

Qin, R. W. (2024). Navigating integration challenges and ethical considerations of AI in e-commerce: A framework for best practices and customer trust. *Technology and Investment*, *15*(3), 168–181. DOI: 10.4236/ti.2024.153010

Qin, X., & Jiang, Z. (2019). The Impact of AI on the Advertising Process: The Chinese Experience. *Journal of Advertising*, *48*(4), 338–346. DOI: 10.1080/00913367.2019.1652122

Rahman, Z. T., Lal, R., & Rena, R. (2024). Challenges of communication with Gen-Z in the era of artificial intelligence-interceded digital economy. In *AI-Oriented Competency Framework for Talent Management in the Digital Economy* (pp. 76–94). CRC Press. DOI: 10.1201/9781003440901-5

Ratnayake, N. (2012). *The Predictive validity of brand-related autobiographical memories on brand commitment.* PhD thesis. Coventry: Coventry University

Ratta, A. A., Muneer, S., & Ul Hassan, H. (2024). The impact of AI generated advertising content on consumer buying behavior and consumer engagement. [BBE]. *Bulletin of Business and Economics*, *13*(2), 1152–1157.

Reisman, D., Schultz, J., Crawford, K., & Whittaker, M. (2018). *Algorithmic impact assessments: A practical framework for public agency accountability.* AI Now.

Resuloğlu, F., & Yılmaz, R. (2017). A model for interactive advertising narration. In Yilmaz, R. (Ed.), *Narrative Advertising Models and Conceptualization in the Digital Age* (pp. 1–20). IGI Global., DOI: 10.4018/978-1-5225-2373-4.ch001

Rettberg, J. W., & Wigers, H. (2025). AI-generated stories favour stability over change: Homogeneity and cultural stereotyping in narratives generated by gpt-4o-mini. *Open Research Europe*, *5*, 202. DOI: 10.12688/openreseurope.20576.1

Reuters. (2022). U.S. Meta Settle Lawsuit Over Discrimination in Housing Advertising Tool. *Reuters.*_https://www.reuters.com/legal/transactional/us-meta-settle-lawsuit-over-discrimination-housing-advertising-tool-2022-06-21

Ricoeur, P. (1984). *Time and narrative* (Vol. 1). University of Chicago Press.

Rıfat, M. (2019). *Göstergebilimin ABC'si*. Say Yayınları.

Ritzer, G. (2011). *Büyüsü Bozulmuş Dünyayı Büyülemek*. Ş.S., Kaya Trans. Ayrıntı. p. 138.

Robin, B. R. (2016). The power of digital storytelling to support teaching and learning. *Digital Education Review*, (30), 17–29.

Rodgers, S. (2021). Themed issue introduction: Promises and perils of artificial intelligence and advertising. *Journal of Advertising*, *50*(1), 1–10. DOI: 10.1080/00913367.2020.1868233

Rodgers, W., & Nguyen, T. (2022). Advertising Benefits from Ethical Artificial Intelligence Algorithmic Purchase Decision Pathways. *Journal of Business Ethics*, *178*(4), 1043–1106. DOI: 10.1007/s10551-022-05048-7

Rodríguez Guerra, A. (2016). Dictionaries of neologisms: A review and proposals for its improvement. *Open Linguistics*, *2*(1), 528–556. DOI: 10.1515/opli-2016-0028

Röhrborn, K. (2001). Artificial idiomaticity in neologistic terms of Republican Turkish. , 20, 1-10.

Şahin Başfırıncı, Ç., & Koç, N. (2023). İletişim alanındaki mesleklerde yapay zekâ uygulamaları: Mevcut durum analizi ve alan yazın taraması. *Karadeniz İletişim Araştırmaları Dergisi*, 121-148.

Şahinci, D. (2021). *Yapay Zekâ ve Reklamcılığın Geleceği*. İstanbul Üniversitesi Sosyal Bilimler Enstitüsü.

Sahut, J. M., & Laroche, M. (2025). Using artificial intelligence (AI) to enhance customer experience and to develop strategic marketing: An integrative synthesis. *Computers in Human Behavior*, *170*, 108684. DOI: 10.1016/j.chb.2025.108684

Salgado-Reyes, N. (2025). User experience (UX) optimization with AI: Integration of artificial intelligence to personalize the user experience in applications and websites, anticipating their needs and preferences. In *International conference on information technology & systems* (pp. 223–231). Springer Nature Switzerland. DOI: 10.1007/978-3-031-93106-2_19

Samuel, A., White, G. R. T., Thomas, R., & Jones, P. (2021). Programmatic Advertising: An Exegesis of Consumer Concerns. *Computers in Human Behavior, 116*, 106657. Advance online publication. DOI: 10.1016/j.chb.2020.106657

Sánchez-López, I., Gifreu-Castells, A., & Roig, A. (2025). AI storytelling & narrative evolution in creative industries. *Systematic Reviews.*

Sanders, T. (2025). Valentino slammed over truly 'uncomfortable' ads. *The Daily Beast.* https://www.thedailybeast.com/valentino-slammed-over-truly-uncomfortable-ads

Sanghrajka, R., Witoń, W., Schriber, S., Gross, M., & Kapadia, M. (2018). Computer-Assisted Authoring for Natural Language Story Scripts. *Proceedings of the AAAI Conference on Artificial Intelligence, 32*(1). Advance online publication. DOI: 10.1609/aaai.v32i1.11420

Sapre, I., & Longani, K. D. (2024). The role of storytelling in advertising: How narrative drives brand loyalty. In *Indonesia Broadcasting Conference (IBC)* (Vol. 1, pp. 187-200).

Sarı, İ. (2015). *Türkçede eklerin dışında kelime yapma yolları ve sözlükselleşme* [Word-formation methods other than suffixation and lexicalization in Turkish] [Doctoral dissertation, Ankara University].

Sarıoğlu, B., & Develi, İ. (2022). Pazarlamada Kampanya Yönetimi Ve Yapay Zekâ Kullanımı. *Uluslararası Halkla İlişkiler ve Reklam Çalışmaları Dergisi, 5*(2), 91–124.

Sarkar, N., & Lal, R. (2023). Changing trends of media ownership: Marketing through community engagement in Hindi television news channels. In *Global Applications of the Internet of Things in Digital Marketing* (pp. 290–309). IGI Global. DOI: 10.4018/978-1-6684-8166-0.ch015

Sarkis, J., Cohen-Rosenthal, E., & Dou, Y. (2020). A review of the emerging COVID-19 pandemic from the perspective of sustainable global supply chains. *Resources, Conservation and Recycling, 162*, 105–110.

Say, C. (2018). *50 questions on artificial intelligence* [50 soruda yapay zekâ]. Bilim ve Gelecek Yayınevi.

Schaltegger, S., & Burritt, R. (2010). Sustainability accounting for companies: Catchphrase or decision support for business leaders? *Journal of World Business, 45*(4), 375–384. DOI: 10.1016/j.jwb.2009.08.002

Schivinski, B., Christodoulides, G., & Dabrowski, D. (2016). Measuring consumers' engagement with brand-related social-media content: Development and validation of a scale that identifies levels of social-media engagement with brands. *Journal of Advertising Research, 56*(1), 64–80. DOI: 10.2501/JAR-2016-004

Schmitt, B. (1999). Experiential marketing. *Journal of Marketing Management, 15*(1-3), 53–67. DOI: 10.1362/026725799784870496

Sephora Italia. (2023, November 28). *mAI colpevoli – Home* [Video]. Youtube. https://www.youtube.com/watch?v=ozO6vqgaRWU&t=39s

Serbanescu, A., & Nack, F. (2023). Human-AI system co-creativity for building narrative worlds. In *Proceedings of the IASDR 2023: Life-Changing Design*, Milan, Italy. Design Research Society: London, UK. DOI: 10.21606/iasdr.2023.293

Sergio, F. (2020). Storytelling in the Luxury Industry: Narratives as a Tool for Experiential Branding-The Case of Christian Dior Couture. Master's Thesis, Università Ca' Foscari Venezia, Venice, Italy.

Serttaş Ertike, A., & Yılmaz, R. (2011). *Reklamcılığın anahtar kavramları*. Kitabevi Yayınları.

Shah, N., Engineer, S., Bhagat, N., Chauhan, H., & Shah, M. (2020). Research Trends on the Usage of Machine Learning and Artificial Intelligence in Advertising. *Augmented Human Research, 5*(1), 19. Advance online publication. DOI: 10.1007/s41133-020-00038-8

Shankar, V. (2018). How artificial intelligence (AI) is reshaping retailing. *Journal of Retailing, 94*(4), vi–xi. DOI: 10.1016/S0022-4359(18)30076-9

Sharma, K. K., Tomar, M., & Tadimarri, A. (2023). Unlocking sales potential: How AI revolutionizes marketing strategies. *Journal of Knowledge Learning and Science Technology ISSN: 2959-6386 (online), 2*(2), 231-250. DOI: 10.60087/jklst.vol2.n2.p250

Shavitt, S., & Cho, H. (2016). Culture and consumer behavior: The role of horizontal and vertical cultural factors. *Current Opinion in Psychology, 8*, 149–154. DOI: 10.1016/j.copsyc.2015.11.007 PMID: 28083559

Sheikh, H., Prims, C., & Schrijvers, E. (2023). Artificial intelligence: Definition and background. *Mission AI*, 15-41.

Shneiderman, B. (2020). Human-centered artificial intelligence: Reliable, safe & trustworthy. *International Journal of Human-Computer Interaction, 36*(6), 495–504. DOI: 10.1080/10447318.2020.1741118

Singh, S. K., Kumar, S., & Mehra, P. S. (2023). Chat GPT & Google Bard AI: A Review. 2023 International Conference on IoT (pp. 1-6). Gorakhpur, India: Communication and Automation Technology (ICICAT).

Singh, A. (Ed.). (2021). *Big data analytics for improved accuracy, efficiency, and decision making in digital marketing*. IGI Global. DOI: 10.4018/978-1-7998-7231-3

Singh, R. K., Prakash, R., & Lal, R. (2021). Adoption of CAB model for instrument development of effectiveness of crime-based reality-shows. *Journal of Content Community and Communication, 14*(7), 230–239. DOI: 10.31620/JCCC.12.21/19

Singh, S., & Sonnenburg, S. (2012). Brand performances in social media. *Journal of Interactive Marketing, 26*(4), 189–197. DOI: 10.1016/j.intmar.2012.04.001

Sivri, O. (2024). Yapay zekâ çerçevesinde görsel sanatların geleceği. *İnsanat. Sanat Tasarım ve Mimarlık Araştırmaları Dergisi, 4*(1), 322–344.

Solomon, M. R. (2018). *Consumer behavior: Buying, having, and being* (12th ed.). Pearson Education.

Soydaş, N., & Çokluk, N. (2023). Kurumsal sosyal sorumluluk projelerinin kurumsal iletişimde rolü: "Shell'de kadın enerjisi" vaka incelemesi. *İstanbul Aydın Üniversitesi Sosyal Bilimler Dergisi, 15*(2), 227–258.

Spanos, M. (2021). Brand storytelling in the age of artificial intelligence. *Journal of Brand Strategy, 10*(1), 6–13. DOI: 10.69554/BANG8294

Srinivasan, N., & Ratchford, B. T. (1991). An empirical test of a model of external search for automobiles. *The Journal of Consumer Research, 18*(2), 233–242. DOI: 10.1086/209255

Srivastava,S. & Muskaan, D. (2023). A Semiotic Exploration of AI-Driven Personalization in Advertising.

Sterne, J. (2017). *Artificial Intelligence for Marketing: Practical Applications.* Rising Media. DOI: 10.1002/9781119406341

Stinchcombe, A. L. (1968). *Constructing social theory*. Harcourt, Brace & World.

Stone, M., Aravopoulou, E., Ekinci, Y., Evans, G., Hobbs, M., Labib, A., Laughlin, P., Machtynger, J., & Machtynger, L. (2020). Artificial intelligence (AI) in strategic marketing decision-making: A research agenda. *The Bottom Line (New York, N.Y.)*, *33*(2), 183–200. DOI: 10.1108/BL-03-2020-0022

Suchman, M. C. (1995). Managing legitimacy: Strategic and institutional approaches. *Academy of Management Review*, *20*(3), 571–610. DOI: 10.2307/258788

Sudi, M. (2024). Semiotic Analysis in Advertising: How Messages Are Communicated To Society. *Jurnal Komunikasi*, *2*(3), 224–235.

Suleiman, D. A., Awan, T. M., & Javed, M. (2021). Enhancing digital marketing performance through usage intention of AI-powered websites. *IAES International Journal of Artificial Intelligence*, *10*(4), 810–817. DOI: 10.11591/ijai.v10.i4.pp810-817

Sung, E. C., Han, D. I. D., Bae, S., & Kwon, O. (2022). What drives technology-enhanced storytelling immersion? The role of digital humans. *Computers in Human Behavior*, *132*, 107246. DOI: 10.1016/j.chb.2022.107246

Suryana, P. (2024). Building a strong brand image: The role of storytelling in marketing. [JECOMBI]. *Journal of Economics and Business*, *4*(02), 107–115.

Sutton, D. H. (2009). *Globalizing Ideal Beauty*. MacMillan. DOI: 10.1057/9780230100435

Tadelle. (2025, May 30). *Mutluluk, lezzet ve Tadelle; Onun adı MUTLU KIRMIZI, Onun adı TADELLE* [Video]. Youtube. https://www.youtube.com/watch?v=YbcLD939Q2A

Tan Çakır, N. (2024). Factual and theoretical development of corporate social responsibility. In Yılmaz, R., & Özer Alper, D. (Eds.), *Innovative models, strategies, and conceptualizations in PR* (pp. 163–174). Palet.

Tang, B. J., Sun, K., Curran, N. T., Schaub, F., & Shin, K. G. (2024). GenAI Advertising: Risks of Personalizing Ads With LLMs. *arXiv preprint arXiv:2409.15436.*

Taşkıran, Ö. N., & Yılmaz, R. (2014). *99 Soruda Reklam ve Reklamcılık*. Derin Yayınları.

Taufiq, A. (2021). Narrative influence in the digital age: How digital literature shapes consumer behavior. *Journal of Society Innovation and Development*, *2*(2), 131–141. DOI: 10.63924/jsid.v2i2.231

Terry, G., Hayfield, N., Clarke, V., & Braun, V. (2017). Thematic Analysis. In Willig, C., & Rogers, W. S. (Eds.), *The Sage Handbook of Qualitative Research in Psychology* (pp. 17–37). Sage. DOI: 10.4135/9781526405555.n2

Tesic, J. (2024). Redeployment of trend forecasting: managing the overproduction challenge in the fashion industry. [Unpublished Doctoral Thesis]

Tesla. (2025). *Tesla official website.* https://www.tesla.com (Accessed: 3 January 2025)

The Guardian. (2024, October 8). US States Sue TikTok Over Mental Health Harms to Children. *The Guardian.* https://www.theguardian.com/technology/2024/oct/08/us-states-tiktok-lawsuit-mental-health

Thomas, M. (2025, April 11). Two Lawsuits Allege The Trade Desk Secretly Violates Consumer Privacy Laws. *People.* https://people.com/mcdonald-s-netherlands-ai-ad-controversy-explained-11867981?utm_source

Thomas, V. L., & Grigsby, J. L. (2024). Narrative transportation: A systematic literature review and future research agenda. *Psychology and Marketing*, *41*(7), 1235–1256. DOI: 10.1002/mar.22011

Thorne, S. (2020). Hey siri, tell me a story: Digital storytelling and ai authorship. *Convergence (London)*, *26*(4), 808–823. DOI: 10.1177/1354856520913866

Time. (2018). Mark Zuckerberg Says He's Still the Best Person to Run Facebook, Despite Its 'Huge Mistake' with the Cambridge Analytica Data Scandal. *Time.* https://time.com/5228542/mark-zuckerberg-facebook-data-scandal

Tıraş, H. H. (2012). Sürdürülebilir kalkınma ve çevre: Teorik bir inceleme. *Kahramanmaraş Sütçü İmam Üniversitesi İktisadi ve İdari Bilimler Fakültesi Dergisi*, *2*(2), 57–73.

Tissera, W. (2025). The Future of Generative Artificial Intelligence in Visual-based Digital Marketing [Undergraduate Dissertation]. Jyaskylan Ammattikorkeakoulu University.

Todd, M. D., & Supa, D. W. (2014). Testing the viability of corporate social advocacy. *Public Relations Review*, *40*(5), 771–783.

Torelli, R., Balluchi, F., & Furlotti, K. (2012). Greenwashing and environmental communication: Effects on stakeholders' attitudes and intentions. *Corporate Social Responsibility and Environmental Management*, *27*(1), 52–64. DOI: 10.1002/bse.2373

ToyBook. (n.d.) AI-generated Toys "R" Us brand film announces first ever AI retail film. ToyBook. https://toybook.com/ai-generated-toys-r-us-brand-film/

Toys"R"Us. (2024, June 21). *The Origin of Toys"R"Us: Brand Film Teaser | Toys"R"Us* [Video]. Youtube. https://www.youtube.com/watch?v=F_WfIzYGlg4

Tregidga, H., Milne, M. J., & Kearins, K. (2014). Governing meaning of sustainability: The discursive construction of the sustainable organization. *Organization Studies, 35*(2), 231–257.

Tucker, C. (2014). Social networks, personalized advertising, and privacy controls. *JMR, Journal of Marketing Research, 51*(5), 546–562. DOI: 10.1509/jmr.10.0355

Türkömer, G. (2018). Yapay Zeka Reklam Sektörünün Geleceğini Nasıl Etkiler? https:// digitalage.com.tr/yapay-zeka-reklam-sektorunun-gelecegini-nasil-etkiler/ . E.T: 27.09.2023

Türksoy, N. (2022). The Future of Public Relations, Advertising and Journalism: How Artificial Intelligence May Transform the Communication Profession and Why Society Should Care? *Türkiye İletişim Araştırmaları Dergisi*, (40), 394–410. DOI: 10.17829/turcom.1050491

Türten, B. (2024). Yapay zekâ ve sinema: Film yapımında olanaklar ve fırsatlar. *Anadolu ve Balkan Araştırmaları Dergisi, 7*(14), 399–425. DOI: 10.32953/abad.1539736

Tyurina, N., Nazarchuk, T., Hurnytsky, O., & Kovalchuk, V. (2024). *Brand communications in anti-crisis management: Theoretical aspects and practical experience of foreign companies*. Innovation and Sustainability., DOI: 10.31649/ins.2024.3.118.127

Uçar, A. (2014). Gülmece ve gülme kaynağı olarak sözcük oyunları [Wordplay as a source of humor and laughter]. *Dil ve Edebiyat Dergisi, 11*(1), 17–43.

Umoren, O., Didi, P. U., Balogun, O., Abass, O. S., & Akinrinoye, O. V. (2022). Strategic digital storytelling techniques for building authentic brand narratives and driving cross-generational consumer trust online. *International Scientific Refereed Research Journal, 5*(3), 238–261.

Unilever. (2025). *Unilever global website.* https://www.unilever.com (Accessed: 9 March 2025)

Vakratsas, D., & Wang, X. S. (2021). Artificial intelligence in advertising creativity. *Journal of Advertising, 50*(1), 39–51. DOI: 10.1080/00913367.2020.1843090

Valls-Vargas, J. (2013). Narrative extraction, processing and generation for interactive fiction and computer games. In *Proceedings of the AAAI Conference on Artificial Intelligence and Interactive Digital Entertainment* (Vol. 9, No. 6, pp. 37-40). DOI: 10.1609/aiide.v9i6.12600

Van Dyck, F. (2017). *Yeni nesil reklamcılık- dijital çağ için yeni kurallar*. The Kitap.

Van Esch, P., Cui, Y., & Jain, S. P. (2021). Stimulating or intimidating: The effect of AI-enabled in-store communication on consumer patronage likelihood. *Journal of Advertising*, *50*(1), 63–80. DOI: 10.1080/00913367.2020.1832939

Van Laer, T., De Ruyter, K., Visconti, L. M., & Wetzels, M. (2014). The extended transportation-imagery model: A meta-analysis of the antecedents and consequences of consumers' narrative transportation. *The Journal of Consumer Research*, *40*(5), 797–817. DOI: 10.1086/673383

Verhoef, P. C., Reinartz, W. J., & Krafft, M. (2010). Customer engagement as a new perspective in customer management. *Journal of Service Research*, *13*(3), 247–252. DOI: 10.1177/1094670510375461

Vidrih, M., & Mayahi, S. (2023). Generative AI-driven storytelling: A new era for marketing. *arXiv preprint arXiv:2309.09048.*

Vidrih, M., & Mayahi, S. (2023). Generative AI-driven Storytelling: A New Era For Marketing. *arXiv preprint arXiv:2309.09048.*

Vidrih, M., & Mayahi, S. (2023). Generative AI-driven storytelling: A new era for marketing. *arXiv preprint.* arXiv:2309.09048. https://arxiv.org/abs/2309.09048

Voorveld, H. A. M., Van Noort, G., Muntinga, D. G., & Bronner, F. (2018). Engagement with social media and advertising: The differentiating role of platform type. *Journal of Advertising*, *47*(1), 38–54. DOI: 10.1080/00913367.2017.1405754

Wahyudin, D., & Tjoa, A. M. (2007). Event-based monitoring of open source software projects. In *Proceedings of the Second International Conference on Availability, Reliability and Security (ARES'07)* (pp. 1108–1115). IEEE. DOI: 10.1109/ARES.2007.84

Wang, B., Zhou, H., Li, X., Yang, G., Zheng, P., Song, C., Yuan, Y., Wuest, T., Yang, H., & Wang, L. (2024). Human Digital Twin in the context of Industry 5.0. *Robotics and Computer-integrated Manufacturing*, *85*, 102626. DOI: 10.1016/j.rcim.2023.102626

Wang, C. L. (2021). New frontiers and future directions in interactive marketing: Inaugural editorial. *Journal of Research in Interactive Marketing*, *15*(1), 1–9. DOI: 10.1108/JRIM-03-2021-270

Wang, H.-J. (2015). A New Approach to Network Analysis for Brand Positioning. *International Journal of Market Research*, *57*(5), 727–742. DOI: 10.2501/IJMR-2015-060

Wang, P. (2019). On defining artificial intelligence. *Journal of Artificial General Intelligence, 10*(2), 1–37. DOI: 10.2478/jagi-2019-0002

Wedel, M., & Kannan, P. K. (2016). Marketing analytics for data-rich environments. *Journal of Marketing, 80*(6), 97–121. DOI: 10.1509/jm.15.0413

Weder, F. (2025). *Strategic sustainability communication: Principles, perspectives, and potential.* Springer., DOI: 10.1007/978-3-031-89486-2

Weila, C., Martin, J. L., & Ruizhi, Y. (2025). Exploring the integration of generative AI in advertising agencies: A co-creative process model for human–AI collaboration. *Journal of Advertising Research, 65*(2), 167–189. DOI: 10.1080/00218499.2024.2445362

Wen, Y., & Laporte, S. (2025). Experiential narratives in marketing: A comparison of generative AI and human content. *Journal of Public Policy & Marketing, 44*(3), 392–410. DOI: 10.1177/07439156241297973

Widiasari, N. (2020). Narration based on corporate social responsibility (CSR) advertisement: The projection and story. *Jurnal Desain Komunikasi Visual Nirmana, 20*(2), 106–120. DOI: 10.9744/nirmana.20.2.106-120

Widiasari, N. (2020). Narration based on CSR advertisement. *Nirmana, 20*(2), 106–120.

Wildenhain, M. (2025). *Yapay zekanın kısa tarihi.* Düşbaz Kitaplar.

Williams, M. (2025). Social media democracy: How algorithms shape public discourse and marginalise voices. *Journal of Media and Rights, 3*(1), a20. DOI: 10.4102/JMR.v3i1.20

Willig, C. (2008). *Introducing qualitative research in psychology.* McGraw-Hill.

Wilson, D. (2016). Relevance theory. In Huang, Y. (Ed.), *The Oxford Handbook of Pragmatics* (pp. 79–100). Oxford University Press., DOI: 10.1093/oxfordhb/9780199697960.013.25

Wirth, N. (2018). Hello marketing, what can artificial intelligence help you with? *International Journal of Market Research, 60*(5), 435–438. DOI: 10.1177/1470785318776841

Woodside, A. G., Sood, S., & Miller, K. E. (2008). When consumers and brands talk: Storytelling theory and research in psychology and marketing. *Psychology and Marketing, 25*(2), 97–145. DOI: 10.1002/mar.20203

World Commission on Environment and Development. (1987). *Our common future.* http://www.un-documents.net/our-common-future.pdf

Wu, C. W., & Monfort, A. (2023). Role of artificial intelligence in marketing strategies and performance. *Psychology and Marketing*, *40*(3), 484–496. DOI: 10.1002/mar.21737

Wu, L., Dodoo, N. A., Wen, T. J., & Ke, L. (2022). Understanding Twitter conversations about artificial intelligence in advertising based on natural language processing. *International Journal of Advertising*, *41*(4), 685–702. DOI: 10.1080/02650487.2021.1920218

Yang, K. C., & Kang, Y. (2021). Predicting the relationships between narrative transportation, consumer brand experience, love and loyalty in video storytelling advertising. *Journal of Creative Communications*, *16*(1), 7–26. DOI: 10.1177/0973258620984262

Yaprak, B. (2024). Generative artificial intelligence in marketing: The invisible danger of AI hallucinations. *Ekonomi İşletme ve Yönetim Dergisi*, *8*(2), 133–158. DOI: 10.7596/jebm.1588897

Yeşilkaya, N. (2022). Ethical issues regarding artificial intelligence [Yapay zekâya dair etik sorunlar]. *Şarkiyat İlmi Araştırmalar Dergisi (Journal of Oriental Scientific Research*), 14(3), 949–964. .DOI: 10.26791/sarkiat.1189864

Yetkin Karakoç, N. (2014). Structural calques in neologism translation and unintelligibility: The case of Generation X. *Turkish Studies*, *9*(3), 1611–1619. DOI: 10.7827/TurkishStudies.6492

Yeung, K. (2017). 'Hypernudge': Big data as a mode of regulation by design. *Information Communication and Society*, *20*(1), 118–136. DOI: 10.1080/1369118X.2016.1186713

Yıldırım, E. (2025). Examining advertisements produced by artificial intelligence from an aesthetic perspective and analyzing a sample advertisement film produced by artificial intelligence. *Journal of Management Theory and Practices Research*, *6*(1), 77–94.

Yilmaz, B., & Ashqar, H. I. (2025). Towards Equitable AI: Detecting Bias in Using Large Language Models for Marketing. *arXiv preprint arXiv:2502.12838.*

Yılmaz, D. (2006). *Sosyal pazarlama anlayışı ve bir uygulama.* [Master's Dissertation].

Yılmaz, R. (2017b, May). *Structural transformation of advertising narrative in the digital age in Turkey* [Türkiye'de reklam anlatısının dijital çağdaki yapısal dönüşümü]. Paper presented at the 1st International Conference on New Trends in Communication, Istanbul, Turkey.

Yılmaz, R. (2017a). Typology of metaleptic uses in television commercials [Televizyon reklamlarında metaleptik kullanımların tipolojisi]. *Gümüşhane Üniversitesi İletişim Fakültesi Elektronik Dergisi*, *5*(2), 691–704.

Yılmaz, R., & Ciğerci, F. M. (2019). A brief history of storytelling: From primitive dance to digital narration. In *Handbook of Research on Transmedia Storytelling and Narrative Strategies* (pp. 1–14). IGI Global. DOI: 10.4018/978-1-5225-5357-1.ch001

Yılmaz, R., & Erdem, N. M. (2016). *150 Soruda Geleneksel ve Dijital Reklamcılık*. Umuttepe.

Yılmaz, R., & Taşkıran, N. Ö. (2013). A model proposal for advertising aestheticization. In Hacıoğlu, Ü., & Dinçer, H. (Eds.), *Globalization and governance in the international political economy* (pp. 264–272). IGI Global.

Yin, R. K. (2011). *Qualitative research from start to finish*. The Guilford Press.

Yuan, R., Liu, M. J., Luo, J., & Yen, D. A. (2016). Reciprocal transfer of brand identity and image associations arising from higher education brand extensions. *Journal of Business Research*, *69*(8), 3069–3076. DOI: 10.1016/j.jbusres.2016.01.022

Yunusov, S., Sidat, H., & Emami, A. (2024). MirrorStories: Reflecting Diversity through Personalized Narrative Generation with Large Language Models. /arXiv.2409.13935 arXiv:2409.13935DOI: 10.18653/v1/2024.emnlp-main.382

Yurdigül, Y. & Yıldırım, A. (2021). Gerçeklik algısına bir müdahale aracı olarak sentetik medya teknolojileri. *İletişim ve Diplomasi*, 5, 105-121.

Yu, Y. (2022). The role and influence of artificial intelligence on advertising industry. In *Proceedings of the 2021 International Conference on Social Development and Media Communication (SDMC 2021)* (pp. 190–194). Atlantis Press. https://doi.org/ DOI: 10.2991/assehr.k.220105.037

Zalando, S. E. (2025). "Annual Report 2024 & Q1 2025 Financial Statements". https://www.annualreports.com/Company/zalando

Zawada, B. E. (2005). *Linguistic creativity and mental representation with reference to intercategorial polysemy* [Unpublished doctoral dissertation, University of South Africa].

Zgoll, A., Cuperly, B., & Cöster-Gilbert, A. (2023). In search of Dumuzi: An introduction to Hylistic narratology. In Konstantopoulos, G., & Helle, S. (Eds.), *The shape of stories* (pp. 285–350). Brill. DOI: 10.1163/9789004539761_013

Zhang, R., ... (2025). *Generative AI for Film Creation: A Survey of Recent Advances*. https://doi.org//arXiv.2504.08296DOI: 10.1109/CVPRW67362.2025.00623

Zhang, J., Li, S., Zhang, J. Y., Du, F., Qi, Y., & Liu, X. (2020). A Literature Review of the Research on the Uncanny Valley. In Rau, P. L. (Ed.), Lecture Notes in Computer Science: Vol. 12192. *Cross-Cultural Design. User Experience of Products, Services, and Intelligent Environments. HCII 2020*. Springer. DOI: 10.1007/978-3-030-49788-0_19

Zhang, J., & Liu, Z. (2023). An empirical analysis of the impact of brand story themes on brand attitude in the context of B2C e-commerce platforms for organic agricultural products. *Sustainability (Basel), 15*(24), 16679. DOI: 10.3390/su152416679

Zhang, L., Li, D., & Zhou, L. (2021). How greenwashing affects consumer responses: A review and research agenda. *International Journal of Consumer Studies, 45*(5), 1250–1265.

Zhang, M., Atwal, G., & Kaiser, M. (2021). Corporate social irresponsibility and stakeholder ecosystems: The case of Volkswagen Dieselgate scandal. *Strategic Change, 30*(1), 79–85. DOI: 10.1002/jsc.2391

Zhang, M., Liu, Y., Wang, Y., & Zhao, L. (2022). How to retain customers: Understanding the role of trust in live streaming commerce with a socio-technical perspective. *Computers in Human Behavior, 127*, 107052. DOI: 10.1016/j.chb.2021.107052

Zhao, Y. (2025). An examination of ethical challenges in the application of AI in marketing. *International Journal of Business and Management, 20*(4), 113. DOI: 10.5539/ijbm.v20n4p113

Zuboff, S. (2019). *The age of surveillance capitalism: The fight for a human future at the new frontier of power*. Public Affairs.

About the Contributors

Recep Yılmaz, Ph.D., is a Professor and Head of the Department of Public Relations and Publicity at Ondokuz Mayıs University, Türkiye. His research focuses on Narrative Theory, Advertising, marketing communication, and theoretical approaches to media and communication studies. His work explores the intersection of narrative structures, persuasion, digital transformation, and emerging communication technologies. Dr. Yılmaz is the author and editor of fifteen scholarly books, several of which are indexed in Web of Science and Scopus. His recent volumes include Developing Digital Narratives in Marketing Communication and AI, Virtualization, and the Future of Marketing, along with earlier works such as Handbook of Research on Effective Advertising Strategies in the Social Media Age. He has also edited and contributed to major reference works, including Narrative Advertising Models and Conceptualization in the Social Media Age, and Handbook of Research on Narrative Interactions. In addition to his books, he has published extensively in peer-reviewed journals, international conference proceedings, and edited volumes, contributing to ongoing debates on narrative mediation, digital storytelling, and AI-driven communication. Alongside his academic scholarship, Dr. Yılmaz is also a fiction writer. His philosophical horror novella Çerçici reflects his sustained engagement with narrative not only as a theoretical construct but also as a creative practice.

***

Oğuzhan Alın is a research assistant at the Department of Public Relations and Publicity at Ondokuz Mayıs University. He was born in Ankara in 1998. He completed his undergraduate education at the Department of Public Relations and Publicity at Ondokuz Mayıs University. He completed his master's degree in the Department of Media and Communication Sciences at the same university. He is pursuing a doctorate in Public Relations and Publicity at Ankara Hacı Bayram Veli University. He began his career as a corporate communications specialist and social media manager at various institutions, and currently continues his work in the fields of public relations, advertising, social media, narrative, and intertextuality.

Mustafa Seçkin Aydın is a Lecturer at Aydın Adnan Menderes University, Çine Vocational School, in the Department of Banking and Insurance. He holds a Ph.D. in Business Administration from Aydın Adnan Menderes University, where his research focused on the impact of customer and user experience on purchasing behavior in e-commerce, utilizing psychophysiological and multi-method approaches. His academic interests include digital customer experience, consumer decision-making, eye-tracking in marketing research, and the application of behavioral economics in digital contexts. He has also pursued education in Business Administration at Baruch College, City University of New York, as part of a professional development program on contemporary American business practices. Dr. Aydın has authored several academic articles and conference papers and continues to explore innovative interdisciplinary methods in digital marketing and consumer behavior research.

Betül Başer is a Research Assistant at Ondokuz Mayıs University, Department of Public Relations and Publicity. She graduated from Cumhuriyet University, Faculty of Communication, Department of Public Relations and Publicity in 2017. In the same year, she started her master's degree at Marmara University Institute of Social Sciences, Department of Public Relations and Publicity with the title "The role of social media phenomena on purchasing decision of Z generation consumers: The example of youtubers in 2020. In the same year, she started her doctorate education at Istanbul University Institute of Social Sciences, Department of Public Relations and Publicity and she is still continuing her doctorate education. Fields of study: Public relations, new media, digital games and consumer behavior.

Nursel Bolat, Ph.D., is a professor at Ondokuz Mayis University, Department of Radio, Television and Cinema. She authored two books (Product Placement: Main Concepts and Channel, Analysing of TV Dramas), and she published numerous papers in several journals, conference proceedings, and chapters in edited books. Her majors are Broadcasting and Digital Media. She also studies Advertising. Some courses she teaches are Broadcasting, Practices in TV Prorammes, Fundamental Technics in Broadcasting, Semiotics and Editing.

Can Murat Demir graduated from the Department of Public Administration at the Faculty of Economics and Administrative Sciences, Selçuk University, Karaman, in 2005. He has been working at the Distance Education Application and Research Center at Ondokuz Mayıs University since 2010. In 2022, he was accepted into the Master's program in Communication Sciences at Ondokuz Mayıs University, and in 2025, he completed his master's thesis titled "Mise-en-Abyme as a Pattern

Tool in the Literary Communication Process: An Examination of the Narratives of Robbe-Grillet, Calvino, and Borges." His work, which integrates philosophy and communication disciplines, has been published in academic journals at both the national and international levels.

Yeter Demir graduated from the Sociology Department of the Faculty of Science and Letters at Dumlupınar University in 2005. In 2022, she was accepted into the Master's programme at the Department of Media and Communication Sciences at Ondokuz Mayıs University and successfully completed her thesis entitled 'An Examination of the Human-Nature Relationship in the Context of Cinema and Anthropocentrism'. She has published academic works at both national and international levels.

Özgenur Reyhan Güler is an academic, researcher, and media professional specializing in communication sciences, public relations, and cultural communication. After completing her undergraduate education in the field of arts and design, she earned a master's degree in cultural management and received her PhD from the Department of Public Relations and Promotion at the Faculty of Communication, Marmara University. Her academic research focuses on intercultural communication, sustainability communication, cultural diplomacy, migration and media representations, ethical communication, and strategic public relations. Dr. Güler has published articles, books, and book chapters in national and international peer-reviewed journals and is actively involved in international academic networks, including COST Actions and United Nations–affiliated initiatives. She currently serves as a faculty member at the Faculty of Communication at İstinye University, where she continues her academic work with a holistic perspective that integrates media, culture, and public diplomacy practices.

Erkan Hirik is a faculty member in the Department of Turkish Language and Literature at Samsun University. He serves as a Professor and holds the administrative role of Vice Head of Department. He is also affiliated with the Department of New Turkish Language. Education He obtained his Ph.D. in 2014 from Kırıkkale University. Prior to his doctoral studies, he completed his master's degree focusing on "Probability Modality in Old Uyghur Turkish" (2010), and his doctoral dissertation is titled "Knowledge Modalities in Turkey Turkish" (2014). Research Interests His primary fields of study include: Morphology (Structure of words) Semantics (Meaning in language) Functional Grammar Linguistic Turkology Language and Culture Relations Pragmatics (Language in use) Professional Activities International Experience: He participated in the Erasmus Teaching Staff Exchange Program at Uppsala University (2012). Memberships: He is a Working

Group Member of the COST Action "European Network On Lexical Innovation (ENEOLI)." Editorial Roles: He serves in editorial capacities for various journals, including International Journal of Uyghur Studies and Journal of Culture Research.

Ebru Özgen is an academic specializing in communication sciences and public relations. She completed her undergraduate, master's, and doctoral education in the field of communication, and her academic research primarily focuses on public relations, strategic communication, media studies, organizational communication, and ethics-oriented communication practices. Having served as a faculty member at various universities for many years, Özgen has taught numerous undergraduate and graduate-level courses, supervised a significant number of theses, and participated in academic jury committees. She has published articles, books, and book chapters in national and international peer-reviewed journals. In her academic work, Prof. Dr. Özgen adopts an interdisciplinary perspective that integrates theoretical approaches with practical applications. She has also held academic administrative positions and actively contributed to scientific research projects.

Tugay Sarıkaya completed his undergraduate studies at Kadir Has University, majoring in the Radio, Cinema, and Television Department in 2012. Following this, he pursued a Master of Arts in New Media at the same institution, dedicating his thesis to examining the limited impacts of social media and exploring the relevance of the opinion leader theory during the Arab Spring. His research focused specifically on the cases of Tunisia and Egypt. In 2019, he gained admission to the Ph.D. program in Media and Communication Studies at Istanbul Commerce University. Tugay successfully earned his Ph.D. from the Institute of Communication Sciences and Internet at Istanbul Commerce University. His dissertation was titled "The Effect of Interaction in Virtual Communities on Social Media: Shaping and Reproduction of Cultural Memory, Neighborhood Identity, and Culture." At present, Tugay Sarıkaya holds a Ph.D. degree and works as a research assistant at Istinye University in the Department of Radio, Television, and Cinema.

Farheen Sayyad is an experienced academician with a Ph.D. in Commerce and Management, specializing in Customer Satisfaction in Micro Health Insurance. With several years of teaching and administrative experience, she currently serves as an Assistant Professor at Sheth NKTT College. Her research interests include micro insurance, customer satisfaction, consumer behavior, and brand loyalty, sustainable business practices etc. She has published extensively in national and international journals.

Esennur Sirer was born in Bursa in 1969. She graduated from Bursa Girls' High School in 1986. In 1990, he graduated from Istanbul University Journalism Faculty of Radio and Television. In 2010, she received her master's degree on Radio-TV Cinema from Istanbul University Institute of Social Sciences with her thesis titled 'The Evolving and Changing Formal Structure of Television Journalism" With her thesis titled "Football as a Popular Culture Product: Image Arrangement from the Viewpoint of the Elements of Construction in Publicity", she was awarded the title of Doctor in Radio-TV at Istanbul University Institute of Social Sciences. From 1992 to 2018, she worked as director in TRT News and Sports Publications Department in Istanbul. In addition to directing, she has been conducting her academic studies since 2007 as a faculty member in the Department of Radio, Television, Cinema and Cinema, Uskudar University, since October 2018.

Nilay Tan Çakır, has been working as Assistant Professor at Ondokuz Mayis University, Public Relations and Publicity Department since March 1, 2019. She graduated from Bahcesehir University Public Relations Department in 2013 with a full scholarship of OSYM (Student Selection and Placement Centre). Also she completed her minor program in Strategic Advertising Planning in the same year. She studied communication at the University of Antwerp, Belgium for a semester with Erasmus exchange program. After graduation, she worked as a copywriter at a digital advertising agency in Istanbul 3 years. Then she received her masters degree from Media and Communication Sciences program at Ondokuz Mayis University. She received her PhD in the Department of Public Relations and Publicity at Istanbul University

Eda Turanci graduated from Hacettepe University, Department of Sociology in 2007, has received her master's degree at Galatasaray University in 2010. She received her PhD. in Public Relations and Publicity from Gazi University in 2017. She is currently working in Ankara Haci Bayram Veli University (formerly known as Gazi University), Communication Faculty, Public Relations and Publicity Department. The courses that she teaches cover the sociology of media and culture, crisis communication, consumption culture and public relations and advertising practices. Her research areas are, public relations, sociology of communication, health communication, crisis and risk communication, crisis and risk management, social media, and consumption culture.

Özge Uğurlu Akbaş graduated from T.E.D. Kdz. Ereğli College. She completed her academic education with a bachelor's degree in Public Relations and Publicity at Gazi University, Faculty of Communication in 2001; a master's degree in the Public Relations and Publicity Program at Gazi University, Institute of Social Sciences in

2003; and a PhD in the Department of Public Relations and Publicity at the same institute in 2008. Since 2009, she has taught a variety of core and elective courses in the Department of Public Relations and Publicity at Maltepe University, Faculty of Communication, where she began working as an Assistant Professor. Receiving the title of Associate Professor in 2021, Akbaş continues her academic career at Üsküdar University, serving as the Head of the Department of Public Relations and Publicity at the Faculty of Communication and the Head of the Public Relations and Advertising Master's Program. Uğurlu Akbaş focuses her work on public relations, consumption philosophy, digital communication, and digital game studies, and she has authored numerous national and international papers and book chapters in both Turkish and English in these fields.

Suman Vij brings over 24 years of diverse experience across corporate, academic, and research domains. Her extensive industry exposure enriches her academic and research pursuits, enabling a strong linkage between theory and practical application. A dedicated academic leader, she is known for her integrity, commitment, and passion for excellence. Dr. Vij actively mentors students and researchers, guiding them toward achieving their academic, professional, and research goals through disciplined effort, teamwork, and innovation.

Elif Yılmaz is a research assistant in the Department of Public Relations and Advertising at Istinye University. She completed her undergraduate studies in Public Relations and Advertising at Niğde Ömer Halisdemir University, Faculty of Communication, graduating as the top student in 2017. She received her master's degree from Marmara University, Institute of Social Sciences, Department of Public Relations. Since 2022, Yılmaz has been pursuing her doctorate in Public Relations at Marmara University, Institute of Social Sciences.

Index

A

C

D

E

F

G

H

I

L

M

N

O

P

S

T

www.ingramcontent.com/pod-product-compliance
Lightning Source LLC
La Vergne TN
LVHW062324300926
849161LV00007B/1565